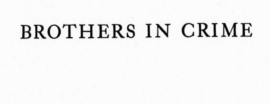

BROTHERS IN CRIME

BROTHERS IN CRIME

CLIFFORD R. SHAW

With the Assistance of

HENRY D. McKAY and JAMES F. McDONALD

With Special Chapters by

HAROLD B. HANSON and ERNEST W. BURGESS

WITHDRAWN

THE UNIVERSITY OF CHICAGO PRESS
CHICAGO and LONDON

THE UNIVERSITY OF CHICAGO PRESS, CHICAGO & LONDON
The University of Toronto Press, Toronto 5, Canada

© *1938 by The University of Chicago*

Published 1938

Third Impression 1966

Printed in the United States of America

FOREWORD

It has become increasingly apparent in recent years that the task of securing a thorough understanding of the delinquent entails the collaboration of workers in various fields of study. The case study reported in this volume has resulted in large part from such collaboration. This study comprises the results of examinations of five delinquent brothers by physicians, psychiatrists, psychologists, social workers, and sociologists. It is to be hoped that a closer collaboration of workers in these fields will become increasingly widespread in the study and treatment of delinquents and criminals.

Another important feature of this study is the fact that it gives a picture of the experiences of the brothers from early childhood to adulthood. In addition to autobiographical documents, it utilizes the reports of observations, interviews, and examinations by workers who have had contacts with the brothers in various situations during a period of fifteen to twenty-five years. Upon the basis of these materials it is possible to observe the evolution of the careers in crime from the first simple acts of stealing in early childhood to the more serious crimes which took place many years later. Such long-time, continuous study is extremely important in securing an understanding of the successive influences which contribute to the development of delinquent and criminal careers.

It is important to observe that this study is not concerned alone with research. It is a concrete illustration of effective rehabilitation obtained by an intensive and continuous program of therapy. Four of the brothers, despite their long careers in delinquency and crime, have been for a number of years satisfactorily employed in private industry.

This study is presented as an example of one of the types of work carried on by the Division of the Criminologist of the Illinois State Department of Public Welfare. It is a valuable contribution to criminology because it throws light upon the processes involved in the development of criminal careers in deteriorated urban areas, because of its implications with regard to the need for developing community-wide preventive programs in these areas, and because it is a demonstration of successful therapy as applied to cases of habitual offenders.

PAUL L. SCHROEDER, M.D.

July 25, 1938

AUTHOR'S PREFACE

This volume is the third in a series of detailed case studies which have been published as a part of the program of sociological research of the Institute for Juvenile Research and the Behavior Research Fund. The cases included in the series are selected to focus attention upon some particular aspect of the problem of juvenile delinquency or to illustrate the use of a special method in the analysis and treatment of cases.

The first case in the series, *The Jack-Roller: A Delinquent Boy's Own Story*, was published to illustrate the use of "own story" material in the analysis and treatment of cases of juvenile delinquents. The boy's own story which comprised the major portion of the case history is supplemented by materials pertaining to the mental and physical condition of the subject and of successive social situations in which he lived. Thus, in this case, as in the other cases included in this series, the "own story" is presented as an integral part of the total case history and is interpreted only in the light of all the available facts in the case. The "own story" is of particular importance since it reveals the sequence of experiences in the life-history of the individual and the interpretations which he makes of these experiences and the situations in which they occurred.

The second case in the series, *The Natural History of a Delinquent Career*, is a study of a young male recidivist who was sentenced to a state penal institution a few months prior to his seventeenth birthday, after having been convicted on a charge of robbery with a gun and rape. At the time of the trial the case was given considerable publicity in the local press. In the news stories the crime was ascribed to alleged depravity of the defendant. He was characterized by such epithets as "young brute," "moron," and "beast." While such a dramatization of a criminal act may serve to promote the financial interest of the newspapers, it contributes little to an understanding of the nature of the act. Actually, the crime for which the youthful offender in question was committed to the reformatory was the product of a process of social conditioning which extended back into the early years of his life. Important in this conditioning process were his experiences in the family, delinquent play groups, and criminal gangs; his contacts with the junk-dealers, fences, and residents who purchased his stolen merchandise; the disorganized condition of the community in which he lived, economic insecurity, and the influence of the juvenile institutions in which he had been confined. The act of armed robbery was a symptom of the kinds of social experiences which had characterized the life-history of the offender throughout his childhood and early adolescence.

The study presented in this volume pertains to the social background and delinquent careers of five brothers. These brothers were the children of foreign-born parents. Their cases are published to suggest the relationship between delinquency and the culture conflicts which often confront the immigrant family in the physically deteriorated and socially disorganized communities in large American cities.

The writer's contact with the brothers has extended over a period of sixteen years. The case histories have been compiled from the records of case-work agencies, courts, correctional institutions, schools, behavior clinics, from interviews with friends and relatives of the brothers, and from autobiographical documents and personal interviews with the boys themselves. The cases are published with the full consent of the brothers and all names and dates which might disclose their identity have been disguised.

The writer wishes to express indebtedness to the Institute for Juvenile Research, the Local Community Research Committee of the University of Chicago, the Behavior Research Fund, the Rockefeller Foundation, and the Chicago Area Project for providing a large portion of the money used in the study.

Gratitude is due members of the Chicago Woman's Club for providing funds for the special-treatment program of the brothers; Mr. Harry Hill, chief probation officer, Cook County Juvenile Court, for giving access to the records in that institution; Joseph

Healy, officer in charge of Juvenile Police Probation Officers, for permission to use the police records; Mr. Maurice E. Moore, formerly of the Institute for Juvenile Research, for securing certain of the original biographical documents; Mrs. Lilian Davis, Institute for Juvenile Research, for editorial assistance; and Miss Lillian Benjamin, Institute for Juvenile Research, for stenographic assistance in the preparation of the manuscript.

Gratitude is also due Dr. Paul L. Schroeder, state criminologist and director of the Institute for Juvenile Research; Mr. John C. Weigel, formerly administrator of the Institute for Juvenile Research and the Behavior Research Fund; Dr. Harold B. Hanson, psychiatrist, Institute for Juvenile Research, for preparation of a special chapter, "Clinical Summaries"; and Professor Ernest W. Burgess, University of Chicago, for his helpful suggestions during the progress of the study, his examination of the manuscript, and his preparation of the chapter on the "Personality Traits of the Brothers."

CLIFFORD R. SHAW

May 9, 1938

TABLE OF CONTENTS

TABLE OF CONTENTS

LIST OF ILLUSTRATIONS

PART I

THE EXTENT AND SPECIFIC CHARACTER
OF THE DELINQUENCIES AND CRIMES
OF THE MARTIN BROTHERS

INTRODUCTION

This volume is concerned with a study of the lives of five brothers, all of whom have long records of delinquency and crime. In the case of each brother the career in delinquency began in early childhood and continued for a period of approximately twelve to twenty years, despite the persistent efforts of public and private agencies and institutions to effect a rehabilitation.

To preserve anonymity fictitious names, dates, and places have been used; the brothers are referred to as John, Edward, James, Michael, and Carl Martin.

This study is published in detailed form to indicate the process in which the delinquent careers of the brothers had their origin and development. It reveals further the marked limitation of individualistic methods of treatment as applied to cases of delinquency in which the behavior problem is a function of social processes which are community-wide in their scope and influence.

In presenting the materials of the case study it is desirable to give at the outset a detailed description of the specific delinquencies and crimes in which the brothers were implicated. The official records in chapter i provide a formal characterization of these offenses in their chronological order. A more detailed description of these offenses in terms of the way in which they took place, the situation in which they occurred, and the meaning ascribed to them by the brothers and their companions is given in chapters ii, iii, and iv. Consequently, a limited number of excerpts from the various autobiographical documents of the brothers have been utilized.

CHAPTER I

OFFICIAL RECORDS OF DELINQUENCY AND
CRIME OF THE BROTHERS

This study of the Martin brothers has extended over a period of fifteen years, and the materials which comprise the case history have been secured directly from the members of the family and from the records of the many social agencies, behavior clinics, and institutions which have attempted to provide for the economic, medical, and social needs of the family. Along with the study of the case continuous effort has been made during recent years to assist the brothers in making adjustment to conventional standards of behavior. Four of them, for a period of six to ten years, have been engaged in self-supporting activities of a legitimate character.

At the present time the ages of these five brothers range from twenty-five to thirty-five years. The extent of their participation in delinquent and criminal activities is clearly indicated by the fact that they have served a total of approximately fifty-five years in correctional and penal institutions. They have been picked up and arrested by the police at least eighty-six times, brought into court seventy times, confined in institutions for forty-two separate periods, and placed under supervision of probation and parole officers approximately forty-five times.

An important practical consideration in this case is the cost to the community of these five careers in delinquency and crime. Obviously it is not possible to determine precisely or to approximate closely the total cost of institutional care, the salaries of public and private workers, and the value of merchandise secured by the brothers in their numerous thefts. It is known, however, that the cost of fifty-five years of institutional care is in excess of twenty-five thousand dollars, as calculated upon the basis of the per capita cost in the different institutions in which the brothers were confined. The value of the jewelry, clothing, and money secured in more than three hundred burglaries in well-to-do homes amounted to many thousands of dollars, since in the specific burglaries in which the police placed an evaluation upon the stolen merchandise the estimates ranged from three dollars to twenty-six hundred dollars. The value of the forty-five or more automobiles which were stolen and the salaries of the various workers who were assigned at various times to supervise the brothers would comprise another substantial item in the total cost entailed in this case.

JOHN MARTIN

John Martin, the eldest of the five brothers, is now thirty-five years of age, unmarried, and resides with his mother. He is a friendly, sociable, carefree, and easy-going person, with a good sense of humor. He gives the distinct impression of being indifferent about his personal appearance and inclined to accept his meager circumstances without any complaint or anxiety. During the last ten years he has not been arrested for any offense. His employment during this period has been irregular, although for the most part he has been self-supporting.

When John was eleven years of age, Dr. William Healy and Dr. Augusta Bronner of the Juvenile Psychopathic Institute reported that he was "fairly bright in school work. . . . . We should class him as having good ability and poor advantages, the latter because of much truancy and language difficulties. . . . . The outlook is good with constructive work done. If the boy continues to live in the same neighborhood he will probably continue the same way. If the mother moves much might be done."

John's initial experiences in stealing occurred when he was seven years of age, and his first court appearance took place when he was eight years and six months old. He was picked up by the police fourteen times, appeared in court ten times on charges of delinquency and crime, served six periods of confinement in correctional and penal institutions (a total of eight years), and was placed under the supervision of probation and parole officers seven times. As indicated in the following official record, almost all his delinquencies were offenses against property.

1. *Eight years, six months of age:*

John was picked up while begging in the South Water Street Market. He had accompanied his father to the market on this and other occasions for the purpose of securing food for the family. It was also reported that he had been truant from school and had stayed away from home several nights during the previous month. He was released to his parents at the police station.

2. *Nine years, seven months:*

While in the company of Samuel Ludlow, age 14 years, 7 months, Joseph Sargent, age 14, Victor Bolar, age 11, James Reiley, age 10 years, 8 months, Michael Sheperd, age 11 years, Howard Philips, age 11 years, 6 months, John was picked up by the police and charged with petty stealing. He was released to his parents at the police station.

3. *Ten years, five months:*

In company with his brother, Edward, 8 years and 10 months, he was arrested and brought to court on a petition alleging truancy from school, begging, and petty stealing. He was committed to the Chicago Parental School.

4. *Ten years, eight months:*

He was paroled from the Chicago Parental School.

5. *Ten years, ten months:*

He was arrested and brought to court on a petition alleging truancy from home and school. He was recommitted to the Chicago Parental School.

6. *Eleven years:*

He was paroled from the Chicago Parental School.

7. *Eleven years, eleven months:*

He was brought to court on a delinquency petition alleging truancy from home and school, and petty stealing. In this connection the court record states:

John has been away from home. He cannot be sent to the Chicago Parental School because his brother Edward is there. The parents have no control over the boy and the influence of the boys in the neighborhood is very bad. The yard back of the house in which they live is used as a hangout by boys who are not working.

The court ordered the delinquency petition dismissed and a dependency petition filed.

8. *Eleven years, eleven months:*

He was brought to court on a dependency petition. The parents were not in court but had previously indicated their desire to have the boy sent to an institution. He was placed in a home for dependent children.

9. *Twelve years:*

He ran away from the home for dependent children.

10. *Twelve years:*

He was picked up by the police and returned to the home for dependent children. He ran away from there twice during the next few months.

11. *Twelve years, nine months:*

He was released from the home for dependent children and placed under the supervision of an officer of the Cook County Juvenile Court.

12. *Thirteen years, two months:*

While in the company of his brother, Edward, 11 years and 7 months, and William Stock, 11 years, 2 months, John was arrested and charged with stealing a bicycle. In regard to this charge the court record states:

The aforesaid boy, John Martin, he is incorrigible. The said boy and his brother, Edward, they are charged with stealing a bicycle from F. J. Ellwood, 8— F—— Ave. The said bicycle was received and turned over to the owner. Also the home surroundings are not very good.

He was returned home and placed under the supervision of a probation officer of the Juvenile Court.

13. *Thirteen years, two months:*

In the company of his brother Edward, 11 years, 7 months, John was arrested and brought to court on a delinquency petition charging burglary. In connection with the offense the court record states:

John and his brother Edward entered the basement of H. Plymouth, 65— W. G—— Avenue, August 2, 19—, between nine and twelve P.M. and stole one bicycle worth $10.00 which was recovered and turned over to the owner. A tricycle worth $3.00 was taken by Edward but it was not recovered. There is a brown suit of clothes worth $8.00 and a spring coat worth $5.00 still missing which they said they did not take. These boys are here on a delinquency petition and there is a bad dependency situation in the family. We have had several complaints about the family. Four days ago the police removed all of the children from the home because conditions were so bad. The father and mother work on a farm and come home very late at night.

Edward was returned to his parents and the case of John was continued for two weeks, at which time he was committed to the St. Charles School for Boys.

14. *Thirteen years, three months:*

He escaped from the St. Charles School for Boys.

15. *Thirteen years, three months:*

He was arrested in Chicago and returned to the St. Charles School for Boys.

16. *Fourteen years, eleven months:*

He was paroled to a farmer who resided near the St. Charles School for Boys.

17. *Fourteen years, eleven months:*

He ran away from the farmer to whom he was paroled, thus violating his parole.

18. *Fifteen years, four months:*

He was arrested and charged with violating his parole from the St. Charles School for Boys. Released to his parents under the supervision of a parole officer.

19. *Fifteen years, five months:*

He was arrested while in possession of a stolen bicycle. The officers reported to the judge:

This boy has been to Juvenile Court and has been to the Parental School. He was arrested at the Illinois Central Railroad Station at

12th Street and Park Row at 3:10 A.M. for having a bicycle in his possession which he claimed he bought. He told your petitioner that he stole the bicycle from a janitor at the E—— Hotel, but I failed to find the janitor. This boy also has been 22 months in St. Charles School for boys.

He was placed under the supervision of a probation officer of the court.

20. *Fifteen years, six months:*

He was arrested while in the act of stealing lead pipes from a vacant building. The offense is described in the court record as follows:

Yesterday this boy was caught in the act of cutting lead pipes out of a building at 20—B—— Street. While being questioned, he admitted he cut the lead pipe out of the building. The total damage was estimated at about $150.00. He sold the lead pipe to a junkman for $5.00.

He was recommitted to the St. Charles School for Boys for violation of parole.

21. *Sixteen years, eight months:*

He escaped from St. Charles School for Boys. Two months later he enlisted in the United States military service, in which he remained for a period of approximately three years and three months.

22. *Twenty-one years, eight months:*

He was arrested with John Hefner, age 22 years, in a small town in an adjoining state on a charge of burglary. He and his companion had burglarized a lumber-camp office. He was committed to the state reformatory in this adjoining state.

23. *Twenty-four years, six months:*

John was discharged from the above-mentioned state reformatory.

EDWARD MARTIN

The second brother, Edward, is now thirty-three years of age, married, and has one child. He is industrious, ambitious, and shrewd. He has very definite plans for the future and is eager to improve the economic and social conditions of his family. He has not been charged with any offense during the last eight years. Throughout the depression period he has supported himself and family on his wages in private industry.

At the age of fourteen years and seven months Edward was given an examination by Dr. William Healy of the Juvenile Psychopathic Institute. The summary of the findings of this examination is as follows:

At the time Edward was fourteen years and seven months old, a clinical report stated that "he displays no gestures or suggestive mannerisms. Answers questions in an intelligent manner. . . . . Patient is neat and clean in his appearance and fairly well dressed for his station."

Edward's career in delinquency and crime has extended over a period of approximately eighteen years, his earliest experience in stealing occurring when he was about six years of age. During the eighteen years in which he was actively delinquent he was arrested twenty-three times, appeared in courts on delinquent and criminal charges eighteen times, served ten periods of confinement in correctional and penal institutions (a total of fourteen years), and placed under the supervision of probation and parole officers thirteen different times. As revealed in the following official record, Edward's delinquencies were almost without exception offenses against property.

1. *Eight years, ten months of age:*

He was arrested and brought to court in company with John, 10 years, 5 months, on a petition alleging truancy from school, begging, and petty stealing. He was placed under the supervision of a probation officer of the Juvenile Court.

2. *Nine years:*

He was arrested and brought to court on a petition charging truancy from school, begging, and petty stealing. Committed to the Chicago Parental School.

3. *Nine years, nine months:*

He was paroled from the Chicago Parental School.

4. *Ten years, two months:*

He was arrested and brought to court on a petition alleging truancy from school. He was recommitted to the Chicago Parental School.

5. *Ten years, eleven months:*

He was paroled from the Chicago Parental School.

6. *Eleven years, seven months:*

In company with his brother John, age 13 years, 2 months, and William Stock, 11 years, 2 months, Edward was arrested and brought to court, charged with stealing a bicycle. He was placed under the supervision of a probation officer of the Juvenile Court. (See No. 12 in the official record of John.)

7. *Eleven years, seven months:*

In the company of his brothers, James, age 6 years, 8 months, Michael, 4 years, 8 months, and Carl, 2 years, 10 months, Edward was picked up by the police while he was wandering about the streets at ten o'clock P.M. In reporting this case the police officer stated:

The mother and father go to work early in the morning and return late at night. They work on a farm. They both go away and leave the children all alone.

The children were released to the parents. Dependency petitions were filed for all the children.

8. *Eleven years, seven months:*

In the company of John, 13 years, 2 months, Edward was arrested and brought to court charged with burglary. The delinquency petition in the case of Edward was dismissed and a dependency petition substituted. He was released to his parents to remain at home until the date of the hearing on the dependency petition. (See No. 13 in the official record of John.)

9. *Eleven years, seven months:*

With his brothers James, 6 years, 8 months, Michael, 4 years, 8 months, and Carl, 2 years, 10 months, Edward was brought to court on a dependency petition. Placed under the supervision of a probation officer of the court.

10. *Eleven years, nine months:*

He was reported for begging with James, 6 years, 10 months. The complaint was filed with a family-case-work agency by a woman living in a well-to-do residential community located about five miles from the Martin home.

11. *Eleven years, nine months:*

Reported begging with James, 6 years, 10 months. The complaint was filed with a local case-work agency by a resident of a well-to-do residential community.

12. *Eleven years, ten months:*

Reported begging with James, 6 years, 11 months. The complaint was filed with a local case-work agency by a resident of a well-to-do residential community located about five miles from the Martin home.

13. *Eleven years, ten months:*

He was reported begging with James, 6 years, 11 months. A minister who filed the complaint with the family-case-work agency reported: "The boys are begging again. They beg every morning and go to school every afternoon."

14. *Eleven years, eleven months:*

He was reported begging with James, age 7 years, at the home of a resident in a well-to-do community. When reporting the incident to a family-case-work agency this resident stated that the boys said that their "father was sick and that they had nothing to eat."

15. *Eleven years, eleven months:*

While in the company of James, age 7 years, Michael, 5 years, and Carl, 3 years, 3 months, Edward was brought to the Juvenile Detention Home charged with truancy from home and school, begging, and petty stealing. Released to the parents under the supervision of an officer.

16. *Twelve years*:

He was reported begging with his brother James, age 7 years, 1 month. The children told the woman who filed the complaint that "our father is ill and the family has nothing to eat."

17. *Twelve years:*

He was reported begging with his brother James, age 7 years, 1 month, at the home of a resident in a North Side community. The records reveal that they told this resident that "their father had been ill for six months and their mother had rheumatism and that they sent them out to beg."

18. *Twelve years:*

He was reported for begging with James, age 7 years, 1 month, at the home of a resident of a well-to-do North Side community. The records show that the children reported to this resident that "their father was out of work and that he sent them out to beg."

19. *Twelve years:*

He was reported for begging with James, age 7 years, 1 month. The complaint was filed with a family-case-work agency by a resident of a North Side community.

20. *Twelve years, one month:*

He was reported for begging with James, age 7 years, 2 months. The complaint was filed by a resident of a well-to-do neighborhood who reported that "the children were loaded with things."

21. *Twelve years, one month:*

He was reported for begging alone in a well-to-do neighborhood on the North Side of the city. The records indicate that the complainant reported that "the boy claimed that his father was out of work and his mother disabled with rheumatism."

22. *Twelve years, two months:*

He was reported for begging with James, age 7 years, 2 months, at a church on the North Side of the city. The pastor of the church filed a complaint with the Juvenile Court and with a family-case-work agency.

23. *Twelve years, two months;*

He was reported for begging with James, age 7 years, 2 months. The incident was reported by a resident of a well-to-do neighborhood about five miles from their home.

24. *Twelve years, two months:*

He was brought to court on a petition alleging truancy from school. The court ordered a dependency petition filed. The case was continued and Edward was released to his parents.

25. *Twelve years, three months:*

At a hearing in court the case was continued for one week, as the parents and Edward were not present. A warrant was issued for Edward and his parents.

26. *Twelve years, three months:*

Edward was reported for begging with James, age 7 years, 4 months. The complaint was filed at a family-case-work agency by a woman living in a well-to-do neighborhood. The complainant reported: "The children had a basket of food and some money which they had begged from residents in the neighborhood."

27. *Twelve years, three months:*

He was reported for begging with James, age 7 years, 4 months, in a well-to-do neighborhood two miles from his home. The following statement is taken from the records of a family-case-work agency to which the incident was reported:

One of the boys had a pair of boxing gloves which he said were secured through a trade. The person reporting the incident said: "The boys were very inquisitive." They tried on his boys' skates and poked around under the porch. His boys have seen them several times in the neighborhood. The complainant is afraid they are learning habits of pilfering as well as begging.

28. *Twelve years, three months:*

In the company of his brothers Michael, age 5 years, 4 months, Carl, 3 years, 7 months, and James, 7 years, 4 months, Edward was brought to court on a petition alleging dependency. In reporting the case to the court the probation officer stated:

These children were brought to court a few weeks ago on dependency petitions. Since that time they have been out begging. Edward habitually begs. Edward, Michael, and James have been out of school. Edward has not attended school for the past six months. Their parents have not made any effort to put them in school but send them out to beg. A woman on the North Side called and told me that these boys were out begging and had told her they needed food and clothing and had begged 90¢ today. The father takes the money. He consents to have them go out to beg. The children have been helping to support the father in this manner.

Edward was placed on probation under the supervision of a probation officer who had an order to place him on a farm.

29. *Twelve years, three months:*

The principal of X—— School reported as follows:

Edward Martin and two companions have been in the habit of coming to the school yard at noon and at recess and taking from the school boys anything that may be of value, especially pennies and other pieces of money. After taking what they can get they command the little boys to bring a nickel apiece the next day. These boys loiter around the school premises and cause a great deal of annoyance in every way.

The complaint was referred to the Juvenile Court for investigation.

30. *Twelve years, seven months:*

He was brought to court charged with running away from home and begging. The probation officer explained that he had been "unable to place Edward on a farm as he was too small. He is only 12 years old. The mother is here. I talked

with the family supervisor last week and she wouldn't recom-
mend his going back home because he is a professional beggar,
and the father sends him out and he earns $2.25. The father
won't work when the boy is begging." Edward was committed to the Chicago and Cook County School for Boys.

31. *Twelve years, eight months:*

He was released from the Chicago and Cook County School
for Boys under the supervision of an officer of the school.

32. *Twelve years, nine months:*

Edward was reported begging with James, age 7 years, 10
months, in a prosperous neighborhood on the North Side of
the city. The woman who filed the complaint with the family-
case-work agency reported that "the boys were at her home
begging with a basket; they had gone from house to house in
the neighborhood."

33. *Twelve years, ten months:*

The principal of X—— School reported to a worker of a
family-case-work agency: "Edward is an habitual truant. He
obstinately refused to go to school." Complaint was referred
to the Juvenile Court for investigation.

34. *Twelve years, ten months:*

Edward was reported begging with James, age 7 years, 11
months, in a residential area four miles from his home. The
man who filed the complaint with the family-case-work agency reported: "The boy said his father was ill and the family
was in need." The case-work agency referred the complaint
to the Juvenile Court.

35. *Twelve years, ten months:*

He was reported begging with James, age 7 years, 11
months. The woman who filed the complaint with the family-
case-work agency reported: "The children were begging after
dark last evening. They had a basket and went from house
to house in a near-by residential district."

36. *Twelve years, eleven months:*

He was reported begging with James, age 8 years. A resident of a well-to-do community on the North Side of the city filed a complaint with the family-case-work agency.

37. *Twelve years, eleven months:*

He was reported begging with Michael, age 6 years. Three residents of a prosperous North Side community filed a complaint with a family-case-work agency and reported that two boys with a small white dog were begging from house to house. The agency reported the complaint to the Juvenile Court.

38. *Twelve years, eleven months:*

A delinquency petition was filed charging incorrigibility. The court record states: "Edward is beyond the control of his parents. The boy begs constantly and will not attend school. Complaints have been numerous about his conduct in this regard." The court hearing was continued because the parents failed to bring Edward into court. A bench warrant was issued to insure their appearance.

39. *Twelve years, eleven months:*

He was reported begging with James, age 8 years. A resident of a residential community about five miles from his home filed a complaint with a family-case-work agency.

40. *Thirteen years:*

He was brought to court with mother by a police officer who had served them with a bench warrant. The court record states:

This case was continued so that a warrant could be issued for the parents. The warrant was issued, but the parents failed to bring the child to the court. The boy has been out of school during the last four months. He habitually begs. Because the boy has been in the Chicago and Cook County School for Boys, the Department of Compulsory Education refuses to take any action in the case at this time. The condition in the home has steadily grown worse. The boy tells me that he goes out to beg four times a week. When the court asked the boy who sent him out to beg, the boy answered, "my mother." After a review of the case the judge stated: "I think that it would be an act of justice to send him to St. Charles!"

Committed to St. Charles School for Boys.

41. *Fourteen years, six months:*

He was paroled from the St. Charles School for Boys.

42. *Fourteen years, nine months:*

While in company with William Stock, age 14 years, 4 months, and Stanley Runcer, 11 years, 11 months, Edward was arrested and charged with burglarizing five residences in a well-to-do neighborhood located three miles from his home. He was held in the Detention Home.

43. *Fourteen years, nine months:*

He escaped from the Detention Home but was returned the next day.

44. *Fourteen years, nine months:*

He was brought to court on a charge of burglary. In presenting the case to the court, the officer stated:

On September 30, 19—, Edward Martin, in company with Stanley Runcer, age 11 years, and William Stock, 14 years, entered the residence of M. K. Lester, 12— M—— Avenue, and stole twelve dollars and fifty cents in money and an Eastman Kodak; and on the same date entered the residence of J. Wright and stole jewelry to the value of seventeen dollars and fifty cents. On Sept. 29th they entered the residence of W. R. Ross 1— P—— Avenue, and stole jewelry to the value of $330.00. On October 4th, entered the residence of S. P. Wagner, 10— C—— Avenue and stole a quantity of jewelry and other articles. On October 1st they entered the residence of H. Leach, 9— W—— Street and took two diamond rings valued at $2,500.00.

Edward was held in the Detention Home to be returned to the St. Charles School for Boys as a parole violator.

45. *Fourteen years, nine months:*

He escaped from the Detention Home.

46. *Fourteen years, eleven months:*

While in company with James, age 10 years, William Stock, age 14 years, 6 months, and Joseph Wyman, 13 years, 1 month, and Edwin Mitchell, age 14 years, Edward was arrested and charged with the burglary of two stores. The delinquency petitions stated:

The aforesaid boy, Edward Martin, he is incorrigible. The said boy and others did break into the saloon of S. Gardner, 10— H—— Avenue, and did steal and take away whiskey and cigars and other goods from the said saloon on December 19th, 19— at the hour of 2 A.M. Also December 27th, 19—, the said Edward Martin and others did break into the barber shop of A. Walters, 19— D—— Street, night time.

Edward Martin and Joseph Wyman entered the home of C. Nagle, 19— K——, and took a violin valued at $200.00 and a pencil at $4.00.

Edward Martin and William Stock, about 4 P.M. entered the residence of J. Jordan, 20— L through a rear door with a skeleton key. Stole a lady's watch valued at $15.00 and $20.00 in currency. The watch was recovered.

About 12 P.M. Edward Martin, William Stock, and Edwin Mitchell entered the residence of W. Kenyon, 4— K—— Avenue, through rear window, stole one pair trousers, $5.00, one vest, $2.00, 1 gold locket and fob, $5.00, 1 quart bottle Old Rose whiskey, $2.00, and a telephone box containing $3.50. They were discovered and arrested before they could get away with the property.

Edward Martin and William Stock were returned to the St. Charles School for Boys as parole violators; Joseph Wyman was committed to the Chicago and Cook County School for Boys; and Edwin Mitchell was placed on probation.

47. *Fourteen years, eleven months:*

He escaped from the St. Charles School for Boys but was returned two days later.

48. *Fifteen years, five months:*

He escaped from the St. Charles School for Boys.

49. *Fifteen years, five months:*

He was arrested while in the company of Adam Runcer, 14 years, 2 months, in the act of breaking into an empty house. Both boys were taken to the Juvenile Detention Home.

50. *Fifteen years, five months:*

He escaped from the Juvenile Detention Home.

51. *Fifteen years, five months:*

While in company of his brother, James, 10 years, 7 months, and Michael, 8 years, 7 months, Edward was arrested in a suburban community in the act of burglarizing a home. Although involved, James was not apprehended. Edward was held in the police station and escaped the next morning; Michael was turned over to his father and returned to the orphanage. The following article appeared in a metropolitan newspaper reporting this incident:

BOYS, 15 AND 9, JAILED AS "CRIME FAMILY" MEMBERS

Two more members of the Martin "crime family," Edward and Michael, aged 15 and 9, were arrested yesterday while robbing the home of Mrs. R. S. Early. They were captured at the point of a revolver by Mrs. Early. There are five brothers in the family, and all have been arrested several times.

52. *Fifteen years, six months:*

With Stanley Runcer, age 12 years, 8 months, and Adam Runcer, age 14 years, 3 months, Edward was arrested and brought to court charged with the burglary of several residences. The court record states:

On July 16th, the above named boy, in company with Adam Runcer, 14 years old, burglarized the residence of A. S. Middleton, 63— K—— Avenue. Also burglarized the flat of Mr. J. Sanders, 52— W—— Avenue. Also C. J. Elder, 62— K—— Avenue. Attempted to burglarize the residence of M. Simon, 14— P—— Blvd., and M. M. Green 54— S—— Road. Burglarized residence of A. Hunt, 59— S—— Road. Is wholly beyond his parents' control and should be sent to an institution.

He was returned to the St. Charles School for Boys. Stanley and Adam were sent to the Chicago and Cook County School for Boys.

53. *Fifteen years, seven months:*

Escaped from the St. Charles School for Boys but was returned the same day.

54. *Seventeen years, six months:*

He was paroled from St. Charles School for Boys.

55. *Seventeen years, eight months:*

Arrested on suspicion in California. He was released to a representative of the Chicago Police Department, where he was wanted as a witness in a criminal case involving one of his companions in crime.

56. *Seventeen years, eight months:*

While on the train about one hundred and fifty miles west of Kansas City, Edward escaped from the police officer.

57. *Seventeen years, ten months:*

He was arrested and brought to the Boys' Court and bound over to the Grand Jury. He was indicted on the charges of burglary and receiving stolen property. He was tried in the Criminal Court and placed on adult probation.

58. *Eighteen years, five months:*

He was arrested and brought before the Criminal Court with Joseph Wyman, 16 years, 8 months, Earl Wooms, age 17 years, and William Sloan, 18 years, charged with burglary and receiving stolen property. Edward was committed on a sentence of 1 to 10 years to the Illinois State Reformatory.

59. *Twenty-one years, six months:*

He was paroled from Illinois State Reformatory.

60. *Twenty-one years, eleven months:*

In company with James, age 17 years, Edward was arrested while tampering with a car in a well-to-do suburban community. He was returned to the Illinois State Reformatory as a parole violator.

61. *Twenty-three years, seven months:*

He was paroled from the Illinois State Reformatory.

62. *Twenty-four years:*

He was arrested in the company of John Olson, age 25, and charged with carrying concealed weapons and committed for one year to the Chicago House of Correction. Olson was fined $100 and costs.

63. *Twenty-four years, eleven months:*

He was released from the Chicago House of Correction and returned to the Illinois State Reformatory as a parole violator.

64. *Twenty-five years, eight months:*

He was discharged from the Illinois State Reformatory.

JAMES MARTIN

James, the third of the Martin brothers, is now twenty-nine years of age. He is married and has one child. He is shrewd, alert, aggressive, industrious, ambitious, affable, and loyal. He establishes normal relationships with other persons and assumes responsibility for the care of his wife and child. During the last five years he has been employed and has earned sufficient money to support himself and his family. At the time he was eleven years of age a clinical report described him as being "a very alert child, who does not let much pass his notice. He has a great deal of initiative, and wanted to make up his own problems for his intelligence tests."

James's long career in delinquency and crime, which has extended over a period of approximately nineteen years, had its origin during his fifth year. At that time he began to accompany his older brothers on begging expeditions to distant parts of the city and to engage with them in simple forms of petty stealing. According to official records his career began at the age of six years and eight months, at which time he was picked up by the police for wandering about the streets late at night. In the course of his active career in delinquency James was apprehended by the police and arrested on twenty occasions, appeared in courts on dependency and delinquency complaints thirteen times, served ten periods of confinement in correctional and penal institutions (a total of thirteen years), and was formally placed under the supervision of probation and parole officers seven different times. The chronological sequence of his offenses, appearances in courts, and commitments to institutions is indicated in the following official record.

1. *Six years, eight months of age:*

James was picked up by the police wandering about the streets at ten o'clock P.M. in the company of Edward, age 11 years, 7 months, Michael, 4 years, 8 months, and Carl, 2 years, 10 months. Released to his parents. Dependency petitions were filed for all of the children. (See Edward, No. 7.)

2. *Six years, eight months:*

He was brought to court on a petition alleging dependency with Edward, 11 years, 7 months, Michael, 4 years, 8 months, and Carl, 2 years, 10 months. He was placed under the supervision of a probation officer of the court.

3. *Six years, ten months:*

He was reported begging with Edward, 11 years, 9 months. Complaint filed with a family-case-work agency by a woman living in a well-to-do residential community about five miles from their home.

4. *Six years, ten and a half months:*

He was reported begging with Edward, 11 years, 9 months. The complaint was filed with a family-case-work agency by a resident of a well-to-do residential community about five miles from their home.

5. *Six years, eleven months:*

He was reported begging with Edward, age 11 years, 10 months. The complaint was filed with a family-case-work agency by a resident of a well-to-do residential community about five miles from their home. (See Edward, No. 12.)

6. *Six years, eleven months:*

He was reported begging in a well-to-do residential neighborhood about five miles from their home, with Edward, age 11 years, 10 months. (See Edward, No. 13.)

7. *Seven years:*

He was reported begging in a well-to-do community on the North Side of the city with Edward, age 11 years, 11 months. (See Edward, No. 14.)

8. *Seven years:*

James was arrested and brought to the Juvenile Detention Home with Edward, age 11 years, 11 months, Michael, 5 years, and Carl, 3 years, 3 months, charged with truancy from home, begging, and petty stealing. James was released to the parents under supervision of an officer. (See Edward, No. 15.)

9. *Seven years:*

Reported begging with his brother, Edward, age 12 years, in a well-to-do community on the North Side of the city. (See Edward, No. 16.)

10. *Seven years, one month:*

He was reported begging with Edward, age 12 years. The complaint was filed by a resident of a North Side community in Chicago. (See Edward, No. 17.)

11. *Seven years, one month:*

He was reported begging with Edward, age 12 years, in a North Side community. (See Edward, No. 18.)

12. *Seven years, one month:*

James was reported begging with Edward, age 12 years, in the North Side community. (See Edward, No. 19.)

13. *Seven years, two months:*

He was reported begging in a well-to-do neighborhood with his brother, Edward, age 12 years, 1 month. (See Edward, No. 20.)

14. *Seven years, two months:*

James was reported begging with Edward, age 12 years, 2 months, at a church on the North Side of the city. The pastor of the church filed a complaint with the Juvenile Court, and a family-case-work agency. (See Edward, No. 22.)

15. *Seven years, two months:*

He was reported begging with Edward, age 12 years, 2 months. The incident was reported to a family-case-work agency by a resident of a well-to-do neighborhood about five miles from their home. (See Edward, No. 23.)

16. *Seven years, four months:*

He was reported begging in a well-to-do neighborhood with Edward, age 12 years, 3 months. (See Edward, No. 26.)

17. *Seven years, four months:*

Reported begging with Edward, age 12 years, 3 months, in a well-to-do neighborhood two miles from their home. (See Edward, No. 27.)

18. *Seven years, four months:*

James was brought to court on a dependency petition with Edward, age 12 years, 3 months, Michael, 5 years, 5 months, and Carl, 3 years, 7 months. The petition was continued, and all the children, except Edward, were placed under the supervision of a probation officer of the Juvenile Court. (See Edward, No. 28.)

19. *Seven years, ten months:*

He was reported begging with Edward, age 12 years, 9 months, in a prosperous neighborhood on the North Side of the city. (See Edward, No. 32.)

20. *Seven years, eleven months:*

He was reported begging in a residential community four miles from his home with Edward, age 12 years, 10 months. (See Edward, No. 34.)

21. *Seven years, eleven months:*

He was reported begging with Edward, age 12 years, 10 months, after dark in a near-by residential district. (See Edward, No. 35.)

22. *Eight years:*

James was reported begging with Edward, age 12 years, 11 months. A resident of a well-to-do community on the North Side of the city filed the complaint with a family-case-work agency.

23. *Eight years:*

He was reported begging with Edward, age 12 years, 11 months. A resident of a prosperous residential community about five miles from his home filed the complaint with a family-case-work agency.

24. *Eight years, one month:*

James was arrested, charged with begging and truancy from school. When questioned by the police he explained that his parents had been sending him out to beg. He was released to his parents pending investigation.

25. *Eight years, three months:*

He was reported begging with Michael, 6 years, 2 months. The incident was reported to a family-case-work agency by a resident of a well-to-do community.

26. *Eight years, three months:*

He was reported begging with Michael, age 6 years, 2 months, and Carl, 4 years, 5 months. The incident was reported to a local case-work agency by a resident of a near-by community.

27. *Eight years, four months:*

James was arrested and brought to the Detention Home, charged with burglary. He admitted that he, in the company of William Stock, age 12 years, 10 months, had burglarized a flat at 36— North H—— Street. He was held in the Detention Home and brought to court three weeks later on a dependency petition. In presenting the case to the court the officer made the following statement:

James has had 41 unexcused absences from school during the last three months. There are a number of children in the family. The two older boys are now in St. Charles. The mother and this boy have been out begging. Sometimes both the father and the mother and this boy go to different houses begging. He used to go out with his two older brothers until they were sent away. The home is in a very bad shape. The mother works out on a farm and there is no one home all day.

James was placed in a home for dependent children.

28. *Nine years, four months:*

He escaped from the home for dependent children.

29. *Nine years, eight months:*

He was reported begging with Michael, age 7 years, 8 months. The complaint was filed with a family-case-work agency by a resident of a well-to-do residential community.

30. *Ten years:*

He was reported begging in a North Side residential community with Michael, age 8 years. The complaint was filed with the Juvenile Court by a family-case-work agency, but no official action was taken.

31. *Ten years:*

He was arrested and brought to court on a delinquent petition charging burglary of two stores. Involved with his brother Edward, age 14 years, 11 months, and William Stock, 14 years, 6 months, Joseph Wyman, age 13 years, 1 month, and Edwin Mitchell, age 14 years; Edward and William Stock were returned to St. Charles, and the case against James was dismissed. (See Edward, No. 46.) Wyman was committed to the Chicago and Cook County School for Boys while Mitchell was placed on probation.

32. *Ten years:*

He was reported begging with Michael, age 8 years, in a Loop office building. The complaint was filed with a family-case-work agency and in turn reported to the Juvenile Court. No official action was taken.

33. *Ten years:*

He was reported begging with Michael, age 8 years, on the Near North Side. The complaint was filed by a resident of the community with a family-case-work agency. This organization reported the incident to the Juvenile Court, but no official action was taken.

34. *Ten years:*

James was reported begging with Michael, age 8 years, in a Loop office building. The complaint was filed with a family-case-work agency. This organization reported the incident to the Juvenile Court, but no official action was taken.

35. *Ten years, one month:*

He was reported begging in a well-to-do residential community with Michael, age 8 years, 1 month. The complaint was filed by a local resident with a family-case-work agency, and in turn the agency reported the incident to the Juvenile Court, but no official action was taken.

36. *Ten years, one month:*

He was returned to the home for dependent children by his father.

37. *Ten years, two months:*

James escaped from the home for dependent children.

38. *Ten years, two months:*

In company with Michael, age 8 years, 1 month, James was arrested and charged with burglarizing three homes. He was held in the Detention Home.

39. *Ten years, three months:*

James was brought to court with Michael, age 8 years, 3 months, and Carl, 6 years, 5 months, on a petition alleging dependency. James was committed to the home for dependent children.

40. *Ten years, three months:*

James, with Michael, age 8 years, 3 months, escaped from the home for dependent children but was returned the following day.

41. *Ten years, four months:*

With Michael, age 8 years, 4 months, James escaped from the home for dependent children but was returned the following day.

42. *Ten years, seven months:*

With Michael, age 8 years, 7 months, James escaped from the home for dependent children. In reporting the escape the superintendent of the school stated: "I do not wish to have these boys sent here any more—so please send us release slips."

43. *Ten years, seven months:*

James, with Michael, age 8 years, 7 months, was found begging in a suburban community. They were brought to Chicago and turned over to the police who released them to their parents. The complaint filed with the Juvenile Court reads:

Upon my return to a suburban community, I received a report about two little boys found begging. When I finally found them, they gave their names as Michael Lake, eight years, and James Lake, ten years [James and Michael Martin]. When I located them, I left them at the elevated station and asked the guard to watch them while I went home for my pocket book. When I returned the boys were just sneaking out of the station. They saw me and started to run. I ran after them and caught one. Some boys caught the other one. I gave them a good shaking and brought them to the city. I took them to the Juvenile Court rooms about five o'clock, but found everything closed [Saturday afternoon]. I then asked the officer in the corridor on first floor if he would send some one home with the boys. He took me to the police station on L—— Street. Boys were to be taken home. James gave a different name at the station, and said he "guessed" he lived on B—— Street. I wish the Judge could talk to them. They said their mother was in Cook County; that their father is sick. The boys do not look like brothers. The younger one, eight years, can neither read nor write.

44. *Ten years, nine months:*

He was brought to court with Michael, age 8 years, 9 months, on petitions alleging truancy from home and school, habitual begging, and petty stealing. The judge asked if the father was paying the six dollars per month assessment for the care of the children in the home for dependent children. The court clerk stated:

The father did pay $18.00 for each of them for the month, but nothing since. They are chronic beggars and the institution won't take them back, so we don't know what to do with the children. We think that a petition should be filed on the older boy [James] and have him sent to St. Charles. He is constantly begging.

The dependent petition relative to James was changed to a delinquent petition and he was committed to St. Charles School for Boys.

45. *Thirteen years, nine months:*

He was paroled from the St. Charles School for Boys.

46. *Thirteen years, ten months:*

Mother requested the court to return James to the St. Charles School for Boys. The probation officer referred the request to the managing officer of the industrial school. The request reads:

I am informed by the mother of the above named boy [James] that since his return from the St. Charles School some months ago he has been exceedingly troublesome, and has led his younger brother Michael into mischief at frequent intervals. James has been entered in the eighth grade at K—— School. His teacher, Miss F——, tells me that he is habitually truant and frequently leaves school at recess during the rare intervals when he does attend, and does not return for the day. His mother states James and his brother Michael stay away from home for days at a time. She would like steps taken to have the boy returned to St. Charles in case he is on parole.

No official action was taken.

47. *Thirteen years, eleven months:*

He was arrested and brought to court with Michael, age 11 years, 11 months, on a petition alleging delinquency. They were charged with burglary and truancy from school. The two brothers had entered and burglarized five homes in a suburban community. The probation officer, in presenting the history of the case to the court, said:

They were picked up in one of the suburban communities. Michael has been on probation to me for a year. James was released from St. Charles a short time ago. His mother tells me that ever since his coming home there has been trouble. He takes Michael away and they just bum the streets. They were going to school. James isn't very speedy, but his teacher tells me he is alright if left to himself. I understand they were picked up for theft. This is the mother. She has had trouble with both boys.

Returned to the St. Charles School for Boys as a parole violator.

48. *Fifteen years, eight months:*

He was paroled from the St. Charles School for Boys to Mr. C. Johnson, a farmer near the school.

49. *Fifteen years, eight months:*
He ran away from the farmer.

50. *Fifteen years, eight months:*
He was picked up in Chicago and returned to the St. Charles School for Boys as a parole violator.

51. *Fifteen years, nine months:*
James escaped from the St. Charles School for Boys.

52. *Fifteen years, nine months:*
James was arrested for burglary and held in the Detention Home for investigation. Returned to St. Charles School for Boys as a parole violator.

53. *Sixteen years:*
He was paroled from the St. Charles School for Boys.

54. *Sixteen years, three months:*
Returned to the St. Charles School for Boys as a parole violator on the complaint of his mother, who stated that he was abusive and had tried to hit her.

55. *Sixteen years, four months:*
James escaped from the St. Charles School for Boys.

56. *Sixteen years, seven months:*
He was arrested and brought to court charged with larceny of an automobile. James claims that another boy was involved but does not know the name of the other boy. According to statements in the record of the court hearing, the judge asked James if he should return him to the St. Charles School for Boys. James answered:

"I don't; it didn't do me no good being out there—I was there four years—if you will give me a chance I think I can make good."

James was committed to the Chicago and Cook County School for Boys.

57. *Sixteen years, seven months:*
He escaped from the Chicago and Cook County School for Boys.

58. *Sixteen years, eight months:*

James was arrested while attempting the larceny of an automobile, and was held in the Juvenile Detention Home. Two weeks later James was brought before the Juvenile Court. The record reads in part:

COURT CLERK: This case is brought in for a rehearing. On July 6th, James was committed to the Chicago and Cook County School for Boys. He had escaped from St. Charles. The Managing Officer, through error, was not notified that the boy was coming into court. There was no one to represent him here. James ran away from the Chicago and Cook County School six days after he went there. He now says he won't run away again.

THE PROBATION OFFICER: Yes, it is an unusual case. I do feel it would not accomplish very much to have him go back to St. Charles. I think he is fed up on that. He promised me before the hearing that he would stay out there for the longest period, do exactly what I wished, if he was given another chance.

THE PAROLE OFFICER: Yes sir, he was committed to St. Charles six years ago. He has been paroled from there three times and escaped twice.

James was returned to the Chicago and Cook County School for Boys.

59. *Sixteen years, eight months:*

He escaped from the Chicago and Cook County School for Boys.

60. *Sixteen years, nine months:*

While in the company of Milton Smith, age 17 years, 9 months, and Ralph Palmer, age 14 years, James was arrested loitering about some parked automobiles. Returned to the St. Charles School for Boys.

61. *Seventeen years:*

He escaped from the St. Charles School for Boys.

62. *Seventeen years:*

In the company of his brother Edward, who was 21 years, 11 months, and on a parole from the Illinois State Reformatory, James was arrested while tampering with a parked automobile in a well-to-do suburban community. He was returned to the St. Charles School for Boys.

63. *Seventeen years, five months:*

He was paroled from the St. Charles School for Boys.

64. *Seventeen years, six months:*

Arrested and charged with violation of parole. The parole officer brought him before the Boys' Court and charged him with disorderly conduct. The officer told the court that he "had not exerted any effort in finding a job." He was fined $31.50. As he could not pay the fine he was confined in the House of Correction to work out the fine. After being held twelve days his brothers paid the difference of the fine due.

65. *Seventeen years, six months:*

He was released from the House of Correction.

66. *Seventeen years, seven months:*

In the company of Francis Berman, age 16 years, 10 months, and Elmer Jolson, 23 years, 11 months, James was arrested in a stolen automobile. James was brought to the Boys' Court and charged with larceny. The two associates were released by the police as James admitted the theft. He was committed to the House of Correction for ten days.

67. *Seventeen years, seven months:*

He was released from the House of Correction.

68. *Seventeen years, eight months:*

He was arrested and charged with larceny of an automobile. Sentenced to thirty days in the House of Correction.

69. *Seventeen years, nine months:*

He was released from the House of Correction.

70. *Seventeen years, nine months:*

James was arrested and brought to court with Francis Berman, 17 years, and Clyde Jones, 18 years, charged with larceny of an automobile. James and Berman were committed to the Illinois State Reformatory for an indeterminate sentence of from one to ten years; Clyde Jones was committed to the House of Correction for a period of one year.

71. *Twenty-four years, three months:*

Released from the Illinois State Reformatory.

MICHAEL MARTIN

Michael, the fourth brother, is twenty-seven years of age and is still confined in a penal institution. Michael is a tall, slender, and attractive young man who gives the impression of being an intelligent, sensitive, quiet, and reserved person. When he was nine years of age he was described in a clinical report as "a bright, alert, promising child, wide-awake, with a great deal of energy which, unfortunately, had been misdirected for a long period of time."

During twenty-two of Michael's twenty-six years of life he has been engaged in delinquency or confined in institutions. His first contact with the police occurred at the time he was four years and eight months of age, when he was found by the police wandering about the streets late at night. In the course of the last twenty-two years he has been picked up by the police fifteen times, taken into courts on thirteen occasions, served eleven periods in institutions (a total of more than seventeen years), and has been placed under the supervision of probation and parole officers at least six times. The official record of his arrests, court appearances, and commitments to institutions follows.

1. *Four years, eight months of age:*

Michael was picked up by the police while begging at the South Water Street Market. He had been in the company of his older brothers, but was separated from them at the time the police found him. Released to parents.

2. *Four years, eight months:*

In the company of Edward, age 11 years, 7 months, James, 6 years, 8 months, and Carl, 2 years, 10 months, Michael was found wandering about the Streets at 10 o'clock P.M. Released to parents. Dependency petitions were filed on all the children. (See Edward, No. 7.)

3. *Four years, eight months:*

The dependency petitions were heard before the Juvenile Court. Michael was placed on probation.

4. *Five years:*

While in the company of Edward, age 11 years, 11 months, James, 7 years, and Carl, 3 years, 3 months, Michael was arrested and brought to the Juvenile Detention Home charged with truancy from home, begging, and petty stealing. Released to parents under the supervision of an officer.

5. *Five years, four months:*

With Edward, age 12 years, 3 months, James, 7 years, 4 months, and Carl, 3 years, 7 months, Michael was brought to court on petitions alleging dependency. All the children except Edward were released and placed under the supervision of a probation officer of the Juvenile Court. (See Edward, No. 28.)

6. *Six years:*

He was reported begging with Edward, age 12 years, 11 months, in a prosperous North Side community. (See Edward, No. 37.)

7. *Six years:*

He was reported begging in a North Side community.

8. *Six years, one month:*

He was reported begging in a well-to-do residential community about five miles from his home.

9. *Six years, two months:*

He was reported begging in a well-to-do residential community.

10. *Six years, two months:*

He was reported begging with James, age 8 years, 3 months. The incident was reported to a family-case-work agency by a resident of a well-to-do residential community.

11. *Six years, two months:*

He was reported begging in a well-to-do residential community approximately five miles from his home. Carried a basket well filled with canned goods, bread, and the like— evidently contributions from the neighborhood.

12. *Six years, two months:*

He was reported begging with James, age 8 years, 3 months, and Carl, 4 years, 5 months. The incident was reported to a family-case-work agency by a resident of a near-by residential community.

13. *Six years, three months:*

He was reported begging in a well-to-do residential community approximately five miles from his home.

14. *Seven years, five months:*

He was reported begging at homes on the Near North Side.

15. *Seven years, five months:*

He was reported begging in a well-to-do residential community about three miles from his home. He told the resident who reported the case a very pitiful tale but one that she was sure was memorized and had been used before.

16. *Seven years, five months:*

He was reported begging in a well-to-do residential section about two miles from home.

17. *Seven years, seven months:*

He was arrested and brought to court on a petition alleging dependency. The history of the case indicated truancy from home and school, and habitual begging. Michael was committed to a home for dependent children.

18. *Seven years, seven months:*

He ran away from the home for dependent children.

19. *Seven years, seven months:*

He was returned to the home for dependent children.

20. *Seven years, eight months:*

He ran away from the home for dependent children.

21. *Seven years, eight months:*

He was reported begging with James, age 9 years, 8 months. The complaint was filed with a family-case-work agency by a resident of a well-to-do residential community.

22. *Eight years:*

He was reported begging in a North Side residential community with James, age 10 years. The complaint was filed with the Juvenile Court by a family-case-work agency but no official action was taken.

23. *Eight years:*

He was reported begging in a Loop office building with James, age 10 years. Complaint was filed with a family-case-work agency and in turn was reported to the Juvenile Court. No official action was taken.

24. *Eight years:*

He was reported begging in the Near North Side with James, age 10 years. Complaint was filed by a resident of the community with a family-case-work agency. This organization reported the incident to the Juvenile Court but no official action was taken.

25. *Eight years:*

He was reported begging alone in a Loop office building.

26. *Eight years:*

He was reported begging in a Loop office building with James, age 10 years. The complaint was filed with a family-case-work agency. This organization reported the incident to the Juvenile Court but no official action was taken.

27. *Eight years:*

He was reported begging alone at 18— North W——Street.

28. *Eight years, one month:*

He was reported begging with James, age 10 years, 1 month, in a well-to-do residential community. The complaint was filed by a resident with a family-case-work agency and in turn the agency reported the incident to the Juvenile Court but no official action was taken.

29. *Eight years, one month:*

Michael was arrested with an unknown companion while in the act of breaking into a residence located at 37— W—— Avenue. He admitted breaking into a residence located at 36— W—— Avenue earlier in the day. Released to the parents at the district police station.

30. *Eight years, one month:*

Michael was arrested in the company of James, age 10 years, 2 months, and charged with committing three burglaries. He was held in the Juvenile Detention Home.

31. *Eight years, three months:*

He was brought to court with James, age 10 years, 3 months, and Carl, 6 years, 5 months, on a petition alleging dependency. Committed to a home for dependent children. (See James, No. 39.)

32. *Eight years, three months:*

He escaped from the home for dependent children with James, age 10 years, 3 months, but was returned the following day.

33. *Eight years, four months:*

He escaped from the home for dependent children with James, 10 years, 4 months, but was returned the following day.

34. *Eight years, seven months:*

With James, 10 years, 7 months, Michael escaped from the home for dependent children. (See James, No. 42.)

35. *Eight years, seven months:*

While in the company of his brother, Edward, 15 years, 5 months, and James, 10 years, 7 months, Michael was arrested in a suburban community in the act of burglarizing a home. Although involved, James was not apprehended. Edward escaped from the police station the following morning. Michael was later released to his father by the police. (See Edward, No. 51.)

36. *Eight years, seven months:*

He was arrested while begging with James, age 10 years, 7 months, in a suburban community. Released to the parents. (See James, No. 43.)

37. *Eight years, nine months:*

With James, age 10 years, 9 months, Michael was brought to court on petitions alleging dependency. Michael was committed to a home for dependent children. (See James, No. 44.)

38. *Ten years, ten months:*

He was paroled from the home for dependent children.

39. *Ten years, eleven months:*

He was reported begging in a well-to-do neighborhood about six miles from his home.

40. *Eleven years:*

He ran away from home. Michael was apprehended a few days later and placed in the Juvenile Detention Home.

41. *Eleven years:*

He was brought to court on a petition charging truancy from school, habitual begging, and petty stealing. Committed to the Chicago Parental School.

42. *Eleven years, six months:*

He was released from the Chicago Parental School.

43. *Eleven years, eleven months:*

With James, age 13 years, 11 months, Michael was brought to court charged with burglary and truancy from school. The two brothers had entered and burglarized five homes in a suburban community. Returned to the Chicago Parental School. (See James, No. 47.)

44. *Twelve years, four months:*

He was released from the Chicago Parental School.

45. *Twelve years, seven months:*

With his brother, Carl, age 10 years, 9 months, Michael was arrested and brought to court charged with burglary. The court record reads:

Michael Martin, in company with his brother Carl, entered the apartment of Wilson Greenman, 16— F—— Avenue, through a partly open window, taking and carrying away jewelry and other articles to the value of $356.00 and two checks. All recovered but one check. Also entered the apartment of Dr. Mason in the same building through a partly open window, taking and carrying away jewelry and other articles to the value of $200.00. All property recovered. They also admitted that they committed three burglaries on M—— Avenue and three burglaries on L—— Boulevard. No property recovered.

Committed to the St. Charles School for Boys.

46. *Thirteen years, nine months:*

He escaped from the St. Charles School for Boys.

47. *Thirteen years, nine months:*

With Carl, age 11 years, 10 months, and Joseph Herman, age 14 years, 7 months, Michael was arrested and brought to court charged with burglary. They had entered a residence located at 44— North S—— Street and stolen articles valued at $45. Returned to St. Charles School for Boys.

48. *Fourteen years, eight months:*

He was paroled from the St. Charles School for Boys.

49. *Fourteen years, eight months:*

He was arrested and charged with larceny of an automobile. Recommitted to the St. Charles School for Boys.

50. *Fourteen years, eleven months:*

He escaped from the St. Charles School for Boys but was returned the same day.

51. *Fifteen years, eight months:*

He was paroled from the St. Charles School for Boys.

52. *Fifteen years, nine months:*

In company with Francis Berman, age 17, Clyde Jones, age 18, Alfred Schwartz, age 26, Michael was arrested and charged with robbery with a gun, burglary, and larceny of automobiles. The Grand Jury returned five indictments against the group. Three indictments were stricken off with leave to reinstate. Michael was committed to the Illinois State Reformatory on two sentences of from one to ten years, to be served concurrently. However, when he was received at the Reformatory, he was rejected because he was under the committable age. The sentence was suspended and he was returned to the St. Charles Training School for Boys. Francis Berman was committed to the Illinois State Reformatory on two sentences of from one to ten years, to be served concurrently. Clyde Jones was committed for one year to the House of Correction and fined $100 and costs, and Alfred Schwartz was committed to the Illinois State Penitentiary for an indeterminate sentence of from ten years to life.

53. *Sixteen years, three months:*

In company with Joseph Siegel, age 18, John Bolton, 18, and Fred Jensen, 17 years, 5 months, Michael escaped from St. Charles. They stole an automobile and drove it to Chicago.

54. *Sixteen years, three months:*

While in the company of John Bolton, age 18 years, Michael stole another automobile in Chicago, and, while being chased by the police, crashed into an electric-light pole. Michael was returned to the St. Charles School for Boys as an escapee.

55. *Sixteen years, three months:*

Michael was removed from the St. Charles School for Boys and brought to the Criminal Court as he was now committable to the Illinois State Reformatory. Two indictments for robbery with a gun and larceny of an automobile, which had been stricken off with leave to reinstate at his last appearance in the Criminal Court, were reinstated. He was committed to the Illinois State Reformatory on two indeterminate sentences of from one to ten years, to be served concurrently.

56. *Twenty-one years, four months:*

He was released from the Illinois State Reformatory.

57. *Twenty-one years, seven months:*

In company with Cyril French, age 25 years, Michael was arrested and charged with robbery with a gun. They were identified as committing two armed robberies. Michael was committed to the Illinois State Penitentiary on an indeterminate sentence of from one year to life.

CARL MARTIN

Carl, the youngest of the Martin brothers, is twenty-five years of age, unmarried, and resides with his mother. As compared with his brothers, Carl is a much more stolid and reserved person. His work record during recent years has been quite irregular, although different employment opportunities have been provided for him.

According to the records of the Juvenile Court and family-case-work agencies, Carl was picked up by the police for stealing when he was about three years and three months of age. These early experiences occurred when he was in the company of his older brothers. His active career in delinquency continued over a period of approximately thirteen years, during which time he was picked up and arrested by the police on fourteen occasions, appeared in courts sixteen times, served six periods of confinement in institutions, and was placed under the supervision of probation and parole officers twelve times. The detailed record of his arrests, appearances in court, and commitments follows.

1. *Two years, ten months of age:*

In company with Edward, age 11 years, 7 months, James, 6 years, 8 months, and Michael, 4 years, 8 months, Carl was picked up by the police wandering about the streets at 10 o'clock P.M. He was released to the parents. Dependency petitions were filed on all the children. (See Edward, No. 7.)

2. *Two years, ten months:*

He was brought to court with Edward, age 11 years, 7 months, James, 6 years, 8 months, and Michael, 4 years, 8 months, on petitions alleging dependency. Carl was placed under the supervision of a probation officer of the Juvenile Court.

3. *Three years, three months:*

While in the company of his brothers, Edward, age 11 years, 11 months, James, 7 years, Michael, 5 years, Carl was brought to the Detention Home charged with truancy from home, begging, and stealing. Released to the parents under supervision of an officer.

4. *Three years, seven months:*

He was brought to court with Edward, age 12 years, 3 months, James, 7 years, 4 months, and Michael, 5 years, 4 months, on dependency petitions. The petition was continued and all the children except Edward were released and placed under the supervision of a probation officer of the Juvenile Court. (See Edward, No. 28.)

5. *Four years, five months:*

He was reported begging with James, age 8 years, 3 months, and Michael, 6 years, 2 months. The complaint was filed with a family-case-work agency by a resident of a near-by community.

6. *Five years, eight months:*

Carl, in company with Michael, age 7 years, 5 months, was arrested and brought to the Juvenile Court charged with begging and petty stealing. He was released to his parents under supervision of a probation officer of the court.

7. *Five years, ten months:*

Carl was ordered brought to court on a dependency petition. The court record reads:

This is the Martin case. The mother is present, but she did not bring the children in with her. The judge ordered dependency petition filed, but neither of the children is present this morning. The brother, Michael, was committed some time ago to the home for dependent children. The mother came in this morning without the children.

When the mother was asked by the judge why she didn't bring the children to court she said: "I don't know why they want them here; they haven't done anything." The owner of the building in which the Martins live was present and said:

"I am the landlord. She is living in my building. The woman is alright and I have no fault to find; here is a plan of my building. I am going to give her another room to live in. I have no complaint to make against her. They are good people as far as I know."

The judge continued the case for three weeks and said:

"See if you can move into that other room and take good care of your children. The next time you are ordered to have them here, bring them in."

When Carl was brought to court he was released to the parents under the supervision of a probation officer.

8. *Six years, five months:*

He was brought to court with James, age 10 years, 3 months, and Michael, 8 years, 3 months, on petitions alleging dependency. Carl was committed to the home for dependent children. (See James, No. 39.)

9. *Seven years:*

Carl's father visited the home for dependent children and took Carl home without the consent of the authorities.

10. *Seven years, four months:*

He was picked up by the police in a railway station and returned to his parents. The incident was reported in the metropolitan press:

With 60 cents he had accumulated for the occasion, 7-year-old Carl Martin, 44— B—— St., started out yesterday to "see Chicago first."

He boarded an elevated train and apparently rode all over the city. His "roll" was exhausted late in the evening, so he walked to the Polk St. railway station, where he was picked up by the police. It was a tired but educated Carl who was turned over to his parents.

11. *Ten years, nine months:*

While in company with Michael, age 12 years, 7 months, Carl was arrested and brought to court on a delinquency petition alleging burglary. He was released to his mother under the supervision of a court officer. (See Michael, No. 45.)

12. *Eleven years:*

The mother was ordered to bring Carl to court on a petition alleging truancy from school, begging, and petty stealing. The court record reads:

Officer reports that the mother started with the boy who jumped off the street car at corner and ran away. Officer states he [Carl] has done fairly well.

The probation officer was ordered to continue supervision of Carl.

13. *Eleven years, four months:*

He was brought to court on a petition alleging truancy from school. The court record reads:

Officer Howard reports boy is under supervision; has been guilty of serious truancy; that he understands the school authorities have instituted truancy proceedings but does not know the date of same.

He was released to his mother under supervision of the court officer.

14. *Eleven years, five months*

He was brought to court on a petition alleging truancy from school. Carl was committed to the Chicago Parental School.

15. *Eleven years, eight months:*

He was paroled from the Chicago Parental School.

16. *Eleven years, ten months:*

While in company with Michael, age 13 years, 9 months, and Joseph Herman, 14 years, 7 months, Carl was arrested and brought to court charged with burglary. Michael was returned to the St. Charles School for Boys. The hearing was continued in order that an investigation could be made in the case of Carl and Joseph Herman. Carl was released to his mother pending the investigation. (See Michael, No. 47.)

17. *Twelve years:*
Returned to the Chicago Parental School for violation of parole.

18. *Twelve years, six months:*
Paroled from the Chicago Parental School.

19. *Thirteen years, two months:*
Arrested and brought to court on a delinquency petition alleging the theft of an automobile. The court record reads:

At 9:30 P.M. Monday this boy stole a Studebaker automobile from the ground of a suburban country club—touring car valued at $950.00—the property of Frank Johnson. Two days later he was caught in possession of the aforesaid car in the vicinity of E—— and H—— streets by officers P—— and G—— of the Police District. Auto recovered although the tools and an auto robe had disappeared.

Carl was committed to the Chicago and Cook County School for Boys.

20. *Thirteen years, three months:*
He escaped from the Chicago and Cook County School for Boys.

21. *Thirteen years, four months:*
He was arrested and returned to Chicago and Cook County School for Boys.

22. *Thirteen years, five months:*
He escaped from the Chicago and Cook County School for Boys but was returned two days later.

23. *Thirteen years, five months:*
Paroled from the Chicago and Cook County School for Boys.

24. *Thirteen years, nine months:*
In the company of Joseph Herman, age 16 years, 6 months, Walter Kohler, age 14 years, Adam Krancer, age 22 years,

John Olson, 24 years, and Homer Luda, Carl was arrested and brought to court charged with larceny of two automobiles. In presenting the case to the court the probation officer charged:

On July 9th, 19—, at 1:00 A.M., the above named boy and Joseph Herman, 16 years, Walter Kohler, 14 years, did steal and drive away a Chevrolet touring car from the curb in front of 13— North H—— Ave., the property of Greta Lohner. The above named boys were arrested at E—— and M—— avenues while riding in the aforesaid automobile. Carl and a boy known as Ralph Palmer [never identified] did steal and drive away a Chevrolet sedan from the curb in front of 12— North O—— St., and drove it to an alley on B—— Street, where it was stripped of tires by Adam Krancer, 22 years old, John Olson, 21 years old, and Homer Luda, 21 years old. The car was the property of I. Greenberg, 40— North L—— Avenue.

Adam Krancer was committed to the House of Correction for a period of sixty days, John Olson was committed to the House of Correction for a period of four months, Homer Luda was fined $100 and costs, Joseph Herman was committed to the Chicago and Cook County School for Boys, and Walter Kohler was placed on probation. Carl was committed to the St. Charles School for Boys.

25. *Fifteen years, two months:*

Carl was paroled from the St. Charles School for Boys.

26. *Seventeen years, eight months:*

He was arrested on suspicion and charged with disorderly conduct but was discharged the same day.

27. *Twenty-one years, five months:*

Carl was arrested on a charge of disorderly conduct and discharged.

28. *Twenty-two years, five months:*

He was arrested on suspicion and charged with disorderly conduct but was discharged.

The foregoing official records reveal certain marked similarities in the delinquent careers of the five brothers. Both the specific forms of their delinquency and the sequence of their delinquent experiences were similar. In the period of early childhood all of them engaged in begging, played truant from home and school, and were involved in various forms of petty stealing. From this early beginning there was in each case a progression to more serious and complicated types of delinquency and crime. These similarities are not surprising in view of the manner in which each boy involved his next younger brother in his delinquent practices. While the official records do not reveal how delinquent patterns were introduced into the family, they do suggest that these patterns were transmitted from the older to the younger brothers as soon as the latter became old enough to engage in begging and stealing expeditions. Thus Michael and Carl were engaged in delinquent activities before they reached the age of establishing significant relationships with children outside the family. Apparently the influences which were most immediately responsible for their earliest delinquencies were inherent in the home situation.

It is important to observe also that the problem of juvenile delinquency in this case was of such a character that it was not susceptible to the methods of treatment employed by the Juvenile Court, the behavior clinics, the correctional institutions, and social agencies. Despite the therapeutic efforts of all these organizations, the five brothers continued in delinquency throughout the period when they were wards of the Cook County Juvenile Court and four of them served sentences in penal institutions.

CHAPTER II

THE FIRST STEPS IN THE CAREERS
OF THE MARTIN BROTHERS

The official records included in the preceding chapter revealed in chronological sequence the specific delinquencies and crimes of the Martin brothers. In these records the successive offenses were described as separate, concrete acts, with a minimum regard for the dynamic life-processes in which they occurred. To understand more fully these delinquent acts as human experiences it is necessary to indicate the circumstances in which they took place, the manner in which they occurred, and something of their meaning and significance as interpreted by the brothers. In short, it seems desirable to describe the offenses, not simply as isolated acts abstracted from their social context, but as aspects of the whole system of interpersonal relationships and social practices which comprised the social world of the brothers. Viewed from this standpoint, the offenses may be regarded as a function of the efforts of the brothers to secure certain common human satisfactions in the particular situation in which they lived.

To give a picture of these more dynamic aspects of the delinquencies and crimes in the five careers a limited number of excerpts from the autobiographical documents of the brothers will be used. These excerpts have been organized into three groups, in each of which is described a particular phase of the process of education in delinquency and crime in the five careers. Those in the first group pertain to the initial delinquencies—the simple acts of petty stealing which occurred in early childhood. The excerpts in the second group give a description of the practice of burglarizing residences in well-to-do neighborhoods—the form of delinquency in which the brothers were jointly involved during the period of later childhood and early adolescence. Subsequent to this period their careers developed along rather widely divergent lines. John and Edward continued in burglary, James and Carl became implicated in the larceny of automobiles, and Michael embarked upon a career of robbery with a gun. These later divergent developments are described in the third group of excerpts. The first group of excerpts will be presented in this chapter, while those included in the second and third groups will be reserved for chapters iii and iv.

JOHN MARTIN

Although John was first taken into custody by the police for theft during his tenth year, his earliest experience in stealing actually took place at least three years previously. As he states in the following excerpts, at approximately the age of seven he began to steal from cars located in railroad yards near his home. He engaged in this practice in the company of many other persons in the neighborhood. Along with this activity he became involved in begging, making raids on local stores, and petty burglary in the neighborhood. By the age of twelve he was involved in the larceny of bicycles in well-to-do neighborhoods in distant parts of the city.

BEGGING

. . . . In times of stress when father was out of work and there was nothing to eat in the house, he and I would go to the old South Water Street Market [which is now Wacker Drive] with a burlap sack or two and collect the dead chickens that were discarded but which were still palatable and fetch them home. Also, we would bring home anything else that we could secure undiscovered, such as bananas, oranges, apples. After we brought the chickens home we would all commence to remove the feathers and after cooking them we would all have a feast fit for the gods. That would be one of the rare instances when our inordinate appetites would be appeased. When I was older we got started begging in rich neighborhoods. . . . .

STEALING FROM RAILROADS

. . . . The earliest recollection that I have of going outside the pale of society was about the age of seven. I and Sam Ludlow, Victor Bolar, James Reiley, Michael Shepard, and several more boys went up on the railroad tracks near our home and broke into a box car loaded with cases of beer. We carried away several cases, but what we did with them I don't remember. The railroad bulls questioned me, but I shut up like a clam. Anyway there was nothing done about it on account of my extreme youth. I should like to see more coppers like that. . . . .

Another one of our acts, which according to convention is wrong, was the securing of coal. George Dyer, Michael Shepard, Fred Kilmer, and my brother Edward, myself, and lots of other kids would go up on the railroad tracks and after assuring ourselves that we were unobserved, especially that no railroad bulls were about, we would clamber upon a gondola and throw off the coal. Certainly we stole the coal. Why should one have it all while the other has nothing? It is a sad state of affairs that a man who has a family and is willing to work can't do so, through the fault of a few mercenary dollar chasers. . . . .

After stealing coal from railroads, William Stock, my brother, Edward, and I stole iron and lead pipes from old buildings in the neighborhood and sold them to the junkman. We went around all over the neighborhood getting anything that we could sell. We didn't make big money but we got enough for candy, shows, and other things that kids all want.

MAKING RAIDS ON NEIGHBORHOOD STORES

. . . . When I was young, our family was in dire circumstances most of the time and the family larder wasn't always full, so I visited various neighborhood department stores to purloin foodstuffs from the counters. In those days the counters weren't glass encased and it was a comparatively simple matter for us boys to grab anything that we craved. One time a clerk saw us removing some smoked sausages from a counter. In order to avoid public attention and to avoid embarrassing me, he took me to a back room and made me empty my pockets and shirt and after giving me a lecture and a dime sent me home. So that put the ban on that particular store. . . . .

I and my pals and my brother, Edward, continued these depredations on the stores for several months until we were finally nabbed and sent to the old Juvenile Detention Home at Gilpin and Halsted Streets just opposite the Hull-House. I always think of this joint with pleasant memories. It was quite a constrast to my home life. At home I didn't eat very often, while here I got plenty to eat, and was kept cleaned and all that rot. . . . .

PETTY BURGLARY IN THE NEIGHBORHOOD

. . . . Another one of my exploits and sources of revenue in childhood was stealing of rabbits. A pal of mine from the neighborhood, Samuel Ludlow, came up to me when I was about eight and asked me if I wanted to make some easy dough. Of course no one will pass up an opportunity to make money, especially "easy" money, so I replied in the affirmative. The three of us would then wait until nightfall (when every good crook puts in his dirty work) and venture out into the community to the scene of the proposed burglary, wherever it might be. After we'd get there we would force our way inside, secure what rabbits we thought best, and dispose of them for what we could get. We sold them to store keepers or to the other kids in the neighborhood.

EDWARD MARTIN

The earliest delinquencies in the career of Edward Martin were strikingly similar to those of his older brother and included stealing from railroads, making raids on neighborhood stores, stealing lead pipes and iron from vacant buildings, begging, and larceny of bicycles. These similarities were quite natural in view of the fact that Edward and John were not only jointly implicated in many of their early delinquencies, but also were associated with the same companions.

STEALING FROM RAILROADS

A lot of the kids and women living in our block would go over to the railroad tracks for coal. A whole flock would be there, twenty-five to forty. On Sundays, however, only the kids would be there. The kids would jump on the moving cars and throw the coal off. . . . .

I knew that my brother, John, started out to steal coal and break into coal cars with these kids in the neighborhood. They asked me to help, but I said it was too cold. I didn't want to get killed by the train. So one day they finally came around. They had some candy and offered me a piece. I thought it was good, and they told me I could pick up some coal and sell it and get some money for candy. So, you know how a kid is for candy. He'd give anything to get it. I went with them and picked up some pieces of coal. Then I got cold and wanted to go back home. They said that I had to pick up some more coal for the candy they gave me. I told them I would not do it and went home. The kids wanted their candy back. I told them I ate it and couldn't give it back. . . . .

We stole coal from off of the moving coal cars, and I had to learn to fight to defend my hard-earned bag of coal. We always went with a cement bag to steal coal, sometimes selling the bag for a dime, but most of the time I'd bring the coal home to ma.

JUNKING

From stealing coal, John, William Stock, and I would go junking. We would swipe lead pipes, gas pipes, and copper boilers. We'd go to empty flats and cut out lead pipes. It was a good day's work when we got into a vacant house and got the lead pipes, brass, faucets, and copper wire.

Some of my pals were always going out picking rags and they told me to come along and not to go to school, that they weren't going. So I would hide my books and go junking. After school I would go back to get my books and take them home. These same kids began to come around the house quite a bit and instead of me going to school, we'd go out on the railroad tracks and to the granaries and pick up coal and wood and sell it. You could always sell it for a nickel a bag, sometimes a dime, if you got hard coal. We used to buy candy with it, which at that time was two or three pieces for a nickle. I got to be a truant pretty regular then because I didn't like school. The kids were telling me whenever you are truant that if you go to a show the truant officer wouldn't catch you as they didn't look for you in shows. So we usually managed to make some money about every other day or so, and we were in shows almost all the time. Sometimes we'd find out where to swipe a brass boiler on back porches and get a dime for it. This way we had enough money for candy, shows and other things that kids like to have.

BEGGING

When I was a kid about seven years old, my pa used to go out to the old Water Street Market when he wasn't working and we would try to buy old stuff for a few pennies. I used to go with him and thought it was a lot of fun to go down in the dark basements and look over old fruit and vegetables with pa. Sometimes we asked if they had anything to give us. I went down for fun to get bananas and oranges to eat. The stuff tasted good and we didn't have much food at home. Pa would try to get old chickens and meat that they couldn't sell and they would give it to pa. Ma used to make soup out of this.

After I got out of Parental School at ten years of age, John was running around now and then with William Stock. I remember one time they were going to split a chocolate layer cake, which was shaped like a loaf of bread. He got it from a bakery. I thought that cake was good. I asked him, "Where did you get the cake, gee, your ma must have a lot of money to buy you a cake like that." He said, "Ma didn't buy it; I went out and got it." I said, "Yea, how did you get it?" He said he went out with a basket and over to people's stores and houses and asked them to help him out. He used to tell them nobody in his family was working and they were poor. So I asked when he was going again and he said that day, that afternoon. He let me go with him and showed me how to do it.

MAKING RAIDS ON NEIGHBORHOOD STORES

When I was about six or seven years old, my brother James and I and other boys did shop-lifting in the five and ten cents store in the neighborhood. We'd pick up a ring and tell the lady we didn't want it and then put it on and walk out. We'd show the ring to the kids and tell them what a swell diamond we had. We didn't have much money and candy tasted good. We took candy whenever we could take it. When it was already in bags, we'd grab a bag and walk out. First we'd sample butter kisses and then we'd take a whole bag.

Another thing we used to do was to take somebody's grocery store credit books and go to the store and get something to eat. These books were good for anybody who wanted credit in the store. I was five or six years old at the time we did this.

William Stock used to take anything he'd put his hands on. By doing these things with him I got into the habit of taking things too. A lot of the kids used to have a bicycle and William Stock, John, and I got some. William and I used to get rides off of John's. I couldn't ride a bicycle, but I had a tricycle that I stole and used to paddle along. The time I got it, I rode it five miles to my home.

JAMES MARTIN

The initial stage in the career of James Martin was similar to that of his older brothers, with one striking exception. Whereas John and Edward served a period of apprenticeship of five or six years in petty stealing in the neighborhood and begging before they became regularly involved in the burglary of residences, James, through the influence of Edward, was inducted into this practice prior to the age of seven. At that age he was already burglarizing residences in well-to-do neighborhoods in distant parts of the city and in suburban communities which were located five or more miles from his home and was first taken into custody for this form of stealing at seven years and four months. Simultaneously with the burglary of residences he participated with his brothers and their companions in begging and in the usual forms of petty stealing in the neighborhood.

I started stealing when I was about six or seven years old. I ran around with my brother [Edward] and his pals, William Stock and Joseph Wyman, who were older than me. With them I used to steal fruit from the peddlers' wagons that used to parade along the streets. As I grew older, I started to shoplift with my buddies and many times with my brothers. We used to go into large department stores, look around and snatch anything that caught our fancy. We used to do this many times because we did not like to go to school, and whenever we got tired of staying in the class, we would sneak out and run away at recess time and hide our books and then go riding on the "L" to some well-to-do district or to the Loop. I was kind of experienced when I quit associating with these older fellows.

While going to school one day, I was accosted by William Stock and my brother, Edward. I was about nine years old. They told me if I would do them a favor, they would give me some money. I agreed to do this favor for them. That night, the three of us burglarized a barber shop. The window was boarded up. William Stock and my brother tore one of the boards away. They then pushed me through the small opening they made, and I opened the back door for them. I knew I was doing wrong, but to my youthful fancy, I thought it was brave to do such things then.

BEGGING

When I was about six years old, my brother Edward and a neighbor's kid, Joseph Wyman, taught me how to beg. I was so small and innocent looking that it was easy for me to deceive people. I would go to the door of a cottage or apartment and knock on the door or ring the bell. If someone would answer, I would tell the person how poor my parents were. In this I was telling the truth. Seldom did I turn away without some money, food, or clothing. If no one answered my call, I took it for granted that the people were not at home. I again made sure by knocking, ringing the bell and making a lot of noise. If no one answered then, I told my older accomplice, and we would break in.

From begging alone, I would procure sometimes three, four, or five dollars in a day and always a lot of food. The food I would almost always take home. Sometimes I would leave it on somebody's doorway. I did this mostly when I was "out of the house." . . . .

STEALING BICYCLES

We stole bicycles when we were small. As we grew older, we started to stealing automobiles just for the fun and the rides. Later on it became a business proposition.

MICHAEL MARTIN

The early phase of Michael's career in delinquency was almost identical with that of James. At the age of five he began to accompany James and Edward on begging expeditions to well-to-do communities. Sometime during his sixth year he was involved with his brothers in the burglary of residences, although his first arrest for this type of offense did not occur until he was eight years and one month of age. Contemporaneously with these experiences he engaged in pilfering in the neighborhood, shoplifting in department stores, and stealing pocketbooks at the bathing beaches.

BEGGING AND PETTY STEALING

When I was about seven years old, ... my brother then took me to the rich districts in Chicago and taught me how to beg. I started doing this and I liked it very well because it gave me a chance to see how rich people lived and sometimes I would make about $3.00 or $4.00 a day. To do it I would usually go to the rich neighborhoods with my brother at about 8 or

9 o'clock in the morning by either sneaking on the "L" lines or hopping trucks and wagons. When we decided the neighborhood was good looking enough we would get off. Then my brother would tell me at which houses he wanted me to beg. I would go to these houses and ring the door bell, while he waited for me in the alley till I came out. If the people were at home I was to tell them my story and then if they were kind people they usually gave me food, clothing or money, and sometimes I got both.

PETTY STEALING IN THE NEIGHBORHOOD, SHOPLIFTING, AND STEALING PURSES AT BATHING BEACHES

I was still a youngster when my brother, who was a few years older than me picked me as one of his companions. He and I and Frank Pepper, who later became my partner in crime, started going out together and to bum from school. I was taken all over the city by them. We usually hopped on wagons, trucks, or any vehicle which seemed to be going in the direction in which we wanted to. My brother and partner both were older than I and more experienced in ways of stealing, so whenever we came in front of a news stand on the street corner we would look and see if there should happen to be a few odd pennies on it and if there were my brother and partner would take them, while I would watch them. After they would take the pennies, we would run away from the news stand before the owner came out. It was this way that I learned to steal from news stands and any other kind of magazine stands. At the time I first started stealing pennies from news stands, my brothers who were older and a lot more experienced were already in a different racket. They were burglarizing homes over in the rich neighborhoods with their buddies. During the time I was stealing with my brother James and my partner, whose name is Frank Pepper, I did not take things seriously and it seems only natural that I was following right in my brother's steps because I was being taught by him and my other buddies. The only thing I thought of when I was stealing pennies from news stands and fruits from peddlers was not to get caught because I did not want my father to give me a whipping because whenever he did whip us we usually got a hard beating.

After my eleventh birthday I started to go with older boys to the beaches, where we would steal pocketbooks till finally I tried it alone and was caught. The way I stole pocketbooks was when I saw some people leave their clothes on the beach. After they would go in swimming, I would keep my eyes on them, search their clothes till I found the pocketbooks, then I put them in my pockets when nobody was looking and went some place to see how much money I stole. If it was enough to last me for a few days I would quit and spend it, but if I didn't get enough I would go back to the beach and steal more till I got enough. Well I kept this up for about two weeks, until I was caught by the people from whom I was stealing and they turned me over to the police. . . . .

CARL MARTIN

The beginning of Carl's education in delinquent techniques and practices occurred at an incredibly early age. He was picked up by the police for stealing at the age of three years and three months (see No. 3, p. 43), and was already involved in the burglary of residences at the age of six. Most of these early experiences took place when he was in the company of his older brothers.

BEGGING AND STEALING BICYCLES

When I was about five years old I used to go with my brother Michael and his pals to rich neighborhoods to beg. In these neighborhoods we would go from house to house and ask people for food, old clothes, and money. Sometimes we would get food, sometimes old clothes, and very often they would give us money. Michael knew just how to get things from people.

After I started to school I kept wanting to go out begging. I didn't like school. I would take a day off now and then and not attend school at all. On these occasions I would hide my books in the school lavatory on the top of some steam pipes, out of sight. Then I would go out with Michael to beg and steal. We had a grand time on these trips and always got things that we wanted.

When we were begging, we would steal everything we could get. At first I wanted toys and things like that. This was the way I got bicycles and tricycles that I would ride back to our neighborhood. We would get these out of yards and basements. Michael and I kept this up until we were caught and put on probation.

PETTY STEALING IN THE NEIGHBORHOOD AND SHOPLIFTING

One of my first experiences in delinquency that I can remember was one morning when I was walking along M—— Avenue with my brother Michael. As it was pretty chilly that day, we stepped into a department store to warm up. As we were walking through the store Michael showed me the candy counter. He walked right up to the counter and took some candy from it, and I, seeing how easy he did it, went up and took some too. That as far as I remember, was one of my first experiences in stealing. It seemed so easy to do that I did not think anything of it, and I did it again and again.

After taking candy, I would go back to the store to see if I couldn't get something else. On arriving there I would take chewing gum, toys, capguns, and such other petty stuff.

. . . . Then I again started stealing from the department stores when I did not go to school. Well I kept this up until I was sent to the Parental School for not going to school.

ATTITUDES OF THE BROTHERS TOWARD THESE EARLY DELINQUENCIES

It is important to observe that at the time these earlier delinquencies occurred the brothers were only vaguely aware of their implication from the standpoint of conventional society. The available evidence suggests that they were habitually engaged in various forms of stealing before they were distinctly aware of the fact that their activities were in violation of the laws and moral standards of the larger social order. Apparently they engaged in stealing because it was one of the forms of activity which prevailed in the groups to which they belonged; from the standpoint of these groups stealing was an accepted and approved practice. Naturally, as active members of these groups and in the absence of any effective contradicting group influences, the brothers accepted stealing as a form of normal behavior. The realization that there was a larger conventional society whose standards of conduct were in opposition to the standards of their immediate social world was not distinctly impressed upon the brothers until they were taken into court and committed to correctional institutions. The following statements give support to this assumption.

At the time we were taking lead pipes, it wasn't stealing to me. I didn't know I was doing anything wrong. I figured it was alright to take it. Several times when we would sell something to the junk man, when he would go in the back, we would take something from the front. Then we would go to the show. Shows were the big idea. We liked Western and Cowboy shows.

We used to hear about the big guys going out and burglarizing stores. Most of our friends in the neighborhood used to talk about stealing. We heard it was done by big people and whatever they did was right and if we could follow them we'd be good people. Even when the police came looking for them, I was told that they came to get part of the proceeds. Most of the kids in the neighborhood I knew were involved in stealing.

Up to the age of eight or nine I never even used to think that our stealing was anything wrong. If you did anything or got anything you were just doing the right thing and were clever enough to do it, that's all.

When I went out to burglarize and steal with older boys, I naturally neglected going to school. Reports from the school to my parents were getting frequent when I missed school day after day. It was then that I started to lie to my parents. I was threatened with a spanking many times from my mother. This scared me a little and I wanted to go back to school and behave but the older fellows always taunted me saying I was a sissy, etc. Then I would go with them to do "jobs." As I was small and young, I got away with a lot of thefts before I was finally apprehended by the police and learned that it was wrong. . . . .

. . . . My brother, Edward, was not a novice at the burglary racket. I'm sorry to say that he influenced me not a little, in regard to stealing. William Stock and Edward were buddies and Michael and I were taken out to steal many times by them. I thought what they did was alright. I'm sorry to say that my younger brother Michael was influenced by me later on. I think that if my folks had lived anywhere but in a big city like Chicago, I or any of my brothers would never have seen the inside of any institution or prison.

The way each member of my family started to steal was probably by being led by one another. I don't know much of my oldest brother's ways, because at the age he started to steal I was still a child. Since then I haven't seen or known much about his ways in crime. But my brother, Edward, was largely responsible for mine, as well as my other two younger brothers' faulty and criminal ways. My brother, Edward, used to pal around with a number of associates his age, and they stole things together. They taught my brother James the art of burglary and many other tricks of stealing as soon as he was old enough. Naturally when Edward got caught and sentenced to St. Charles my brother James would select the next brother to help along in begging and stealing and breaking into people's homes. I was picked out as the one to go with him. I usually obeyed his orders because I trusted him. The guys used to go around, me with them, and we would naturally become friends too, so that's about the way I started to learn how to steal. Through James and his pals, who came to be my pals, I got started stealing and later Carl got started through me. I used to take him out stealing whenever James and Edward were arrested and sent away. I taught Carl the tricks that had been taught to me.

The fellows I went with to rich suburbs to break into homes would associate with Carl and when I was ever arrested and sentenced to Parental School or St. Charles they usually would continue to break into homes whenever they wanted to and my kid brother would be with them, so that is the way I and my two younger brothers were led into crime. It was through the teaching of our older brothers and their friends they picked for us to associate with. We did all of these things together and we didn't think they were wrong.

The experiences described in the foregoing autobiographical excerpts comprise the initial phase of the development of the delinquent and criminal careers of these youthful offenders. These delinquencies consisted primarily of rather simple acts of stealing, which required relatively little planning, skill, or dexterity. They were, in most instances, forms of social behavior in which two or more of the brothers, or their companions, were implicated. And, it is apparent, as suggested before, that each brother was instrumental in introducing each succeeding one into these early delinquent practices.

CHAPTER III

FROM BEGGING TO BURGLARY

It is the purpose of this chapter to give a description of the offenses in which the Martin brothers were implicated during the period of late childhood and beginning adolescence. Roughly this phase of their careers comprised the period between the ages of nine and fifteen years. As indicated in the official records the burglary of residences in well-to-do neighborhoods constituted the most common type of theft in which the brothers were engaged during this period in their lives. Their description of these offenses gives evidence of the employment of more refined techniques, of greater deliberation and premeditation in planning offenses, of increased utilization of professional fences for the disposal of stolen goods, and of more definitely crystallized attitudes of suspicion and hostility with regard to the police, the courts, and the officers to whom the brothers were assigned for supervision while on probation and parole. The transition from the initial experiences in petty stealing to the burglary of residences was a continuous process of education, habituation, and increasing sophistication in the art of stealing. The first simple acts of stealing were preparatory to the more serious and more carefully planned depredations which succeeded them.

It appears that the burglary of residences developed as an adjunct to the begging in which John, Edward, and their companions were involved. Originally their primary object in begging in the South Water Street Market and in the well-to-do neighborhoods was to secure food, clothing, and money. Later, probably because of their earlier experiences in stealing in their own neighborhood, John and Edward began to steal tricycles, bicycles, and other playthings from the yards and basements while on begging expeditions. These stolen articles they retained for their own use or sold in their neighborhood for small sums of money. Proceeding from this simple form of stealing they began to burglarize any apartments which they could easily enter. In the beginning they gained access to these apartments through unlocked doors, windows, and transoms; later, however, they learned to employ burglar's tools as a means of forcing an entrance.

In this chapter, as in the preceding one, excerpts from autobiographies will be presented to show in particular the way John and Edward became implicated in the burglary of homes in distant parts of the city, the techniques they employed, and the manner in which they involved their younger brothers in this form of delinquent behavior.

JOHN MARTIN

Aside from begging in the South Water Street Market, John's delinquencies before the age of twelve were confined almost exclusively to petty stealing in the immediate vicinity of his home. At about that age, or soon thereafter, he and William Stock, Edward, and their companions began to make expeditions into wealthy neighborhoods for the purpose of begging and stealing bicycles. Simultaneously with this practice they were engaged in burglary of places of business located in their own neighborhood. John has described certain of these experiences in the following manner.

STEALING BICYCLES

After all of our stealing in the neighborhood and begging at the market, we got started begging in rich communities. On our trips to these communities we would pick up everything we could steal in yards and basements. My pal, William Stock, Edward, and I, and sometimes other boys went on these trips. We saw other boys in our neighborhood with bicycles. We got a liking for them ourselves. We learned that they stole them in rich communities, so we went out to these neighborhoods to get some for ourselves. I, and William Stock, and Edward would go to a swanky community about five miles away and patrol the alleys on the lookout for any bicycles that some unsuspecting boy had left outside as a gift to us. One day as my pal and I were walking down the alley we spied two brand new bikes standing in the yard back of the house. I suggested that we grab them. William Stock objected at first. He said that as the bikes were new we wouldn't get away with them. Finally, however, I persuaded him to seize one and I took the other. We got on them and headed south towards our neighborhood. All went well until we got under the railroad viaduct about a half mile from home. We were riding blissfully along when I happened to glance back over my shoulder. I noticed a car tearing along as though the devil were chasing it. It dawned upon me in a flash that they were chasing us. So I warned my pal. To keep going ahead would mean certain capture; but at about that time we came to R—— Street. This is a street about one block long that extends to the Chicago River. My colleague kept going straight ahead while I turned into this street. I sped up it until I came to the river with all avenues of escape seemingly cut off. What to do now? I was in a dilemma, but only for a few seconds. Now, if one has noticed how the piling is built along the banks of the river he will notice that one section of timbers runs but a couple of inches above the surface of the river. Don't forget that my pursuers were hot after me. So as I said, I arrived at the river and without an instant's hesitation I jumped off the bike and went head first into the river and swam under the piling. That left my body completely submerged with but enough space between the lower timber and the surface of the water for me to protrude my nose, so that I could breathe. In the meantime my trailers arrived at the water's edge and looked about for me. "Now where the hell did he go?" asked one. "Don't know, Bill. Looks like he went and got himself drowned," answered the other. Wasn't that a hot one. I certainly did give them the merry ha ha! My ruse was successful, while my co-worker got nabbed. I don't like to pat myself on the back but I think that was pretty slick.

Another time my pal, Edward, and I went on a stroll up to the rich neighborhood for the purpose of getting some more bikes. I entered the basement of an apartment building and was prowling around when my sixth sense caused me to turn around. At first I noticed a shadow on the floor and looking up saw the janitor of the building. "What are you doing here, kid?" he growled. "Well, I felt kind of thirsty and in walking by I noticed that the basement door was open, so came in to get a drink." "Well, it may be so," he said, "but you'll have to come along with me." He escorted me to his quarters and upon arriving there called up for the "Black Maria." I waited until he finished talking and said: "Say, mister, where's the wash room?" He told me to go with him, and so I started to the wash room with him two feet behind me. When I got to the stairs that lead from the street down to his quarters, I went up them like a shot out of a gun, and down the alley like a bat out of hell with him after me. As I went along I kept gaining on him and turned into a yard with the intention of going out into the street. That is where I made an error; the yard had no outlet to the front. If I had kept going ahead I'd have made good my escape. As it was, I was cornered, as there was no way in or out except the way that I went in. As it was, he got me and held me until the wagon made its appearance. However, as I wasn't caught with anything contraband on me, I was turned loose as no charge could be placed against me. . . . .

Another time my pal, Edward, and me went out to get some more bicycles. After we got some I was riding down B—— Street on a hot bike.

When arriving at the elevated structure crossing B—— my handle bars were seized by a plain-clothes man. He took me to the station house where I was booked. "I'll bet this is the kid that's been swiping all them bikes on the north side," said one. I denied it vigorously. They had the right guy all right only they didn't know it. Well, there was no way of beating the rap as they had me dead to rights. In due time I and my brother and pal were taken before his honor and after a perfunctory trial I was committed to the St. Charles School for Boys. . . . .

BURGLARIZING PLACES OF BUSINESS IN THE NEIGHBORHOOD

When we were stealing bicycles in the rich neighborhoods we were also burglarizing places in our community. Some of the places we made were nickelodeons. Well, one night when I was about twelve years old, I effected an entrance into a nickelodeon through the basement window. After I got in I made a bee-line for the cashier's booth, but I didn't find anything there. So I started fooling around with the lights with the intention of lighting the interior of the theatre so I could look about. I felt that I could do this safely as the lights wouldn't be visible outside. So I pushed a button and to my amazement, I lit up the front of the theater. As I did so a harness bull who happened to be approaching saw this, what to him appeared a phenomenon of seeing lights being turned on at three o'clock in the morning. So he tried the doors and fortunately for me he was unable to get in, so after that I didn't procrastinate a bit but beat a hasty retreat. Another about the same time was when I happened to be walking through an alley in this same block, with no good intention, I must admit. It was about 2:00 A.M. when I heard a noise and stopped and listened. The noise also ceased. I listened for half a minute or so and heard nothing, saying that it was probably my imagination and was ready to proceed when I heard the sound again and it advanced towards me and the next thing I saw was a flashlight and a policeman's pistol stuck in my ribs. "You had a mighty close call then, kid. I was ready to shoot," he said. "What are you doing here this time of the morning?" he growled. I told him that I was taking a short cut home. He asked me where I lived and to prove the veracity of my story he escorted me home. I always shiver when I think of how close I came to shaking the hand of the Grim Reaper. . . . .

EDWARD MARTIN

After his release from the Chicago and Cook County School for Boys at the age of twelve years and seven months, Edward engaged in the burglary of a large number of residences in well-to-do neighborhoods of the city and in certain suburban communities. In these burglaries he was implicated with William Stock, Stanley and Adam Runcer, and his younger brothers, James and Michael.

He gives the following description of the delinquent activities in which he engaged during this period in his career.

When I came back home on parole from the Chicago and Cook County School for Boys at the age of thirteen, I went out with William Stock some more times on the same old racket, which was begging and prowling. The burglary stuff started when we went begging. If, while begging, we would see some thing we liked, we would get into the habit of taking it. Some of us older kids used to take pennies from other kids. This we would do in our own neighborhood and around the school yards. Later we got started begging and prowling homes in rich neighborhoods. In doing this we would go on an elevated train to the rich places and ring door bells in the front and if no one answered we would go around the back and ring the door bell. If no one was at home and we could get in, we would prowl the place. We got caught a lot of times.

When we were out begging, we would take everything that we could get our hands on that could be sold. Any house that was empty or any house where no one was at home, we would get into. Sometimes we would ring the front door bell and if no one would answer we would try the back door to make sure no one was there. If we got no response we would go into the basement and crawl through the screen. We took mostly jewelry and money. We would give the jewelry away or sell it to some of the people in our neighborhood. If they wanted a ring we would steal one and sell it to them; if they wanted a watch we would steal a watch and sell it to them. I kept on burglarizing homes with William Stock until I was finally arrested and sent to St. Charles.

On leaving St. Charles at the age of fifteen, after my first term there, I went back home and met William Stock again. He didn't have a hard time in trying to get me for his partner in begging and burglary. Having gained some experience through Stock, I went into burglary on my own, if Stock didn't feel broke enough to go along.

In our burglaries we used many systems of gaining an entrance into homes. After using the begging as an excuse, to see if anyone was at home, we would make sure that our actions were those of kids at play, but looking the house over for the best possible place of entrance. A residence was the easiest place to enter. The many screened porches or shrubberies growing around the home, gave us all the cover we needed. If we found the basement windows the easiest place to get through, we would place a piece of cloth near the latch, and with a pointed instrument we would strike the cloth hard and break a small hole in the glass, big enough to unfasten the window catch, thus making our entrance easy and fairly quiet. If the home had a screened porch, we used the shadiest and least conspicuous place of entrance. We would enter the porch either by using a skeleton key, by snapping back the window catch with a knife, or by breaking the window. If a transom window happened to be open we could crawl in through there. If the basement door was the only approach and couldn't be opened with a key, we would force the door in by back and leg pressure. If utmost quiet was needed, and the basement door or window had to be opened, we would either scrape off the putty and remove the glass, or open the door by cutting out a panel with a sharp knife.

After entering the basement we would find many of the doors leading to the basement locked from the inside, with the key left in the lock. In this case we pushed a piece of newspaper over the space where the key might fall, then pick the key out of the lock, have it fall on the paper, pull the key and paper towards ourselves, and thus gain entrance. Sometimes these doors would have a latch and in that case we had to crack a panel with whatever came handy. We usually entered the flats by the rear door or window. If the flats were on the first floor, the side window was the easiest. In many cases no force had to be used, as many a window and door were open just inviting us. Most of the jobs were picked at random; whatever one appeared the easiest and safest we took. If noise had to be made, we would pick a time when the "L" ran by, or if around street car lines, we would wait until a street car rumbled by.

For a store with barred windows we used a small jack to spread the bars enough to let us squeeze through. In this begging and burglary work we took in all the wealthy communities on the north side of the city and the suburbs on the north and west sides of Chicago. Many a chase and close call we've had while in the act of burglary. Many were the shots fired upon us by the police, but luck must have been with us.

Many of these burglaries would not have happened if someone had given me a helping hand to show me where I would end. Being a young fellow with lots of pep, I took to burglarizing as a form of exciting exercise, never giving a thought to the future or the consequence. I just lived from day to day, cautious of every cop and ready to run at the least suspicious move he would make.

During this time we prowled a flat just off the Lake Front. Making sure no one was home we spied an open window facing the Lake about eight feet above the ground. Three of us were working that day. My partner and I being the tallest and strongest, we boosted the other boy up until he caught the ledge, worked himself inside and opened the door for us. As soon as we got in, we always would go to the bedrooms first, as we usually found most of the valuables there. After the bedrooms were searched the rest of the house would be split up in three searching sections. If two of us were working we would both search the bedrooms together, and then split the search, so as to be in a position to be able to get away quickly, should anyone come in either the front or back door.

We always made sure no one surprised us, as we managed to avoid capture this way several times. During this burglary, while searching through a closet, I spied an open wall safe. Making sure it was no trap or camera, I saw two big diamonds. Not knowing they were the real stuff, I gave them away.

Because of the valuable things we were stealing the police reinforced their vigil for the burglars who were raiding all those numerous homes in these districts. After a few more burglaries and several narrow escapes from the police, I decided to lay low for a spell, as I always had enough money on hand to take things easy. I warned my regular partner and the different boys I worked with and made myself scarce around my various hangouts, because I didn't want to be picked up. After staying away about ten days, I happened to stroll by one of my hangouts, and right into the arms of the police, who were waiting there.

The lad who was with us on the job when we got the rings went out on a prowl, was arrested, confessed the ring job with William Stock and me, and pointed us out to the police. After several days of grilling I still denied any connection or knowledge of the whereabouts of the rings. Although I participated in this burglary I refused to confess my part, because it would get some friends into trouble. I agreed to find the rings for them if they would take my word of honor to let me go alone for them. They refused to take my word. Through the checking of all known persons and help of the partner that caused my arrest they found the rings. For this offense I was to be sent to St. Charles, but I escaped from the Detention Home.

My partner was arrested for some burglaries and was there when the police brought me back. After about three months in the Detention Home, we managed to escape again through the girls' section by forcing a heavy window screen, and after eluding at least a dozen people, on the street who saw us breaking out, we outwitted them and got away.

Laying low for a few days until the cops quit looking for us, we began to pull more burglaries. Much of the stuff we took, we either sold to the older fellows for whatever we could get for it, or some of it we gave away to fellows we liked. I always had to be on the go, as I couldn't sit around.

After six months of burglaries I was finally caught by a bunch of fellows who saw us coming out of a friend's house, with bundles of clothing, boxes of cigars, and wearing sweaters, belonging to their friend. After being chased for a mile through yards and alleys, they overtook me and handed me over to the police. We had entered this place with a skeleton key. There were three of us on this job, the other two got away, but of all the luck one of these chasing boys of six feet four inches took out after me. How I kept out of that gorilla's reach for a mile I don't know. For this offense I was sent to the St. Charles School for Boys.

A few days after my arrival at St. Charles William Stock was also to be sent there but he managed to escape from the officer who was taking him. Getting lonesome for my pal I managed to escape from St. Charles three weeks later with a fellow named Lester Thomas. After supper Lester and I were able to sneak up to the officers' bathroom on the second floor and through the bathroom window we managed to slide down the rain pipe. In our sneaks and socks we made our escape to the railroad tracks. Running across open fields we had lost our footwear in the ooze and mud of a late January evening. Boy! how them railroad ties and stones can blister feet. We walked all the way down to Wheaton, a distance of about fifteen miles over a period of a day and a half, as we had to hide during the day. Arriving in Wheaton during the night, hungry and tired, with burlap bags wrapped around our feet, we found an open basement window throwing out warm heat. Crawling into the basement we lay down near the furnace, and soon fell asleep. About one o'clock in the morning we were awakened by the noise of creaking stairs. Afraid to move, we lay still hoping we wouldn't be seen; but Lester, in lying down happened to pick the place in front of the furnace door. The noise we heard was the owner of the place coming down to fix the furnace for the night. He walked towards the furnace in the dark, and not using the flashlight in his hand, he almost stumbled over Lester. With a very surprised and scared cry of "Oh" and several more "Oh's" and a hasty departure as if a ghost were on his heels, he managed to reach the upper stairs. Reaching the stairs he turned the flashlight on the spot where he bumped into Lester. Seeing Lester he stopped his hasty exit, saying, "Why it is only a kid," and then seeing me he asked, "Is that a man?" After being told I was also a boy, with a sigh of relief he came back, but first making sure we were boys by asking us to stand up. When we explained that we were cold and wished only to sleep near the furnace till morning, he told us to come upstairs with him. We had a private talk with the lady of the house and she promised us train fare to Chicago. He left the room on some excuse, while the lady gave us a sardine sandwich and a cup of coffee. In the meantime he made arrangements with the sheriff, although he made believe he would buy us tickets, walked us to the depot, and turned us over to the sheriff. After placing us in the Wheaton jail, he called the St. Charles School and we were taken back.

Arriving at St. Charles that afternoon, we were taken to the tool shed and placed under guard of an inmate. We were made to stand in a corner, with our arms placed behind our necks, and told to stand still. At each slightest move we received a barrel stave over our differential, or a poke in the ribs. After about two and a half hours of this, till the close of the afternoon work period, we were marched with the rest of the boys back to the cottage. We were made to stand before the boys without supper, while they ate theirs. About six o'clock that evening the house father himself took charge of us. After taking personal charge of us, the first thing he did was to speak to us separately and gloat over our capture. After the speech of gloating was over, we would be called again separately, and round number two would consist of blasting oratory mixed with cuss words until he worked himself into a frenzy, which would be about the third round of speech. The fourth round was the expectation round, in which he would make fast, jerky movements with his arms, making us duck expecting blows. After soothing our fears and making us think that we had nothing to fear an unexpected right swing would come over with jarring impact, which shook us to our toes. After several more sudden wallops, we would trade places until he felt satisfied that his boxing was up to par.

Feeling we had enough of his boxing practice, our next punishment was to carry a heavy swab upon our shoulders, and made to run in a big circle in the basement. Before this type of punishment began he would ask us how far we intended to go when we ran away. When I told that I intended to reach Chicago, and Lester was to reach his home, in a small town in the southern part of the state, we were told to place these heavy, awkward swabs on our shoulders and run as fast as we could, and when we figured we had covered the distance to our homes, we were to cover the same thing coming back.

As an inspiration to us, he would set himself in a position where we had to pass him at a turn. After many minutes of torturous running, I began to slow up. But when I received a swishing sock across the seat of my pants, which made me jump three feet, I ran faster for the next several minutes than I did at the start. After running for at least two hours and receiving many blows, we were told to get ready for bed with the rest of the boys, as it was bed-time. After donning night-gowns we were made to stand up all night. The hardest and dirtiest work was ours for months to come, until I ran away again, and made my escape good for a month. Escaping early in the morning, I managed to reach St. Charles town, where I caught a cattle train coming into Chicago, and managed to get in in time for breakfast. Soon after arriving home I learned that my two younger brothers were placed in an orphan home. I decided to get them out the next visiting day. Discarding my reform school clothes, I went out and found my partner, William Stock, from whom I borrowed some street car fare. Then I went out and burglarized two places in which I took some jewelry and a little money. I sold the jewelry to a friend of mine. The following Sunday I went to the orphanage and brought James and Michael home with me.

The following Tuesday I went to a western suburb to go to work prowling. James and Michael told me how they had gone with William Stock on several jobs, and wanted to come along. Not wanting to leave them at home alone, I took them along. In prowling the seventh and last home for the day, we entered by using a skeleton key on the rear door. While in the process of searching, the lady of the house came home. Hearing us in the upstairs rooms, she called some name. When no one answered her, she became suspicious and called the police.

While she phoned the police, James walked out the back way; Michael became frightened and ran the wrong way, and in trying to help Michael, I stayed too long. Thinking Michael was safe until later on, I began to creep out the back door, when this lady stepped from behind the curtain and put a gun in my back, and told me to hold it as the police would soon be there. She was right; they came immediately. She held me while the others searched the house. Michael was found in the attic hiding behind a trunk. While we were at the station, they notified pa to get Michael and take him back to the orphanage. They notified the St. Charles authorities of my capture. Next morning, through their carelessness and my scheming, I managed to walk out like a free boy, and did I run from there!

A week later I was captured for a runaway, and taken to the Juvenile Detention Home, pending my return to St. Charles. While here, with a hidden saw in a hollow belt, I sawed my way out of the linen room. This was the way I had made my first escape, by forcing the heavy screen enough to permit me to squeeze through. They had replaced the broken lock with a chain around the damaged part, so it was an easy matter to saw a link of chain, and make another escape.

I managed to stay away for three months, until I broke into a home that happened to be equipped with a burglar alarm connected with the neighbors next door, who in turn notified the police. A sixth sense told me something was wrong. Sure enough I saw a janitor guarding the rear exit. Knowing my hunch was right, I dashed out of the front window screen jumped to the porch and nearly into the arms of a guard stationed there, whom I evaded by slip-rolling. Then the chase started in earnest. Some lady athlete got on my heels, and stayed there until she drew a big pack with her yells of Robbers! Help! and Burglars! It didn't take long for the pack to be in full swing and they closed in on me, and the police had me in tow again. With a few more burglaries pinned on my ticket, the Juvenile Detention Home closed me in again.

Knowing that I had escaped from St. Charles, the judge sent me back on several other charges. Arriving there again I was returned to the cottage I had run away from. Although punished again, my punishment wasn't as severe as the first time. Behaving and being a good boy, I stayed there twenty-two months, and had worked my way up as the baseball team's star pitcher, and on my release I was major of our battalion, a high ranking officer.

JAMES MARTIN

James Martin was initiated into the practice of burglarizing homes in well-to-do neighborhoods by his older brother, Edward, and the latter's companions, particularly William Stock. He engaged in this form of delinquency until he was approximately fifteen years of age. His description of certain of these offenses is given in the following excerpts.

When I was a very young boy I was taken out to rich neighborhoods by my brother Edward and William Stock to beg and steal. After they were put into institutions, my brother Michael and I teamed up together. I was about eight years old at that time. Michael and I were very successful together. We stole and begged as often and as much as we could. In order to find out if anybody was in a home, we would beg. If someone would answer the doorbell or my knock, I would beg for food, clothes, or money. Sometimes we would have so much food that we would throw away some of it. If no one would answer my call, we would break into the home. We were very successful in prowling people's property. We each took turns in "begging." I must admit that Michael was a better house breaker than I. He could crawl through small openings much easier than I could, as he was small and skinny while I was a little taller and much huskier. He found no trouble at all in climbing telephone poles, crawling through transoms above the doors, etc. I did the heavy work, such as lifting him up to the transoms, jimmying the windows or doors, handling the dogs, etc.

The only trouble we seemed to have was the people's curiosity in wanting to know why we were not in school instead of "begging."

As to burglarizing, Michael and I were very erratic. One day we would burglarize five, ten, or sometimes fifteen cottages or apartments a day. On other days, we would play with these people's children. We would go in some backyard and play with them in their sand piles, go in their tents and use their toys with them. Sometimes, we were "snubbed" by these children, but that did not worry us because we played with their toys anyway. Usually when we were not wanted, the boys or girls would yell for their mother. When this happened, we would go away before she came out, but this did not happen very often. I can remember only two occasions when this happened. Other times we would spend lots of time on the beaches. Sometimes we would do nothing but play a week straight at the beach. . . . .

Most of the time when I went out stealing, Michael would accompany me, but sometimes Edward would come along, also sometimes William Stock. On one occasion all three of us boys, Edward, Michael, and myself went to one of the suburbs west of Chicago. I "begged" for about fifteen minutes before I came to a house. I thought no one was home. I rang the bell, knocked and kicked at the door, but no one would answer. I had every reason to think that no one was home. I told my brothers Edward and Michael so. The access to the house was easy enough, and no one tried to impede our way in. While canvassing one of the bed-rooms, I heard a commotion in the hall outside of the room. Frightened a little, I ran out to the hallway just in time to see Edward running swiftly in my direction. He told me that a woman was sleeping in the room he went into and accidentally woke her up. She screamed, ran to the telephone, and called up the police. Edward told Michael and me to run upstairs. I ran, but not upstairs. I ran into the kitchen and out of the back door. The police responded so quickly that I was just out of the house when they ran in. Some went through the front door and some came into the rear yard. One of them asked me where my mother was. I pointed to the house and told them she was in there. I then casually walked out of the yard. . . . .

One time when we were out prowling we spotted a house and after our usual way of finding out if no one was home at the front of the building, we went to the rear of the place to use the same formality. But, our way into the back yard was impeded by a big German police dog. The dog growled and barked when we tried to get in the yard. I tried making friends with him, and for a little while I thought I would not succeed. While talking and edging in close to him, I noticed a name on the dog house which was in the corner of the yard. The name was "Prince." I called the dog by his name and he pricked up his ears. I knew then that it was the dog's name. Getting a little braver, I kept edging up closer to the dog all the while calling his name. Still having a box of bon bons which I stole that day, I opened the box and offered "Prince" some of the candy. After he ate several pieces I gave him more. In a little while I won his friendship. After Michael and I played awhile with "Prince" we broke into the house and burglarized it with a "watch dog" tagging at our heels all the while.

Another incident that I remember well was when Michael and I burglarized a place on the North Side. It was late in the afternoon when we broke into the cottage. We were in the house about five or ten minutes when we heard some one unlocking the front door. Michael and I were in the parlor. We ran upstairs to the attic and stayed there awhile wondering who came into the house. In a little while we heard children's voices. We snuck downstairs to investigate. In a small room we saw two girls about our own age playing with toys. Taking two penny banks which belonged to these children, we snuck out of the house. We broke the banks open and took out five or six dollars in change.

For several months Michael and I were together burglarizing almost all the time. We associated with other boys, but not very much. We would get on the elevated trains and ride out to a neighborhood that looked rich and prosperous. Here we would get off and go from home to home ringing bells until we spotted a place. By jimmying the door or window we would get in. We could get into almost every place. One day we were begging and burglarizing around five or six o'clock in the evening. As it was in the fall of the year, darkness settled in about this time. After repeated attempts to find a cottage or apartment that we could burglarize, we finally came to one. We broke in, and were in the house only a short time when I heard someone trying to get in the front door. I called Michael and started to run towards the back of the house. In the semi-darkness of the rooms, I got lost in these rooms. Hearing a person coming in my direction, Michael and I ran into a bedroom and under the bed. As we already raided this certain room, it showed signs of our hasty searching. The person who walked in the bedroom was a young man about twenty-five years old. Michael and I were pretty excited there under the bed. The man finally walked out, but came in a minute or two later. I thought he did not know that we were under the bed until he started whacking at us with a long curved sword. He could not reach us with the sword, but when I saw the end of it so near to me, I had a strong desire to be somewhere else. Seeing the end of that sword only two or three inches from my face, was, I think, one of the greatest thrills I had.

In the end he got us from under the bed. While he was questioning us, a woman came into the room and talked to him and us boys. The man finally decided to call up the police and turn us in. Michael and I had a very good reason to fear the police, because every time we were arrested, the courts never failed to send us to some institution. So after hearing this man's decision, I searched my mind for a way to escape from the man. As he did not hold us and had no other weapon in his hands, but this long curved sword, I jumped through an open window while we were walking through one of the rooms on the first floor. The man hollered and ran to the window after me. Meanwhile Michael bolted through the front door while this was going on. Michael and I met a block or so away from the scene of our adventure.

When I was little, we used to sell iron, lead, and all kinds of things to the junkmen. They always bought most everything we had. When I was burglarizing homes with Edward, Michael, and our pals, we had a lot of local places where we could sell jewelry, watches, and other things which we stole from rich homes. One fellow by the name of Jack Adams who worked in a garage would get rid of the jewelry and other stuff which we sold. He gave us a pretty good price on the stuff and we kept doing business with him for a long time. We had other regular places like this where we could always get rid of our things for a good price.

MICHAEL MARTIN

As clearly indicated in the preceding excerpts, Michael was given his original instructions in the practice of burglary by his older brothers, especially James. This fact is further substantiated by the following short excerpts from Michael's autobiography.

Sometimes when I went out begging with my brother, James, we would keep going from house to house till we would finally come to one that did not have anybody at home. Well, I usually made sure that nobody was home by ringing and knocking at both the front and back doors. If nobody was there we'd look around and see if the doors or windows were open and I'd call my older brother who told me how to get in. Sometimes we got in houses by the doors, windows, transoms, ice boxes and even basement doors that led into the kitchen. Then I'd open the kitchen door for my brother, who would help me search the house. We took anything that we thought was valuable, such as jewelry, ties, and money and many other things. . . . .

I then took my younger brother Carl with me to the very rich neighborhoods in Chicago and showed him how to beg and steal like I was shown by my older brothers.

. . . . We would go to school in the morning and at recess we would quit and go to the rich places and would start to beg again. We did this for about two weeks till we got caught again in a house. We were again taken to the police station and searched and shipped to the juvenile where we enjoyed ourselves till we went to trial. . . . .

From the first time I ever stole money and broke into people's homes I never thought about what the consequences were if I ever got caught. I remember when I was still a young kid about nine years old we had a dog by the name of Topsy and my brother Edward trained him so that he could come along with me and my other brothers and beg with us. He was trained to sit up and beg by sitting on his hind legs and placing his forepaws together and then he would bark at a sign from one of my brothers. Whenever I went out with my brother Edward, we used to take the dog along and he was a great help in begging or burglary because he was so well trained. Whenever we went on a street-car my brother Edward, would tell Topsy to jump into the basket he carried and then cover him up with a towel or napkin. Topsy used to be able to do most anything which was possible in the dog kingdom because he was so well trained by my brothers or me. The police in several towns and in Chicago heard about him and us and caught us begging several times and took us to the police station. We used to make the dog do so many funny tricks that the police got a big laugh out of it and would forget about our crime and sometimes let us go. Many of them offered to buy the dog from us, but we didn't care to sell him and besides he was too valuable to us. For about a year and a half the dog went out with either me or my brothers and helped us get some money off of many people who were against begging, but when I told them how smart my dog was they asked to see him do tricks and they always gave me money or whatever they had and did not have any use for. And they wouldn't suspect us. The kids would be interested in Topsy and play with him and they wouldn't get suspicious of us when we would get into a house.

CARL MARTIN

As indicated in the official records in chapter i, Carl's initial experience in stealing occurred when he was about three years and three months of age. He was engaged with his brothers in the burglary of homes when he was approximately seven. The manner in which James and Michael implicated him in this form of delinquency is indicated in this brief statement from his own story.

James and Michael used to take me on their trips to rich neighborhoods when I was very young. We would go begging from door to door asking for food, clothing, and money. I would ring doorbells to find out if the people were at home. If they were, I would beg. If they were not at home I would call my brothers and they would help me break into the home by way of windows, ice boxes, and transoms. Then we would take something to eat if we were hungry and anything that we thought we could sell. This way I learned how to get into homes. I was caught several times on these trips but was let go because of my age.

The burglaries described in the foregoing pages comprise only a small proportion of those in which the brothers were implicated during the second phase of their career in delinquency and crime. Those presented are sufficient, however, to reveal the social process by which the brothers were initiated into burglary, their consuming interest in stealing as an adventure and as a means of securing the money, clothes, food, and playthings which they desired, and their growing sophistication with regard to stealing, evading the police, and the disposal of stolen goods through professional fences.

CHAPTER IV

DIVERGENT DEVELOPMENTS IN THE FIVE
CAREERS DURING ADOLESCENCE

Following the period in which the brothers were involved in begging and the accompanying practice of burglarizing residences, their careers progressed along somewhat divergent lines. John and Edward continued to engage in burglary, James became involved in the larceny of automobiles, Michael in armed robbery, and Carl in the theft of automobiles. These divergent developments, which occurred after the brothers were approximately fifteen, were coincidental with certain important changes which took place at that time.

In the first place at that age they began to encounter great difficulty in using begging as a guise for the prowling of residences. Because of their size, their presence in well-to-do neighborhoods aroused suspicion and they could no longer elicit a sympathetic reaction from the persons to whom they appealed for aid. In the second place the brothers were separated from each other during adolescence because of long terms of confinement in different correctional schools and penal institutions. During this period it was seldom that as many as two of the brothers were at home together for a long enough period of time to engage jointly in delinquent activities. This separation had the effect of dissolving the combinations of relationships between the brothers which had obtained in their previous delinquencies. Consequently, as each brother returned home under parole supervision from correctional schools and reformatories, he established contacts with other offenders in the neighborhood and with these companions engaged in new forms of delinquent and criminal conduct. A limited number of these later offenses are described in the following pages of this chapter.

JOHN MARTIN

After escaping from the St. Charles School for Boys at the age of sixteen, John Martin enlisted in the United States Army. At the end of three years he was honorably discharged. Three months later he enlisted in the Marine Corps from which he deserted and returned to Chicago. Shortly thereafter he met an ex-convict with whom he left Chicago in search of work and while out of the city committed the burglary for which he was committed to a state penitentiary.

When I was about fifteen years old, I was paroled from St. Charles to a German farmer. On this farm I had to get up at 4 o'clock in the morning and work until 8 in the evening. I went to that farm on a Wednesday and when Sunday rolled round, the square head said to me, "Well, John, I suppose you want to go to church, seeing as today is Sunday, so here is four bits." I took the dough and kept on going. Three days of that kind of work was enough for me, especially at 50 cents a day. I suppose that farmer must have thought that I went to China to church. Four months later I was picked up and sent back to St. Charles. . . . ."

A year later John escaped from the St. Charles School for Boys and enlisted in the United States Military Service.

About a week after my desertion from the Marine Corps I happened to get picked up by the squad, packing a rod. Well, I was thrown in the "can" overnight. The same night that I was in the station house, four or five members of the Marine Corps went down to get me at home. Wasn't that a break for me? I was safely locked up in a police cell and they didn't know it. Neither did the coppers know that I was wanted by the marines. As the gun wasn't actually found on me, the next morning the police captain turned me loose.

Well, I worked at odd jobs after deserting from the army until I happened to meet a guy with whom I was acquainted. The place that I met him was on West Madison Street in Chicago. As there wasn't much work in town at that time, we shipped out of Chicago for the lumber camps in an adjoining state. After a twenty-four hour ride we arrived in this state. We went to work for a lumber company. As we were without proper clothing for that kind of work and broke, we were compelled to get goods on time and pay what I thought was an exorbitant price for them. I worked for this company for three weeks.

While there, I held different jobs some of which were: swamper, sawer, road-donkey, bullcock, etc. The last named was the final job I held. The duties were to clean out the shacks, chop wood for the kitchen, and so forth. That last job didn't exactly suit my nature. However, one of the duties of this job was furnishing wood for the foreman's shack and building a fire in the stove early in the morning. On that job I had an opportunity to observe things. One of the things that I observed was the place where the camp boss kept the dough. So as I said, my pal and I quit the job after three weeks. We went to town where we recuperated for a couple of days. It certainly was cold in that part of the country. I remember one Sunday morning the thermometer registered 45 degrees below zero.

Well, after a couple of days my pal suggested that we go back to this camp that we quit and get this money that the foreman kept in his cabin. I was for returning to Chicago and objected to the idea. After a good deal of talk on his part I was finally persuaded to fall in with the scheme. We left town on a Saturday and after walking all day we finally covered the thirty miles to the camp which is at the head of the narrow gauge railroad, which the company uses to transport its logs to the sawmill. As there were a good number of men who go from camp to camp to work, our appearance didn't cause any particular flurry. It was taken for granted that we came there to work.

After the long tramp through the snow we were pretty well exhausted. So we stayed in camp that night and all day Sunday and slept the sleep that men do who are really tired. Sunday night we crawled into the hay early in the evening and about 1:00 A.M. Monday morning we got up. The reason that we got up so early in the morning was because in the first place we had a six mile hike to the scene of operations. The second reason was that we had to time our arrival to just within a few minutes before the man got up who built the fires in the foreman's shack and the other cabins. We reasoned that in case the foreman happened to wake up when I entered the cabin he would think that it was the regular man on his round of duties and he wouldn't pay any attention.

Well, we finally got there. First, however, we got a lantern and lit it. Then we put a piece of cardboard on one side so that when I entered I would place the lantern on the table so that the bright side would face towards the bed where the foreman was sleeping and leave me in total darkness so that I could do my dirty work unobserved.

After we got everything ready we approached the cabin and stood outside listening for a minute or two to assure ourselves that everything was as it should be. The snoring of the camp boss punctuated the stillness. I grabbed for the door-handle in a bold matter of fact manner and I walked in. I placed the lantern so that I would be in total darkness. I took the cash-drawer and a watch that belonged to the boss and walked out.

There was about thirty dollars in cash and this watch which was valued at seventy-five dollars. I suggested that we go to the nearest rail point and grab a rattler south, but my pal was a weak-kneed cuss and said that we ought to take a little rest. So I acceded to his wishes again and, when we got to a little town which was only three miles from the robbery, we entered a boarding house there. Stopping off there proved to be our waterloo. If we had kept on travelling as I wanted to do everything would have been jake. But I listened to this ignoramus and we got nabbed, convicted, and sentenced to the state penitentiary.

EDWARD MARTIN

During the final period of his career, Edward continued in the burglary of homes and places of business. These burglaries, as compared with those in which he was implicated in earlier years, were more definitely planned, entailed greater skill and more elaborate techniques, and were not committed under the guise of begging. In many respects they resembled the techniques of older and more experienced burglars.

When I came out of the St. Charles School for Boys the last time, I was past seventeen years of age. The kid days were over, when we stole for the fun and excitement and to get a few pennies for shows. I had no intentions of behaving myself nor quitting my burglaries. Having exchanged stories about crimes with older boys in St. Charles, I had learned to be more careful and cautious. I also knew that since I was past seventeen years, I would not be taken to the Juvenile Court if arrested again, but would be brought before the Criminal Court from which I could be sent to prison.

On arriving home in Chicago, I began mixing with the bunch of older fellows, and from them I heard about their burglaries. I decided not to make any attempt to commit any burglaries until I had a market for my stolen articles which would give me a good income and, being more wary, I made up my mind to use more caution when pulling a job. My burglaries would be fewer and through my contacts with the older mob my loot would be fenced for a fair profit. . . . .

. . . . Some five weeks after arriving home, one of the boys I had been friendly with was given an order for a lady's engagement ring, which some fellow wanted to get for his girl. First making sure that the fellow would pay a fair price, I stated I would get him a good ring that would be worth the price he was willing to pay. Having a week's time to get it, I rode about the north side district, looking the homes over, trying to pick one out where I was sure I would get what I wanted on my first burglary. Walking around the north side, looking at the homes as I passed them, I had a feeling of someone watching me. Walking to a corner, I caught sight of a man trying to hide behind a tree. Not wishing to get run in I took my person from here and went back home.

While at home I recalled most of the districts I had worked in and where I got most of the best stuff. Recalling I had been in a wealthy suburb north of the city, I decided to go there on the morrow.

Getting up about nine o'clock the next morning, I cooked myself some breakfast. Finishing this, I checked over my assortment of pass-keys and several small jimmies, which I figured I might need. Placing them where I could easily throw them away if I was spotted by any cops watching me, I took the "L" to the north side suburb I had in mind. I had put on my best clothes so that I would not be conspicuous and arouse suspicion. When I reached the residential district, where the town's "400" lived, I picked a great mansion with a large lawn and statues, where I knew I could get what I was after. Since it appeared that no one was at home, I walked to the servants' and chauffeur's quarters first, as I knew that the danger of being caught would come from here. Getting no response here, I walked to the back door of the house. Getting no answer here, I began looking for the best means of entering. The rear door gave me the most protection from prying eyes, so I went to work on the kitchen door. Using a pass-key I opened the kitchen door lock, but found it bolted from the inside, and I couldn't get in. I then went to the basement door and opened it with another pass-key. I walked up the stairs and stood here for a few minutes and listened for footsteps from above. Making sure that no one was there, I gently crept upstairs. Finding the door unlocked, I opened it a trifle and listened some more. Not making any noise while walking over the thick rugs, I went from room to room, trying to locate the people, if any were sleeping. Finding the rooms unoccupied, I went through the bedrooms and the boudoir, and picked up a man's fine watch, a ruby ring, a necklace, and a diamond ring which I wanted. I also found about thirty dollars in cash. Although the house was lavishly furnished with expensive rugs and furniture, plus everything else, I took only what I could dispose of easily.

Making a safe departure I came back home and made a deal for selling the ring, which was a good one. I sold it for $125.00. The ruby went to a saloon-keeper for $35.00; the watch sold for $20.00; the necklace, being too hard to dispose of, I gave to a friend. Making over $200.00 I quit burglarizing until I made my trip to the west coast. I had made enough to supply my needs for some time.

I now began going to poolrooms where I learned how to shoot pool. While here I used to hear from some of the fellows about their trips out to the West Coast. On hearing this I decided to join some of them the next time they went. I always felt the urge to travel. History and geography were my favorite studies, and I had become fond of books on exploring.

When the opportunity came, I took it. Having made the acquaintance of two fellows going west, I was offered the chance of stringing along with them. Picking out that night as the best time to start, we rode a street car to the vicinity of Cicero Avenue and 16th Street, where I followed them to the tracks of the Santa Fe Line. We had a short wait until the mail train came along. Watching it slow down at the crossing nearby, we managed to get on before it picked up much speed.

Catching the first mail car just back of the engine, we stayed here until we came in sight of Joliet. One of the boys who knew the stops this train would make, told us to follow him. Following him, I crawled over the top of the train. Crawling on hands and knees we were told to lie down as soon as the train pulled into the depot, so as not to be seen. Having reached the third car in back of the train, we stopped crawling. Sitting down we saw the depot approaching. Knowing it was time to make ourselves as small as possible, we lay down flat. We lay this way until the train started again. On pulling out of town we would crawl back to the blinds, or sit on the tender out of sight of the engineer and fireman.

On reaching another town we repeated the crawl again. At the next stop, the fellow who knew the road fell asleep, and refused to get up when I warned him of the approaching of a big town. He was a hard sleeper, and once falling asleep he was hard to wake up. For this we got kicked off by the fireman who saw us when he came back to check the water in the tank.

We were seen by a couple of railroad bulls while getting off, who in turn chased us up a country road trying to catch us. Evading them, we stayed in town about two hours, and then caught a westbound freight. Finding an empty refrigerator, we crawled into the end where the ice was placed when the car is full. Finding it dry here, the three of us lay down and went to sleep. On waking up we were but a few miles from Kansas City. Also, on waking up I found that one of these fellows had gone through my pockets and had taken some money from me. On finding I had gone with sneak thieves, I told them to go their way and I would go mine.

Travelling alone, I listened to the experiences of some of the fellows who were on the same train. I heard about the hot spots on the road where the bulls were tough. Having covered some fifteen hundred miles of road, I began to hear about the bulls in California. Hearing that they would make you walk from town to town if you didn't have the price of a railroad ticket, I decided I would have to stop off somewhere and prowl a place for a little cash, as I had spent my last quarter for lunch in the depot at Lincoln, Nebraska. Coming to a western division point, I had enough time to get into a one-story place, where I found between six and seven dollars in change. Feeling better with money in my pocket, I caught the same freight west. . . . . .

The next afternoon the train was boarded by two tough bulls, one a fairly tall fellow and the other a little, short guy. Riding on a tank car my first warning came, when the chap to whom I was talking got pale around the gills. Wondering if he was getting sick, I questioned him. Not answering me, because he was looking up at the box car above me, he made me curious. Looking up on an impulse, I almost fell off the train. Shorty was pointing a big .45 right at me; the hole looked like the mouth of a cannon. Not thinking a runt like him could be a bull, I started to climb the car to take the gun and give him a trimming for pointing a gun at me. As I started up, Shorty said, "Hold it!" and the chap whispered, "He is a railroad bull."

Stopping the train the bulls separated the boys who had no train fare and sent them on their way up the tracks to the next town, from which they would be escorted by other bulls, on down the line. Those of us who had money were made to buy tickets. . . . .

I bought a fifty-cent ticket to the next town, where I planned to catch another freight train. The next passenger train was due at midnight. Loitering around the station, our train finally came. After giving the conductor my ticket, I began to scheme as to how I could stay on as long as the ones who bought five-dollar tickets. I noticed most of them sitting in one section of the car. Thinking that if I sat with them the conductor would believe me a $5.00 ticket man, I found an empty seat with these men, and when my station was called I made off I was asleep. Still making off, I saw the conductor come through again asking for tickets. Asking the fellows around me their destination, he thought me the same, and thinking me asleep, he didn't bother me. Shortly after this I really fell asleep, and was awakened with the other boys when the train pulled into San Bernardino, their destination.

Feeling in fine humor over the long fifty-cent ride, I had some breakfast at the depot, then began to hitch-hike my way to Los Angeles. Getting to within fifty miles of this city, I got tired of this slow means of travel. So I purchased a ticket and rode the electric line into town.

I had always pictured L.A. as a wonderful city, much better than Chicago. After spending a day looking the town over, my bubble broke, as a pin breaks a baloon. I didn't care for this town. Pickings were poor, and after four days of it here and in its suburbs, I started back for home. Getting as far as N—— , I was arrested by one of the railroad bulls for riding freights and charged with vagrancy. Finding some jewelry on my person, I was ordered held at the county jail pending investigation. Being the biggest county in the country, the county jail was about two hundred miles from where I was pinched.

Under guard of the officer who had arrested me, I was placed aboard a train and taken there. Giving an alias, I was found out by a letter that William Stock had sent me while in Chicago, which they found in the lining of my coat. It was a funny thing, this letter. When on my way west, I had looked for it several times, as I wanted to throw it away because it contained my right name. I looked through my pockets several times without finding it. When I arrived at the county jail, I was searched again, and the letter was found in the lining of my coat.

In it I was asked to see the fellow who accused Stock of robbing his home, and to ask him to be lenient with Stock, as this fellow was going to get him the maximum sentence possible for this type of burglary. This letter was a contraband, being sent out without the permission of the authorities of the reform school.

This letter was the cause of a lot of misunderstanding and trouble. When I first received this letter I had answered Stock in another letter, in which I stated that I had received that, "you know what I mean." Meaning, of course, the contraband letter. When my letter arrived at St. Charles, addressed to Stock, it was censored and held. My statement of, "I got that, you know what I mean," was interpreted in a different manner. Not knowing that Stock had sent me a contraband letter, they misunderstood it as a statement that I had recovered the jewels he had stolen on the $25,000.00 charge of which he was accused. Not having been recovered by the police, he was believed to have hid the jewelry, and I having been released from St. Charles had recovered them.

I stated in my letter I was bound for California and that on my return I would go and see the man as he had asked. My letter was turned over to the police. On finding Stock's letter on me, the police here got in touch with the Chicago authorities. In reply, they were asked to hold me until I could be brought back by extradition.

Two weeks later, I was turned over to a Chicago policeman, Sergeant Jackson, whom I knew through one of my arrests in Chicago. On the way back we stopped off at W——, Arizona. He turned me over to the sheriff for a day, while he went to see the Grand Canyon. Before stopping here, he promised to take me along if I told him where the jewels were. Not having any knowledge, only what I had heard, I couldn't tell him anything. I had often read about the Grand Canyon and wanted to see it. I was tempted to give him a cock-and-bull story in order to go along, but on second thought I figured I might get myself into trouble.

Spending the night in a dark two-by-four jail, I was given breakfast at the town's only restaurant, under the eyes of the sheriff and his dog. After breakfast, I went back to jail, and waited several hours until the cop came back and we boarded the train again for Chicago. . . . .

. . . . After boarding the train, and being told I was supposed to have recovered the jewels that Stock was accused of, I figured I was going to be sent away for something I had nothing to do with. Knowing I could get away any time I was ready, I waited until the train was in a populated section of the country. Arizona, Texas, and Oklahoma had too many open spaces; towns were too far apart, and it was much too easy to be recaptured. . . . .

. . . . About eighteen hours from Chicago where the towns were much closer together, my time came. I waited until I was sure the officer was sound asleep. I stood up and gently stepped over his beer-belly and into the aisle. I walked to the end of the car as if I were going to the washroom. Finding the washroom locked I entered the next car. Here I opened the small window near the end of the car which had a small bar above it. I grabbed the bar and stood up, managing to kick the window within a few inches of closing, so as not to leave any clue of my escape. Succeeding in this and being very limber and athletic, I swung myself atop of the Pullman car. I ran the four car-tops and reached the tender and stayed there until the train stopped for coal and water. When I got off I hid myself near a bunch of coal cars and watched the policeman get off to search for me. Losing sight of him in the early morning darkness, I waited for the train to fuel up.

After hearing the engineer give the highball signal, I waited for the first chug of the starting engine, then running swiftly, I hopped on and rode it into the Kansas City yards, where it reduced speed, which allowed me to jump off after a 122-mile non-stop ride. Being day-light when I jumped off, I lay down close to the tracks, letting the train pass before getting up, so as not to take any chance of being seen from the car windows. From Kansas City I caught a hot shot, that is a train with perishable goods, that ran on a very fast schedule, and hit Chi in fast time.

Arriving in Chicago, I stayed at a friend's house till I got the news that the coast was clear for me to go home. After I arrived home, I heard how the policeman from whom I had escaped had been looking for me, and how he had tried to bribe the folks with money for information concerning me. Knowing this, I had a hunch he would be told of my coming. Expecting him, and having a strong hunch I prepared a means of exit.

That night, knowing he would come, and instructing my family in what to say if questioned, I lay myself across the bed waiting. I was awakened about one o'clock by a heavy pounding on the door. Knowing who it was, I slipped into a sub-basement, which had a screened opening under my bed. Getting in just in time, I heard the cop tramping through the different rooms, saying, "Where is he? Where is he hiding. I know he's here; I had someone watching who told me. Where is he?"

Not finding me, and coming to the bedroom where the kids were lying, he offered different sums of money if they told him where I was hiding. Having told them what to say, they gave him their stories of my last being there, in a sing-song fashion, that almost anyone but he could see that it was made up.

Not being able to get his hands on me, he left in a huff and with a threat. I managed to keep away from him in his day and night search for me, until some two weeks later. Knowing that he had visited all of my known friends at their various homes, I arranged several signals with them, which when heard were to let me know if the coast was clear, so I could come in.

After a burglary in which I managed to get myself a new suit, shoes, ties, and shirts, I went over to one of my friend's home. Concealing myself in an alley, I gave the signal for an O.K. sign. Not getting any, I tried again. After several more attempts I decided no one was in. Knowing I could get in anyway, I crept up the stairs quietly. Reaching the third floor, I listened at the door; not hearing anything, I quietly stepped inside. Taking my attention off the door-knob, I glanced into the room and caught sight of Sergeant Jackson who at the same time saw me. Catching sight of each other so suddenly, we just stared at each other, unable to move. Being first to break the spell, I jumped back, slammed the door which I was holding all the time, throwing the bundle I had been carrying on the rear porch, I practically flew downstairs into a basement and into concealment before he was halfway down. I did not wish to take any chances of running through the long gangways, and possibly being shot, so hiding was my best bet. After listening to his noisy search, I stayed in hiding a good half-hour. Making sure the chase had moved by, I then hid myself in the next building until it began to get dark. The coast being clear, I left my place of hiding.

Knowing I had had a close shave, I stayed away from my usual hangouts until my capture and arrest on a burglary of a dentist, who, by the way, chased me all over the northwest side, until his yells for help caused my capture by a Federal dick who helped chase and get me, when I stumbled and fell over the uneven ground of the prairie I had been running through.

As a result of this, I was taken to the police station where I was questioned and held there for several days. Although I had been running around under an alias, I was recognized by two policemen who had me there sometime back. Since they were not sure about my identity, they questioned me about many things, using various ways to trip me up. However, not succeeding very well, they still continued to believe that they had had me before, in which case they were correct; but not having been fingerprinted before, they didn't have that means of checking up.

After checking up on my alibi, and still certain that I was the one they suspected, they decided to take me to my mother's address and ask her. They placed me in a squad car and drove to the house. By chance, a little boy was in the yard, who knew me and called me by name, as we were walking to our door. Stopping me, the policeman said to the boy, "Do you know him?", the boy said, "Sure, that's Eddy." Then asking ma, who couldn't answer in English, they brought me back and sent an officer who could speak the same language to her, and found out all the dope about me and Sergeant Jackson.

They immediately notified Sergeant Jackson of my capture who came down, together with two officers, to take me into custody of his district. They handcuffed me and the two officers escorted me to the paddy wagon where a third officer was told to keep his gun trained on me during the ride to the station. This was one fellow who was really afraid of my escaping again, and took no chances. At the station I was locked up and placed under guard of a special policeman.

The next morning I was brought before the Boys' Court, bound over to the grand jury, then placed in the County Jail awaiting trial before the Criminal Court. During my three months of waiting for trial, I met many of the big shots of that era and some who rose up later on.

Finally when my case came up in court, I won my freedom, because the lawyer who took my case had a high political standing. The Sergeant Jackson case was thrown out by the grand jury as there was no evidence to link me in that robbery, because I had been in St. Charles when it happened.

William Stock, my pal, was released from St. Charles, tried in a criminal court, found guilty, and sentenced from one to twenty years in the State Reformatory.

After winning my freedom, I met several of the boys whom I knew at St. Charles. These boys were pulling big jobs and I began to work with them. My companions on these burglaries were Earl Wooms, Bill Sloan, and Joseph Wyman. About two months after our meeting Bill and Earl were prowling a policeman's flat. When the cop came near his home, he saw them. Dashing in suddenly, he captured Earl, while Bill made his getaway. Under a third degree, Earl confessed several robberies with Bill, and on bringing the police to Bill's room, they recovered about $800.00 in stolen goods. After an intense search, Bill was arrested and indicted by the grand jury along with Earl. While they were held by the police, I was named in one of their burglaries. While walking with Wyman, I was betrayed by a police stool pigeon, who helped set a trap into which I walked.

After being held at the Detective Bureau for eleven days, I was finally booked on a burglary charge with Earl, Joseph, and Bill. Joseph, having a wealthy brother-in-law, was given one year's probation; Earl and Bill were given one to twenty years in the reformatory, and I received one to ten years in the reformatory on a charge of receiving stolen property.

JAMES MARTIN

When James was fifteen years and four months of age, he escaped from the St. Charles School for Boys and returned to his home in Chicago. At that time all of his brothers, with the exception of Carl, were in penal institutions. John was in a state prison, Edward was serving a sentence in a reformatory, and Michael was confined in the St. Charles School for Boys. In the absence of Edward and Michael, with whom he had previously engaged in delinquency, James resumed his contact with a former companion and through him was brought into association with other delinquents in the local neighborhood. In the company of these boys, James became implicated in the larceny of automobiles, which to him was a new form of delinquent experience. One of these boys, Anton Macy, whose nickname was "Chrysler Kid," was particularly skilled in the practice of stealing automobiles.

The exact number of thefts of automobiles in which he was involved is not known, although he has estimated that the total was in excess of forty. It is known, however, that he was recommitted to correctional schools and served sentences in the Chicago House of Correction and the Illinois State Reformatory for this form of delinquency. His account of these experiences is given in the following statements.

It was after I was paroled from the St. Charles School for Boys at the age of fifteen that I started stealing cars. Although I never had driven a car before, I knew how one was operated. A fellow by the name of Anton stole a Buick sedan one day. I accompanied him and when he went home to eat I took the car and started on one of the wildest experiences I had. I knew what I should do to make a car run and I knew the standard gear shift, but the Buick's gear had a universal shift. To begin with after starting the motor I had all I could do to put the gear in first, or what I thought was first, but was high instead. The car started to shake and quiver at first, but it finally picked up and gathered speed. It was around February and the streets were wet and slippery. I started a few times to put the car in what I thought was second, but every time I bent over to try and shift the gear, the car would seem to swerve a little and it scared me, so I contented myself by leaving it in that gear. At crossings I would push on the clutch and brake and the car would stop.

On one of the street crossings I guess I wanted to show off a little and I would push down the hand throttle to make the motor roar. While doing this I unconsciously took my feet off the clutch and the brake. The fun then began. The car, after a few hesitating movements, went forward like it was shot out of a cannon. Why I did not kill any people or kill myself, God only knows. The car ran down the avenue at forty or fifty miles an hour. Swerving in and out among the other autos and street cars gave me time to think of nothing but the driving ahead of me. I was too excited to think anyway. Three or four times I sent pedestrians running to safety on the side walk. I finally ended the mad drive by shutting the switch and braking the car to a stop. That was my first lesson in driving and I rather liked it after I recalled the events in my mind later on.

I stole cars with Anton Macy [the "Chrysler Kid"], Jack Gleason, and Slim Casey. All three were in prison at one time or another, but Slim was the only one that did not go to Pontiac or Joliet. Anton was in Pontiac and now is in Joliet. Jack Gleason was in Pontiac for about 3 or 4 years. Slim Casey and I and Anton used to be more or less partners. I seldom went out with any one else. Our technique was not one of opening the ignition through some mechanical means, that took too long and was too hazardous. We would look for cars with keys left in the ignition lock. We did however have a set of master keys for Chevrolets.

I first stole cars for the thrill and pleasure of just driving. Later on I stole the cars for the tires and accessories that I could dispose of. We had one garage where we could sell all the tires and other parts which we were able to steal. At times stealing a car was exciting. On one instance Slim Casey and I boarded a street car and went to a suburb to get a Hudson "with balloon tires." We could get $15.00 apiece for the tires if they were in good shape. As we walked around in Oak Park in the evening we "spotted" just the kind of a car we wanted. Not only were the tires in good shape but the car had a Lorraine Spotlight worth about $35.00. Being smaller and younger looking than Slim Casey, I looked in the car to see if the keys were in the ignition. Sure enough they were in the car. Slim and I walked around the street planning a way to steal the car. We had to talk things over because the owner of the car was watering his lawn right in front of the building where the car stood. After we watched him go to the side of the house to water the grass, Slim and I went into the car. We no sooner had the motor started when the man ran out and started yelling at us. I got a little excited and killed the motor. I started the motor again immediately but the man had jumped on the running board of the car, and was yelling for all he was worth. I started to drive but he still clung to the doors. It took Slim over a block before he could push the man from the car. Boy, did I have to step to get out of the neighborhood.

Another time Jack Gleason and I went out to get a car, any car. As it was dark, it would be easy. We went around the neighborhood of P—— and H—— Streets. I saw a Willys Knight, a new job with keys in it and we decided to take it. We both sat in the front seat and I started the motor when suddenly someone grabbed me by the back of my coat. I looked around and there was a man holding both Jack and me. Gee! I got scared. Jack twisted away and hit the man with a pair of pliers he had and we both jumped out of the car and ran. When we entered we did not see the man lying in the back seat. You can be sure we looked in the back seat from then on.

The more cars I stole the nervier and more careless I became. One time I went out alone and stole a Buick Sedan. In the back seat there were two pans of cakes that I gave to some of the boys in the neighborhood.

An incident that struck me very funny at the time was when Anton Macy and I were walking along and a Willys St. Claire model drove up with a man and a woman. The man no sooner walked in the store with the woman when Anton took his car and drove away. I didn't accompany him because I had my eye on a Jordan roadster. Anton just drove away when the woman came out to where the car was and started looking for it. After seeing it gone she got excited and called to her male companion. After asking a lot of people questions and getting no satisfaction she gave the fellow a heck of a bawling out, right there on the street. I felt sorry for the fellow. After things quieted down a little I got in the Jordan car and stole it. . . . .

During the summer that I was sixteen years of age, I continued in the stealing of automobiles, was arrested and served two short sentences in the House of Correction. During that period of my life I was not staying at home, though I did go over to see my mother once in a while. The "Kid" [Anton

Macy] and I lived for a while with two girls who were about two years older than we were. The "Kid" was living with these girls and invited me to make my home with them. I was living there at the time of my commitment to the House of Correction.

After my release from the House of Correction the second time I continued to steal automobiles. Another friend of mine came out the same day. We went over to his house to get something to eat. I lingered there for about two hours before I finally boarded a street car for home. A few houses away from home, I met Alfred Schwartz and Francis Berman. These two fellows were out on various "jobs" with my younger brother, Michael. They told me that the St. Charles parole agent had just arrested Michael. I went home, changed clothes, and then went out and stole a Buick sedan. Francis Berman was with me. I drove over to the police station and wanted to see my brother. They told me he wasn't booked, so I couldn't see him. As I had no money at the time, I borrowed a couple of dollars off Alfred Schwartz and Francis Berman. Later on that day I stole a Chrysler roadster, stripped off the tires and sold them.

A few days later I stole the automobile for which I was committed to the Illinois State Reformatory. That evening Francis Berman and I rode the "L" out to a swell suburb. We did not go out there to steal automobiles, because we knew we were wanted by the police, and we wanted to keep out of the neighborhood as much as possible. We could have just as well gone to some theater to spend the evening, but I liked to stay out in the fresh air, preferably in a quiet and secluded neighborhood. So I picked a western suburb.

I liked to walk along the quiet streets, looking at the nice cottages, glancing in through the windows for a sight of some home-like scenery. I liked to listen to the music that I heard sometimes as I passed the cottages. I used to wonder how it would feel to live as these people did. Sometimes I would envy them and compare their homes with the home I had always known. As Francis and I were walking along a street, a car drove up to one of the cottages across the street near us. We stopped and watched them get out of the car. As they alighted I noticed that the driver of the car did not bend over to lock the gear shift. The car was a Chrysler make, a brougham sedan. As they walked into their home, I told Francis that I was going to steal the car. I walked across the street and to the car. I tried the gear shift and found it unlocked. Stepping into the car, I started it and drove off, picking Francis up on the next block. We drove around awhile then went back to our neighborhood. We parked the car in front of a large apartment building, and then went to our rooms and to bed. Next morning I went down looking for "my" car. I found it and drove it to a friend's garage. That night Francis, two other fellows, and I went out to a small town north of Chicago in this car. We were to visit a friend and stay with him on his farm over the week-end. We did not reach out destination because we lost our way. After an experience of being stuck in the mud, we drove back to Chicago. The next day I was arrested on suspicion, squealed on by Francis Berman's cousin, and charges of automobile thefts were placed against me. After four days in the Detective Bureau, I was taken to the County Jail and indicted on two charges of automobile stealing. I was given a trial in the latter part of November. I pleaded guilty on one charge and was given one to ten years at the Illinois State Reformatory.

MICHAEL MARTIN

A few days after Michael was paroled from the St. Charles School for Boys at the age of fifteen years and nine months, he became associated with three older delinquents, Francis Berman (aged 17), who was one of his former companions, Clyde Jones (aged 18), and Alfred Schwartz (aged 26). These young men were engaged in armed robbery and solicited Michael's participation in this activity. After some hesitation he consented to accompany them and became involved in a series of incidences of armed robbery. He was arrested one month after his parole from St. Charles and brought to court charged with robbery with a gun. He was returned to St. Charles, while his companions were committed to the House of Correction and the Illinois State Reformatory. After escaping from St. Charles he was brought into the Criminal Court and committed to the Illinois State Reformatory. After serving a sentence of five years in this institution he was paroled but again became involved in armed robbery and was sentenced to the Illinois State Penitentiary. His description of certain of these experiences is given in the following quotations from his autobiography.

Well, after I got acquainted with the group around the corner, one of them asked me if I cared to burglarize some stores at night, but I was afraid because I had just been paroled from St. Charles and was afraid to get caught; besides these fellows were almost strangers to me and I did not care to go with them. So I told them no, I did not care to try it, because I had just come from St. Charles and was afraid I'd get caught doing it. So they let me go and they went by themselves and burglarized and held up several places.

About a week later I met another fellow who knew my brother, James, and used to go out with him. He and I got pretty well acquainted. After knowing him a few days, he asked me if I cared to go and hold up a bakery shop which he had spotted for some time before. Well, I kind of stalled him off for a few days, because robbery with a gun was a new racket to me and I didn't care much about it.

The only racket I ever played was burglary and that was when I was a kid. When I got out of St. Charles the second time, I knew I couldn't go back to begging and prowling houses, because I was pretty big and my line of begging would not work, because people would tell me I was old enough to work. So ever since then I quit breaking into people's houses.

.... So after a few times of asking me to go and rob this bakery shop I consented to go, because I was broke and I did not have a job; and besides, all my former associates were either in jail or had moved out of the neighborhood. My brother, Edward, was still in the reformatory and my other brothers, James and John, were in jail too, so that left my mother and my youngest brother at home with me.....

.... After a few days of going out with this fellow, he got a gun from a man who lived near our home. This man wanted $25.00 from each of us after we got through robbing the bakery shop.

That night I did not go home because I had to stay up all night with this fellow. We walked the streets until about 4 o'clock in the morning and then went to the bakery shop, which was located only about two blocks from my home. When we got there we waited until the bakery opened. While we were waiting, my partner told me just what to do, because this was the first time I ever tried holding up anybody. I was shaking all the time and wanted to go home, but it was too late then, because I promised him and besides the store was just opening. The street lights just went out and I guess it was about 5 o'clock. As soon as the store opened, one customer went in and came out, and then my partner and I went across the street and he told me to put my handkerchief across my face as soon as we hit the door, but I was so excited and scared that I forgot all about the handkerchief.

As we went into the bakery, my partner who had the gun, went in first and I followed him. A woman was taking care of the store and as she turned around to wait on us, my partner told her to throw up her hands and face the wall, while he told me to get the money out of both places. I started out of the bakery with my partner and ran down several yards and alleys till we thought we were safe. Then we went to a hotel and divided the money between us. Then we went to bed and slept till about 10 o'clock in the morning. Then we went back to the neighborhood and I went home and left a lot of change I had at home. I did not tell my mother what I had done and when she found the change, she asked me where I got it, but instead of telling her the truth, I told her I had a job and told her to keep the change, which amounted to about $30.00 or $40.00. She kind of thought I stole it, so she didn't take a penny of it, because she would rather starve than receive a penny of stolen money from me. I don't know what happened to the change and I didn't care because I had about $200.00 in bills on me.

Well, after that holdup things seemed to brighten up before me and I thought if the rest of the holdups were going to be that easy and profitable

I figured on making it my future racket. So after the first week of spending part of my easy money on all sorts of amusements, we met up with another fellow whose name was Alfred Schwartz. He was about 25 years old. He is now doing time in Joliet. He was sent there on the robbery charge for which I was sent to the reformatory. After the three of us got together, we planned on pulling off big robberies. . . . .

After each holdup, I usually came home either at 3 or 4 o'clock in the morning, and then I usually slept till about 8 or 9 o'clock in the morning. Then I would meet my two partners and we would loaf around the rest of the day. At night we would again rent a car and start out for a good time. . . . .

. . . . A few days before my brother, James, came home I went with my two buddies, Alfred Schwartz and Francis Berman, on a few more robberies. I was fifteen years old and the youngest of the three. About a week before I was arrested, I had bought a big revolver, belt and holster for $15.00 from an acquaintance who had stolen them. I let my partners have the gun whenever we went on a robbery, because I never used one of the guns before, and besides I was so afraid that I wouldn't shoot anyone if I did have the gun. My pals decided to take it away from me. What I was used for mostly was to spot the money after we got into the place. Whenever we went to hold up a place I would go in first. I usually bought something and gave them a $10 or $20 bill and told them that was the smallest bill I had. If the store owner changed it, I gave my two buddies the signal and they would come dashing into the store and hold up the owner, while I got the money. Then we would dash right out again into the running car and turned a few corners till we thought we were safe from pursuit and then go to one of my buddies favorite hotels and split the stolen money into three equal shares. Then each of us would take one-third of the total amount.

The night before my brother, James, was supposed to come out of the House of Correction, I went with my two buddies and we held up a store that looked good for a haul or stickup, but we didn't get any, so at 3 o'clock in the morning I went home and the other fellows the same. We had a date to meet each other at 8 o'clock the next day so with that in mind I crept into my home at 3 o'clock in the morning and I was so tired and sleepy that I did not take time to undress. I remember just taking my coat, cap and shoes off and falling into bed with the gun holster and belt still on my person. I went to bed with the intention of getting up about 8 o'clock and meeting my two rap partners, and then go to the Bridewell and get my brother, James, because his time was up then. But I must have overslept because at 8 o'clock I was still sleeping. I had not had a good night's sleep for about a week before, so that's the only reason I can think of for oversleeping. The first thing I knew was when I woke up a couple of detectives were in my room with my parole officer and one of them had my gun and was taking the shells out of it and putting them in his pocket. . . . .

CARL MARTIN

The specific form of delinquency in which Carl was implicated during the period following his participation in the burglary of residences with his brothers was similar to that of his brother James. During this later period his delinquencies were limited largely to the larceny of automobiles. After Carl was paroled from the Chicago and Cook County School at the age of thirteen years and five months, he became associated with an older boy, Joseph Herman (16 years), who was a former companion of Carl's older brother James. In the company of this boy and a younger companion Carl became implicated in the larceny of automobiles and was subsequently committed to the St. Charles School for Boys.

After I came out of the Parental School about the age of thirteen I went back to school for a little while and then stopped. I met two friends of my brother James. These fellows were in the car racket. They asked me if I wanted to go out with them. I said yes, so I got started going out with them to steal cars. These fellows knew how to get into cars. Sometimes we found cars unlocked, with the ignition key in place. All we had to do was to get in and start the car and drive away. Sometimes we used master keys. Other times we would break the lock in the door, connect the ignition and start the car. I got interested in stealing cars and learned how to steal them through these older fellows.

After taking cars with these fellows, sometimes I would go out alone to get a car. One time I got a craving to drive a car. So one night I went out to a country club in one of the suburbs north of Chicago. I knew the community well, because I used to go there with my brother to prowl apartments. I saw a new Studebaker touring car which I wanted. I took the car and drove it around all evening. It was a wonderful machine and I got a great kick out of driving it. I drove it all around in our neighborhood and got caught with it a day or two later, and sent to the Chicago and Cook County School for Boys.

After I came out of this institution I met my old friends again stealing cars. We would steal cars and sell them to a man in a garage. He would strip the car and sell the tires and accessories. We got only a few dollars out of each car, but it was enough to help in spending money. We kept on taking cars and selling them to the garage man until we were arrested and I was sent to the St. Charles School for Boys.

Perhaps one of the most important facts revealed in the ex-cerpts included in the preceding pages of this chapter is the manner in which the divergent forms of delinquent and criminal conduct of the Martin brothers during adolescence reflected the varied contacts which they established during this period in their lives. In the case of each brother the specific kind of delinquency and crime engaged in during this period conformed to the type of criminality which was current among the other offenders with whom each brother became associated on his return from correctional institutions. Thus, while James and Carl became associated with automobile thieves and embarked upon a career of stealing automobiles, Michael, on the other hand, formed an association with two experienced robbers and with them became implicated in armed robbery. This fact is suggestive of the social characteristics of the delinquent experiences of the Martin brothers which were a part of the interpersonal relationships and social practices comprising their social world.

PART II

THE SOCIAL BACKGROUND OF THE
MARTIN BROTHERS

INTRODUCTION

In the foregoing chapters the delinquencies and crimes of the brothers were described by means of official records and by excerpts from their autobiographies. Since it is assumed that to understand the nature of these offenses it is necessary to study them in their relation to their social context, careful consideration will be given to a description of the social world in which the brothers lived. This will entail, among other things, a characterization of their community, their family, their play groups and gangs, and the more general social processes which were instrumental in determining the character of these smaller social groupings.

Although for this purpose the community, the family, and the play groups will be dealt with separately, it should be remembered that such a separation is, in many respects, artificial. The Martin family and the play groups and gangs were integral parts of a larger social complex. They were not only related to each other but they were interrelated with various other elements in the life of the community. Each of these groups becomes understandable when regarded in terms of its varied functional relationships. In like manner, the physical, economic, political, and cultural conditions which obtained in the community were functions of larger processes of competition, segregation, and differentiation within the life of the city as a whole.

CHAPTER V

THE COMMUNITY BACKGROUND

In this chapter a description will be made of the local community in which Mr. and Mrs. Martin have resided since they established their home in Chicago more than three decades ago. Particular emphasis will be placed upon three major aspects of the community: (1) its physical deterioration and low economic status, (2) the confusion and diversification of its cultural standards and patterns of behavior, and (3) its delinquency traditions.

PHYSICAL DETERIORATION AND LOW ECONOMIC STATUS

The community in question is adjacent to a center of heavy industry located along one of the branches of the Chicago River— a drab, unattractive, and deteriorated community. When the Martin family established their home here, the community was inhabited almost exclusively by persons of their own nationality. Since that time despite the great population changes that have taken place in many other similar areas in the city, the population in this community has undergone little change as regards its nationality composition. It is a community of first immigrant settlement with the physical characteristics common to the so-called "blighted" or "slum" areas.

For the most part the dwellings are old and dilapidated structures accommodating two or more families, as few new residential buildings have been constructed during the last three decades. An analysis of the distribution of the residential structures which have been condemned by the Chicago Department of Public Works shows that this community is among those communities in which a disproportionately large number of the dwellings are under condemnation for demolition or repair.

The presence of a large number of old deteriorated buildings provides an appropriate situation for the practice of junking, which is one of the most common initial forms of delinquency in

98

which boys in this neighborhood engage. This practice consists of stealing iron, lead pipes, and lumber from vacant buildings and disposing of them to junk dealers or to residents of the community. As indicated in chapter ii, this form of stealing was among the earliest delinquencies in which the brothers were implicated.

Three decades ago this community was characterized by a relatively great density of population with approximately one hundred thousand persons per square mile. Since that time the total population has decreased continuously to the extent that in 1930 the number of its inhabitants was less than half as great as it was in 1900. This marked decrease has been due to the combined influences of many factors operating in the community and in the city as a whole, among which may be mentioned the reduction in the number of buildings available for residential use because of demolition, the gradual change from residential to industrial usage of land, and the movement of many families out of the community as they have prospered sufficiently to be able to pay higher rentals in communities of higher economic status. The community is in a process of transition and deterioration, with little evidence of any effort on the part of property owners to make improvements in its physical condition.

The obvious physical deterioration is suggestive of the low economic status of the population residing in this community. Rates of unemployment, poverty, and economic dependency have been relatively high for many years. For the most part the residents are unskilled laborers who have been forced to work at those types of employment which are relatively unremunerative and provide little security. Even during periods of prosperity the standards of living have been generally low, while in times of depression a large segment of the population has been unemployed and dependent upon charity for subsistence.

With regard to economic insecurity the Martin family was not unlike many other families in the community. Studies of the distribution of the families who received financial assistance from the United Charities and Jewish Charities in 1921 revealed that this community was among those in the city in which the

highest proportion of the families were receiving financial assistance. In 1934 the Cook County Statistical Service of the Illinois
Emergency Relief Commission made an analysis of the proportion of families on relief rolls in each of the 120 subcommunities
in the city. It was found in this study that the community under
consideration was among the fifteen with the highest proportion
of families on relief. At that time more than one-fourth of the
families in the community were dependent upon public agencies
for financial assistance.

The universally low economic status of the families in this
community stands in sharp contrast to the standards of living
which are maintained in a large proportion of the communities
in the city. In general the families of this community are seriously
handicapped in providing for their children the educational opportunity for successful achievement in business and the professions in the highly competitive world outside of the community. With relatively few exceptions the children are forced to
accept whatever employment is available regardless of how irregular, uninteresting, or unremunerative it may be or how little
it may offer for the future. In this situation, however, they are
exposed to the luxury standards of life which are generally ideal-
ized in our culture but which are beyond their attainment. They
observe older persons in their community who have acquired
money and personal prestige in business, in the professions, in
politics, or in crime and the rackets. To many of them the fact
that they cannot possess the things which they see others enjoy
does not nullify their eagerness and determination to secure these
things—even by illegitimate means when such means have the
support and sanction of the groups to which they belong.

The inability of many of the young men in the community to
secure remunerative employment in private industry appears as
an important factor in the problem of delinquency and crime.
Very often crime and the rackets offer the only means of achiev-
ing even the minimum of economic security. Only a small proportion of the men who return to the community on parole from
penal institutions are able to secure any kind of remunerative
work; employment opportunities are limited and employers are

often skeptical with regard to the employment of men who have criminal records. That many of these men in the community return to a life of crime is inevitable, not only because of their inability to make an adjustment in industry but because they are again brought under the influences which were responsible for their delinquencies in the first instance.

In discussing the low economic conditions which characterized this community it should be indicated that the delinquent children represent families of widely divergent economic status. They represent those that are poverty-stricken as well as those that are in the highest income groups in the community. In fact there are families representing all economic groups in the community in which there are both delinquent and nondelinquent siblings. Presumably, therefore, the effect of economic conditions in any given case of delinquency is a relative matter; apparently its significance is dependent upon its relationship to many other things in the total situation.

CONFUSION AND DIVERSIFICATION OF STANDARDS

Perhaps one of the most important characteristics of this community, particularly with regard to delinquency, is the confusion and wide diversification of its norms or standards of behavior. The local population comprises many natural groupings, with widely divergent definitions of behavior, standards, and expectations. The moral values of these different social worlds range from those that are strictly conventional to those that are delinquent and criminal in character. Thus, acts of theft are sanctioned in certain groups and condemned in other groups. They are defined as good, proper, and desirable by certain groups and as bad, improper, and undesirable by others. In some groups personal status may be enhanced by manifestations of skill, courage, and dexterity in the execution of acts of theft, while in other groups the commission of an act of theft on the part of any member results in ostracism. What is approved in one situation is condemned in another.

The children living in this community are exposed to a variety of interests, forms of behavior, and stimulations, rather than to a relatively consistent pattern of conventional standards and values. In this community situation, with its confusion of standards, there is more than one type of moral instruction and education available to the child. A career in delinquency may emerge as a product of the natural processes of learning and habituation under certain group influences, just as attitudes, interests, and habits of a conventional character may be formed in other group situations. As Frank Tannenbaum states, "The alternatives between the criminal and non-criminal ways of life are, so to speak, on a par, and each is open to new recruits."[1]

The diversification and inconsistencies in the patterns of life in this community appear in many forms. There is, in the first place, the disparity of interests, standards, and philosophy of life as between parents and children. For the most part the parents were born in Europe and their attitudes and interests reflect their Old World background. The children, on the other hand, were born in Chicago and their attitudes and interests stand in sharp contrast to those of the older generation. In 1920 approximately 85.6 per cent of the heads of families in this community were listed as foreign born in the United States Census. At the same time, 84.0 per cent of the persons under 21 years of age were classified as American born of foreign or mixed parentage. This preponderance of foreign-born adults and of native-born children is a contributing factor in the cleavage between the older and younger generations and reflects a break in the transmission of cultural heritage from the parents to the children.

The parents, who were reared in homogeneous communities in the Old World, have come to America as adults, brought with them the ideas of morality, of workmanship, and of children's responsibility to their parents which were inculcated in them in that situation. To a great extent the children are not receptive to those values because their attitudes, interests, and ideas are products of a very different social world. In this situation the parents are often helpless in their efforts to instil into their children the values which to them seem essential to a normal,

[1] Frank Tannenbaum, *Crime and the Community* (New York: Ginn & Co., 1938), p. 217.

stable life. Conflicts arise with regard to a wide range of matters pertaining to family life, employment, leisure-time activities, school attendance, and delinquency. To enforce conformity the parents often resort to severe corporal punishment. In the absence of effective community sentiments in support of the wishes of the parents, the severe punishment often has the effect of further alienating the child from the parents.

While on the whole the parents are slow to make adaptations to the demands of the community situation, the children readily learn the language and adopt the practices of the community and learn how to get about in the city and meet situations which are strange and bewildering to their parents. Thus, the children become increasingly more sophisticated than the parents and often assume the role of interpreters for them. Naturally, the parental control in this situation is weakened and the family is rendered relatively ineffective in developing the attitudes, habits, and interests in the child which might serve as a safeguard against any demoralizing influences he might encounter in the gangs and play groups outside of the home. A young delinquent described this situation in the following manner.

These parents send their kids to school. The kids get a little education, which is a little above that of their parents. The life in the community and in the city is fast; in fact it dazzles these parents. The kids try to explain to their parents things about their school and play. The parents have no interest because they do not understand. As the parents cannot understand, the kids think themselves superior to them and do things according to their own figuring and neglect the teachings of their parents. They follow their own views and their minds, which are far from maturity, are filled with ideals and ideas of worthlessness.

The misunderstanding and conflicts between parents and children reflect divergent group experiences. In many instances the children belong to street crowds, play groups, or organized gangs in which the absorbing interest is in varied forms of delinquency. The free, spontaneous, colorful, and glamorous life in these groups is stimulating, exciting, and enticing. These groups afford satisfactions and exert an influence and control upon the lives of their members with which the family, the school, and the character-building agencies in the community can scarcely compete. In these groups, as indicated by a member of the gang to which the Martin brothers belonged, "the young kids hear tales of how cars, furs, jewelry and other things are stolen. They see the easy way the older fellows flash their rolls and strut their stuff. The other kids get the impression that life isn't so tough and they go out and try to get these things for themselves."

The attitudes on the part of the adults in the community with regard to delinquency are varied, although, undoubtedly, the preponderant attitude among individual parents is one of disapprobation. The attitudes of certain of the adults, however, are characterized by indifference, tolerance, or tacit approval of stealing, and in many instances the adults are directly involved in the delinquent activities of children. Among these are the professional fences who dispose of stolen merchandise, the parents who send the children out to steal, those who receive these stolen things from their children, and other residents who purchase stolen goods from the young delinquents. This practice among local residents is an aspect of the community life which is important in the problem of delinquency. It not only serves as a market but it gives sanction and justification to the child for his participation in delinquent practices.

A young delinquent who resided in the vicinity of the Martin home gives the following description of the way in which the delinquents disposed of their stolen merchandise.

Almost any week day gangs of boys from 8 to 17 years old go out stealing in department stores and other places. They work these stores for everything that is valuable and everything that they can sell to people in the community. Many times they sell them to older guys in the rackets. These are well known to the boys and they either buy their loot for about one-third of its original value, or the boys give the loot to them and pay them for selling it. Sometimes the boys take their loot to some pool room where they know the guys and sell it to them. Often they sell all their men's wear to these guys. These fellows may buy the women's wear and jewelry to sell or sometimes they buy the things to give to their girl friends. [There are local dealers around in the district who buy the loot and junk dealers who give a small price for iron and lead.] Any left overs of dresses, hosiery, and jewelry the boys will sell to women or girls in the community or give them to their own sisters. For several hundred dollars worth of merchandise they may get only $50.00 or $60.00 in cash to split among themselves.

The character of the moral values and expectations which obtain in these delinquent groups is indicated by the extent to which personal status of their members is enhanced by demonstration of skill in committing acts of theft, cunning and ingenuity in circumventing the police, and loyalty to their group associates. Assimilation into the life of these groups entails participation in delinquent activities, education in the technique of stealing, and conformity to moral standards which are diametric to the norms of conventional social groups. Thus a member of one of these groups in the community stated: "Every kid in these little gangs tries to swipe more stuff than anybody else so he will be looked upon as the best guy."

It appears from what has been said in the preceding pages that this community comprises a varied assortment of social groupings and forms of moral conduct. As a social environment for the child it presents an opportunity for widely diverse forms of character formation, ranging from those that are delinquent to those that are conventional in nature. The extent and character of delinquency and crime in the community will be presented in the succeeding pages.

DELINQUENCY TRADITION IN THE COMMUNITY

The community in which the brothers resided has been characterized by a disproportionately large number of school truants, juvenile delinquents, and adult offenders each year for a period of at least forty years. During this time delinquency has become established as an integral part of the pattern of life of the community; it is in a very real sense one of its social traditions. This tradition is assimilated by groups of young boys and transmitted by them to succeeding ones. The careers of the Martin brothers illustrate in a concrete manner the transmission of this tradition of delinquency through the medium of group relationships.

With regard to the percentage of boys aged ten to seventeen years who are dealt with by the police for alleged delinquency, or those who are taken into the Cook County Juvenile Court on petitions alleging delinquency, or those who are committed to correctional institutions, the volume of delinquency in this area has been for many years among the highest in all the local communities within the city. At the time the brothers were being initiated into delinquency only eleven of the one hundred and thirteen local areas of the city had higher rates of delinquency; in 1900, 1920, and 1930 this community was among the 10 per cent of the communities with the highest rate of delinquency.

During the years that the brothers were active in delinquency approximately 12 to 15 per cent of the boys aged ten to seventeen years residing in this community were dealt with by the police for alleged delinquency each year. When it is realized that the number of boys dealt with by the police does not include all of those who are actually engaged in delinquency, it is clear that the prospect of contact between young boys and older delinquents in this community was at that time very great. The greater probability of such contact in this community as compared with other local communities is indicated by the fact that more than 85 per cent of the boys aged ten to seventeen years in the city resided in communities that had lower rates of officially recorded delinquency.

It is important to observe, also, that this community is characterized by a very high rate of crime among young men aged seventeen to twenty-one years. During the period 1924–26, fifteen young men per hundred in this age-group were taken into the Boys' Court on felony charges. Only ten of the one hundred and thirteen areas of the city had higher rates of criminality for this age-group. The presence of such a large group of older offenders in the community is again indicative of the great possibility of contact between the younger boys and older offenders.

For the most part the delinquencies in which the boys and young men of this neighborhood engage are offenses against property. Among the very young boys stealing from railroads, junking, and shoplifting in local stores are most prevalent. Among the older boys shoplifting in department stores in the Loop, burglary of homes and places of business, the larceny of automobiles, and armed robbery are the most common.

As already suggested these varied forms of delinquency are perpetuated in the neighborhood through interpersonal relationships within play groups, street crowds, and gangs. This process is briefly characterized in the following excerpts from the autobiography of a young delinquent in the community.

The kids I knew around the neighborhood who were able to avoid stealing were monuments of character because for every encouragement for right living around there, there were ten good arguments in favor of being crooked.

When a kid did make up his mind to go straight there was always a friend to tell him of some easy thing that would pay a lot of money for only a few hours work. There was scarcely one of the kids who at some time or other in his life was not a thief.

As the kids get older they take in the shows and learn to play up to the girls until it becomes the favorite pastime. After leaving school the average boy's day around that neighborhood consists of the following. He is awakened in the morning by the father and given fifteen cents carfare with the command to go and get a job. He makes a trip down to the pool room where he lounges all day, in the winter. In the summer, he goes to the park. At about 2 o'clock, he returns home and tells the folks of his failure to secure work. He then listens to a berating for a few hours and eats his supper and putting on his coat and hat returns to the corner. Met in the pool room by his friends there is always a way to make a few dollars. Taking on a "sucker" at the pool tables. Maybe a petty burglary with a net of ten dollars. Then later in the evening, they attend a show with no other thought than that maybe they can pick up a "broad."

The revenue sometimes comes from stealing and stripping of cars. There are some fellows that are just bums. Never do these fellows break out into the larger fields of crime. They are too lazy to work and too yellow to steal. They are the panhandlers. They can sense when you are holding a few dollars with unerring accuracy. They would be first-class con-men if they were only possessed of a little spunk but all the ambition they have is to bum six-bits for a bottle of bum booze.

All kinds of fellows follow this path around that neighborhood. They start with the petty things and gradually grow into a larger scale. The kids hear the older guys talking of the things they have stolen. This ability is admired by the younger kids and generally admiring, they tried to imitate. They would learn from the older boys the method that was used and then go out and do it. No certain branch of stealing was done by all of the boys. There were different types. Some stole cars; others burglarized stores; and still others snatched pocketbooks.

Attention has been focused upon two general aspects of the community situation in which the Martin brothers resided. In the first place it was indicated that it comprises a variety of social worlds and diverse codes of conduct; both conventional and delinquent forms of conduct here are fostered and approved. In the second place along with the inconsistencies in the social traditions within the community, many of these traditions are at variance with the culture, practices, and norms of conventional society at large. Thus the child is surrounded by a bewildering assortment of definitions of what constitutes proper and improper conduct. Whether he becomes a delinquent or a nondelinquent seems to depend, in many cases at least, upon which of the varied social worlds or systems of relationships he becomes associated with. From the standpoint of his own social world the boy who engages in delinquency may be regarded as a "right guy," but from the standpoint of the court he is regarded as a law-violator and a delinquent.

CHAPTER VI

THE MARTIN BROTHERS AND THEIR COMPANIONS

As was pointed out in the preceding chapter, delinquency and crime have been for many years part of the social tradition of the community in which the Martin brothers resided. For the most part, play groups, street crowds, and gangs are the bearers of this tradition. Its perpetuation is dependent upon these natural social groupings and upon a community milieu in which there is low resistance to delinquency and in which the residents in various ways give sanction and encouragement to the child in his delinquent activities. The process of transmitting traditions of delinquency from group to group is illustrated by the play groups and gangs to which the brothers belonged. A partial account of the activities of these groups was given in the autobiographical excerpts presented in chapters ii, iii, and iv. A more detailed description will be given in this chapter.

THE EARLY PLAY LIFE OF THE BROTHERS

When John Martin was approximately seven years of age, he became identified with one of the many play groups in his community, a group composed of at least twelve boys ranging in age from five to twelve years. Their playgrounds were the alleys, streets, and railroad yards; their activities were largely spontaneous, random, and unsupervised; simple forms of stealing were interspersed with nondelinquent activities with little realization of their moral implications.

As a means of supplementing the brothers' account of the activities of this group, a brief excerpt will be presented from the autobiographies of one of the other members. This quotation suggests that stealing was simply one of the forms of interesting play life in which the group originally engaged.

My earliest recollections of the neighborhood go back to the time I used to play with a small group of kids. We played Cowboy and Indians and very often we would go to the river and throw stones in the water and play around in the railroad yards. We would spend all day fooling around in this way, only going home to secure our meals. Our mothers would worry about our whereabouts on these days when we did not appear and would scold us and threaten to have our fathers give us a licking, but the next day we would go back again doing the same things.

We lived next to a lumber company and we used to go around there and talk with the men. They often played jokes on us. One of the men once gave me some booze; it was only enough to burn my throat and I ran away. One day we were fishing in the river and I fell in while trying to get a fish. I almost drowned but one of the older boys grabbed me by the pants and pulled me to the shore.

I started to school when I was a little past six years of age which is the time when most of the boys in the neighborhood started school. After school all of us kids would play all kinds of games in the streets, alleys, or on the school playground. After we had our supper all of us kids would get together and go to shows. There was no restraint exercised by our parents. In those days two of us used to get into a show for a nickle. We always managed to get our hands on a few nickles. If we didn't have any nickles and sometimes even if we did, we would manage to sneak through one of the back doors. All of us kids liked Cowboy and Indian pictures and when one of these was showing there was nothing that could keep us away from the shows.

As I said, one of our favorite places of play was the railroad yards, but the cops from the railroad always tried to make us leave because we would get noisy and very often we would break into the box cars. I shall never forget one time when we were playing in the yards and we broke into two cars that were loaded with pickles. The cars were on different tracks and some of the kids got into one car and some into the other car and one of the greatest free-for-all pickle battles ever staged took place. Pickles were strewn from one end of the yard to the other. Now I ask you what kid would not prefer the company of the gang when such interesting events took place? Very few of of them, I believe, would not like it, especially boys of spirit. And that poor railroad cop! That poor fellow deserved whatever salary he received. I imagine that many times he stood on the carpet before the officials because of the many depredations that we committed. Expense meant nothing to us. We always acted and then considered the consequences after we were caught.

Another time when we were playing in the railroad yard there was a car filled with horses on a side track. Some kids said that we could have a lot of fun if we opened the door and let the horses out. Every kid dared the other kid to open the car. For a long time everyone was afraid to, but finally one boy got enough nerve and opened the door. The horses didn't even wait until we put the runway up to the door; they just jumped out. What a rodeo we had! We really enjoyed ourselves watching those horses run up and down the railroad yard. Every thing went well until the railroad policeman came around. He tried to chase all of us kids and at the same time tried to corral the horses. At that time the real fun began. The horses ran out of the railroad yard and into the streets. In a few minutes there were stray horses all over the neighborhood. They were in people's front yards, alleys, streets, and vacant lots. Finally the fire department was called and came out and rounded up the horses. They found all of the horses and the only bad effects noticeable were that they were full of burrs and stickers. There was so much excitement and so many people on the streets that the policemen were not able to find the boys who had done the deed.

We used to have a great time on the railroad tracks fighting with other gangs of kids. There was one gang in particular from across the river who were our mortal enemies and we fought them every time we could. The fights usually took place on the railroad tracks where all the gangs would congregate for the purpose of taking coal. Each gang would fight the other gang to see who could get the best coal or the most coal. Stealing coal from the cars on the tracks was one of the things that we did most. It was more fun than anything else.

This bunch of kids was made up of roamers. They managed to roam around everywhere and do all kinds of things. During the summer-time we would sleep out in the public parks and wait for the milkmen and bakery wagons to start their deliveries in the morning. As they would deliver their milk, bread, and cakes in front of the neighborhood stores, we would lie in wait and be ready as soon as they would leave so we could rush the place and grab what we wanted. If the bread boxes were closed we would use a jimmy to open them. When we got a little more experienced we had keys made to do away with the jimmys. It was a great life to me while it lasted.

The members of this group took advantage of every situation which afforded an opportunity to steal anything that appealed to their imagination. In the beginning, delinquency was not differentiated from the many other fascinating activities with which the group was preoccupied.

One day when we were walking through the alleys we came upon a yard with a fence around it. In the yard were some police dogs. There were seven little puppies and the mother. We got through the gate and took all of the puppies together with the mother. We divided up the puppies and I sold mine for $5.00 a piece. One of the kids was smart at this kind of a racket. He got the newspapers and after looking through the lost and found columns discovered information about people wanting lost dogs. As they only wanted the mother dog back, they offered a reward to anyone who would find the mother. This other kid and me took the mother dog back to the owner. As soon as we got there they called the police. After taking us to the police station and after some masterful lying by us, the coppers believed our story that we had caught the dog while it was running around on the street. They took us back to the people where we stole the dogs and had the owners give us $10.00 reward. I at once thought this was a good racket. I claim this was my real start in crime.

The older and more experienced delinquents in the neighborhood provided the example and the encouragement to the younger delinquents to engage in more serious crimes.

In our neighborhood the older men congregated in the corner saloons and many of them were habitual drunkards. The kids in our bunch would stand on the corner ridiculing them as they staggered home from the saloon. We often watched the older boys who were constantly on the alert to "roll or rob" these men of the few dollars that had been left them by the saloon keepers.

One summer when I was little I had a job working in a sporting-goods concern. One of the fellows in our gang asked me if there was very much money in the office of the store. I told him I would find out. After I looked around I told him that there was a lot of money. Together we planned to rob the place. The plan was for me to leave the fire-escape door open one evening after work so that we could all go in that night. Ten of us burglarized the place and after doing considerable damage to the safe and the office, we left with the loot including a 25-gauge automatic pistol and bullets. I got the pistol and the bullets and sure had one grand time shooting the globes on the street lamps around in the neighborhood.

When I was a little bit older we got in touch with some big guys in the neighborhood. We knew these fellows and they told us they would pay us if we would burglarize a certain radio store. The owner of the store always left his car parked in front of the building. Very often he left his keys in his car. It was my job to steal these keys. After we had the keys we waited for a few days and made arrangements to get a truck which we were going to use to haul away the radios from the store. The evening we picked for the burglary we parked the truck in the rear of the store in the alley. I and another kid went to the front of the building to open the door with the keys and we were to go to the back entrance to unlock the door there so that we could put the radios on the truck. When I went to the front door I found that the key would not work in the lock. After trying for a long time I noticed a man was watching us from across the street, but we didn't pay any attention to him. We tried our best to turn the lock but the key broke in the lock. Meanwhile the man who had been watching us from across the street called the coppers. When we saw the coppers coming we started to run away but they caught us after we had given the truck driver jiggers. This was the first time I was ever arrested and I was then started on my real crime career.

John's initial contact with this play group at the age of seven marked the beginning of his career in delinquency. It was in the company of the members of this group that the early acts of stealing occurred which he and Edward described in chapter ii. The names and ages of the members of this group were as follows: Samuel Ludlow, 12; Joseph Sargent, 11; Howard Philips, 9; Victor Bolar, 8; Vincent Langley, 8; Michael Sheperd, 8; James Reiley, 8; Charles Duggan, 8; Fred Kilmer, 8; John Martin, 7; Edward Martin, 6; and George Dyer, 5. Thus, ten of these boys were older than John, while Edward Martin and George Dyer were younger. Three of the members, Samuel Ludlow, Joseph Sargent, and Howard Philips, were already experienced in stealing and had been in the Juvenile Court on petitions alleging truancy from school and delinquency.

Of these ten associates of John and Edward, nine were taken into the Juvenile Court on petitions alleging truancy and delinquency, nine served periods of confinement in juvenile institutions, and of the nine who reached adulthood, eight served sentences in institutions for adult offenders. A brief summary of the official records of these early associates is presented below.

Samuel Ludlow.—He was brought to the juvenile court for truancy from school and theft; confined in the Chicago Parental School and the Illinois Industrial School for Boys, at St. Charles; served two sentences in the Illinois State Reformatory for burglary, one sentence in the Illinois State Penitentiary for robbery, and one sentence in the Federal Penitentiary at Leavenworth for passing counterfeit money.

Joseph Sargent.—He was taken into the juvenile court for playing truant from school and stealing; confined in the Chicago Parental School; and served one term in the John Worthy School. He is now serving a long sentence in the Illinois State Penitentiary for criminal assault.

Howard Philips.—He was taken into the juvenile court five times for truancy from school and stealing; confined in the Chicago Parental School, and the John Worthy School; served two terms in the Chicago and Cook County School; and was incarcerated for two terms in the Chicago House of Correction for burglary.

Victor Bolar.—He was taken into the juvenile court for theft on two occasions; confined in the Illinois Industrial School for Boys, at St. Charles for stealing; and served a term in the Chicago House of Correction for burglary.

Vincent Langley.—He was taken into the juvenile court on four occasions for truancy from school and theft; confined in the Chicago Parental School; and served one term in the John Worthy School.

James Reiley.—He was taken into the juvenile court on two occasions for truancy and theft; confined in the Chicago Parental School, and the Industrial School for Boys, at St. Charles; and served one term in the Illinois State Reformatory and one term in the Illinois State Penitentiary.

Charles Duggan.—He was not taken into the juvenile court nor did he serve periods of confinement in juvenile institutions. He served a term of eight years in the Illinois State Reformatory for robbery. He was killed by the police in an attempted robbery.

Fred Kilmer.—He was taken into the juvenile court for playing truant from school; confined in the Chicago Parental School four times; served one term in the Chicago and Cook County School for Boys; and was incarcerated for three terms in the Chicago House of Correction for burglary. He escaped from the Chicago House of Correction and is now a fugitive from justice.

Michael Sheperd.—He was taken into the juvenile court on three occasions for truancy from school and theft; served terms in the Chicago Parental School, the John Worthy School, and the Illinois Industrial School for Boys, at St. Charles. He is now serving his second sentence in the Illinois State Penitentiary for armed robbery.

George Dyer.—He was taken into the juvenile court on two occasions for playing truant from school and served two periods in the Chicago Parental School. He was killed at the age of sixteen while stealing merchandise from freight cars.

These official records have been presented to confirm the statements which were made by John and Edward that their original experiences in stealing took place in the company of older delinquents. As they stated in chapter ii, their first thefts were part of the varied activities of this group. The above records give official confirmation to these statements.

RANGE OF CONTACTS WITH DELINQUENTS AND CRIMINALS

Following their contacts with the delinquent group described in the preceding pages, John and Edward, along with their younger brothers, became associated with a large number of other delinquents in the community. In the course of their careers the five brothers were directly implicated in theft with at least 103 other delinquents and criminals. The brothers' initial contacts with most of these offenders were made in the course of their activities in the local community, although in a limited number of instances the first contacts were established in juvenile institutions. The location of the places of residence of these 103 companions at the time they were implicated with the brothers are indicated on Figure 1.

Among the juvenile delinquents and adult offenders with whom the brothers were implicated in theft, the names of twenty-eight

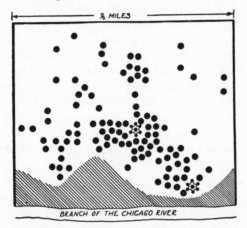

FIG. 1.—Geographic distribution of home addresses of one hundred and three offenders with whom the brothers were implicated in delinquency, in relation to two places of residence of the Martin family.

appear in the official records in chapter i. Because of the significance of these associates in the lives of the brothers, a brief summary of their records is presented below. (The records of six of these were presented previously in this chapter.)

Francis Berman.—He was taken to the juvenile court on two occasions for burglary and was committed to the State Industrial School for Boys at St. Charles. His adult record shows that he was arrested many times for burglary and robbery and that he served a sentence in the state reformatory and is now in the state penitentiary.

John Bolton.—He was taken to the juvenile court on three occasions on charges of larceny and burglary and committed to the Chicago and Cook County School and to the Illinois Industrial School for Boys, at St. Charles. His adult record includes three appearances in court for minor offenses.

Cyril French.—He was taken to the juvenile court on six occasions for truancy, larceny, burglary, and larceny of automobiles. He served two terms in the Chicago Parental School and one term in the St. Charles School for Boys. As an adult he served a sentence in the state reformatory and he is now serving a one to life sentence in the state penitentiary.

John Hefner.—The juvenile court record is not known. As an adult he served one year in a Federal Prison for fraud and desertion from the army; five years in a state reformatory for burglary; one year to life for armed robbery in a state penitentiary from which he escaped three years later. He is now serving a term of twenty years for armed robbery.

Joseph Herman.—He was taken to the juvenile court on four different occasions charged with truancy, burglary, and larceny of automobiles. He served terms in the Chicago Parental School, and the Cook County School for Boys. As an adult he was taken to the Criminal Court for larceny of automobiles on three different occasions. He was placed on probation for one year and he is now serving a term in the state penitentiary.

Fred Jensen.—He was taken to the juvenile court five times for burglary and larceny of automobiles. He served three terms in the St. Charles School for Boys and was later placed in the Lincoln State School and Colony. He is now serving a sentence in the state penitentiary.

Elmer Jolson.—He was taken to the juvenile court for burglary and incorrigibility. As an adult he was arrested and taken to court on charges of burglary, larceny, bastardy, and non-support. He served one year in the House of Correction and one term in the state penitentiary.

Clyde Jones.—As an adult he was arrested for disorderly conduct, larceny and robbery. He paid two fines and served one year in the Cook County Jail.

Walter Kohler.—He was taken to the juvenile court for burglary. He was brought into the Municipal and Criminal Court nine times on charges ranging from disorderly conduct to burglary. He served one sentence in the House of Correction.

Adam Krancer.—As an adult he was arrested for election fraud, receiving stolen property, and assault with a deadly weapon. He served two terms in the Chicago House of Correction.

Homer Luda.—Arrested and taken to the juvenile court on a delinquency petition. As an adult he served a sentence in the Chicago House of Correction for larceny.

Edwin Mitchell.—He was taken to the juvenile court on a delinquency petition and placed on probation.

John Olson.—Arrested and taken to the juvenile court on two occasions charged with truancy from school, larceny, and burglary. He served one term in the Chicago Parental School. As an adult he was arrested several times for disorderly conduct, receiving stolen property, and carrying concealed weapons. He served four terms in the Chicago House of Correction.

Ralph Palmer.—He was arrested and brought to the juvenile court on two occasions for larceny of automobiles. His adult record reveals that he was arrested twice for larceny of automobiles, and three times for disorderly conduct. He served one term in the Chicago House of Correction.

Adam Runcer.—He was twice taken to the juvenile court on petitions alleging delinquency. As a juvenile he served one term in the Chicago and Cook County School for Boys and as an adult he was taken to court charged with disorderly conduct on at least five different occasions.

Stanley Runcer.—He was taken to the juvenile court on petitions alleging truancy or delinquency on six different occasions. He served one term in the Chicago Parental School, two terms in the Chicago and Cook County School, and one term in the St. Charles School for Boys. As an adult he was arrested and taken to court five times for either disorderly conduct or burglary, and he served one term in the state penitentiary.

Alfred Schwartz.—As an adult he was arrested for grand larceny and burglary. He served one term in the Chicago House of Correction and is now serving a term in the state penitentiary for robbery.

Joe Seigel.—He was taken to the juvenile court on three occasions for larceny and burglary. He served terms in the Chicago and Cook County School and the St. Charles School for Boys. He is now serving a long sentence in the state penitentiary for robbery and murder.

William Sloan.—He was taken to the juvenile court on four different occasions for truancy and delinquency. He served two terms in the Chicago Parental School and one term in the St. Charles School for Boys. As an adult he appeared three times in the criminal court for burglary and he has served one term in the state reformatory.

Milton Smith.—Arrested and brought to the juvenile court five times for larceny and burglary. He was committed to a state school for the feeble-minded and the Chicago State Hospital. As an adult he was repeatedly arrested for larceny. He paid three fines, was placed on probation, and served two terms in the Chicago House of Correction.

William Stock.—He was taken into the juvenile court nine times on petitions alleging truancy from school or delinquency. He served two terms in the Chicago Parental School, two terms in the Industrial School for Boys, at St. Charles, one term in the Illinois State Reformatory, and one term in the Chicago House of Correction. Subsequently he was arrested and taken to court five times for disorderly conduct. For one offense he was placed on adult probation for one year.

Earl Wooms.—He was taken to the juvenile court once on a truancy petition and once on a delinquency petition. He was committed to the Chicago Parental School for one term. His adult record includes a sentence to the state reformatory.

Joseph Wyman.—He was taken to the juvenile court five times on truancy and delinquency petitions. He served terms in the Chicago Parental School, the Chicago and Cook County School, and the St. Charles School for Boys. As an adult he was placed on probation for burglary, and served one term in the state reformatory.

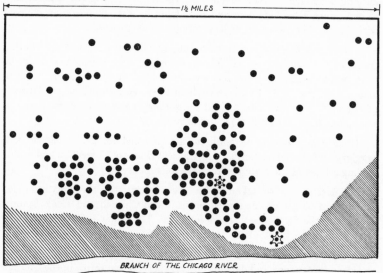

Fig. 2.—Geographic distribution of the home addresses of one hundred and ninety-one juvenile offenders with whom the five brothers had personal contacts during the period when they were active in the Juvenile Court but with whom they are not known to have engaged in delinquency, in relation to two places of residence of the Martin family.

In addition to the one hundred and three offenders with whom the brothers were directly implicated in theft, they had personal contacts with at least one hundred and ninety-one other delinquents from their community who appeared in the juvenile court during the period in which the brothers were active in delinquency. The home addresses of the delinquents in this larger group, concerning whom specific identifying data are available, are indicated on Figure 2.

Figures 1 and 2 are presented to show the wide range of personal contacts which the brothers had with other officially known delinquents in their community. It is obvious from these maps that the range of such contacts was community-wide in scope. This fact gives added support to the assumption that the delinquencies of the brothers were not isolated, individual phenomena; they were, rather, part of the organized social practice and mode of life which existed throughout the community. Their intimate relationships with more than two hundred and fifty known delinquents and adult criminals, along with a much larger group of unofficial delinquents and other residents who in various ways aided and abetted the brothers in their crime, provided the morale, *esprit de corps*, and moral sanction necessary to sustain their interest in crime and the market for their loot. They lived in a social world in which delinquency served a dual purpose—on the one hand, it was a means by which they secured the friendly regard, approval, and approbation of their fellows, while on the other hand, it served as a source of economic gain. In short, their delinquencies may be regarded as an adjustment to the social world in which they lived, and their social world was an adaptation to the life of the local community.

The brothers not only had direct relationships with a large number of contemporary delinquents in their community, but the groups to which they belonged were related, through a continuity of contacts, to a succession of groups which had been active in delinquency and crime during preceding years. The brothers' delinquent groups were part of a sequence of group relationships which extended far back in the history of the community. As indicated in Figure 3, the final group with which Carl Martin was implicated was thus related, through one sequence of relationships, to nine preceding delinquent groups. In this chart, Carl and the companions with whom he was last implicated in stealing, comprise Group 10. The groups which were historically related to Group 10 are numbered from 9 to 1. Each of these groups is composed of boys who were known to have been implicated together in delinquency. The continuity of relationships between these groups is indicated by the fact that beginning with Group 1, the

Fig. 3.—The historical sequence of group contacts in which the Martin brothers were involved as revealed in the records of the Juvenile Court.

names of one or more of the boys in each group appear in the next succeeding group, as indicated by the arrows in the chart.

When Carl was thirteen years and nine months of age, he was taken into the juvenile court in the company of Walter Kohler and Joseph Herman on a charge of stealing automobiles. These three boys constitute Group 10 on the chart. Carl Martin and Joseph Herman had been involved with Michael Martin and his companions in Group 9, while Michael and Carl had been involved with the boys included in Group 8. Michael, James, and Edward earlier had been associates of the boys in Group 7. Of the boys in this group, Edward and William Stock had been involved with the boys whose names appear in Group 6, while John had been a companion of the boys in Group 5. Five of John's companions, Joseph Sargent, Victor Bolar, Samuel Ludlow, Vincent Langley, and Michael Sheperd had been implicated with Group 4, and two of these, Sheperd and Langley, had been members of Group 3. Langley and Roger Fulton had been implicated with George Levy and Jasper Tuttle in Group 2. Levy had previously been associated with Clay Porter and Frank Peters in Group 1. This sequence of group contacts covered a span of approximately eighteen years. At the time Carl was brought to the juvenile court at the age of thirteen, many of the persons whose names appear in Groups 1, 2, and 3 had graduated from juvenile institutions and were serving sentences in reformatories and prisons.

The transmission of patterns of delinquency from more experienced offenders to the younger delinquents is illustrated in still another way in the case of the brothers. During their early career in delinquency, the brothers had personal contacts with offenders who represented a wide range of chronological age groups of varying degrees of habituation and sophistication in delinquency and crime. Their intimate associates included certain older offenders who had not only graduated from juvenile institutions but had served sentences in reformatories. For example, it will be remembered that Michael, at the age of fifteen, was implicated in armed robbery through the influence of two adult criminals, one of whom was twenty-six and the other twenty-two years of age. It is through such contacts that the young delinquent not only is involved in more serious crimes but acquires added knowledge and sophistication with regard to the criminal world.

THE CRIMINAL GANG VERSUS CONVENTIONAL SOCIETY

The influence which the gang exerts in holding the youthful offender in a career in delinquency is concretely illustrated in various instances in the careers of the five brothers. A specific illustration of this point is provided in the problems which Edward encountered in attempting to make an adjustment in private industry when he was about fourteen years and six months of age. While on one of his many begging expeditions in well-to-do neighborhoods he met a wealthy woman who volunteered to secure employment for him. She made arrangements for such employment in one of the large banks in the Loop. Edward's account of the difficulties which he encountered in this work situation reveals the conflict between the pressure exerted by the social world of his companions in the community and the attitudes of his fellow-employees. Although he had a genuine desire to succeed in his work, the ridicule which he received from his fellow-workers, because of his language, manners, and ragged clothes, and the constant solicitation on the part of his companions to return to delinquency made it impossible for him to hold his position.

This experience also illustrates the common attitude of suspicion with which the habitual delinquent often regards persons in conventional society who express an interest in his welfare. Because of his previous experiences he often assumes toward such persons the same attitude of distrust which characterizes his feeling toward the police, probation and parole officers, guards in institutions, and court workers. Not infrequently such persons are considered by the delinquent as inimical to his own welfare and the security of his group.

While begging on the North Side I was stopped by a lady who asked me what I was doing with such a basket under my arm, and why I wasn't in school. She was dressed in a gray, two-piece suit, and in the way she asked the questions I thought she was a truant officer and was ready to run. Reading my thoughts, she assured me I had nothing to be afraid of. Telling her of conditions at home, she told me to come over to her home the coming Saturday as she had some clothes and things she wanted to give me. Reading my doubts as to my coming, she made me solemnly promise I would be there Saturday.

My word was my bond. Although being suspicious of her good intentions and thinking that I would walk into a trap, I, nevertheless, though with great misgivings, went there that Saturday. After giving her my word of honor, I had to go. To my great surprise it was no trap, and after spending several hours at her home, in which she asked about everything at home, she gave me some clothes, a basketful of edibles, and a dollar. With another promise that I was to return the following Saturday, I bade her goodbye. The many following Saturdays proved to be days of friendship for me and the rest of the family. She drove over to our home; found conditions as I had told her. She proved a good friend and a helping one. All of us kids received presents from her and help in many forms.

After making her friendship, I got into trouble over my truancy. Out of a wintry sky I was arrested at home by a policeman, taken to the Juvenile Home, and brought to court a few days after. Having no idea as to the reason or suddenness, I heard some woman employed by the court tell the judge that I was a beggar and wouldn't go to school; that I was a little blackguard and should be sent to St. Charles for eighteen months. Upon her recommendations, the judge sent me there. Turning me over to some parole officer, I was taken aboard a train for St. Charles. Arriving at the depot we were met by an officer of the school. Getting into his model T Ford touring car, he drove the three miles to the school, and I nearly froze to death getting there.

. . . .

When I got back home from St. Charles, I met my younger brother, James. I heard that most of the family was scattered in various orphan homes. Due to pa's drinking, the juvenile authorities had taken the kids away; the reason I saw James was that he had run away from one. During the conversation that followed he told me that he had continued going to see the lady who had befriended me, and when I was sent to St. Charles he told her that I had been killed by a street-car. Hearing this, I bawled him out for lying to her, and the same coming Saturday, I took James along and went to see her. When she saw me she thought I was a ghost. Hugging and kissing me, to my embarrassment, she upbraided James for lying, and had me tell her all about myself and just what had happened to me. Always recalling her as the finest lady I knew, I told her everything. Telling her that I was going to try to find work, she said she would try to find one for me, and for me to come back Tuesday morning. Spending most of the day with her, we left for home late that evening.

Coming back Tuesday morning, she said she had a job for me. After dining with her, she drove downtown. Parking the car we walked into a big bank and into the auditor's office where I was asked a few questions and given a job as a messenger boy in the bank. Working here, I carried notes from cage to cage and helped the cashier get large sums of money out of the vault every morning. At closing time, I would help again by carrying the money back to the vault, and it was nothing to carry between twenty and fifty thousand dollars at one time. Not only did I carry money, but also liberty bonds, as the War was on, and carrying between two to three hundred thousand dollars in bonds was a daily occurrence. Was I tempted? Not in the least. I held the trust of my friend far above all the money there. To me, it was as if I were carrying a bunch of paper instead of money. If I cared to have stolen any money it would have been easy; we messenger boys were all over the three floors of the bank, and also outside of it. Not only was my lady friend too nice, but the people working here were fine to me from the president down.

My best clothes were rags compared with the new suits worn by the other boys I worked with. Seeing how I had won the friendship of the people I came in contact with, a couple of the spoiled brats working here began to jibe me about my clothes, and would ask me if I had come from 33rd and the tracks. Taking the thing as a joke, I would smile at the joker. After a week of wise-cracking, it began to get under my skin. The jokes became more pointed and they were said when all the boys were around. Knowing it was against the rules to fight, I held myself in check until lunch-time, when another wise-cracker was insulting me. Putting my sandwich down, I walked over to the joker, told him and the rest of the boys that the joking was being carried too far, and I wouldn't take many more. One of them asked me what I would do. My reply was that they would see the next time I heard a wise-crack. In reply, one of the boys asked if I was getting tough. I answered that they would be shown just what I meant. The instigator of the whole thing, not liking my challenge, told me to shut up or he would bust me in the nose. Not knowing if I would have to fight all eight of the boys or him alone, I knew this had to be a showdown. Telling him to go ahead and sock, I walked within reach of him. Standing in front of him, I challenged him to sock me. Refusing my offer, I called him a few choice names. Telling him to keep his big mouth shut about anything concerning me, I turned my back and caught a punch in the back of my head. Turning around, I sailed into him, fists flying. I hit him as hard and as fast as I could, knocking him into the lockers.

The noise carried into the assistant auditor's office. Hearing the noise and investigating, he found the two of us fighting. Stopping the fight, we were told to report to the auditor after lunch. Hating myself for having to tell, I, nevertheless, was in the right, as I had asked the fellow to quit trying to be funny several times. Hearing my story, he upbraided me for fighting instead of reporting to him. Telling the boys that they would be fired if this happened again, he ended the matter by telling me to report any boys who thought more of their wise-cracks than their jobs. With this warning, the matter was closed. Except for a few cold shoulders from the instigators I got along fine.

A few days after the fight I was taken to one of the downtown department stores where the assistant auditor bought me two shirts, a tie, short pants, and stockings. Not knowing why he had me go along, I said nothing. Arriving at the shirt counters he asked me what size shirt I wore. Buying two shirts and a tie he led me to the pants department. Asking what size I wore, I began to get fidgety, thinking that if I had to pay for the clothes bought I had no money to pay him and it would take about two weeks' pay in order to pay back. Interrupting the saleslady, I told him I had no money with which to pay for these things, and that I didn't need them. I refused to let him buy me these things, thinking that he was spending his own money on clothes for me. Explaining to me that the bank was buying the clothes, I didn't know what to say. Donning my new clothes the next morning, I thanked the vice-president who was responsible for my good fortune.

While working at the bank, William Stock would come over to the house after my working hours, and tell me what a good time he was having, the places he was robbing, and the money he was making. He would come over every few days and tell me to steal some money from the bank, or quit, and go robbing with him. After about three months of working in the bank, he finally made up a glowing tale of the dough and the easy life he was living while I worked all day. I quit my job for his lousy companionship. The devil must have weakened me that day, or either loaned Stock his tongue, because I am sorry to this day that I let him talk me out of a good job and environment. Making no report as to my absence, the bank sent a fellow to my home to find out why I hadn't come to work. Coming during the presence of Stock at my home, I was at a loss as to what to say. First telling him a story, which was a poor excuse, I began to tell him that I would be down in the morning and to hell with this bumming. Then Stock spoke up and told him I didn't want to work, and that the bank was too cheap to work for. Saying this to a man I had come in contact with during my work at the bank, he embarrassed me so much that I was ashamed to look at the fellow. Taking my silence for the truth, he left me. Agreeing in silence, I almost came to blows with Stock over his statements. Knowing the damage was done, there was no need of being sore with Stock. Patching up our quarrel, I began going with Stock and a kid named Stanley. Stock had gotten friendly with Stanley while I was at St. Charles. During my absence he had turned to burglary and begging.

It has been indicated in the foregoing pages that John and Edward learned to steal in the company of the play group with which they became identified when they were approximately six and seven years, respectively. Stealing was one of the undifferentiated activities of this group, which included in its membership older boys who were already playing truant from school and experienced in stealing. The practice of stealing was a social heritage which the group acquired from the preceding groups in the community and from other contemporary delinquent groups. As John, Edward, and William Stock grew older they became implicated in stealing with scores of other boys, including the younger Martin brothers. The control which was exerted through their relationships with numerous delinquent and criminal groups in the community was a compelling influence in the lives of the brothers, as indicated in the inability of the family, the school, the church, the juvenile court, and family case-work agencies to alter their conduct.

CHAPTER VII

FAMILY DISORGANIZATION AND CULTURE CONFLICT

The parents of the Martin brothers were born and reared in a rural community in Europe. They emigrated to the United States five years after their marriage and established their home in the community which was described in chapter v. Their efforts to establish a home and to provide for the physical and social well-being of their children in the complicated life of this new community will be briefly described in this chapter. Four general aspects of the family will be considered: (1) the maternal and paternal ancestors; (2) economic maladjustment; (3) conflict of attitudes and interests as between parents and children; and (4) social isolation of the brothers from conventional neighborhood institutions.

THE MATERNAL AND PATERNAL ANCESTORS

As stated above, both Mr. and Mrs. Martin were born in an agricultural community in Europe. Mr. Martin's family was composed of peasants whose educational advantages were extremely meager, while some members of Mrs. Martin's family were educated and held minor public offices. Both parents were members of large families which were well integrated in the cultural life of the Old World community. Aside from a half-brother of Mrs. Martin, no other members of either family emigrated to Chicago, although some of her relatives settled elsewhere in America.

Albert Martin, the father of the five brothers, was one of eleven children, five of whom are still living. The paternal grandfather supported his wife and children by working as a tenant farmer. The paternal grandfather is now dead, but the paternal grandmother still lives in the village in which her ancestors resided for many generations. All of the father's five living brothers and sisters are married and reside in Europe.

The mother was a member of a family of ten children, three girls and seven boys. The maternal grandmother was married twice, and one son born of her first marriage came to Chicago some years prior to the emigration of Mr. and Mrs. Martin. It was he who loaned the money to the Martins for their passage to America. After the death of her first husband, the maternal grandmother married a postman in the local village. The salary from this office and supplemental income from a small farm provided a comfortable living for the family. Of the ten children of the maternal grandmother, only two, in addition to Mrs. Martin, are living. Joseph, one of Mrs. Martin's living brothers, makes a comfortable living for his family working as a blacksmith. The other brother is an invalid and is supported by his seven children.

An investigation which was made in Europe indicated that the parents and the members of their families were of good repute. Their relatives were never involved in criminal practices, as indicated in an official report which stated that "about those above-mentioned people nothing unfavorable can be reported."

Statements which were secured from the pastor of the local parish and from relatives and neighbors in Europe confirmed this official report. In a recent interview Mrs. Martin stated that "there are not, thanks to God, any bums, robbers, or thieves in our families in Europe." It should be added, further, that none of the twenty-three known cousins of the Martin brothers have been involved either in delinquency or crime. These include the four children of Mrs. Martin's half-brother who were born and reared in Chicago.

In accordance with custom the marriage of Mr. and Mrs. Martin was arranged by their parents. Mrs. Martin states that her mother and the father of her husband had decided that she and Mr. Martin should be married; the paternal grandmother also favored the plan, but her own father was opposed to the marriage because he did not approve of either Mr. Martin or his father. At the time of their marriage, Mr. Martin was twenty years of age and his wife was six years his senior.

Mr. Martin was employed as a common laborer for five years before he and his wife came to the United States. At the time of emigration there were three children in the family, all of whom died in infancy. John, the oldest living son, was born after the parents established their home in Chicago.

The community in which the parents of the brothers were reared was a small village, the economic life of which was chiefly agrarian and as such required little technical skill. The mores were relatively consistent and homogeneous. Most of the families of the community had lived in close proximity to each other for generations. In view of the homogeneity and stability of the culture, the community had little difficulty in maintaining its identity and transmitting to successive generations its sentiments, forms of conduct, and institutions. Each new generation assimilated through informal, personal contacts the conventional social heritage of preceding generations and was subject to the control of the common sentiments and public opinion of the local community. The moral attitudes of residents regarding the conduct of children were more or less uniform throughout the community and largely consistent with the mores of the general social order.

In this situation parental control was much less difficult to maintain than it was in the type of community situation in which the brothers were reared, for in the Old World community, the interests and expectations of the parents were consistent with and supported by the attitudes and interests of the community at large. In contrast with this situation, the community in which the brothers grew up was marked by a diversity of practices and standards, many of which were inconsistent with the mores of conventional society in America and with the cultural standards which prevailed in the Old World community in which the parents were reared.

ECONOMIC MALADJUSTMENT

Upon his arrival in Chicago Mr. Martin faced the immediate task of finding employment in a complicated and mechanized industrial system. Obviously, his previous occupational experience did not serve as an appropriate apprenticeship for successful adjustment to the requirements of this new industrial order. New skills and a familiarity with the city and its highly competitive economic life had to be acquired.

During the early years the father worked as an unskilled laborer in tanneries and slaughter-houses. During the periods in which he was able to secure employment, his wages ranged between $25 and $35 per month. With this income provision had to be made for food, clothes, and medical care, payment of a rental of $4.50 to $10 per month, and reimbursement of Mrs. Martin's half-brother for the money he had advanced to the Martins for their passage to America. Along with these expenditures, legal fees which the father had to pay in connection with a litigation placed an added financial burden upon the family.

As a result of its extremely low economic status, the family was forced to reside in the most deteriorated buildings in the community. Of the nine buildings in which the family lived four have been demolished because of their dilapidated and unsanitary condition. The various places of residence of the family have been briefly characterized as follows by Edward.

From my earliest recollection, we were always in dire need. Our places of domicile were always of the cheapest, usually of the basement type. Many of the recollections of my childhood are of periods of sickness in these basement flats. From the smell of leaking gas to stinking garbage I pulled through it all until the age of seven, when I received my first bath and first breath of clean, fresh air at the Parental School. Although homesick for awhile I was made to feel at home there. To me it was better than home. The good food that I received here I never had at home.

1. The place where I was born was in a four-story brick house. We occupied the first floor in front, and had four rooms. A few doors away was a public school and the railroad was a little over a block away.

2. The next place we moved to was about six doors east and on the same side of the street. This building was a two-story frame house and we had the rear flat on the first floor. We had four rooms here.

3. Our third home was an old frame house built for two families. We occupied the top flat and had four rooms. The house sat between the alley on one side and the railroad on the other. This building has been demolished.

4. A four-room basement flat in a brick building was our fourth home. The front rooms facing the street were ours. This building faced the street on one side and the railroad in the rear. This building has been also wrecked since then.

5. The flat here was in the basement of the rear building. It consisted of four rooms, with a toilet outside.

6. Our next home was another four-room flat in a brick building next to the alley. We occupied the basement flat in the rear of the building.

7. Our next home was another basement flat in the rear of the rear building. This was a frame house and had four small rooms and was very dark. This building has also been demolished.

8. This place was a five-room cottage in the rear building. The rooms were fairly well lighted. The entrance was at the rear of the place facing the alley. This place has been wrecked.

9. This was a four-room flat in a three-story brick building. We occupied the rear basement flat. After living here about six years the landlord put in electric lights, and installed toilets inside of each flat.

During the first six years of his residence in Chicago, the father's wage was sufficient to support the family on a low standard of living. From that time, however, the economic stress became increasingly severe, since the number of children increased without any enlargement of the family income. The funds available for the support of the family were further reduced by the father's illness and excessive drinking which was accompanied by increasing irregularity of employment with still further reduction in income. The financial circumstances became such that it was necessary for the mother to appeal to a family case-work agency for assistance. The following excerpts from the records of this agency give a concrete picture of the economic conditions which obtained in the family during the childhood of the brothers. The first family visit reported here was made when John was seven years, six months; Edward five years, eleven months; and James, one year, and seven days of age.

Worker visited Martin home today. Mr. Martin had a very bad foot. It was swollen. County doctor ordered but not arrived. Man has been out of work for some weeks, there was no coal in home and almost no food. Ordered quarter ton soft coal be sent them and left groceries.

Three days after first entry.—Worker visited home and left money, $1.50, for food and for a pair of shoes.

Twenty-two days after first entry.—Mrs. Martin was in the office today, asks for clothing. Gave her two pair children's second-hand shoes, one pair stockings, one sweater, two old suits of underwear. Gave her a grocery order for 75¢.

Twenty-six days after first entry.—Visited Mrs. Martin at home. Advised her to take in washing. Gave her 50¢ for food.

One month after first entry.—Mrs. Martin was in office. Gave her $1.00 for food.

Two months, 14 days after first entry.—Mrs. Martin was in office with John and Edward. Fitted John with new shoes. Advised mother to get shoes from the County for Edward. Husband still sick.

Two months, 20 days after first entry.—Mrs. Martin in office for shoes. Worker gave her a pair of second-hand shoes. Mrs. Martin said they had not a cent in the house to buy food. Husband still sick. Promised visit.

Later—same day.—Worker visited. Man out. Woman cleaning. Said she had a few odd jobs. Earns very little. Children have nothing to wear. Mother said she owes money to grocery. Three months in arrears in rent. Gave woman 50¢ and two pair of pants, two pair stockings, one pair old slippers.

Two years, 11 months after first entry.—Mrs. X—— (another agency) reports by phone that Martin case has been known to them and that the husband has been ill for a great length of time.

Two years, 11 months after first entry.—Worker visited home. Man said he had no definite promise of work, although he hoped to get a job in a few days.

Two years, 11 months after first entry.—Worker visited home. Man had not yet secured work. Later visited grocery store. Purchased 57¢ worth of groceries.

Two years, 11 months after first entry.—Worker visited home. Woman said man was working.

During an interval of two years, when the father had fairly regular employment, the family was self-supporting. At the conclusion of that period, however, the family again applied to the relief agency for financial assistance.

Four years, 9 months after first entry.—Mr. Martin was in office asking for food. He has not worked for over a month. Rent is three months in arrears. Received a five-day notice to move. He has borrowed money from neighbors. Said his wife has only 30¢ for the last two days, which she got from a neighbor. Children cried this morning for food. Gave 50¢ and promised a visit.

Four years, 9 months after first entry.—Worker visited home. Family in four rooms. Mr. Martin out looking for work and Mrs. Martin could give little information. Man had been employed in a machine shop. Was paid $7.00 a week. Mrs. Martin stated he drank very little but spent all his money on friends borrowing right and left. They had a great deal of trouble with the children. John and Edward were both away in some school. Mrs. Martin could not give address or name. She claimed that the family had no relatives at all in this country. Stated rent was due for two months and that an eviction notice has been served.

Same day.—Worker visited Mrs. B——, the landlady. She stated that Mr. Martin did not work steadily and always drank. Family owe her $21.50. Mrs. B—— is not willing to keep family even if the rent was paid.

Same day.—Worker visited address where Martins had lived two years previous. Landlady said Mr. Martin drank a great deal and worked unsteady. Rent was paid very irregularly in part payments. The landlady felt much relieved when family moved.

Four years, 9 months after first entry.—Mr. Martin in office. Cannot give work record as he said he always worked short hours and at different places. Later he remembered that he worked for cement company. Says his wife has a brother living on T—— Street. Could not give the exact address. Mrs. Martin's mother died last year. Mr. Martin is a tall, healthy looking fellow. Seems slightly intoxicated. Has left eye blurred. Mr. Martin insisted that if he was given a loan of $10.00 he would repay it very soon and take care of his family entirely. Mr. Martin agreed if he was not able to raise a loan he would be willing to place his wife and children in an institution temporarily.

Same day.—Later: Phoned R—— company. The man who answered the phone said the place was almost closed, foreman was discharged and he could not look up the records for a visitor.

Four years, 9 months after first entry.—Phoned Mr. B——, bailiff, asking if he would hold eviction off. Gave report on case. Mr. B—— promised that eviction would not take place until the 20th.

Four years, 10 months after first entry.—Mr. Martin in office. Said they had moved on the 21st to A—— Street. Received $3.00 from M—— society and had two days work. Paid his rent, $6.00, on the 7th. Owes the express man $4.00. Express man has threatened to take furniture.

Four years, 10 months after first entry.—Worker visited home. Woman making supper; soup, potatoes, bread, and a can of beer on the table. Mr. Martin had not been home the entire day. Thought he probably got work.

Four years, 10 months after first entry.—Mrs. Martin in office asking for aid. Says rent was due on the 22nd. Woman begs at grocery for stale bread. Mr. Martin cannot find work.

Five years, 10 months after first entry.—Mrs. Martin is a strong woman. Apparently has bad eyesight. She admitted that Edward has been begging but did not think there was anything wrong in it. Said people asked him to come. Promised not to allow it any more. Mr. Martin and she have worked on farms during the summer. He worked regularly last winter and had applied at the charity office. They received county supplies three times last winter. Mr. Martin is working on a farm. Gave address of I.I. & E.D. and diagnosis blank for Mrs. Martin to go to I. & E. dispensary.

Six years, 2 months after first entry.—Visited home. Found family living in low basement rooms for which they pay $6.00 per month rent. Woman and two smallest children at home. Children and rooms appear to be clean and tidy. Mrs. Martin said her husband had been out of work all winter.

He last worked for a furniture shop, but she couldn't give the name of the firm. He was employed there for only one week. Later both man and woman worked on a farm picking onions. Said that John had stolen a bicycle last summer and was arrested and committed to St. Charles Training School for Boys where he is at the present time. Family receives county supplies. Left card for man to go to I.F.E.B. and told Mrs. Martin to send her husband to our office if he does not obtain work in a few days. They owe two and a half months' rent.

Six years, 10 months after first entry.—Visited. Unable to locate family on A—— Street. Called at previous address and was directed to R—— Street. Father employed at M—— company on N—— Street. Earning $2.00 a day. Mother knew nothing of begging of children. Thought it was Edward with neighbor's child.

Seven years, 2 months after first entry.—Mrs. Martin in office asking assistance for rent. Will be evicted Saturday. Mr. Martin has been ill for two months. Worked at L—— Piano Company for three weeks and hurt side. Has no doctor. Found work on the 19th. Will not be paid until the 12th of next month. Mrs. Martin asks for loan. On the 19th they were in court and will be evicted within five days. They owe a month and a half rent. Mrs. Martin thinks husband is working now for a railroad company as a laborer.

Eight years, 4 months after first entry.—Michael came to office asking for aid saying that his father is unable to work and that he drinks heavily and that two of his brothers were at St. Charles. He was put on street-car and sent home.

Eight years, 7 months after first entry.—Mrs. P—— phones asking report on family. Boy at settlement which reported that the father was unemployed due to illness. Worker referred her to Juvenile Psychopathic Institute.

Eight years, 7 months after first entry.—Mr. Martin injured his leg while working at the Stock Yards. Said a 500-pound piece of meat had fallen on it. Worked only one and a half days and received no compensation although company paid hospital bills. Spent two weeks at hospital and left the latter part of December, using crutches. Mr. Martin not satisfied with what company has done for him, but thinks they should have paid part of his salary during his illness. Gave him a card to lawyer. Mrs. Martin is working in a pickle factory. Mr. Martin does not know what she is earning. They have been getting groceries on credit and the landlady is willing to wait for the rent until he goes back to work. She gave the visitor the impression that he was able to take care of the family until he found work. The father has been looking for work during the last few days.

These excerpts indicate the limited economic resources of the family during the childhood of the brothers. According to their statements there were periods when the supply of food was extremely meager and their wearing apparel consisted chiefly of used clothes which they secured from the relief agency or from begging. It was during these periods of stress that the father often went to the market to get discarded fruits, vegetables, and poultry. The meager provisions of the family were also supplemented by the coal, food, and clothes which the brothers secured by begging and petty stealing.

CONFLICTS OF ATTITUDES AND INTERESTS BETWEEN PARENTS AND CHILDREN

Another outstanding feature of the Martin family was its lack of cohesion and unity. The attitudes and sentiments of the parents reflected their Old World culture; they were unfamiliar with the customs and institutions of the American community. Their intimate contacts and social intercourse were limited largely to other adults who were equally unfamiliar with the customs and practices of the New World. In contrast, the children became incorporated into the street crowds, play groups, and gangs of children in the community, where they acquired the language of the New World, a knowledge and sophistication about the life of the local community and of the city, and attitudes of superiority toward the foreign-born adults of the community. This life of adventure and novelty in which the children participated was largely unknown and inaccessible to the parents except as it was interpreted to them by the brothers; it was as foreign to the parents as their Old World culture was alien to the brothers.

As the brothers became incorporated into the neighborhood groups, they developed forms of conduct of which the parents disapproved. As the latter attempted to enforce conformity to their standards, conflicts developed, arising with regard to religion, truancy from home and school, the companions with whom the brothers associated, and stealing. Since the mother was a devout member of the church, she attempted to inculcate her religious precepts in her sons. Because of the counteracting influences to which they were exposed outside of the home, they were not receptive to her religious instructions, as indicated by the following excerpt from the autobiography of one of the brothers.

My stay at home with the parents was one of arguments over my lack of religious tendencies. A day seldom passed when I didn't receive a bawling out from Ma about religion. Coming home was not as pleasant as it sounds. Anything I would say, concerning religion, would be the start of another argument.

In our family the church was first. Whatever the church said we were to do. Ma would do as the church said, but trying to get us boys to do the same was a different matter; therefore, the daily religious arguments.

Although I never tried to hurt her feelings, I would be driven almost frantic by the endless religious squabbles, and often left the house for hours at a time, just to get out of reach of her voice.

The conflicts which developed in relation to the refusal on the part of the children to attend school and to abstain from stealing are described in the following statements by two of the brothers. In an effort to cope with the problem of truancy, the parents resorted to severe corporal punishment. This punishment, particularly in view of the fact that it was inflicted to impose standards of conduct which were in opposition to those which prevailed in their gang, tended further to alienate them from the parents, to induce protective lying, and to give rise to more subtle means of circumventing the parents and the school authorities.

While playing hookey from school one winter, a kid brought a note home asking mother why I haven't been in school for the last several months. I had spent that day with the other kids on the railroad tracks. We built a fire, stole some spuds from a box car, and had barbeque spuds. We then spent the day flipping rides on and off the different freights that pulled in. Between this we had a bunch of snowballs, and from our hiding place we would throw and try to knock off someone's derby. If the man happened to see us, we would run like hell. If the man caught us he would kick us in the pants. Derbies used to be our weakness during snow-time. After I had cleaned up, and getting my books together, where I had hid them, I started home with a cheery whistle on my lips.

Not suspecting I had been found out as a truant, the cheery whistle soon became a squawk of pain. After getting a good licking from Ma, I was promised a better one from Pa. Knowing the weight of Pa's hand, I made myself scarce before he came home. Afraid to go home that night, I found a warm entrance, a back hallway, where I lay down and fell asleep. The hallway got a little chilly and I woke up. Looking for a warmer spot, I walked to the top of the stairs. Finding an open door, I walked into what seemed to be an empty, warm room. I started to lay down when I bumped into an obstacle. Lighting a match to see what I had bumped, I nearly jumped out of my skin, in getting out of this place. Of all hallways to pick from, I picked an undertaking parlor, and the room I was about to lay down in was full of caskets. Leaving in a big hurry I walked around for about a half-hour until I spotted an empty milk wagon setting in a vacant lot. Climbing into the back of it, I lay down, and shivered through the rest of the night. That morning, with my teeth chattering and froze stiff, I wended my way to a friend's house, where I sat before the fire, thawing out. Afraid to go home, I passed the day around the river and railroad tracks sitting before a fire, cooking spuds.

That night I found a warm hallway, and slept contentedly until a night watchman saw me, and turned me over to a cop. After being questioned as to why I was sleeping in a hallway, I was given a ride in the paddy-wagon and turned over to Pa. Knowing what to expect, I wasn't disappointed. Ten minutes after the wagon left, my yells woke up most of our neighbors. With my hand on my sore seat, I nevertheless was glad to crawl into bed with the rest of my brothers and fall asleep.

. . . .

We got along very nicely until my mother and father started to get notes from our school, telling them how I would go to school half a day and run away the other half. My father found out what I was doing when I wasn't in school, and one evening when my brother, Carl, and I came home, he searched us and found some jewelry and money and also a pistol and bullets which we stole out of some house. Well, he took all of the stuff away from us and asked us where we got it. We told him because it was no use denying it, and then he gave us an awful beating and took all the stolen property to a police station. The police wanted to know where we stole the stuff from. They asked us if we could show them the houses. We gave them an idea of the place we stole the stuff from. The police found the people and told them how they got it from my father. They agreed to let us go on account of my father returning the stuff, so we went back to school.

The lack of understanding and conflict which existed between the brothers and their parents is very concisely expressed in the following quotation from James's autobiography. With regard to his father he states:

. . . . He always treated us fairly and did everything he could to prevent us kids from going wrong, but he was bucking the surrounding neighborhood and it was too strong for him. Our contacts and companions were stronger than his pleas. He often told us that the things we were doing would lead us into a lot of trouble from which we would not be able to extricate ourselves, but we were young and thought we were pretty smart and ignored his pleadings.

Another factor which probably contributed to the lack of solidarity in the family was the separation of the parents and the brothers during long periods of time. In their childhood the brothers were separated from each other and from the parents by their repeated commitments to various institutions. Furthermore, the mother, as well as the father, was forced to seek employment outside of the home to supplement the meager family income. Very often she worked in vegetable gardens outside of the city limits, when it was necessary for her to leave home very early in the morning and to remain on the farm until late in the evening. During these absences the children remained at home without adult supervision, the younger children being left under the care of the older ones. As indicated in the following quotations from the records of the family case-work agency, this condition continued for a period of more than eight years during the period of childhood of the brothers. The first visit reported here was made when Carl was one year and six months of age.

Worker visited home. Mother not at home.

Nine months after first entry.—Worker visited home. No one home but little ones. Mother had gone to store. Home conditions remain the same.

One year, 1 month after first entry.—John is home from school, says he is going to school Monday. Mrs. Martin was not at home or I would have insisted on boy going right to school.

One year, 3 months after first entry.—Worker visited home; found the little children at home playing on the door-step. The mother was working on the farms and the father was out looking for work. The landlady complained that the children were neglected in this way very often. John was arrested again.

One year, 3 months after first entry.—Worker visited home; found children at home alone. Rooms were dirty and damp. Landlady reports that the children are neglected like this very often. John was again arrested and was at Detention Home.

One year, 8 months after first entry.—Worker called at Martin home but found no one there but the boys. Mr. B—— of the I.H. Society stated that Edward has been out begging again. A lady reported that Edward said his mother told him to go out among the rich people and beg. Mrs. Martin promised me faithfully she would never allow child to go begging again.

Three years after first entry.—Worker called; no one home but Michael and Carl.

Three years after first entry.—Worker called; parents not at home, Michael and Carl home. Children and home very dirty.

Four years, 1 month after first entry.—In response to Mrs. L——'s letter: Called at home, found no one at home. The neighbors thought the children must be indoors but wouldn't open. The parents both work, but they don't know where.

Four years, 6 months after first entry.—Worker called; Michael and Carl were spinning tops in the yard. Michael has not been in school since he broke his arm; the splints will be removed November 2nd. He will return Monday. Promised him a gift if he will be regular in school until Christmas. Carl goes to kindergarten afternoons and is too interested to miss a session.

Four years, 7 months after first entry.—Michael and Carl were at home. The former has not been in school since he broke his arm. It is all right again. His mother works daily. This A.M. she locked the spare room, and Michael was left without clothes to wear.

Four years, 9 months after first entry.—Called at 4:30 P.M. No one at home. Children in the yard informed me that both parents are working and that the boys go to M—— avenue. Michael is not in any school that they know of.

Six years, 8 months after first entry.—Worker visited; no one at home. Neighbors reported mother at work. Carl at play.

Six years, 8 months after first entry.—Worker visited; no one at home. Neighbors reported father and mother out of work. Carl at school. School has no record of Carl.

Eight years, 3 months after first entry.—Worker visited. Mrs. Martin at work. Boys playing somewhere in the neighborhood.

It seems clear from the foregoing material that the parents and the brothers belonged to diverse social worlds; hence, because of the differences in their group experiences, the family lacked the unity which is usually regarded as being essential to normal family life. As an agency for providing training, guidance, emotional satisfaction, and security for the brothers, its ineffectiveness is amply demonstrated by the repeated delinquencies of the brothers. These delinquencies occurred despite the good intentions and continuous effort of the parents to instil in their children conventional ideals. Probably these efforts were particularly ineffective because they were not supported by a corresponding sentiment, public opinion, and practice in the community.

ISOLATION OF BROTHERS FROM CONVENTIONAL NEIGHBORHOOD INSTITUTIONS

Presumably, the problems which the parents faced in rearing their children in the American community were quite different from what they would have been in the Old World community from which they emigrated. There they would have had the support of the large family of relatives and the common sentiments and public opinion of the community in their effort to train, guide, and control their children. On coming to Chicago they settled in a community in which primary group controls had largely disintegrated and the social groupings were characterized by widely divergent traditions, moral norms, and practices, and where traditions of delinquency were already established. As the brothers became incorporated into the life of the neighborhood groups, whose norms and mode of life were opposed to those of the parents, parental control was weakened and the parents were unable to transmit the value of their tradition to the brothers. The social heritage of the parents was not carried over to the children; there was a sharp break in family tradition. At the same time, the educational, social, and recreational institutions, which represented the conventional culture of the New World, failed to provide a system of values, sentiments, and practices sufficiently persuasive and vital in character to establish a form of control appropriate to the demands of conventional American society.

With the exception of the mother, the members of the Martin family were not incorporated in any conventional American or Old World neighborhood institutions. From the time of her arrival in America Mrs. Martin has been a devout church member, the father has been irregular in his church attendance, while the brothers have been indifferent to the church and have never been identified with it or with any of its societies. Thus, the brothers did not have the stabilizing influences which might have resulted from an intimate relationship with this institution. As they became involved in the random play activities and delinquencies of the gang, they repudiated all institutions which sought to enforce conformity to conventional standards of conduct. They rejected the church, played truant from school, were indifferent to character-building institutions, and recreational agencies, and defied the police, the courts, and the truant, probation, and parole officers. These reactions, it is assumed, were a product of their experiences in a delinquent milieu and the arbitrary and coercive methods employed by many agencies to enforce their allegiance to conventional norms of conduct which were inconsistent with the values in their own social world.

PART III

THE FORMATION OF THE ATTITUDES, INTERESTS AND BEHAVIOR PATTERNS OF THE MARTIN BROTHERS

INTRODUCTION

It is the purpose of Part III to give a brief description of the chronological sequence of personal experiences in which the gradual formation of the attitudes, interests, habits, and forms of conduct of the brothers took place. Autobiographical documents have been used for this purpose. These documents, although presented in abbreviated form, suggest the manner in which the varying experiences in the family, the gang, the school, and other social groupings in the community conditioned the personal development of the brothers. As revealed in these documents, the specific delinquencies appear as events in the process of interaction between the brothers and the constantly changing influences that impinged upon their life during their early childhood and adolescence. It is in relation to this process of adjustment of the brothers to successive social situations that their delinquent acts become intelligible.

These more complete documents, as compared with the fragmentary excerpts presented in preceding chapters, afford a more satisfactory basis for analyzing the delinquencies of the brothers in terms of their efforts to secure common human satisfactions and to make an adjustment to the circumstances of life in which they were placed. Their delinquencies appear not simply as isolated acts but as aspects of dynamic life-processes.

In writing these life-histories the brothers were motivated by an interest in their own lives, monetary considerations, and a genuine hope that the documents might be useful in preventing other boys from becoming involved in delinquency and crime. No guidance or direction was given them except that they were encouraged to give a detailed description of their experiences during early childhood and adolescence. At the time of writing they did not have access to their official records, nor were they aware of what the others had written.

Each of the brothers has written a number of autobiographical documents during the last ten years. These documents range in length from fifteen to one hundred and fifty typewritten pages. In so far as possible, the excerpts used in previous chapters were taken from the short documents, while the longer documents have been reserved for the chapters in this part. This selection of materials was made to avoid unnecessary duplication. In a few instances, however, excerpts which were previously used will appear again in the documents presented in the following chapters.

In making comparisons between the documents included in Part III, the time and place of writing should be taken into consideration. The life-histories of John and Edward were completed recently, while those of James and Michael were written about eight years ago when they were incarcerated. It should be remembered that references to age, family conditions, and particular delinquencies are given as of the time of writing and not as of the publication date. Since the documents were written at different times, many of the references to specific events will vary from one document to another.

With the exception of modifications that were necessary to disguise the identity of the brothers, a few changes in paragraphs and punctuation of some of the documents and omissions that were made to reduce their length, these life-histories are presented essentially as they were written. Aside from deletions and identifying information, John's document is presented exactly as it was prepared. Edward's story was reparagraphed and in many instances repunctuated to facilitate reading. Few changes were made in James's life-history, except that its length was reduced greatly. Michael's autobiography has been reparagraphed, repunctuated, and considerably reduced. Aside from punctuation, Carl's document is presented as it was written. Such changes as were made have not altered the original meaning of the documents.

The life-histories of the five brothers will be presented in the following chapters with a minimum of interpretation. Many of the points of special interest relative to their early experiences in delinquency, their family life, their activities in the gang, have been discussed in the preceding chapters. A limited number of interpretive comments in connection with each document are made by means of footnotes.

CHAPTER VIII

THE LIFE-HISTORY OF JOHN MARTIN[1]

I

I was asked to write a brief account of my early youth.[2] I'm afraid that I won't be able to say much as nothing unusual or out of the ordinary ever took place in my life; I lived a quiet, normal life of the average boy of that day. That is, it was quiet outside of a few exceptions.[3] Well, to begin, I was born some thirty-five years ago in Chicago. The place of my birth was in a frame shack on W——

[1] John Martin wrote the life-history presented in this chapter a few months prior to its publication. Approximately ten years had elapsed between his release from prison and the time of writing. He was induced to write this story for a small monetary consideration while he was taking a short vacation from the company for which he worked. He wrote rapidly and without direction. The tendency to moralize and philosophize about his own experiences and about life in general, so evident in this document, is common to all the shorter life-histories that he prepared. These documents closely resemble one another in literary style, content, and point of view.

[2] For discussions of the value of life-history documents in the study of delinquents and criminals see C. R. Shaw, *The Jack Roller* (University of Chicago Press, 1930) and *The Natural History of a Delinquent Career* (University of Chicago Press, 1931); E. H. Sutherland, *The Professional Thief* (University of Chicago Press, 1937); W. I. Thomas and F. Znaniecki, *The Polish Peasant in Europe and America* (New York: Alfred A. Knopf, 1927); John Dollard, *Criteria for the Life History* (New Haven: Yale University Press, 1935); B. Karpman, *Case Studies in the Psychopathology of Crime* (Washington, 1933).

[3] This introductory paragraph suggests the point of view of the entire document and at the same time epitomizes John's whole philosophy of life. He is a carefree person who is more or less indifferent to success as measured in conventional terms. His philosophy is fatalistic and he is apparently reconciled to the events and circumstances of his life whatever they may be. As suggested here John treats his experiences in delinquency very lightly and with considerable emphasis on the humorous aspects of the different episodes. He reveals that he has few if any mental conflicts about his delinquencies and crimes and that he is not greatly concerned about the moral implications of his behavior. It is probable that from the point of view of the local situation in which he lived there was nothing very "unusual" about his life. It is only when one accepts the point of view of conventional society that John's behavior becomes "unusual or out of the ordinary," and John seldom views it from that perspective.

Avenue, near the railroad tracks. Out of a total of eight children in the family, I was the fourth offspring. It seems that all the foreign families run into large figures. The poorer they were the more children there were in the family. My mother told me that if she had waited another three months I would have been born in the old country. You see, my parents emigrated from Europe a short time previous to my birth.

When I was about five or six years old my older brother, who was my senior by three or four years, contracted diphtheria and died. I suppose it is kind of tough for a person to go out before they've tasted a little of life. But, sometimes, I think it is for the best that a person goes out early rather than go through all the hell that we have to endure in this world. Now that I can reflect on my past life I'm sorry it wasn't me instead of him. As the old adage goes: "It's only the good that die young." Well, it certainly was true in my brother's case. He was a good kid, if there ever was one. Of course, I didn't think so at the time, because any time I did anything wrong or disobeyed my Ma, why he'd whale the tar out of me. So, being too young to know better, I told my Ma that I was glad that he died because, that way, I wouldn't get any more lickings from him. I'm pretty sure that if he had lived he would have been an upright, honest, useful citizen, and would have changed the course of all our lives and I wouldn't have had to spend several years of my life in state and city institutions. As it was, he left and we were left without a guiding hand. My Pa used to lick us but we paid no attention to him, as we did to our brother.

My parents were very poor. My Pa had no trade or experience in any line of work but worked as a day laborer in a coal yard or tannery along E—— Avenue or along the tracks. His weekly pay was about twelve dollars, which seems small nowadays, but it could go a long way thirty years ago as the prices on commodities came within the means of his salary. We would have gotten along quite well on what he earned, as my Ma knew how to balance the budget. The only thing wrong was that he was a slave to Demon Rum, and he always did have an insatiable thirst on or about paydays; then we wouldn't see him for two or three days, and when he did come home, why, he'd be cleaned. They didn't have any taverns in those days; they were known as saloons. That word is so seldom heard now that it is becoming obsolete.

To continue, when he was out on a spree and the saloon happened to be closed, why, he'd bang away on the door until the proprietor opened up, and he'd buy the house a drink. As he was known as a free-spender, a good-time Charlie, he always had three or four parasites along with him to help him spend his money quicker. Outside of that one inconsequential trait, he was a pretty good Pa. He wouldn't get drunk every payday, but it was too frequent for the family's good, and us kids would have to go hungry at times, and a growing kid can surely eat, especially us. It seemed that we were always hungry, and that made it kind of tough for our Ma. She always did worry about things and she still does and she's in her sixty-ninth year. After all, her life wasn't a bed of roses, so who could blame her for worrying about where the next nickel will come from.

But, to get back to the old man: He couldn't get away from his weakness, although I know he'd stay on the wagon for four or five months in a vain attempt to lay off the stuff. That was in the latter part of his life, although he didn't know that his days were numbered. That's the way it is with life, it's so uncertain. How can anyone know when he'll go? As I said, he'd quit drinking for awhile, but when he would fall he'd fall hard. It was during prohibition that he was making his fight to shake off the habit. But after a lifetime of doing the same thing it's pretty hard to quit anything; even for the strongest minded person. After a certain number of defeats, you figure: "What's the use?" and you follow the line of least resistance.

They really sold some great whiskey during the prohibition era. That stuff would burn out the inside of a barrel. What I'm leading up to is a little over fifteen years ago one of his real, good, saloon-keeper friends sold him some "bonded" whiskey, and told him that when he drank that he wouldn't go anywhere else. Well, he drank it, but the saloon-keeper misinformed him about it being good alky, because my Pa went to the cemetery all unknown to himself. I kind of hated to see him go. In my earlier days, he was stern with us, but in the last year of his life he became real sociable and human. He seemed to get over some of his old-country ways. He seemed to get more Americanized. Before, he used to disapprove of us even going to a movie, but he, himself, started to go to the movies. I think that his going to the picture-shows kind of changed his viewpoint on life, broadened his mind. As I said, I really got to like him in that last couple of years of his life. It was too bad that he had to go in his prime. He was only forty-six when the Angel Gabriel blew his horn.

II

When I was seven or eight years old I started to go to school. The first school I entered was the kindergarten class at the public school. In fact, I live right in the shadow of it at the present time. They had quite a time keeping me in school however.[4] I would ditch school with some of the older fellows around the neighborhood. Some of these guys were Jim Reiley, Joe Sargent, Howard Philips, and Sam Ludlow.[5] Every other day the truant officer would be hot-footing it after me. At times, I wouldn't show up at school for three or four days. During such a time I'd be afraid to go home because the old man would lay it on me, as he often did, with the raw-hide. So, instead of going home at night to sleep, I would crawl into some hallway and get what sleep I could under

[4] The attitudes of John and his brothers toward the school must be analyzed with reference to the conflict of cultures in the area in which they lived. Since free public education was not a traditional aspect of the culture of the foreign-born people in this area, the public school from their point of view was essentially a foreign institution. They were unfamiliar with the curriculum and the purpose of education. This lack of understanding was further complicated by the fact that the teachers came almost entirely from outside the local neighborhood and represented cultural backgrounds which were alien to the local parents. It was, therefore, quite natural that the children should reflect in their behavior the fact that the school was not an institution in which the people were vitally interested or one that was closely integrated in their life-experiences.

[5] In the original document these persons were designated either by their first names or by descriptive nick-names. The aliases are given in full here so that they can be identified in the chapter in which the official records of companions are presented.

the circumstances, which was no picnic.[6] One time, while I was out like that, some copper picked me up and took me into a restaurant for something to eat. When I was through eating he offered to pay for it, but the proprietor wouldn't take his money. That is just an illustration to show the difference between people now and what they were twenty-five years ago. I suppose they change with the times; I don't know.

When I was about nine years old, I had a habit of getting up around four A.M. We didn't have much to eat in the house, so I'd get up about the time the bakers would come around to make their morning deliveries of cakes, bread, and various sundries to the local grocery stores. Nowadays, they take the stuff inside, but at that time they used to leave the stuff outside. The world was more carefree then, and the people had a trusting nature. After the wagon would pull away I would first go up to the trays of cakes and bread and after first feasting my eyes upon them—and they sure looked good to a hungry kid—I would feast my stomach. Then I'd take what I thought would be enough for the rest of the household and go away. After making my delivery at home, I would once more sally forth, and make the rounds of two or three back porches and come home with four or five quarts of milk which altogether combined lasted throughout the day.[7] So, one

[6] Truancy from home and school are often symptoms of the beginnings of a delinquent career. A study of the boys who were taken to the Cook County Juvenile Court during a ten-year period has revealed that 55 per cent of the individuals taken to court as truants reappeared in the court charged with juvenile delinquency.

[7] As indicated here and in the other life-stories the family was maintained for weeks at a time through the begging and stealing of the five brothers. The parents received the bread, cakes, milk, and coal which their children brought home, without making any explicit distinction between the practice of begging and the practice of petty stealing. Their acceptance of these necessities does not necessarily mean that they approved of stealing. It must be recognized that they confronted a very difficult and complicated task. They were in dire economic need; they were largely unfamiliar with the activities in which the children were engaged outside of the home; and they faced problems with which they were unfamiliar. Various forms of stealing were generally accepted in the neighborhood. Stealing from railroads, for example, was a common and accepted practice. Apparently the parents accepted many of these activities as part of the common practice of the new community situation in which they were placed without appreciating the consequences which might result

can see that I recognized my responsibilities at an early age and contributed my share towards the maintenance of the household.

My series of depredations were brought to a halt temporarily when I was picked up and sent to the old Juvenile Home at G—— Street and H—— Street. What the offense was I don't recollect. It might have been incorrigibility, truancy, insubordination or what have you? But I think it was a bit of all combined. Whatever it was, it was only a misdemeanor. I kind of liked the place. That was the first place I'd ever been in and I thought the food was swell. When I first entered there, I was given a bath, some clean clothes, and a physical examination. I stayed there about three days and was hailed before the magistrate who let me go home in the custody of my parents on a promise to behave.

After I got home I resumed my old life where I had left off, and after a few weeks I was back in the Detention Home. When I went before the judge the second time, I didn't fare so well. He sentenced me to the Chicago Parental School, where I stayed for three and a half months for truancy. While I was there, I really had to toe the line. I caught plenty of hell, if I didn't. The fellow who was in charge of the cottage I was in, who was known as a housefather, had a playful habit of picking you up around the neck and banging your head up against the ceiling for any slight infraction of the rules. They really neglected the boys' health in the place, because while I was there I had an acute case of kidney trouble and nothing was done to alleviate my condition, let alone, cure me. The pain used to shoot through me as though someone stuck a knife in me, and I used to have to double up from it. But I suffered in silence.

We had morning and afternoon sessions of school, and in the evenings we'd sit around and read, or whatever was on the program, and then we'd retire about nine o'clock. On Sundays, we'd attend Sunday School. I guess I used to be a pretty tough punk while I was there. At times, I used to swear like a mule-skinner. One time the housefather overheard me using a few choice words

---

from them. In later years, when the brothers brought home jewelry and other merchandise which obviously had been stolen, the parents refused to accept it and in many instances turned it over to the police.

of my own concoction, and he made me chew on a bar of soap to purify my language. So, after that I looked about twice before I deemed it safe to express myself orally. And, I was only ten years old at the time, so my periods of incarceration started quite young, don't you think? After being there for three and a half months my parents came and took me home. And, I was sure happy.

But a short term in that place didn't dampen my zeal or fire. I remained a model boy for a few days; then I started cutting up once more.[8] I refused to attend school regularly, and got into all kinds of petty mischief. So, a few months later I was returned to the same place. I was eleven years old then and a lot more smarter. On arriving there I went through the same routine and after staying there for about four and a half months this time, I was released.

The next two and a half to three years were uneventful. I managed not to get into any jam—that is, no one ever caught up with me. I was getting restless and wanted some outlet for my excess energy. So, I got in with Howard Philips, William Stock, Sam Ludlow, and Joseph Sargent. We made the North Side our stamping ground. We figured that's where the rich and well-to-do people lived, so that would be the logical place to roam. We were after nothing big—just bicycles. Of course, if an opportunity presented itself where we could snare anything else without the risk of apprehension,[9] we wouldn't hesitate to take that chance. As they say, ignorance is bliss, and being ignorant, we knew no fear. As we knew that the bicycles were usually kept in the back yards of the residential dwellings, our method would be to walk down

[8] One of the inherent limitations of individualistic and institutional treatment outside of the local neighborhood is that the person must return eventually to the situation in which he became involved in truancy or delinquency. The study of cases has revealed that even if the boy has resolved to keep out of trouble after his release the chances are that after a few days of restless inactivity at home he will return to his former companions and participate in the forms of activity that are common to the group.

[9] There is little evidence to indicate that either John or his brothers were concerned over the moral implications of their behavior. As indicated here the major consideration in deciding upon the advisability of an act of theft was the possibility of apprehension and the probable value of the article to be stolen.

the alleys until we spotted one. If the opportunity was right, we would borrow the bicycle then and there. If we saw that we couldn't make it, and the bike looked good to us, why, we'd memorize the house and come back after dark. In the meantime, we'd go out and look for easier prey. After darkness arrived, we'd go back to the place we had spotted earlier in the day. Sometimes we'd have a little difficulty in securing this certain bike, especially if it was locked up. But, no matter what the difficulty, which was never too great, we'd always manage to get the bicycle.

As we worked in pairs, we'd usually grab two bikes. We'd never be satisfied with one. Of course, if we couldn't get two that day, why, we'd both ride on one. But a day seldom passed that we failed to get two. I wouldn't hesitate in taking anything. I'm not patting myself on the back, but it's true nevertheless. My motto was to make hay while the sun shined. My colleague William Stock was a little more shy than I was. If he saw a new bicycle anywhere, he'd hesitate in taking it. Then I'd have to bolster his courage for him and argue with him before he'd acquiesce. He always figured a new bike was too hot to handle. I remember the first time that I tried to ride a bike. You see, I had never ridden one before and I certainly had a tough time of it. I'd go from one side of the street to the other, into light poles and everything, but after a few sessions on it I got the hang of it. Incidentally, that was the first bike that I ever went south with. Imagine anyone taking anything and not being familiar with it.

As I wanted to say I think I was about thirteen years old when all this happened. That was probably our best year, so our stocks soared to a new high. To give a rough estimate, we must have gotten about sixty bicycles all told, the majority of which yours truly takes the credit for. The whole North Shore was in arms against us. I know that because I was picked up by the police and put in a station on the North Side. They said, "I'll bet you're the one that's been stealing all these bicycles." Of course, they didn't know for sure; they were just guessing, as I was picked up with no contraband on me, which was a break for me. They had the guilty culprit but they didn't know it. What a laugh on them. Anyway, they took my name and address, which I was chump enough to give them, and instead of locking me up, they threw a blanket on the floor down beside the turnkey's desk, and ordered me to go to sleep. They figured I was too young to be locked up. As I had been walking practically all day without cessation, I was pretty tired; so I took their advice and fell asleep with the turnkey sitting there beside me, keeping his weather-eye peeled on me. After I had slept four or five hours, I should judge, I woke up and saw no one about. After looking about for a minute while I was lying there, I took stock of the situation and saw that there were no barred doors between me and freedom. So, what would be the natural thing to do? I got up and, after first peeking into the garage and seeing no one there, I nonchalantly walked out and started for home. But, on arriving there a few hours later, I took a look from a block distance and there's a big harness-bull standing in front of the house. I had a hunch that they would show up and that's why I took my time about getting home. How could the cops be so dumb as to advertise themselves that way? I can just imagine their consternation when they walked in where I was sleeping and found that the bird had flown the coop.

I remember one time during our expedition for bicycles, I and my colleague spotted two brand new bikes. I remember that they were "Rangers," that is, it was the name of the bicycles. My associate was hesitant about taking them figuring that because they were new they'd be too hot. He always did seem to be lacking in courage and it was up to me to pep him up. So, after a lengthy argument, I finally presuaded him to take one and I grabbed the other.

We both got on and started to liven up the asphalt in order to put a little distance between us and the former owners of the bicycles. We headed south towards our own neighborhood. We managed to get out of the North Side all right and had no trouble on the way such as being accosted by the heat which we always had our eyes peeled for. If we happened to spot the law anywhere, why, we'd duck down the first convenient alley or intersection. Our exercise of constant vigilance, I can say, kept us from being apprehended. It enabled us to stay out of the clutches of the law for quite some time. But, in time, everyone meets their Waterloo and we were no exception to the rule.

As I was saying, we were pedaling along serenely with not a worry in the world. As the old saying goes: "Ignorance is Bliss." We happened to be riding along H—— Avenue and had just passed under a viaduct and were approaching R—— Street. I happened to look behind me and saw a car coming towards us hell bent for election. I didn't pay particular attention at first but as it was rapidly overhauling us and slowing down as it neared us I became uneasy. It dawned on me that they might be after us. My suspicions proved to be correct. There were two fellows in it and the look they gave us as they neared us indicated that the least they'd do would be to tar and feather us. I knew that we had no chance of getting away from a car and as these two fellows were ready to pounce on us I quickly changed my course and started pedaling in the opposite direction. As it takes a minute or so for a car to turn around I was able to go a block or so before they again caught up with me. It was unfortunate for us that we were stopped in that particular spot. As I said, H—— Avenue runs under a railroad viaduct and there are no side streets. There couldn't have been a worse spot in the city. So that left us in a predicament. As they came abreast of me the second time I again repeated the maneuver and started pedaling up-hill as fast as my legs would move the pedals. When I reached R—— Street I turned east into it. It is only a short street about a block long. It only runs east of H—— Street into a branch of the Chicago River. But during this moment of excitement I didn't think of that. The uppermost thought in my mind was how to get away from these two fellows.

I'm riding down R—— Street as if the devil were chasing me and they were right behind me coming like a bat out of hell. I came to the river's bank and thought to myself, "What shall I do?" "I've either got to take a ducking or get pinched." I had the choice of two evils and decided that a ducking would be preferable to getting arrested. So I quickly unloaded from my bicycle and into the river I went, clothes, shoes, and all. If you've noticed the construction of the Chicago River bank docks you'll notice that the bottom beam running the length of the bank is only a matter of four or five inches above water. After I lowered myself into the water I crawled under this bottom beam with not much more than my nose protruding from the water. I stayed in the water for a half hour or so. They stayed up there for fifteen or twenty minutes waiting for my body to come up. I had them wondering how anyone could stay under water that long. The cops debated as to what could have happened to me. I think that they were filled with just a little remorse to see a young fellow like me drown. Come to think of it, it would have been best for a lot of people concerned, including myself, if perhaps, I had gone down. There would have been less evil taken place in this world, because a lot of people have suffered through my indiscretions. Perhaps it wasn't intentional on my part, but they suffered just the same. It's the innocent that suffer the most for our wrong-doings and it hurts me just as much, especially if it's someone I really care for and I am the direct cause of their being hurt. Perhaps I have been bad and been in jail. That shouldn't cause people to look down on me. I've done some good in this world, something that nobody will know except the party or parties concerned. It will die a secret with me. As it is said one half of the world doesn't know how the other half lives.

After what seemed like an endless wait these two fellows took their departure taking the bikes along with them. In order to make sure that they weren't quietly sitting around and waiting for me to come up I stayed in the water a few additional minutes. Then I crawled back on the dock dripping like a sewer rat caught in a deluge. As it was a nice warm summer's day I felt no after-effects from my prolonged stay in the water. In fact I really would have enjoyed my enforced dip in the river——but. If one has ever taken a look at the surface of the river one will know what I mean by that word, but. With all the filth and scum floating on the surface, the river actually stunk. The river looks much cleaner now than it did twenty-five years ago. If I remember right I think that my partner was nabbed by these two guys because I didn't see him for a long time after that.

I guess that I took part in all the trivial, mischievous things that a small boy does who isn't brought up in the proper manner. One of my playful habits when I was short of a little ready cash was to go junking. Only the junking that I did wasn't exactly within the law. To me, however, nothing was outside the law. Whatever I did I never thought twice of whether it was right or wrong in the average person's eyes. The junking that I'm referring to was fairly lucrative. It was procuring lead. Only I didn't use a hit or miss method such as going through the alleys on the chance that I might stumble onto some lead lying around. That would be a waste of time as that stuff is too valuable to be left lying around. There are only two places where lead is found. One is in the earth. The other is in old, abandoned houses. But I didn't go to the mines in Montana for my mineral. That would require too much effort, and think of the distance that I'd have to cover. Besides, I'd have to pay freight charges if I did that, so it wouldn't be worth the trouble. Instead of going to all that trouble I decided to remain in Chicago and get a corner on the lead market here. As there was a plentiful supply here, I decided it was the best thing to do. Other kids in the neighborhood did the same thing.

Whenever I felt the urge I'd go walking through the neighborhood until I'd see some old, empty shack that looked as if it was ready to fall over. Sometimes I went alone; other times kids from my gang went with me. As a rule there were always lead pipes in these old buildings, but at times I was too late as some other vandal—or shall I say competitor—had beaten me to it. However when I did go into a house and there was any lead in it, why, I'd help myself. Usually, I would only take it out of the cellar, but as competition grew stronger I would have to climb up to the first and second floors for my lead as the lead in the cellar would be gone. Even the houses in good order didn't escape my tour of inspection.

Even though they were empty but were ready for occupancy I would force my way into them and take all the lead that I could carry.[10] As there were plenty of vacant houses in the neighborhood one had no trouble. In speaking of the neighborhood the area where the park now stands was nothing but a prairie. It was used as a city dump, and whenever the wind was right we certainly got a beautiful aroma in our nostrils. B—— Street wasn't paved then and whenever it rained, why, we'd walk in mud. And the flies were thicker than mosquitoes. The surrounding streets were the same, and if I remember correctly we still had board walks instead of concrete. That was close to thirty years ago as I was very young at the time.

There was one certain method that I had of getting money, and it wasn't by breaking the law either. That was by mooching, or in plain English, begging. I would stroll through the rich neighborhoods and pick out some likely looking house and knock on the back door. Usually it would be a woman who would answer my knock. I would give her a hard luck story, magnified a hundred times, and it rarely failed that I went away empty-handed. Sometimes I'd see a woman in the backyard, and, if she had a kind face I'd put the bee on her. Due to my youth it was easy to win their sympathy. It was a cinch for me to receive from ten up to fifty cents sometimes. If I didn't get cash I'd receive the equivalent in articles of clothing or anything else that the lady didn't think she'd need. Quite a few would invite me into their kitchens for a bite to eat first. Some would take my name and address and would promise to look me up. Everything considered it was a sweet little racket. My brother Edward went along with us on many occasions. He also went with William Stock and me to steal bicycles.

As we lived in the vicinity of the M and M railroad tracks we got our coal fairly cheap. In fact it cost us hardly anything at all.

[10] This description of the way in which junking developed into burglary is not unlike the way in which begging developed into burglary as outlined in chapter iii. Obviously from John's point of view the development of the less serious offense of junking into the more serious offense of burglary involved no sudden changes in motivation, moral evaluation, or techniques. To him there was little difference between these acts, whereas under the law or from the point of view of popular opinion they are assumed to vary widely in relative seriousness and in their moral implications.

As there was a small freight yard near our house, we would go inside of it after first seeing where the yard-bull was. Then we'd climb up onto a gondola and throw off whatever we could carry and depart. Sometimes we would wait for a train that was pulling in and while it was still moving we'd climb up onto a car and throw off some big lumps over the embankment into the alley below. As the train used the outside track next to the alley it was a cinch to get all the coal we wanted for the duration of the winter. We certainly had the yard-bull running wild. All he needed was a ring in his nose.

So I worked myself up the ladder of life. Of course, there was nothing serious done. All I did was borrow a little coal now and then, chop off a few lead pipes, or purloin a bicycle here and there. Nothing but all small stuff, nothing worth writing about. However, my behavior got so that I was sent to the St. Charles School for Boys. Somebody told the judge that I had swiped a bicycle. Of course I was prosecuted and as I didn't know what a mouth-piece was I was railroaded to the reform school.

III

I first entered that joint at the age of thirteen. It seemed like a pretty nice place when I first saw it and got to like it more after I was there a while. When I got there I went through all the necessary red tape of getting a physical examination and the rest of that bunk. I was put in a cottage that was in charge of an old couple. They were about the nicest old couple there. The old man was almost blind. Whenever he moved about he'd have to keep his hands in front of him. Whenever he wanted to punish someone why he'd take a pencil and put it between the offender's fingers and then squeeze them. That was the extent of the pun-ishment. Whenever he did that to me I'd holler to the high heavens when I really didn't feel it at all.

I was placed with a detail that worked in the south garden. After about three days there I began to get homesick. Being city bred I didn't know how to look a cow in the face. One afternoon we were working in the south garden picking grapes. There were about thirty of us in the group and we decided to take French leave. There was only one man in charge of us. So we formed a plan. One of us was to leave unobserved and after he had gotten about five hundred yards away he was to show himself running. Our plan worked according to schedule. We called the farmer's attention to the fact that a kid was running away and he took another one of the kids from our gang and hightailed after this runaway kid. Before he went he left one of the conspirators in charge of the rest of us. As soon as he got out of sight the whole bunch of us took it on high for the tall corn. Well, they got out the whole county to look for us. They caught the most of them before nightfall but I managed to stay away for three days before they grabbed me. An hour after the wholesale break I almost got caught myself as a couple of farmers passed within twenty yards of me. But I heard them talking between themselves and I quickly ducked down behind some tall stalks of corn.

After it got dark I left the protection of the cornfield and started heading east for Chicago. I trudged along the country roads for three days and nights without any shoes on my feet. It was warm so I didn't mind. About the second night I came to some railroad tracks and put one foot on the track to cross over and imagine my surprise when I was tossed up into the air for about six feet. I had stepped on the third rail of the C. A. & E. electric Railroad. After that experience I gave all tracks plenty of room. It's a miracle how I escaped death. That's as close as I've ever been to it. During my three days of freedom I subsisted on ears of corn, apples, and whatever varieties of fruits and vegetables that I could obtain. On my third night out I was walking along a country road near Wheaton, Illinois. A farmer came along driving a horse and wagon in the opposite direction. This was about nine o'clock in the evening. As he came near me he made a sudden dive for me, almost catching me off my guard so quickly did he leap. But I managed to elude his grasp and hightailed it for the tall corn. He began to run after me but as I could run like a scared jackrabbit when necessary I quickly outdistanced him. As there was a slight reward for the apprehension of any escaped inmate from the school, he tried his best to coax me out of the cornfield. He told me to be a good boy and come out

and he'd give me something to eat. In fact he promised me everything under the sun to get me to come out, but I just stood there
like a mouse not saying a word. He finally became discouraged
and went away.

After he had gone I cautiously advanced out into the open and
after making certain that he had gone I started walking up the
road once more. He must have notified the sheriff's office, however, because about twenty minutes later a car came down the
road. The driver seemed real pleasant and asked me if I wanted
a ride. I told him yes as I had a weakness for automobiles and
thought nothing of his being on the road at that time of night.
Furthermore, being on the road for three days and nights, and
sleeping in odd places had rather tired me out. Imagine my surprise, though, when he took me into the sheriff's office. I wasn't
exactly unhappy when he did bring me there, however. I was
rather hungry and my body craved some real food. When I got
inside they must have suspected that I was hungry so they gave
me a big bag of biscuits and a big pitcher of coffee with real country cream and did I do justice to it? I never really enjoyed anything as much since then as I did those cakes and coffee.

I was returned to the institution and the old man asked me why
I beat it. I told him that I was homesick. Well, I stayed in that
cottage for a few months and was promoted to cottage boy. That
is, instead of going outside to work with the rest of the boys, my
duties would be inside such as making up the beds, washing the
dishes, cleaning the floors, woodwork, and numerous other duties
about the cottage. However, my spirit was still unbroken and I
became too tough for the old couple to handle. I was insubordi-
nate and disobedient. I was with the best couple in the school but
didn't realize it. So I was transferred to a different cottage. This
one was in charge of a younger man, who happened to be an ex-
army officer, and who still held a commission in the reserves. He
was the toughest guy in the joint and we were all afraid of him.
He'd punish us for the least little infraction of the rules. I sure
had to toe the mark while I was in his charge.

After a short period with him he figured that I was tame
enough so I was transferred to a more permanent housefather.

This man was also strict but he was fair to everyone. He played no favorites. That was a good point in him. However, when he punished anyone why the victim would rarely come back for a second treatment. He didn't believe in sparing the rod and spoiling the child. He'd punish the boys as their own fathers would. For that purpose he kept a rawhide strap about two feet long, an inch and a half wide, and a quarter inch thick. Considering the fact that he weighed about two hundred pounds you can just imagine whenever he laid that strap into anyone why they really knew that they were being punished. I was with him for a couple of years and I managed to avoid that strap. I considered myself very fortunate indeed.

Our work used to vary according to the season. In the winter we would shovel out the spur track leading to the powerhouse. As we had some real winters in those days and it being out in the country, it was nothing unusual for the track to be buried under a ten foot drift of snow. In the summer I was on the extra detail and I was assigned to unloading coal cars in back of the boiler room. It was hot, dirty work and I could never wash the coal dust out of my eyes. The extra was composed of those kids who weren't assigned to any steady work. For awhile there, I was working in the barbershop and was becoming fairly proficient in my work. Whenever I'd get some kid in my chair I would ask him how he wanted his hair cut. He would instruct me on how to go about it and I would listen to him attentively. When he got through explaining how to cut his hair I would grab the clippers and proceed to give him a thorough scalping. We had no choice but to cut hair under the head barber's orders. Sometimes we'd get some kid who would object strenuously to having his golden locks clipped and then we'd have to hold him in the chair by force.

From the barbershop I was given a job as steamfitter's helper. From a nice, easy, clean job I went to a hard, back breaking job. I sweated plenty on some jobs before but they were mild compared to this one. One time during the summer we had to change a pipe under the sidewalk. As the steam was on at the time one can imagine how hot it was. It must have been at least two hundred degrees under that sidewalk. I stayed on that job for about nine months and as the housefather got to like me a bit and knowing that I was due for a parole, he gave me the job of taking care of the ice-plant working the night shift. He put me on my honor and I didn't betray his trust.

After I had been there for about one and a half years, I was paroled to a farmer. My hours of work were from five in the morning until nine o'clock in the evening for which I was to receive the magnificent sum of three dollars per week. I didn't stay there long, however. Just about three days, I believe. The work was too hard and the hours too long. It probably would have been a good job for some country lad, but not for me. One evening after I was through working, the farmer gave me his horse and buggy and sent me on some errand to town. What the errand was I forget. He also put in his young daughter of about five years of age in the buggy for the ride. Well, I started for town. But, being a kid and not knowing the country, I soon became lost. So what could I do? I drove that poor kid and horse around all night and, at last, in the morning I finally drove into town. That farmer was certainly a mighty relieved father when he saw us safe and sound.

The farmer himself was all right but the work was too hard for me. So, when Sunday rolled around I decided to give up my work. The farmer, being a religious man asked me if I wanted to go to church. I told him yes and he gave me a half dollar and told me to go. However, instead of going to church I headed for town and the railroad yards. I suppose that farmer must have thought that I went to China to church.

Four months later I was picked up and sent back to St. Charles. About a year after my return to the school I was given back my old job of taking care of the ice-plant at night. While on that job it was customary for me to have breakfast in the kitchen which is in the same building as the ice-plant. All went well for awhile until I went into the kitchen for my usual breakfast. Well, the woman working in the kitchen had baked a cake and I started to take a piece, but she told me to lay off. I desisted temporarily and waited for an opportunity for her to turn her back when again, I started to cut myself a piece. But, suddenly she turned about and caught me red-handed. I felt as guilty as a collie dog caught slaying sheep. She began to throw curses and blasphemy at me working herself into a cat fit, and then grabbed a knife and started to beat me over the head with it. There was nothing that I could do, so I went back to the cottage and told the old man about it. He sympathized with me but the old lady came and told his wife about it and she made me squat for one hour and then I was forced to go to work without my supper, despite the old man's objections. He made a helluva squawk to his wife about it. Well, such treatment made me sore. I was determined to do something about it. So, that night as usual the watchman came at 11:00 P.M. and woke me up to go down to the ice-plant. So I went down and oiled the machinery and saw that everything was in order and, after reconnoitering about the premises for awhile to get the location of the night watchman, I entered the kitchen. On entering I went to the cupboard which I knew contained food. But it had a big strong lock on it. However, locks never did discourage me. So I went to the ice-plant, secured a hammer, and returned. With a couple of vigorous blows I had it broken open. I don't remember just what the closet did contain, but I remember taking a whole bologna sausage and a loaf of bread.

Altogether I'd been there for about three and a half years. So I kissed the St. Charles School for Boys goodbye forever and started towards Geneva. Instead of following the highway I cut across country. As it was in early spring and unusually warm, I can say without exaggerating that I floundered in mud up to my knees. When I got to Geneva I hung around the railroad tracks until a N.W. Ry. freight pulled in and which I boarded and rode into the Proviso Yards. I got off in the yards and in walking through I was flagged by a yard bull. However, I didn't stop to chew the rag with him but took it on the lam. I finally arrived home. No attempt was made to apprehend me.

IV

I stayed home for a few weeks and as the World War had just ended a few months previously, I decided to enlist in the army. Time was hanging heavy on my hands and I didn't know what to do with myself. So I figured that seeing a little of the world and experiencing new adventures would make me all over; it would help me to forget my disagreeable past life. As I wasn't quite seventeen years old I didn't know how I'd be able to manage it. Then I happened to remember that all alien citizens had to be registered during the war, therefore, my pa must have a registration card. So, I went home and got it, then went to the Recruiting Office and gave my name as it showed on the card. My age I gave as 19 when I was just sixteen years old. My army life I shall omit as I have written about it on other occasions. Needless to say it was the most interesting and happy phase of my life. In passing, let it be known to all concerned that I received an honorable discharge at the expiration of my term of enlistment.

I left the service May 13, 19——. On that day I received a few hundred dollars which I had saved during my stay overseas and speculating in the foreign exchange. After I got home, however, I certainly did treat myself and my brothers good. Before two weeks had passed all I had left was a double sawbuck. And I had nothing to show for it. A good time is all I had. As the old adage goes: "A fool and his money soon part."

I obtained a job inside a pie factory, but after three years of open life in the Army it was unbearable for me to be shut in. So after three months of civil life I tired of it, and re-enlisted in the U. S. Marine Corps. As life in the Marine Corps didn't agree with me I went over the hill (deserted). About this time, however, I made the acquaintance of John Hefner, a young fellow on Madison Street. We were both about the same age, therefore we had something in common. He told me that he had done a stretch for deserting from the U. S. Army. We got real friendly and he suggested that we ship out to the north woods of a nearby state as they needed lumberjacks up there. I was no woodsman, but as I was temporarily unemployed at the time I agreed. It was a bit chilly up there, the temperature going down to 45 degrees below zero at times. But I stuck it out for three weeks and I was intending to return to Chicago. However, fate decreed that I wasn't going to see Chicago for a long, long time. At the logging camp where we worked we knew that the foreman of the camp kept a certain amount of cash on hand at all times. After we had quit our job and had already left the camp I told my partner that I'm going back to Chicago. But he suggested that before we go back to town we might as well first take the cash that was in the foreman's shack. I objected to it, didn't have any desire to pull any job. But, as he insisted, I reluctantly agreed. My heart wasn't in it. If I had followed my own judgement and not listened to him I would have been saved a long term of incarceration.

In every lumber camp there is a person known as a bull cook. His duties are to get up in the morning before anyone else and build the fires. So about a half hour before the bull cook was due to wake up we took along a lighted lantern, with a piece of paper on one side. As I was acquainted with the duties of a bull cook, I entered the shack and extinguished the foreman's lamp. Then I placed the lantern that I had brought, on the table so that the light would shine on the sleeping foreman and I would remain in the dark.

I cautiously opened the cash drawer and commenced to rifle all the cash in it. Then I closed the drawer so it wouldn't be noticed right off. I walked out of the shack and we started hiking down the road. I suggested that now we had the cash we keep on traveling, but, he said that he was tired and wanted to stop in the nearest village for a rest. I objected to that again, but he again over-ruled my objections. As I was wearing a flaming red mackinaw I could easily be identified. Even after pulling the job we still could have made our escape if he had listened to me, but, in order to humor him I listened to his bum counsel. So, we stopped in a nearby village, which was only six miles from the robbery. As it was real early in the morning and dark, and in order to avoid suspicion by asking for a room at such an unusual hour, we stopped and took shelter in the village church. After a couple of hours there we went to the local boarding house and got a room. After we had slept we ate and left the hotel. About a half block from it we were stopped by a deputy sheriff and I knew that the alarm had been broadcast for us.

From there we took a sleigh ride to the county seat where we were locked up in the county jail. The county sheriff was a smart punk and didn't give us any breaks at all. We almost made our escape from this joint. We got a couple of table knives and by hitting them together we fashioned a couple of hack saws. Then we sawed away one of the bars that was on the bottom of the chute leading to the sky light. Of course, there were bars at the roof's edge also but if they were as soft as the one below we wouldn't have any trouble with it.

But this smart punk of a sheriff must have suspected that we'd try something like that and we had no sooner finished cutting through the bar and putting it back in place when the sheriff decided to look the jail over. He took a kick at the bar and it fell out so that ended our plans of escape. After that we didn't have a chance to twiddle our thumbs without someone knowing it. We went to court without counsel and because we were from Chicago the judge threw the book at us. Anyone from Chicago hasn't a chance in that lousy state. The judge said "five years in the state prison."

A few days later I entered the stir. I was put in one of the old cell houses thereby joining the bucket brigade. The old cell houses had no running water so one can guess what is meant by that. The first few months were mental torture to me. Time went by so slowly. My cell in the old cell house had an eastern exposure, and every morning during the summer I would wake up in time to see the sun come up over the horizon. It certainly was a pretty view.

There was one old fellow who entered the prison in 1871 and when I walked through the iron gates about four years later he was still there. A matter of fifty-three years! I believe that is a record for imprisonment. When I thought of the time that he spent behind gray prison walls, I almost laughed at the insignificant five years that I had received. After serving my maximum sentence, that is with time allowed for good behavior, the prison gates finally opened up for me. I had served forty-five months, the time prescribed by law, with an additional five days extra that I had to serve for being thrown in the hole once.

V

Once a man has been in prison he is branded. Especially if he lives in a small town he might as well move out. People figure that once a man has been in prison he can't be trusted. Of course, it's true in a lot of cases. Some are just habitual criminals that don't deserve a chance. There are some ex-convicts who want to make good but can't do it. By changing one's name one can get by for some time and perhaps attain a moderate degree of success. But his success is limited, due to his past record. If he has the chance to climb higher he is afraid to do so. He has the fear that his past might come up and slap him in the face.

I was twenty-five years old when I got out of prison. During the long years that I've spent there I had plenty of time to think things over and come to the conclusion that I'd be the loser every time if I tried to buck society. Why should I waste my life in prison or perhaps meet a worse fate? This life of petty crime has cost me a great number of years of freedom that I could have diverted into more useful channels. I could probably have been a success now at my present stage of life. But what am I? Or what can I amount to now? It is too late in life for me to amount to anything. Perhaps I am not so old in years, but if I go to the average business firm they will tell me that I'm too old. They want young blood. However I am reconciled to my fate whatever it may be.

In conclusion, I repeat that the people one mingles with in his early youth influence his life in later years. That is the period in a boy's life when his mind is susceptible to suggestions. If one mixes with thieves why he will also turn out to be one himself.

CHAPTER IX

THE LIFE-HISTORY OF EDWARD MARTIN[1]

I

My mother and dad were born in Europe. Both of them were born in a little village on the outskirts of a large city. The folks on father's side were farmers. Mother's folks have had schooling and occupied positions of importance in the village. About five years after their marriage, they wanted to come to America. Mother had a step-brother who came here some years back, and wrote nice letters about this country. In the exchange of letters, my dad was given the necessary instructions in applying for passage to America.

After mother received the necessary money from her step-brother and friends in this country, they bade their old friends good-bye. They booked steerage passage on an old tramp steamer, and arrived in New York some twelve days later. Completing their quarantine period at Ellis Island, they took a train to Chicago. There they were met by my mother's step-brother at the depot and escorted to a flat which he had rented for them.

During the next four years of adjustment two of us kids were born. Father worked in a tannery at this time and things seemed to be going along fine. The money borrowed by them to make the trip was paid back. But, with the beginning of the following year things began to change. Pa had liked his drinks even in the old country, but he had been moderate. During the first four years he very seldom took a drink of liquor until his debt was paid. Paying his last debt, Pa celebrated the occasion by getting drunk. And

[1] Edward wrote the life-history presented in this chapter a few months before publication and about eight years after he was released from the state reformatory. He dictated a rambling account of his life several years earlier, parts of which were used in other chapters. More recently he wrote a short life-history which he was encouraged to use as an outline for the longer document, about two-thirds of which is included here. Edward wrote primarily for employment but with a developing interest in the fact that his life-story would probably be published. The entire document has been reparagraphed and divided into sections.

from that time on he continued to celebrate. As the saying goes: Pa went to the dogs. He lost all sense of responsibility. His drinking brought us trouble and misery.

The responsibility of caring for the family fell on Ma's shoulders, but it became a little too great for her to carry. Pa lost his tannery job several times, but because of his skillfulness he had been called back time and again; the foreman however got tired of doing this, and fired him for good. We had to move for lack of rent. Moving to a flat a few doors east of the place of my birth, we lived here about ten months, when we were forced to move again. While living here, I recollect my first impression of a drunken man. How he would weave from side to side, fall down heavily, and snore like a buzz-saw hitting a knot. When we moved from here I was a very sick baby and I recall Ma holding me in her arms and pleading with the landlady not to throw us out. With the help of my generous godfather, from whom we received a horse and wagon for moving, we moved to an old ramshackle frame building where the rent was $4.50 per month. We lived alongside the main line of a railroad and the house trembled and the windows rattled every time a train roared by. During the beginning of our stay here, I would get frightened when the trains passed by, as it seemed that the house was falling down on us. We lived in a rear building, facing an alley to one side, and the railroad on the other.[2]

[2] In contrast with John's autobiography which is humorous and replete with generalizations and speculations, Edward wrote a matter-of-fact account of his life in which he describes in careful detail all of his experiences with law-enforcement agencies. He tried meticulously to describe the incidents of his life in their proper sequence and to reproduce faithfully the setting in which each occurred. James and Michael were similarly consistent in presenting their experiences in their correct sequence and in maintaining their time and space relationship. In view of the fact that none of the brothers had access to their official records and the fact that they were writing about events that transpired many years before the time of writing, their autobiographies correspond strikingly well with the official records presented in chapter i. It should not be assumed, however, that the validity of these documents depends upon their correspondence with official records. They are valuable not because they corroborate or fail to corroborate the details of their offenses as reported in official records, but because they furnish the individual descriptions and interpretations of their life-experiences. It is through these individual descriptions and interpretations that the attitudes, values, and philosophy of life of the person are revealed.

As I was too young for school I used to pass the time away by watching the trains go by. In the winter time, after a big snow, I would pass the day by jumping into the snow pile in our yard, or whatever took my fancy. During the first winter here, another baby came, making it a little harder for us all. The winter James was born, I recall the house was cold at least half of the time, for lack of fuel. During these cold spells when Pa came home drunk, we often saw Ma crying, and seeing her cry, we kids also cried. Pa had luck in always finding a job, and would work until he received his pay, and then, getting drunk for several days, he would lose the job. While drunk he had fights with the neighbors and all who came his way.

Being five years old, Ma took me to a parochial school, where she wanted me to attend, but being a little young, the teachers told her to wait another year. Shortly after this we moved again, a half block south, into a basement flat alongside the railroad. Michael was born here. It was here that I first saw the neighbors steal coal from a car standing near the house. To me it seemed that the men and women must have emptied a half car, throwing coal into the yard; then all the neighbors helped each other fill their coal sheds. I recall the railroad bull asking the people about the half-empty coal car, and everyone denying their guilt.[3] When I was a little over six years old, we moved to a place near the river, another basement flat in a rear building. Here my youngest brother, Carl, was born.

It was while living here that I got lost while trying to follow my older brother to a strange part of the city. John and some older boys were going somewhere and because I was too young, they refused to take me along. After chasing me home several times, I followed them at a distance. They spotted an empty wagon going in their direction, and jumped and sat on the tailgate. When I saw them get on, I tried to catch up and get on, too. Being too small, I couldn't run fast enough to catch up with the horse. After I chased the wagon for several blocks, I lost track of them.

[3] Not only is stealing from the railroad accepted in this neighborhood, and in others with similar characteristics, but it is also tacitly condoned by the city police who seldom bring boys to court for this offense. The futile efforts of the railroad detectives in trying to prevent this practice is also mentioned by John.

After what seemed like miles of walking and after numerous stops for rests, I realized I was lost. Not knowing my street address, I tried to find my way home. I walked and walked for hours. I recall walking through the Loop. I recall a big building with a bunch of window lights, which I passed at least six or seven times. No matter which way I turned I seemed to come back here. I wandered into a Negro neighborhood. I was surprised when I saw colored people, never having seen or heard of them. I wondered why they didn't wash their faces. I thought all people were white.

I finally reached a park I had visited with an older boy. Darkness having settled sometime before, and to make matters worse it now began to rain, I went into a nearby hallway to wait until the rain ceased. I sat down to rest, and then knew nothing more because I fell asleep. How long I slept I do not know. I woke up when I felt a weight on my leg. Looking up, I saw a man standing over me. He asked me something in a language I didn't understand. I told him in English that I had become lost, but that I could find my way home now. After telling him this, he refused to let me go home alone, because it was very late. He took me first to his wife, next door, which happened to be a saloon, then with a few directions from me, he carried me home. For this, Pa gave me a licking with a cat-o'-nine-tails.[4]

Pa or Ma tended to all our needs. Pa did the dental work. By this I mean if we had a toothache, he would manage to hide a pair of pliers behind his back, then ask us to show what tooth hurt. He then managed, in some way, to get the pliers on the tooth, and jerk it out.

Ma usually did the barber work. When we went to sleep, Ma

4 The conflict of standards and moral values in the area is reflected in the conflicts between the standards of the parents and those of the groups to which Edward and his brothers belong. In this situation the efforts of the parents to control their children through punishment were futile. The Old-World values of their parents made no appeal to the boys, whereas the unregulated play life of the community, which represented American values to them, was stimulating and exciting. It was natural that the subtle pressures making for conformity to the standards of the groups through which they secured these basic satisfactions should be more effective than the efforts of the parents to secure conformity to their standards through verbal reprimands or corporal punishment.

would get the clippers out, and when daylight came, our heads would be bald and radiant as the moon. We all hated baldheads, because the other kids used to joke about them, and make us feel like two cents. I realize now that it was the best thing for us, because every time we had a head of hair we always had a head of lice. Every time I ran a fine comb through my hair I usually trapped three or four of the black sheep. Never having a bath, the word itself had no meaning. If a bathtub could be found in my block, it would be in someone's coalshed.

Pa appeared to be drunk more often, and Ma began going to work at truck-farming in the suburbs. So we were left alone from early morning until late at night.[5] Ma would give John a dime to buy a nickel loaf of bread, and a nickel's worth of sausage, which had to last until she came home.

I lived here only a short time when I got acquainted with the other roughnecks, picked up most of their bad habits, and learned how to do all the things they did. When Ma started working and there was no one to care for us I learned how to go junking; that's picking up bottles, rags, copper, lead, brass, zinc, or anything that was of value to a junker. Whenever we saw anything of value while walking around aimlessly, we would save it until we had enough to take to the junk-yard ourselves, because we would get a better price here than from the junkman who went up and down the alleys and streets.[6] It was while living here that I learned to fight for everything I got. From stealing coal, wood and junking, I learned to protect the pennies for which I had worked hard. Many of the children here turned out to be bad eggs. Most of them wound up in the Big House. Many still live in this vicinity.

When I heard tales about the way schools punished children, I

[5] During these periods when the mother was absent from the home, the children were left to their own devices. They were without the restraints or guidance that a normal family life would provide. Similarly they were without the stabilizing attitudes and values that might have been developed in a family situation in which there was more unity and integration. As a result these boys were the willing victims of the attractive life of the delinquent groups in the area in which they lived.

[6] The presence of junk dealers, fences, and residents who were willing to purchase material picked up or stolen by the children of the community is a positive influence in the development of attitudes of delinquency among boys.

was afraid to go to them. Ma had taken me there two years previous but being too young, I didn't start. Now, being about seven years old, Ma took me there again. On my second day I received a few blows over my hand, and then began playing hookey with the other boys. While playing hookey, we would walk over to the railroad tracks with coal bags and wait for the coal cars to pull in. We would board them and throw off as much coal as possible, fill our bags, and either carry the coal home and put it in the coal shed, or sell it for ten cents a bag.

When the shows would open at noon we truants were in the front line, waiting to buy a nickel ticket, which would allow three of us kids to see the movie. We always had candy which one of us would buy at the five-and-ten-cent store, for an amount equal to the price of the show, split it in equal shares, and enjoy the thrillers that the nickel shows held. During the winter time, when Ma would be at home, going to the shows was a good place, and the best place to keep out of the truant officer's hands. About the time that school ended for the day, we would leave the show, first cleaning ourselves in the washroom and then return to the places where we had hid our books, get them and go home.[7]

The following days of truancy varied. Sometimes, if it was warm, we would go over to the river and swim or learn to swim in the old swimming hole that was formed by the caving in of the river bank. Taking chances of drowning, we would play many games of follow-the-leader, trying to outdo each other in this swimming hole. On other hookey days, if we weren't stealing coal, we would go junking. Other days saw us playing over on the railroad tracks, jumping on lumber piles, chasing each other, playing "it," throwing stones into the river, trying to outdo each other in everything we played.

During this period, I learned how to fight and shift around for myself, found how to make show money, and pick up articles from

[7] This group truancy does not necessarily imply that these children were maladjusted in school. It suggests, rather, that there was no effective public opinion in the community in support of school attendance. Moreover "bumming school" was and is a traditional practice that has developed and is permitted to persist because of the absence of any concerted resistance to it.

rear porches, which had a value in the junk-yard. By this I mean if us kids would see a washboiler on someone's porch, we would sneak up and take it. We would rip off the bottom, and being copper, we would get from five to ten cents for it from the junk-yard and then we would divide the money up which was usually spent for candy.[8] Everything was split equally. When junking, we would try to get either copper, brass, or lead, as this metal paid a good price, and wasn't too heavy for us, as was iron. Iron was cheap, and you had to get a lot in order to get show money, and it was very heavy to carry. Not having anyone to look after us while Ma was working, it was no wonder that I came to do and learn these things.

Getting to know the truant officer, from the older boys, it was no trouble to keep out of his hands, because the older boys usually saw him first. In the chase through yards and alleys, the older boys would take hold of my hands, and I just seemed to be flying instead of running. He would chase us smaller boys, but we wouldn't try to outrun him. Making sure he wasn't too close, we would run in someone's yard, and secrete ourselves on someone's porch or shed until he ran past.

When I was about eight years old and still playing truant while Ma worked, the truant officer came to our home one evening. After telling Ma of my truancy from school, he stated that the juvenile authorities had sent him with an order from the court for my appearance on such-and-such a day. Arriving at the court, I was impressed by the sternness here, and when Ma led me to the bar, my knees were knocking. Standing before the bar, I heard my name called. The judge called my name again because he did not see me. He began to ask questions, when a policeman standing to my left stated I was here. Being undersized and under-

8 The wants and desires of delinquent children are not unlike those of non-delinquents. For the most part delinquents spend the money which they have se-cured through petty stealing, junking, or begging, for shows, athletic equipment, candy, and other luxuries which are normally supplied by parents when their cir-cumstances permit. For example, our studies of shoplifting among juveniles reveal that children very often steal or attempt to steal articles such as roller skates, flashlights, bats, balls, bicycle parts, and other equipment related to either their own recreation or the activities of the groups to which they belong.

nourished, I recall the judge leaning over his bench and looking at me where I stood without shoes, a torn pair of pants, and a baldhead. I don't know what his thoughts were.

All I recall was that a policeman led me to a sideroom, where they had about ten kids bigger than myself. In here I found out that they were going to take me away from home, and put me in the Parental School. Thinking that they were only scaring me, I sat in the room with the other boys, who were talking with their mothers and fathers. When two more boys were brought into this room, and hearing that they were going to the Parental School, it finally penetrated my head that they weren't joking as the kids in the neighborhood did. When I found this out, oh, how I cried! As bad as I must have been, I didn't realize that what I was doing was wrong. Law and order had no meaning to me, because I only did what the others did.

Whatever you did, whether it was truancy or stealing coal, it was all right as long as you didn't get caught. Having no one to take me in hand, I followed the flock.

Every time I thought of being away from Ma and the rest, I cried all the harder. Finally a policeman ushered us into a horse-drawn carriage, where some of the kids told me to shut up. Passing through the Loop, I stopped crying, as my curiosity got the best of me. The big buildings awed me and I couldn't believe they could build them that high. I recall the City Hall, especially, as it was one of the biggest then. During the ride, the kids' happy spirit got me, and when we reached the school, I laughed and joked with the rest.

On reaching the school, we were led to the main office, where the officers drew lots in picking out the boys they wanted. A man from Cottage E drew me, and led me away to the shower room, where he gave me another baldhead and forced me to take a bath. A bath was something new to me. Never having one at home I thought it was something useless, which I plainly stated, adding a few cusswords to emphasize my point. But a few pokes and blows across my ribs and seat forced me to take one anyway. I was then given school clothes. Later, I was led to my cottage where I saw my brother, John.

Not being used to this kind of life of rules and regulations, I got myself in to plenty of trouble. When being taught how to drill, I got mutinous with one of the kid officers. When first taking up this drill exercise, I took it as a joke; after a spell, when it began to get tiresome, I refused to obey the officer. Getting tough with me did no good, as I got tough myself and told him to put up his dukes. After his refusal, I called him a few bad names. Being an officer, he called my brother, John, and told him to tell me that I couldn't use bad language, and had to obey orders. Leaving John and I together, John told me what they would do to me if I didn't do what I was told.

That evening I had to chew a piece of soap for swearing. I soon found out I had to live quite differently from the life I led at home. Although I felt homesick once in awhile, I really liked this place. I liked the clean clothes, clean bed sheets, and baths, and all the many other things which up to this time I had never known. The meals to me were very delicious, and the atmosphere agreed with me. I liked a lot of things about the place. There was a swimming pool, which I fell in love with. The schooling, and the teachers were more than considerate. I was taught my A B C's and multiplication tables here. I was taught how to plant seeds, how to pick flowers, and do a little truck-gardening.

Although I was punished a few times at the beginning of my first period in the Parental School, the officers polished me down, and at the end of my seven months stay here, I had learned many things. I became a model boy. The folks in charge of my cottage treated me like a son, and I got along fine with the rest of the kids. In a way, I was sorry I had to leave, but the homing call is always stronger, no matter how bad home may be, especially to a little tot like me, who hadn't had any experience of being away from home.

A few days after I came out of the Parental School I was walking down the street with my brother John. We met a friend of his who had just been in a fight with a kid. Hearing this kid swear, I told him it's wrong to swear, and that he would get punished for it. He, in turn, wanted to know since when did I become a sissy and a teacher's pet. I soon found out that I was getting into fights for sticking to the new ideals I had been taught. When some of us kids would get in groups and talk about something, the kids would use a cussword here and there. When it was said in my presence I would resent it by telling the kids that it was a sin and not to swear. As a rule, the kids were a little bigger than myself and would resent my butting in. After a verbal fight, it usually would end up with, "You want a punch in the nose?" After declaring himself, the kids would take sides, for or against him, which usually ended in a fight between the two of us. I found out I would have to fight every kid I knew, because everyone that I knew swore like a trooper.

Eventually this ideal wore away, as I began to mix with the kids. Before long the Parental School was a thing in the past, and I was doing the same things I had done before. While fighting for my new ideals I received a name for being tough. And, because the kids found out I had been in the "bandhouse" as they called it, the tough character stuck.

Only the older and bigger kids would dare get tough with me, as the others had built a sort of legend about me, and warned the rest of the kids about my toughness, and "being in the bandhouse," because that was where the tough guys went. By getting this title through no fault of mine, I was used as a defender of my many young friends.

While playing hookey from school one winter, a kid brought a note home asking mother why I haven't been in school for the last several months. I had spent that day with the other kids on the railroad tracks. We built a fire, stole some spuds from a box car, and had barbeque spuds. We then spent the day flipping rides on and off the different freights that pulled in. Between this we had a bunch of snowballs, and from our hiding place we would throw and try to knock off someone's derby. If the man happened to see us, we would run like hell. If the man caught us he would kick us in the pants. Derbies used to be our weakness during snowtime. After I had cleaned up, and getting my books together, where I had hid them, I started home with a cheery whistle on my lips.

Not suspecting I had been found out as a truant, the cheery

whistle soon became a squawk of pain. After getting a good licking from Ma, I was promised a better one from Pa. Knowing the weight of Pa's hand, I made myself scarce before he came home. Afraid to go home that night, I found a warm entrance, a back hallway, where I lay down and fell asleep. The hallway got a little chilly and I woke up. Looking for a warmer spot, I walked to the top of the stairs. Finding an open door, I walked into what seemed to be an empty, warm room. I started to lay down when I bumped into an obstacle. Lighting a match to see what I had bumped, I nearly jumped out of my skin, in getting out of this place. Of all hallways to pick from, I picked an undertaking parlor, and the room I was about to lay down in was full of caskets. Leaving in a big hurry I walked around for about a half-hour until I spotted an empty milk wagon setting in a vacant lot. Climbing into the back of it, I lay down, and shivered through the rest of the night. That morning with my teeth chattering and froze stiff, I wended my way to a friend's house, where I sat before the fire, thawing out. Afraid to go home, I passed the day around the river and railroad tracks sitting before a fire, cooking spuds.

That night I found a warm hallway, and slept contentedly until a night watchman saw me, and turned me over to a cop. After being questioned as to why I was sleeping in a hallway, I was given a ride in the paddy-wagon and turned over to Pa. Knowing what to expect, I wasn't disappointed. Ten minutes after the wagon left, my yells woke up most of our neighbors. With my hand on my sore seat, I nevertheless was glad to crawl into bed with the rest of my brothers and fall asleep.

Because I played hookey so long, I received another request to see the Judge again. After stating I would not attend school, I received another Parental School term. This time I spent eleven months there. I always recall them as pleasant ones. I had no trouble with the kids. The food was swell, except the codfish we got on Fridays. I didn't like this so well, but the orders were you had to eat everything or be punished. So, with a hand over my nose, I would manage to eat it. . . . .

II

Yes, sir, I will always recall my stay at the Parental School as pleasant. Although I had overstayed the time set by the Court, the authorities couldn't get any answer from my folks in regard to coming there and taking me home. Finally, one chilly autumn day I was dressed up and, in care of an officer, I was brought home.

My folks had moved a half-mile west while I was in the school and I was rather surprised when I was taken to this new address, as I still thought we hadn't moved. The place they had moved into was a basement flat next to an alley. This place was cold as an icebox. Being next to the alleyway, the windows, when open, would bring in the garbage smells. Now and then I would see a rat chewing a hole in the sill trying to get in. To me they looked as big as a cat. When I went to bed I would hear them nibbling on the sill, and us kids were always afraid of them getting through and jumping on us, as the windows were near the ceiling, and above our bed.

I returned to school the following day after my return from Parental. Having no friends in this neighborhood, I stuck to my older brother, John. I got along fine at school and liked it. At least until the time I began going astray. I attended school pretty regular, excepting a period when a slight cut over my eye got infected, and nearly blinded me.

I attended school that winter and the following spring and I made fair headway, up to the time I made friends with a fellow named Stock. Late in the spring, while on my way home for dinner, I found a penny laying in the school-yard. Eating a sandwich, which usually consisted of two slices of homemade bread, a little lard and a slice of onion, I wended my way to the nearest candy store. As most of us know, a candy store is like a magnet when you have money in your pocket. I had a penny in mine. Arriving at the store I saw my brother Johnny and Stock standing in the doorway. Speaking to my brother for a moment or two, he introduced me to Stock. Acknowledging the introduction I had a feeling I had seen this guy before. For some reason or other, I just didn't like him. I remembered that John and he played truant once or twice a week.

On my way to the store later I saw Stock again. Saying, "Hello," I went about my business. I had recalled I had trouble with this chap before. I remembered him and another boy throwing a rock at me. I recalled that I had chased him for five or six blocks trying to catch him and give him a pounding. Although he got away then, I was looking for an excuse to give him one now. I believe he recognized me also, but he was always nice when he saw me. Knowing I had no use for him, he told John about it. The next time I saw him, John was with him. I was on the verge of taking a swing at him, when Johnny talked me out of it, and told me what a swell guy Stock was. He told me about going to shows and eating candy at Stock's expense, and said to forget my grievance and be friends. Having shows and candy in mind I figured he might be a good guy, and I'd better not hit him. To win me over he treated me as he did John. I often wondered if he stole money out of his mother's purse. It didn't take long before I knew how he made this money to spend.

A few weeks later having an infected eye, I was permitted to stay home. Strolling towards the candy store I saw Stock standing out in front, with a basket on his arm. After greeting him, he said he was waiting for my brother. Telling him that John went to school, he asked if I wanted to come along to the city. I recall one thing that he pictured for me in answering my questions of "why" and "for what." That was a sort of glowing picture of a ride on the "L" and the big buildings I would see, and all at his expense. This was like giving me a dish of ice cream for nothing.

I accepted the invitation and all others after that. Going along for about two weeks I began getting curious as to why he received money and things to eat from the different places he would go to. Although I was told these places he went to were people who knew him and his family and were helping them out, I began thinking different, as every time I went along he went to different homes. I went along for the ride. But when he came to the place he wanted, I was asked by him to wait on the corner while he went from house to house in that block. After going to most of the homes, he would come back with money and a basket of food. One day I heard him ask for food at a strange place, and then I knew that what he was doing was begging.

Seeing him get food and money this way, I decided to take a basket the next time I went along. Having only the barest necessities at home a basket of food would really be appreciated by us kids. Seeing me with a basket at our next meeting, he didn't like the idea of me cutting in. During my former trips I acted as his stooge. By this I mean I had to carry his basket when it became full, to repay him for the carfare or "L" fare he spent on me. Although this fellow never cared for school, he was very shrewd and a schemer. In me he had a helper and a companion for almost nothing. As I said before, although he didn't like the idea of me taking a basket, he didn't refuse to pay my fare. John in the meantime, had been sent to St. Charles.

Later on, we seldom paid an "L" fare, as we had learned how to find holes or openings that we crawled through that gave us an inlet to the train. Being small boys we would manage to squeeze through the most impossible places, and take the craziest and some of the most dangerous chances, just to sneak a ride on the "L." Going with Stock I was taught the technique of begging, and getting the hang of it, I helped my family and myself with a bigger and better larder.

During this start of my begging, I began to play truant during the afternoons. Later, it became so I was truant all day. Stage by stage, I quit school altogether in order to devote all my time to begging, having learned the ropes through Stock.

I would go from house to house, as Stock did, and give the folks a long, hard-luck story that would make them sympathetic; for this we would get some eatables, or a little change. Although I gave a hard-luck story, the funny part of it was that, as far as we were concerned, it was a true one. Most of the homes we told our tales of woe were very sympathetic, and usually gave us a helping hand.

Even begging had its humorous side, that is, if you could see the humor of it. After learning all I needed to know, Stock and I continued to stick together. At every other door, he would ask for help in my presence; if we got anything he split. The next place, being my turn, I would ask and if I received anything, I would split, too.

In one place, being my turn, I rang a doorbell in a second-story flat. A well dressed, buxom woman, after hearing my story, felt very sympathetic. With the words of "You poor boys," she took my basket (which I had emptied downstairs). Saying she would fill it up, she disappeared inside. Thinking we had made a good strike, we would smile at each other, and wonder if she would give us any money, too. After a few moments of waiting she came out with my basket full, with a paper covering the contents. Thanking her with all our hearts for her goodliness, she replied that it was nice of me to be grateful, and if we were in this neighborhood at some future date, we were to drop in and she would give us more. Smiling, and thanking her again, we left with the promise that we would return in the future. Getting beyond range of prying eyes, we got ready to split. Setting the basket down, Stock took off the paper cover. Lo and behold! What do you think we got? The nice, kind hearted buxom lady gave us some of the hardest and moldiest bread we had ever seen. A whole basketful, and a promise of more the next time we were in the neighborhood. Although the full basket felt rather light, I didn't express my suspicions until we both had a look. Both of us being big hearted we offered our shares to each other.

Having a good laugh over the lady's kindness, and the lady having a bigger one, no doubt, we emptied the bread in a prairie, picked up our cans of eatables, and went home. The old, stale bread business would pop up every so often. It seemed that the ones of the buxom type, who looked the most prosperous, the most dignified, and were the most sympathetic, were the ones from whom we received the most stale bread.

After begging for about a year, I had more truancy trouble. Taken to court I was described as a habitual truant. The Judge, not knowing how to dispose of my case at the present time, my case was continued for two months, and I was sent to the Juvenile Detention Home at G—— and F—— streets. This was my second time here in the past year, as I was picked up for begging about six months before this, and had spent about seven weeks here before I was sent home.

In this place we had very little to do. Scrubbing the floors was the main item of work. After being awakened in the morning, we had to make our beds. After the beds were made, the guards would pick out the biggest boys, order them to scrub the bedroom, and the smaller boys would push the beds to one side. After scrubbing the open section, the beds would be moved into it and the rest of the whole dormitory was scrubbed. After this was done, we would wash up and march upstairs to the dining room for our breakfast. Before eating, one of the guards would call the roll. We answered our names as being present. After a short morning devotion of thanking the Lord for our daily bread, we ate our breakfast. After breakfast, we would go to the playroom and pass the rest of the day the best way possible (usually fighting).

In the summer time, the kids would spend most of the time in the walled-in yard, walking around, or playing a game of playground ball occasionally. However, we small kids were too small to play ball with the other kids. We spent most of our time fighting. Most of my fights were with the dagoes or shines. When I first came here the shines were the ones I had to fight most of the time. I always had to be on guard because there were two nigger partners with whom I was always fighting. If they caught me unawares they would both gang up on me, and I had my hands full fighting them until the guard, hearing the commotion, would come and break us up. Being on my guard, this didn't happen very often. When I caught them apart, I had a swell time giving them a trimming. After spending most of my seven weeks in this manner, I was turned over to my parents. On my second trip, my time was spent in the same manner, only more fighting. In most of the eighteen months I had spent in the Detention Home, at various times, I recall them mostly as months of fighting.

After a two months' wait, I saw the Judge again, and was sent to the Chicago and Cook County School. A very able and understanding man was in charge, and it is a pleasure for me to say this, as he was like a father to the boys in his care. Although the Parental School wasn't bad, the Cook County School was the best of any school I have ever been in. I really was sorry when I was released. I hated to leave this place. The work was pleasant, not hard at all. The country air, and the fresh food was of the best.

At the time of my detention here, the school wasn't fully built.

The boys sentenced to the Cook County School were being held
in a separate wing at the Juvenile Home, waiting completion.
During the finishing stage, four of us boys were transferred to the
new place to clean the floors and do general work in putting everything in shape for the boys, awaiting their transfer here. I did
most of the housework in the superintendent's home. We ate all
our meals in the basement of his cottage. We ate the same things
that he did, and the whole bunch often ate at his table. After
meals I helped with the dishes, did a little dusting, ran errands
and took the one-horse shay and drove his wife to town, and
picked up the superintendent's daughter at the end of the school
day. After supper I would help feed the two horses. If the horses
hadn't been out that day, the fellow who was the caretaker (also a
fine fellow) would tell us boys to ride around and give the horses
some exercise. Knowing nothing about riding a bareback horse, I
was often left sitting on the ground, while the horse galloped
around the field laughing at me.

When I was told I was going home in the morning, I felt rather
bad as I would have liked to stay here. Being home a short time,
and living at another new address, which, by the way, happened
to be another basement flat in another frame shack (which since
that time has been demolished) I began begging again. Conditions at home were as bad as ever. Our meals were of the very
cheapest and not enough to supply our needs. Not having the
necessary food, and no way of getting it, begging was the only way
I could receive the necessary food and clothes. Begging was a
necessity, because it raised our standard of living to a slightly
higher degree; and it became a means of paying our rent. Although it went against my boyish pride when I got an inkling of
the type of people who did this, nevertheless, I, knew it was
necessary in my case.

While begging on the North Side I was stopped by a lady who
asked me what I was doing with such a basket under my arm, and
why I wasn't in school. She was dressed in a gray, two-piece suit,
and in the way she asked the questions I thought she was a
truant officer and was ready to run. Reading my thoughts, she
assured me I had nothing to be afraid of. Telling her of conditions

at home, she told me to come over to her home the coming Saturday as she had some clothes and things she wanted to give me. Reading my doubts as to my coming, she made me solemnly promise I would be there Saturday.

My word was my bond. Although being suspicious of her good intentions and thinking that I would walk into a trap, I, nevertheless, though with great misgivings, went there that Saturday. After giving her my word of honor, I had to go. To my great surprise it was no trap, and after spending several hours at her home, in which she asked about everything at home, she gave me some clothes, a basketful of eatables, and a dollar. With another promise that I was to return the following Saturday, I bade her good-bye. The many following Saturdays proved to be days of friendship for me and the rest of the family. She drove over to our home; found conditions as I had told her. She proved a good friend and a helping one. All of us kids received presents from her and help in many forms.

After making her friendship, I got into trouble over my truancy. Out of a wintry sky I was arrested at home by a policeman, taken to the Juvenile Home, and brought to court a few days later. Having no idea as to the reason or suddenness, I heard some woman employed by the court tell the Judge that I was a beggar and wouldn't go to school; that I was a little blackguard and should be sent to St. Charles for eighteen months. Upon her recommendations, the Judge sent me there. Turning me over to some parole officer, I was taken aboard a train for St. Charles. Arriving at the depot we were met by an officer of the school. Getting into his model T Ford touring car, he drove the three miles to the school, and I nearly froze to death getting there.

At the school I was taken to the Administration Building, asked several questions, the answers to which were duly recorded. I was then taken to the receiving cottage where I went through a breaking-in and quarantine stage for two weeks. After two weeks I was questioned by the supervisor as to where I came from and the type of work I had done and liked. The supervisor would assign you to a cottage where the boys were about the same height. If you were a little boy you were assigned to the little boys' cottage;

if you were a big boy you went to the big boys' cottage. I don't know why he asked about the work I liked, because you never got what you would like to learn.

Each cottage had a certain type of trade, and if you were transferred to it, you did that line of work unless you were assigned to something special. There were also eight farm cottages and if you came from the country you would be assigned to one of these. In my case, although I was rather small, I escaped the smallest cottage, and was assigned to Cottage R.

The house father of this cottage had charge of a fruit garden, which was called the south garden. This is where I worked with the other boys of my cottage. We worked in split shifts. In the afternoon, the morning detail went to school, and the morning schoolboys worked in the afternoon detail. I was assigned to the morning detail and afternoon school.

After working here about two months I was assigned to work in the main kitchen. The main kitchen is where all the food is cooked for the boys of all cottages, excepting the farms. At certain periods of each day, morning, noon and night, two boys from each cottage would come to the main kitchen pulling a little covered carriage containing several pans about a foot square. We would take and fill these pans with whatever food we cooked for the rest of the boys. Their food was cooked in big steam kettles, and our's over a range.

The kitchen was situated in the center of a low, long building. The storeroom underneath, a bakery at the south end, and a butchershop on the north. We had the choicest cuts of meat, as the butcher ate at our table, and because we supplied the bakery with their food, we also had the best bread and special cakes.

Getting up at five in the morning, the night watchman would escort me to the kitchen. After helping in distributing the morning mush, one of us five boys would set our table. We never made our own meals; we had one of the boys who did nothing else but cook for us. When all the carriages had left with their morning breakfast, we would sit down and eat ours.

Working in the kitchen made me exempt from any of the duties in the cottage. While the other boys were drilling and the new boys learning how, I would sit on the lawn and watch them.

We quit work around 6:00 to 6:30 o'clock in the evening. If I knew the boys were to drill that night, I would prolong my stay at the kitchen until I felt certain the boys were nearly through before I came to my cottage. On evenings of playdays I would manage to be at the cottage a little earlier. I had no intention of running away. The work wasn't hard, the food was excellent. I was getting fat, and was content.

Some eighteen months after my arrival, I was given a blue slip, which meant on the morrow I was going home. After getting the slip, I walked over to the receiving cottage where I received some of my old clothes, sent from home. I took them to my cottage where I put them in the dressing room locker.

The following morning I donned my own clothes, bade the boys good-bye, walked over to the Administration Building where I reclaimed what few possessions I had and got on board the school bus with the other ten boys who were leaving. We rode to the railroad station where tickets were bought for us by a school officer who put us on board the train. That first ride to the depot I will always remember. That was as beautiful a day as I can recall. Summer was in full bloom, trees with their full coat of leaves, the growing crops and the morning sun making the morning dew glitter. I never thought what the future might bring as I lived in the present. Before getting on the train I was given streetcar fare and another new address of where my folks had moved to.

Arriving at a downtown terminal, I walked about the downtown section, looking at some of the improvements that had been made during my absence. This country was at war with the Germans at this time. Spotting a recruiting station, I tried to join the army. I was told to wait a little longer, as this country wanted some of the grownups sent to France before they would start sending kids. Completing my sight-seeing, I decided to walk the four miles home, and save the carfare. When I arrived at my new address, I found the flat that my folks lived in. No one being home I found an open window, crawled in and looked the place over. Another basement flat, but this one in a two-story brick building. Four rooms, toilet in the hallway, and gas for lighting purposes. Although a nice, cool place in the summer, it was hard to heat in the winter.

[Edward renewed his acquaintanceship with the woman who befriended him before his commitment to St. Charles. She persuaded him to accept a position in a large bank in the Loop. He worked in this position a few weeks but became dissatisfied and returned to the practice of begging and burglary with his companions. Edward's description of his experiences in the bank is included in chapter vi, page 123.]

While in the act of begging, if no one answered the bell, Stock would break in, in whatever way he could, and steal whatever he liked. Going with Stanley and Stock, I acquired their tricks. After going with them about three weeks, they picked the neighborhood where my lady friend lived. Knowing how she must have felt about my quitting, I excused myself on some pretext. Ringing her doorbell, I was asked to come in. Telling her I was sorry for quitting, she upbraided me like a mother would a child. In an upbraiding tone I was asked if I would go back. Telling her, I would, she dressed up and in forty-five minutes later we were at the bank and I had my job back.

For some reason or other, the job didn't feel the same. Although I did the same things, it seemed that there was something missing. What it was I don't know. The appeal seemed to be gone. Now and then I caught the auditor's eye on me, and I wondered if the lady had told him what I did since quitting the last time. My lady friend when in the bank on several occasions, seemed to quit giving me smiles as she used to. Because of the feeling that I had lost her friendship, plus the seeming watchfulness of the auditor's eyes, I gave up the job. Although I found myself another job in a shoe factory, I didn't like the work here either and quit after two weeks.

Always meeting Stock in the neighborhood, I let him talk me into going back in the racket with him. It seemed that after leaving the bank job the first time, I became restless; I had to be on the go. From the age of fifteen, until I became eighteen, I seemed to have bugs in the seat of my pants, and couldn't stay put.

I quit the shoe job, and took up Stock's and Stanley's company. What were the number of places we entered I can't recall; they were too numerous to mention. In the beginning when entering a home, I was mostly interested in getting money, and took nothing but that. Later however, until my arrest, I began taking watches and jewelry, as did Stock, who always took everything of value in the jewelry line. Jewelry, such as watches, I sold for whatever I could get. Not knowing its value, I didn't get much. The other things, if we couldn't sell them, we gave to someone we liked, or threw them away. We entered the homes in many ways. On some, we used a skeleton key, in others the windows were open. Still others, we forced our way in by either breaking a window, or breaking down the door as quietly as possible. In some, we would crawl through an open transom. In others, as in flats, the icebox was an easy means of entrance. In several of these burglaries we were nearly caught.

When no one answered the doorbell after a moment of ringing, we would take it for granted that no one was home. Gaining an entrance in a quiet way, we would be surprised in the act of burglary by the owner who had been sleeping. After a hurried exit by way of a window or door, we eluded the man or woman by running through yards and alleys. In one place, on the first floor, which I entered through an open transom, I couldn't open the rear door. Telling Stock to go to the front, I began walking towards the front door. While passing a bedroom I was seized by the owner, who awoke when I began speaking instructions to Stock. Being seized so suddenly, my reactions were those of a frightened animal. Feeling my arm pinioned, I involuntarily stepped back, jerking loose the hold. Seeing a giant of a man (well, he looked like a giant, anyway) I whirled around and ran the way I come. Knowing that I would never get out the way I come, I leaped through a closed window. Shielding my face with my arms, my only bruise was a bump on my elbow which I received when I landed in a heap on the rear porch. Yelling for

Stock to run, I leaped to the ground, jumped over the rear fence, and ran hell-bent for election. After chasing me for three blocks I lost the man through the maize of yards and alleys which I ran through.

After these narrow escapes, we really made sure no one was home by ringing the front and rear doors. Sometimes the bells were out of order, and we would make enough noise to wake up the dead by pounding on the door just to be sure the people had gone.

Prowling houses too numerous to mention or recall, I was finally picked up at the house in late October. What happened was Stanley Runcer and Stock had been picked up while roaming on the North Side. The policemen, finding a bunch of jewelry on their persons, knew they had a couple of burglars. During the grilling process, Stanley gave in and implicated Stock and myself in numerous jobs. All three of us were taken in a car, driven to most of these places we had burglarized, and told to confess that we had been there. If Stanley stated we were there, we admitted our guilt; in others which Stock and I committed without Stanley, we stated we knew nothing. In a flat next to the Lake which Stanley also pointed out, I denied I had been there. I had found two rings in a wall-safe, and thinking them of no value, I gave them to one of my friends.

Knowing if I admitted my guilt I would get others into trouble, I denied all knowledge of being there. Thinking the rings had no value, I failed to tell Stanley and Stock about them. After Stanley admitted being there, Stock did also. I tried my best to convince them we weren't there, or that if they were, I wasn't. My statement of not being there was said in such a manner that I implied a meaning of "no," but the thing went over their heads. They even went to the trouble of recalling how Stock and I had given Stanley a boost to an open window, and how he had broken an egg in the purse when he found no money in it. The police then began to question me about the whereabouts of the two rings I had taken from there. I denied knowing anything about them. After being transferred to the Juvenile Home, the police would come and question us every few days. They came to the conclusion I had taken them without letting Stock and Stanley know about it. Failing to get the address of my friend, they asked Stock. Having taken Stock to this friend several times, they received the address from him and found the rings there.

Held at the Juvenile Home, pending trial, scheming on how to escape from here, I finally found a way out. Being separated from Stock, I couldn't let him in on it, so with the help of another boy we forced two screen locks and escaped by way of the fire-escape on Armistice Day, 19—; two days before I was to appear in court. Reaching my home unmolested I snuck into the house, put on some other clothes, and slept in a hayloft above a stable nearby. The next day I went to the friend, who got in trouble on my account. Hearing that they had to go to court with me, I was told I would get them into more trouble if I wasn't there. Hating to cause them trouble, I let them turn me over to the police, and saved a lot of trouble. At court the following day, I found the rings I had taken were valued at $3400.00. For this I was sentenced to St. Charles again, but managed to escape a few days before my transfer.

In this escape, seven of us boys got away, Stock, myself, and five others. Whether Stanley was in this I don't recall. Using the hayloft for a bedroom we stayed away from home about a week. We sent the different kids we knew to find out if the cops were looking for us. Finding the coast was clear, we used the utmost caution in approaching the house. Not wanting to take any chances, I would send some kid to see if the cops were at the house waiting for me. Being told no one was there, I would come in through the alleyway because the entrance to the house was the nearest from here. Knowing if the police came it was usually at night, I was always ready to flee at the first knock on the door. Half of the time I slept with my clothes on.

Picking up the string where the police broke it, we continued our burglaries, and began breaking into stores as well as houses. A fellow named Shorty and myself broke into a tavern about two o'clock in the morning. Getting what cash was left in the till, we made ourselves a collection of the best wines, liquors, and cigars. Having come into possession of several skeleton keys, we found one of the keys opened the side door of this tavern. Locking the door again, we waited until the place closed before we made our entrance. On the way out we spotted the telephone box where the nickels, dimes, and quarters were held. Not wanting to leave that, we jerked it off the wall. In doing so the owner heard the noise in the adjoining room. Working in the dark, we wrapped the stuff, including the telephone box, into a bunch of newspapers. With the bundles under our arms, we got as far as the door, when the lights were snapped on, and the owner pointed a gun at us. Making us sit down in one of the booths, he called the police. Late that afternoon, we were taken before a judge in a sideroom. Because the fellow got his things back, we were let go with a promise to be good boys. It was a lucky thing they didn't know I had run away from the Juvenile Home.

Meeting Stock, I told him about my experience. Having had some experience with the police, I began to look at them as enemies of my freedom, and when in their vicinity I was always ready to run at their slightest movement in my direction. A few days after Christmas, we went out to a wealthy section of Chicago. Entering a first-floor flat, we found clothes, cigars, whiskey, and another telephone coin box. On the way out we ran into a bunch of boys standing in front of the house. While on their way to see the boy who lived in this flat, they watched us enter through the rear. Getting more boys they surrounded the front and rear entrances. Coming out the front way, we ran into the boys in front. Stopping us at the front of the building, they asked what we were doing there. Not wanting to answer them, we told them to mind their own business. Since keeping steady company with Stock I had many fights while with him, because he would get tough with anyone who got fresh, and I would have to back him up. Though outnumbered by more than two to one, we fought against odds before. Telling them where they could go, we started walking, when one of the older boys said to grab us and hold us while he got the rest of the boys. The three of us having had many such fights, fought free of these boys. Knowing that more help was coming, we knew to stay was to get caught. This place being on H—— Avenue we ran south on H—— Avenue to W——

Avenue. Here we ran in different directions as there were a dozen boys chasing us. Running at top speed, we gained a little lead in the three-block run before separating.

On separating, I ran west to the first alley. Running south here, I began to lose the boys chasing me. Running through alleyways and yards, I shook off all but one tall fellow of nineteen, who stuck on like glue. Tiring out from the hard run, I sought a hiding place. The neighborhood wasn't as dense as it is today. Buildings were in small clusters of mostly two-story apartments, and the clusters a block or so apart. Because it had snowed recently, my tracks were easy to follow. Losing the big boy, and being winded, the only place of concealment I could find was the rear porch of one of the apartments. Finding a place on the second floor, I caught my second wind. If I happened to be seen now, I would have the advantage over my pursuer.

The cards must have been stacked against me. No sooner had I found this spot than the lady of the house saw me on her porch. She opened the door, and inquired as to my business. Watching the alley for signs of approaching pursuers, I tried to tell the lady that I was playing "it," and was trying to avoid being seen. While speaking to the lady the fellow I had lost followed my footprints in the snow to the house where I was hiding.

He told the lady he had been chasing me all over town, and that I had robbed a flat. Being a conscientious lady she called the cops, while I tried to talk my way out of this. But, I was held by this fellow until the police came. This fellow holding me was too big and powerful to fight, weighing about 200 pounds and standing six feet four. The police drove me to their district station and locked me up.

I was grilled and questioned all day but I admitted nothing. While being questioned, some cop recognized me as being over at his station before his transfer here. What he did was tell the officers who I was and who I worked with. Of course I didn't know this. Knowing that I would never disclose the others' identity, they laid a nice trap and used me for bait. Knowing I would join Stanley Runcer and Stock at the first opportunity, they released me that evening, December 30th. Trailing me, they came in contact with a person who knew the three of us and most of our habits. However, figuring I had another lucky break, I slept at home that night. While looking for Stock the next day, I heard that he had gone to the I—— Theatre, a small show and swimming pool combined. Paying the show's admission charge, I stood in the long waiting line. Getting halfway to the ticket collector, I saw the same policeman standing near the collector, looking the people over. Unseen by them, I managed to reach the outer door and make myself scarce.

Meeting Stanley and Stock, I was told how they had been pointed out in the show by someone, but with the help of a kid who was with them, they made good their escape through the rear door. Although being seen in the act of leaving, they, nevertheless, made good their escape. Reciting our experiences during the past two days, we stayed away from most of our usual places, excepting a little restaurant in which we always ate. We never ate home.

After keeping out of sight most of the day, we decided to go go to the restaurant and eat. Entering the restaurant we sat down to eat. Stock ordered a hamburger sandwich, Stanley an egg, and myself a dish of homemade rice pudding. Although hungry for food, upon entering the restaurant, I got a depressed feeling as though something was wrong. Looking around, I saw nothing to cause this feeling. About half-way through with the eating, the door opened. In came a fellow I knew, but never spoke to, with the two policemen that had arrested me, and chased Stanley and Stock out of the show. Whispering "cops," I made believe I didn't know Stanley and Stock. Walking up to me they greeted me by name. I said, "Hello." Having lost what little appetite I had, I stood up, dropped a dime on the counter and started to walk out. Taking a short step or two I was asked to sit down, and not to be in such a hurry. The cops told me I had lots of time. Sitting down, one of the cops asked me who my friends were, sitting alongside of me. I disclaimed all knowledge, and stated I had seen them for the first time. Having been pointed out as to their identity, the cops had to have their fun also, by listening to the tall lies and stories about the great mistakes they were making. After listening to our lies they cut short the comedy and took us to their district station, where they found out about out Juvenile escape and St. Charles sentence.

Taken back to the Juvenile Home the authorities refused to be responsible for our detention, as we were hard to hold and were a bad influence on the other kids. Assuring them I would be sent to St. Charles in a few days, they consented to hold me. Taken to the Juvenile Home on the first of the month I went to the court on the fourth, and was remanded to the custody of the St. Charles authorities on the same day.

My first stay at St. Charles wasn't bad, as I avoided the drilling most of the time. This time I haven't any compliments to write about the place, as I received the full power of the system that was in vogue at this time. I also started my second term by putting out the wrong foot.

Here after less than two weeks, I tried to make an escape with two other boys. Some stool pigeon was let in on the attempt, and reported me to the housefather. Our plan being only in the first stage, I was given an hour squats. I had said a fellow could squeeze through one of the windows. This I mentioned to one of the boys who I figured would make the attempt with me. He mentioned this to his friend, and some other kid overheard it, and reported to the housefather. A few days later I was transferred back to the cottage I had been in my first time. With my transfer went the report about my attempt to escape.

After being assigned to his cottage, I was given a lecture by the housefather on my attempted escape, and told what he would do to me if I tried it on him. I didn't mind the lecture because we were all given one, but the way he spoke of my attempted escape and the punishment I would get gave me the impression that I was supposed to be too yellow to run away while in his cottage. After hearing this speech, I made up my mind to run away the first time I was given a chance. A week later I made friends with a boy who had run away several times before my first release. His name was Lester Thomas and he was from down state. Asking him if he wanted to go again, he said he did. I also asked if he had any ideas of how to escape. Stating he had, he mentioned that the officers' bath room was the easiest place to get out of in the cottage. There was a drainpipe running to the ground, and being on the second floor, we could slide down it to the ground. The windows of all cottages are fixed to a certain extent. The basement windows are either screened or barred. The first floor windows are fixed to open about four inches from the top or bottom. The windows on the top floor, being about 20 to 25 feet above the ground, opened all the way, as the height was a little too great for a boy to take a chance of jumping out. The doors were locked at all times.

I studied the place the next time I was outside and saw it was a safe means of exit. We planned our departure to leave the following evening shortly after eating our supper. After supper the following night, we left the dining room, where we were swabbing the waxed floor, walked upstairs into the officers' bathroom, bolted the door from the inside, and quietly opened the window. Then, getting a good hold on the drainpipe, Harry and I slid to the ground. . . . .

III

After our capture and return to St. Charles we were put in the punishment line for the day. Later we were marched back to the cottage with the rest of the boys on punishment. We then had to stand in the dining room and watch the boys eat their supper. After they ate supper, we were told to go to the basement where the housefather took personal charge of us. Stepping into a small sideroom he called us in one at a time. Being called first, he gloated over my capture. I was watching his hands most of the time, and was ready to duck when he moved his hands. He told me to step out for a moment and tell Lester to come in. After doing the same thing to Lester, I was called in again. Thinking I would get a beating sure this time, I would duck as before. But I was told to step out, and tell Lester to step in again and he kept this up until he lulled our fears, and made us believe he was only giving us a talk for our own good.

Thinking that we wouldn't get a beating I quit ducking when he moved an arm while talking to me. Seeing that he had us where he wanted us, he began to let go with fast, swinging hooks which made me see stars of every hue. Getting about four rounds of his boxing, in which I saw more colored stars than I knew existed, he felt satisfied that his punch still had a wallop, and with a smile he told us to go to the swab room, and for each one of us to bring out the heaviest swab there, which by the way, was plenty heavy. (A swab is a cloth-covered box, made out of heavy wood about twenty two inches long, one foot wide and five inches deep, filled with cement, which has a long, heavy handle used to swab the cottage waxed floors.) Getting one swab apiece, we were asked how far we had intended to go. Asking me, I said, "To Chicago." Lester said to his home downstate. Hearing this, he commanded us to place the swabs on our shoulders, and start running the length of the basement, and when we had figured we had reached our destination points, we were to keep running until we had run the same distance back. From 5:30 to 8:30 we ran continuously. Whenever we began to lag we received a blow across the seat of our pants, which made me grit my teeth in pain, but, nevertheless, I managed to find an extra burst of speed, which seemed to satisfy the housefather, as he didn't hit me again until my tired body began lagging again. Bedtime being 8:30 we were told to put our swabs down. Shoulder aching, and very tired, I knew this was one time I would appreciate a bed. Marching with the rest of the boys we undressed in the cloakroom and put our nightgowns on. We were marched into the dormitory and told to step out of line and stand before the captain's bed. We were told that the housefather had ordered him to have us stand up all night and not to let us sleep. How that man could punish! Tired, sleepy and exhausted, the night never seemed to end. While standing I would fall asleep and bounce my head against the wall when my neck would relax. After what seemed to be ages and ages the morning bugle was heard. The boys got up, made their beds, got dressed, and we marched down to the dining room and had our morning cereal and milk.

Being in the morning school, I went to school with the boys in my period. During the reading class I fell asleep and when it came my turn to read, I didn't know where the other fellow had stopped reading. For this I received a bawling out from this teacher, and another one from the geography teacher. When asked why I was falling asleep in school, I was afraid to tell her as I might receive more punishment for telling her. Coming closer to speak to me, I guess she could see I looked tired and sleepy, because quietly she said, "I can see you haven't had any sleep." Knowing she would cause friction if she reported me to the principal, she said nothing more. Ending the school period the boys marched back to the cottage. I had dinner with the rest and was put to work in the kitchen wiping dishes and scrubbing floors.

The kitchen jobs here are the worst in the cottage. Those who are acclaimed the bad boys are put to work here, and are beaten often as the kitchen is usually in charge of the biggest and toughest inmate, who is given permission to beat the boys, as are all other boy officers. Between the hours of 11:30 and 1:00 P.M. the boys stay in the cottage cleaning up the various sections each working day.

My housefather, having charge of the tool room, assigned Lester and me to his toolroom detail where he could watch us. We were assigned different periods; Lester worked in the morning and I in the afternoon. Marching to the toolroom with a few other boys who worked here, I was made to stand up all afternoon and it seemed an endless one. Being in his presence at all times, the housefather would gloat and throw wisecracks my way, by saying he would have me stand up again tonight. I knew, however, that if he would make me stand up that night I would have dove out the dormitory window into the snow, nightgown or no nightgown. I had already made up my mind as it was the only course left open. I don't know how I stood up under the punishment as long as I did.

We were allowed to eat supper with the rest of the boys. After this I went to the kitchen where I was assigned for the next six months. After cleaning up the kitchen I was given more punishment of carrying the swab, completing the journey I had started. After about an hour and a half we were told to put the swabs away. After putting the swabs away we were made to squat until bedtime. (Squats: A means of exercise providing it isn't overdone. Being overdone it becomes a punishment. In cases here, it is known as punishment. Before starting you have to join your hands at the back of your neck, holding your elbows back as far as possible, and keeping your body stiff, you bend your knees until you touch the back of your heels with the seat of your pants, straighten up, keeping your body and elbows straight all the time). Here you have to do these squats as fast as possible for an hour or more, and you are occasionally hit across your pants to warn you what to expect if you slow down. We squatted till bedtime.

Expecting to stand up again, I was surprised when the captain told us we could go to bed. This night passed all too quickly. . . . .

About six months later I again escaped and I caught an early morning cattle train bound for Chicago, and got home in time to watch the people rush to work, and also early enough to have a bite of breakfast at home. I managed to stay away for a month in which time I pulled a couple of burglaries and some jail breaks. Stock being in the can, I worked mostly alone. After arriving home I had heard that my two younger brothers were placed in another orphan home. I resolved to get them out and went there the following visiting day, and did. I did not wish to let them run loose and get picked up, so I took them along on a few burglaries the next day. Having prowled six places without getting much cash, I entered the seventh one by using a skeleton key on the rear door. While upstairs prowling around the lady of the house came home. Still prowling, we heard the phone ring once and stop. Thinking it rather odd, I excused it as a wrong telephone number. Shortly after this we heard the lady call upstairs. Getting no answer, she heard us scampering around, trying to get out. She then called the police. While calling, one brother went out the back door, and the other got frightened and ran to the attic. Not wishing to leave him here, I ran after him, telling him to follow me, but he was too scared. Opening a roof window, I saw no means of escape here, and knowing that precious time had flown I told him to hide here until dark. Starting down, I got as far as the kitchen door, when the lady of the house stuck a gun in my back. A few seconds later the police arrived. In searching the house, the police found my other brother hiding behind a trunk. At the station, my brother was released to my father to be returned to the orphanage. I was found out as a run away from St. Charles.

Being allowed to walk in the corridor of the cell-block, I schemed a way of getting out by going into my cell and pretending I was closed in. I noticed that many policemen came through the outer door. Letting them think I, the only prisoner, was locked in, they would leave the outer door open. Using this psychology it worked as I knew it would. Early the next morning a policeman came in leaving the outer door open, and when he saw I was locked in he paid no attention to me. Waiting until he went into the next room, I opened my door gently, and after getting out of here, I ran like hell to the nearby "L," snuck in and rode home. While walking home, I met several fellows I knew reading a newspaper. Rather surprised in seeing me, they asked when I had gotten out of jail. Asking what they meant, they showed me a piece in the newspaper stating I had been picked up and arrested yesterday. Reading it myself, I stated it was a mistake of some kind because it couldn't be me as I was here as they could see. Knowing I couldn't go home now, I got myself a furnished room and slept there.

A week after this I was picked up by the police who were looking for me. Taken to the Juvenile Detention Home I escaped again by way of the linen room. Knowing I would eventually be arrested I prepared to have some tool which I could use for this means. Having a belt with a hollow center, I secreted a hack-saw in it, and when I was arrested and shaken down my belt escaped detection. Knowing the hours that the linen room was open, I hid myself. Having made but light repairs of the damage I had done on my last escape from here, it was an easy matter to cut through a link of the chain that had been placed to hold the screen shut, and by cutting the chain, I made good my third and last escape. . . . .

IV

During this last stay at St. Charles I began hating guys like my housefather, and places like this where they treated boys so mean. When I left, I left with a hatred for this place. On my first release I felt no resentment such as this. The day I left I was glad to leave, but I didn't have the happy feeling I had the first time. With the month I had been gone when I escaped, I spent a total of twenty-five months my second time here. During my second stay here, Stock and Stanley Runcer had been arrested on a big jewelry burglary, and were both here in St. Charles at the time I left.

Before leaving this place, I had worked myself up to the highest officer in rank, and was in charge of the kids, having things fairly easy. I still wish to go down in stating that the system at St. Charles is too strict and a detriment in the correction of growing boys.[9] If given more play, more competitive sports, proper and

[9] Delinquent boys present widely different descriptions of St. Charles School in their life-histories. Some boys write favorably of the institution while others are very belligerent and emotional in their condemnation of the institution and its administration. Edward's description indicates what the school meant to him and while that is important with reference to his behavior it does not follow that others would describe the institution in the same way. In fact there is considerable variation not only among the reactions of the five brothers to their experiences in St. Charles, but also between the reactions of the brothers and the reactions of many other inmates. In turn there is a wide disparity between the descriptions of the institution given by inmates and descriptions of the institution given by employees, officials, or visitors.

But the final verdict on the effectiveness of St. Charles or any other training or correctional institution must be stated in terms of its effect upon the subsequent behavior of its inmates rather than in terms of their adjustments during incarceration or the favorable or unfavorable comments made about the institution after release. The autobiographies of Edward and his brothers, in contrast with the autobiographies of other former inmates, indicate that these brothers reacted much more favorably to the institution than do a large proportion of the boys. Yet four of the five brothers continued in crime after their release. This indicates that no permanent modifications were effected in their behavior; in short it indicates that the correctional school did not modify their well-developed tendencies to engage in delinquency. It is probable that no correctional institution should be expected completely to redefine and redirect tendencies which are so well defined and well developed as the tendencies toward delinquency that were exhibited in the Martin brothers. Their delinquencies were a product of attitudes and habits which had been in the process of formation over a long period of time, so that it would be expected that their modification would likewise be a long and tedious process. Moreover it is possible that the training might have been more effective if it had been followed by some consistent after-treatment through which the brothers were assisted in making an adjustment outside of an institution. But such assistance was not furnished and four of the brothers continued to engage in criminal activities.

short talks, illustrations of bad boys, and how they are given long terms in the penitentiary, much will be done towards correcting juvenile delinquents. If shown the difference in the amount of the value of what they had stolen, the number of years they must stay for the offense, and the amount they could have earned in the time they spent in jail, plus loss of freedom and good times—if the boys could be taught these things it will save the state and the public a lot of trouble in caring for boys who will be sent to another institution later on. After all, St. Charles is a reform school, set up for the correction of juveniles, and not as a penitentiary, as the officers here are making it. St. Charles needs more kind and understanding housefathers—not mostly a bunch of farmers who think themselves as kings and lords, who are glad to have landed the job. The months that a kid spends here are more than enough to teach, show, and illustrate the evils of later life. The kids are good pupils, and in this early stage of a kid's life, he remembers things which either make him a good or bad citizen.

On leaving St. Charles I lost the rosy outlook about life. I had a subconscious feeling that I was going to make somebody pay for the treatment I had received here. I had no intentions of behaving myself, and I didn't have any intention of quitting my burglaries. Having exchanged stories with boys about their causes of being here, I learned to be more careful in the future. Being seventeen years of age I knew I would be taken to the County Jail if I were caught again, as I had passed the age of sixteen, which was the limit of the Juvenile Home.

Making friends with the older boys I knew, I made no attempt to commit any burglaries until I had a market for some article which would make me some money.

[After committing one burglary, Edward went to California. While there he was arrested and turned over to a representative of the Chicago Police Department. Edward's own description has been presented in chapter iv, page 79.]

Finding the cop a sound sleeper, I knew I could get away when I chose. Seeing the western towns were so many miles apart, the country sparsely settled, and the risk of capture too great, I bided my time. On the third night of the ride, we began hitting towns closer together. Having followed our course by watching the towns on a railroad map, I saw we were entering the state of Kansas. Knowing the time was ripe to leave, I waited until the wee hours of the morning, when folks sleep the soundest. When the train made periodical stops for lunch, I looked over the cars for a means of escape. At the end of each car, opposite the lavatory, I noticed a small window with a bar mounted on the outside above the window. Studying the distance to the top of the car, I knew I could swing myself on top, as I was pretty active, and had done things much more difficult. Hearing the next stop would be K——, some hundred and fifty odd miles away, I knew my time had come, as the train was due in Chicago that night, and by the time the train hit K—— the cop would be wide awake, and my last chance gone. On getting up I had to step over his outstretched legs to reach the aisle. Successful in this, I made believe I wished to use the lavatory. Watching the cop out of the corner of my eye, I saw him sleeping. Holding a hand across my stomach as if I had cramps, I walked to the lavatory. Getting out of sight of the few people watching me, I quickly opened the small window opposite the lavatory. Reaching up, I grabbed hold of the bar above the window, climbed out and stood on the sill. I managed to force the window down to a few inches of closing, to cover my means of exit. Getting a good grip on the bar, I swung myself to the top of the car. Being four cars back of the engine, I ran the car tops to the engine tender. Occasionally I glanced over the car tops to see if I had been followed, although I knew I was pretty safe here. I was taking no chances, because what I did others could also do.

While riding the freights west, I had learned to balance myself on the tops of moving and swaying freight cars; so running the tops of this train was no trouble. A short time later I noticed the train was slowing down. Looking about in the dark, I saw coal and water chutes. Knowing that this was the reason for the reduced speed, I got off when the train stopped. Spotting a bunch of coal cars about a hundred feet away I ran towards them. Climbing on one, I took a position overlooking the train. Watch-

ing the passenger cars carefully, I saw someone get off, using a
flashlight. The flashlight gave indications of the owner looking
for someone, and being in a hurry about it. Who it was I wasn't
sure, but from all indications, I figured it to be the policeman I
had left.

The area in which the train made the stop was rather desolate,
and I had no intention of missing this train, cop or no cop.
Keeping my eye on the flashlight and the train I soon lost sight
of the flashlight going in the opposite direction. I heard the engineer give the highball but I still sat quiet and waited for the first
chug of the engine. Being quite close I knew I could catch it
even though these passenger trains pick up speed mighty fast.
Hearing the chug, I ran for the tender, jumped on, and stayed
there till the train slowed down when it came to the Kansas City
yards. I jumped off and laid down close to the tracks which pre-
vented me from being seen by the people in the cars passing
above me. After the train passed, I stood up and looked at it.
I saw the conductor get off his seat on the rear platform, and
hurriedly enter the car. Leaving there in a hurry, I made my
way to the other end of town, where I bought myself something
to eat and caught another freight to Chicago. Having caught a
hot shot, I got into Chicago early the next morning.

Knowing I was hot, I stayed at a friend's place. Occasionally I would send a boy to my home to inquire if the police had
been there. Although I knew I wasn't guilty of the charge I had
been brought back on, I expected to be framed into jail on
my past record with Stock. After staying away for a week, I
figured I was pretty safe. Going home one morning, I found the
coast clear. On entering the house, however, I had a very strong
feeling that the policeman I had escaped from would be over that
night. My feeling was as strong as if the policeman had told me
himself. Just how I knew this, I don't know. Preparing myself a
hide-out for this occasion, I felt pretty secure. When bedtime
came, I took off my shoes and layed across the bed, with my
clothes on. About one o'clock the knock came and I knew who it
was. Picking up my shoes, I crawled into my hide-out, just in
time as the door was opened a little too soon. While hiding, I

heard the tread of heavy feet walking about from room to room looking for me. My hide-out was a sub-basement underneath my bed, where a cover of linoleum concealed the opening. Coming into the bedroom I had just left, I heard him questioning my younger brothers as to where I had gone. I heard him say he knew I was here because the lady in front had seen me here and told him. Having expected him, as I have stated, I told the members of my family to say that they had not seen me for three months and to stick to it. Questioning and threatening got him nowhere, so with an angry attitude he finally left the house. Even after he left I stuck to my hide-out, as I didn't wish to take any chances of him spying through the window and seeing me.

After feeling sure that he had left for the night, I came out of hiding, undressed and went to sleep. Though staying at home, I was very cautious in approaching or leaving the house. I would send some one out to make sure no cops were around before I left my home, and I also had somone go to my home to make sure no cops were waiting for me when I came back.

After I had escaped from the policeman and came back to Chicago, I made the rounds of my friends' homes, and told them I had escaped from the cops. I inquired if the cop I had run away from had been around inquiring for me. Hearing he hadn't, as yet, I said to tell him, if he came, that they had not seen me for several months. Expecting the cop to come around inquiring about me, and not wishing to be caught, I made up a signal with my friends, which was to let me know if I had a clear coast. If I got no answer to my signal, they were out, or the cop was there.

About a week after this I went out on my first burglary since coming back.[10] I had an order for some silk shirts and as I was

[10] The results of studies of success and failure of boys who have been treated in juvenile courts, behavior clinics, and correctional institutions indicate that the results of these types of treatment which have been observed in the case of the Martin brothers are not unusual. In a follow-up study of boys who were treated in the Boston Juvenile Court and the Judge Baker Foundation Behavior Clinic, Sheldon and Eleanor Glueck found that 88.2 per cent engaged in additional delinquency or crime within a five-year period (Sheldon Glueck and Eleanor T. Glueck, *One Thousand Juvenile Delinquents* [Cambridge: Harvard University Press, 1934]). Healy and Bronner found that 72 per cent of the boys released from St. Charles

pretty broke, I went out on a prowl. Spotting an easy place on the second floor, with an open window, I walked up the stairs, used my pass-key on the rear porch door, and got in. Having spotted the place from the alley, I had walked to the front first and rang this apartment's bell. Getting no answer I got in through the rear door. While going through all the rooms and closets I found a new suit of clothes, just made for me. Taking the new suit, a pair of new shoes (my size), six silk shirts, some socks, and some jewelry, I wrapped all the stuff into two bundles and left. After I left, I took a street car, which brought me in the vicinity of a home of a friend. I got off on the spur of the moment and went to the vicinity of their home. Finding a hiding place, behind a post in the alleyway, I began tossing small pebbles against the wooden balcony of the third floor where they lived. I would toss a pebble and then hide behind the post, watching the rear porch for my answer; a sign of O.K. or run. Waiting a minute or two, I received neither. Thinking I had thrown too lightly, I threw another stone. Hiding again I waited.

I knew that someone was always at home this time of day and couldn't understand why I received no answer. Thinking that I had not hit the boards the right way to have the sound carry into the house, I threw more pebbles. After throwing between ten to fifteen stones, I couldn't understand why I received no answer. It was too early in the day to take any chances of going home and being seen. I finally decided to go up to the house anyway. I knew where the key was hid and I had access to the place. While creeping upstairs, I tried to figure where my friends might have gone. Knowing that some of the day was spent with a neighbor downstairs, I accepted this as the solution of getting no answer. With the two bundles under my right arm, I crept up the stairs to their door where I stood and listened for signs of life. Not hearing any, I took hold of the doorknob with my left hand and

School for Boys likewise continued their careers in crime (William Healy and Augusta F. Bronner, *Delinquents and Criminals* [New York: Macmillan Co., 1928]). Their general findings were substantiated by a more recent unpublished study of the subsequent records of boys released from St. Charles made by O. G. Connerton of the State of Illinois Division of Pardons and Paroles.

turned it very slowly and quietly. I had done this quiet entry stuff several times and had managed to sneak in unheard, sneak up on my friends, and then scare them. Having this in mind, I turned the knob to its full extent, and I walked in. Still holding the doorknob, and keeping my eyes on it, I released the knob slowly, watching it intently for signs of noise. Standing within the doorway, I looked up.

Looking into the house, I received one of the greatest surprises of my life. I had entered so quietly that I was unheard. Looking up, I caught the eyes of the policeman turning to look my way. Catching sight of each other at the same time, we stood frozen like statutes. My hand on the knob, a bundle of clothes under each arm, I just stood there, staring popeyed at him, and he doing the same. Having run into each other so unexpectedly and catching sight of each other at the same time, the surprise was so great and we apparently so shocked each other that we were unable to move. He was seated in a chair, to the left of the door. He just sat there, his eyes bulging out at me. I was first to break the trance. I jumped back, slamming the door. I tossed my bundles on the porch and went down the three flights with the speed of a scared rabbit. I didn't want to run out of the alleyway or gangway between the houses because he could see me there and I would become an easy target. Not wishing to give him a chance to shoot me, I looked for a place to hide, on reaching the basement. Knowing the landlord lived in the basement flat, and was hard of hearing, I ran to his door. I had a good two-story lead on the copper. I found the door unlocked. Closing the door, I saw a dark bedroom, where I walked into and hid. Hearing the heavy, loud noise on the stairs, I listened to the approach of the copper's steps to the door I had just come in. Knocking at the door, I saw a lady come from the front room and open the door. I heard the cop asking the lady if anyone had come that way. While speaking to her I could see him looking around the room, holding a pistol in his hands. Being assured no one was here he went about his hurried search. Hiding here until I was sure I wouldn't be caught, I slipped out through a side window into the building next door; then hid myself in another basement until darkness came. Although I left my hiding place, I did not return home. Having made some money that day, I rented a furnished room and slept here until I was caught a week or so later.

I spent the money I had received for the shirts (which I had retrieved the following day) and I put on my new suit and went out to make some more money. Going to the northwestern part of the city, I espied a combination home and dentist office. Having the appearance of being closed for the day, I went to the front door. This I found locked. Being too conspicuous, I went around to the rear. The rear porch was rather conspicuous, too, but not the basement door. Being screened by the stairs, I tried my passkeys. I opened the lock and found the door bolted from the inside. Seeing that this was the only way I could get in without being seen, I forced the door in by bracing my back against the wall and feet against the door. I forced the door at its hinges and shoved the door out of my way and walked upstairs. There I spotted a monkey wrench on the way up and took it along as a handy article for protection, or for breaking whatever needed breaking. Seeing a bulldog watching me, I made friends with him. In the dining-room cupboard drawers I found $21.00 in bills. Putting the money in my pocket I heard someone at the front door. When I got to the basement door, I heard the door open just as I closed mine. Because I let the door click in closing, I was heard. After running through the basement and out the back, I heard this fellow coming after me. Since it was a sparsely settled district I was seen by him while running. He yelled and I knew he had spotted me and I began going to town. Reaching a long two-story building about a hundred feet away, I tried to lose him here. It was unsuccessful and saw it was to become a race where the one who ran the fastest and the farthest would be the winner.

Being mostly open prairie, without bunched houses, I began running for the railroad tracks, some half a mile from here, with about a thirty-yard lead, I increased it to about seventy-five yards in the next quarter-mile. Tiring out, I began to lose my lead when I neared the railroad. I was puffing like a locomotive but I kept up a jogging run, trying to catch my second wind.

Seeing I could never crawl up the railroad with him a few yards behind, I tried to scare him away. I picked up a stone and waited for him to get closer. Coming within ten yards of me, I told him to beat it or I'd bounce a rock off his dome. Saying, "Don't you dare," he came for me anyway. Because I did not wish to knock his brains out, I tossed it in the direction of his feet, hoping to scare him. While watching him approach, I could see that he was puffing worse than I. Having had a short rest, my second wind was coming back. My only recourse was to run in the direction of a tenanted section, and lose him. I ran over a fourth-of-a-mile and gained a lead of over a hundred yards. When I got to within a block of the section I was running for, I heard this fellow yell for help, when he espied two men coming in the direction I was running. Hearing his yells of "Catch him! Thief!" they began chasing me. After chasing me a couple of blocks, they caught me when I stumbled and fell over the bumpy ground. Holding me, they waited until my pursuer came up puffing. On stating I had broken into his home, one of the fellows who caught me flashed his badge, stating he was a government officer and would take me to the police.

Because I failed to bribe him with some of the money I had stolen, I was turned over to the police. Using an alias, I escaped recognition until the following day, when I was recognized by the two policeman who had had me here sometime back. At every change of shifts I was brought out of my cell, and made to walk up and down the room of the station before all the policeman lined up at roll call. If anyone recognized me he would speak up and say so. Two in plain clothes did. Running under an alias, I stated that they were mistaken. I had a fairly good alibi and had them guessing. I didn't fall into their little traps and, after three days of detention, they decided to take me to the address they said I lived and prove I was the fellow they had a couple of years back. The more they saw me, the surer they were of having had me before.

So three days later, they put me in one of the private squad cars, and drove to my address, where I was recognized by a little boy. When we got home, one officer got out of the car with me.

We walked into the yardway to our flat and a little fellow in the yard saw me approaching. On coming close to him he said, "Hello, Eddy." The police, hearing this, said to the boy, "Do you know him?" I shook my head at the kid "No," but the kid said, "Sure. That's Eddy. He lives here," pointing to our flat. The policeman with a smile of satisfaction, and I, with a fallen face, walked to the door of my home, where we were admitted by my mother. My mother being unable to understand the English language, the policeman learned little here. We returned to the station and an officer who could speak the same language as my mother was sent to talk with Ma. When he returned he had all the dope he needed about me, and the news that another officer was looking for me. They checked up and then transferred me to another district for safekeeping until the sergeant I had escaped from came and had me transferred to his district.

I was put in the patrol wagon, and handcuffed to two policemen and the sergeant had his gun in his hand pointing it in my direction. Having escaped him so many times, he was afraid I would do a "houdini" on the way to his district, and wasn't taking any chances with me. We arrived without mishap, I was placed in a cell, a policeman stationed to watch me the rest of the day and night, and taken to court the next morning. I was brought to the Boys' Court and found guilty of burglary, and tried in the criminal court about two months later. The charge, on which I had been brought back from California, was thrown out when my letter to Stock was read.

I secured a good attorney, of high political standing and won my freedom after several months of waiting at the County Jail.[11] The judge, having heard of my escape from the sergeant who came to my trial, got a good big laugh when I was told to repeat my escape in the court room. He asked the sergeant a few questions,

[11] This is the closest that any of the brothers came to participating in any aspect of organized crime. For the most part they ran their own risks, took their own profits, and assumed their own losses. There is no evidence that they ever "beat a rap," or that they ever succeeded in fixing a case, or that, with one exception, they ever had a good lawyer to represent them, any one of which might have been indicative of important connections with highly-organized adult crime or the criminal rackets.

laughed some more, which made the sergeant red in the face. Having been discharged, I bumped into the sergeant in the corridor, where he told me he would get even with me for this.

After being placed on adult probation at the age of seventeen, I went home. Having nothing to fear, I tried to find a job. I had no luck, but kept looking for a month. One day when I was answering an ad in the paper, I ran into William Sloan and Earl Wooms at the place where I went for the interview. Since we didn't get a job, we walked out together. Since we had met in St. Charles, being in the same cottage, we exchanged tales as to what happened since we last saw each other. Telling each other where we lived, we made dates to meet the following day to look for work.

Having no success in getting jobs, we began discussing ways and means of getting some money as we were all broke.[12] All of us having burglary experience, we decided to break into a place the next day. Over-sleeping that night I missed my appointment with them. Hoping they had waited I dressed hurriedly, and went to where I was to have met them. I found they had gone. Walking about the neighborhood, I met Joseph Wyman, who I also knew from St. Charles. Telling him I had missed my date with Sloan and Wooms, he said he wanted to come in with us. Meeting them that evening, I told them about Wyman and what he had said. We all agreed to let Wyman in with us, and went to his house to tell him.

Going up north in a bunch, we were chased by someone in plain clothes. Four of us were too noticeable, so we worked in pairs. Going north with William Sloan we entered an apartment by breaking a small hole in a window. Having a better idea of values and a greater means of disposing of stolen articles, I took a fur coat which I knew could be sold for a nice sum. When we split up our spoils, I took the fur coat as a share of my end.

[12] One of the inherent limitations of institutional treatment is that the individual is eventually returned to the situation in which he originally became delinquent. Here he associates either with his former companions in delinquency or with persons whom he became acquainted with while in the institution. When Edward accidentally met some of his friends from the reformatory the major interest they had in common was criminal behavior.

Finding a market through Joseph Wyman I sold it for a hundred dollars, and gave Wyman twenty for getting the sale. Having enough to last awhile, I quit going out, and began running around with Wyman. Running around with Wyman I was taken to my first brothel house, where I sowed my first wild oats at eighteen.

About ten days after selling the coat, Earl and William Sloan were arrested prowling a policeman's home. The officer, coming home, saw them through the window. Dashing in suddenly, he seized Earl while William made a getaway. They beat Earl up and he confessed the name of his partner, his address and all he knew about Wyman and I. Laying a trap, they caught William coming home, and recovered about eight hundred dollars of stolen merchandise. Although they had nothing on me, they nevertheless were looking for me. William Sloan refused to implicate me. Working through a stool pigeon in the neighborhood, the police lay a trap for Wyman and myself. Having been with Wyman until late, I slept at Wyman's home. While sleeping there, I had a dream of the police, and on waking up, I had the funniest premonition of danger if I went to my neighborhood. Wyman wanted to go to his girl's house who lived near my home. When I told him about my dream, he ridiculed me for telling him such stories. I let him talk me into going along but I kept a lookout for the police. Getting to his girl's house safely, I sat in a chair while he talked with his girl. We sat there for about ten minutes and heard a Model T horn in the alleyway. Seeing who it was, I didn't answer it, as I had no use for the owner of it.

Although he did me no harm, I didn't like this fellow. He was a sneaky looking person whom I knew as a stool pigeon. Though I knew him, and he knew me, I never spoke to him, unless necessary. He blew the horn some more and called my name. Hearing him call, I told Wyman to answer, as I didn't care for his company. Wyman walked out to his car, spoke to him a few minutes, and came back, stating that the fellow had something important to tell me. I told Wyman to tell him I wasn't interested. Wyman returned with another statement that it was important for me to see him. Still refusing to go, Wyman said he would go with me to hear what could be so important. I walked to the car in the alley and asked what was so important. The first thing he asked was, "Have you a gun?" I asked him why he said that and he told me of a grocery store where there was only an old man about seventy years old running it. As I listened to him, I thought to myself, "A guy like him is just the type to take advantage of an old man at the point of a gun, and at that I doubted if he had enough courage to even do that alone." Hearing his story, which I figured was phony, I stated I had no gun and didn't hold people up, and wouldn't even try holding up an old man who was trying to get along. I refused his offer of letting me in on his tip and I started to leave, when he pleaded with me to look the place over for him and let him know what I thought of it.

Although I didn't want anything to do with him, I let Wyman talk me into going for the ride anyway. Getting into the back seat with Wyman, I said there was something phony about this. I knew him as the sneaking, ratting type, not to be trusted. The reason soon became apparent. It was a frame-up. He had been watching my movements and, being a cops' stool pigeon, he had reported the coat incident. Having planned a trap, intending to catch or shoot me holding up a store, the police were waiting in their car at the head of the alley, ready to follow his car. After getting me into the car and hearing me say something was phony, he drove in the direction opposite the one he was told to take by the police. The police noting the change of direction, overtook his car, and at the point of pistols Wyman and I were taken to their car and driven to the detective bureau.

Upon being questioned about the fur coat, I denied all knowledge of ever having had one. Going to work on Wyman they got all the dope they needed. One poke at Wyman's jaw and he told everything. He even took them to the party who bought the coat. When they showed me the coat, I denied ever having seen it. After eleven days of seeing the coat, and then their Gold Fish (Third Degree), I still denied seeing the coat. The Gold Fish was their term for taking me into a fairly large room, where I was questioned and beaten—mostly beaten. Using systems of being kind one time then beating me the next, I still denied having seen the coat. The police gave up beating me, and booked me. I was booked for burglary, indicted by the grand jury, and held at the county jail pending trial. At trial, Sloan who was sentenced with Wooms on other burglaries said he had stolen the coat and given it to me to sell for him. On his statement, my charge was changed, and I was sentenced from one to ten years at the reformatory for receiving stolen property. I stayed at the county jail two weeks after being sentenced until they had a bunch of fifteen boys before transferring us. The police handcuffed us three to four in a bunch and we were piled into a paddy wagon, driven to the Chicago and Alton station, and under the care of armed guards placed aboard a train. . . . .

V

On being paroled, I was promised a job with a cab company as a clerk. Arriving home, I visited my sponsor who promised me the job. I was instructed where and when to go to work. I reported for work on the day set and worked here for five months, until my brother James who had been committed to St. Charles, escaped and came home. While taking him to a place in the suburbs of Chicago we were stopped and locked up on suspicion. Finding me a parolee, the cops tried to frame a larceny of an automobile charge on me. Failing to make it stick, they got in touch with the parole office, who sent me back to the reformatory as a violator of my parole, because I had left the city limits. I had understood when I left the reformatory that I could go anywhere in the county.

On my return to the reformatory, I was given my same number back, followed the same routine the other new boys do, and did the same work at the tailor shop as I did before my parole. For this violation, I stayed here twenty-two months before I received another parole. Being released this time, the sponsor said I would have to find my own job. Being unable to account for all of the past five years, or supply satisfactory references, I didn't land any job, excepting one that was temporary. Getting discouraged by not being able to land a job, I began hanging around with petty stick-up men who held up anyone or anything that was easy. Never having any liking for holding up people, I turned down several offers of being in on a heist. These fellows were what is known as the dancehall type. Most of their evenings were spent at a cheap dancehall in the neighborhood. Keeping their company, I began passing my time here, too. Though I knew nothing about dancing, I liked to listen to the orchestra. I always did like music. By keeping their company, I got into several fights in the dancehalls.

Some three months after my release, there was a big free-for-all in which we ran out a half dozen dagoes, because of their boasting and familiarity with some of the dancing teachers. A half hour later, one of the boys saw these fellows coming back with reenforcements. Seeing we were outnumbered a good two to one, we made a quiet exit. After this some of the fellows came here carrying guns. A few days later one of the boys carrying a gun was challenged to a fight. Thinking he had put the gun in his overcoat in the cloakroom, he placed it in mine instead. Our coats were of the same color and hanging close to each other. On leaving here, I placed the overcoat on my arm and walked home. The day had been mild. When I hung the coat up at home, I heard a heavy sound where the gun hit the wall. Investigating, I found the gun. Knowing whose gun it was, I tried to return it the following day. I was unable to see the owner and I brought the gun back home. Then, having several days of mild weather, I forgot about the gun. Some days later I got into a conversation with a friend about theatres and decided to see one with him. After picking a new theatre on the north side, I took a street car with him that evening. The weather being still fairly mild I carried the coat over my arm, forgetting that the gun was in the pocket. On the way home because I got tired of carrying the overcoat on my arm, I slipped it on. Fishing for cigarettes, I felt the gun.

Not wishing to get caught carrying a gun, we took a side street to the carline. When we got to within a block of the carline we were stopped by two plain clothes men. While talking to us they patted me around the pockets, and overlooked the gun. After shaking us down, we tried to talk them into letting us go. This they refused, and said we would have to go to the station. Having the gun was no consolation. Although I knew how to use a gun, I didn't care to kill anyone and not being a killer, I was in a quandary. Having been ordered to walk to their call box, I was tempted to use the butt end on the cop's head closest to me. Night having fallen, I made up my mind to throw the gun to the ground at the first opportunity. But I made up my mind too late, as we passed the only open space of ground. Thus, missing the only opportunity of disposing of the gun, I was on the verge of using it at the call box. One policeman went to the phone to call the patrol wagon; the other took up a position to the left of us, my partner being in the center.

As I knew I would be sent back to the reformatory if I were caught with a gun, I figured my chance of getting away was now or never. Having watched for my chance, I slid my hand into my pocket. Pulling the gun out slowly I had just started saying, "Stick," when the policeman who was watching us stepped back getting my partner between us. Having just started the words of, "Stick 'em up," I cut short the words when I saw my chance fail. The policeman didn't know how close he was to a peaceful surrender or a gun battle. On entering the paddy wagon, I had no chance of hiding the gun here. Hoping to get locked up in a cell without another search was my last chance of disposing of the gun. I had no such luck. My partner did. He was locked in a cell and I was held out for questioning, and another shakedown. The funny part of the search was that they left the pocket in which I had the gun in till the last. Being the only pocket that wasn't searched, when the cop put his hand on the gun he was looking me in the face. As he felt the gun I could see his eyes bulge out a little. He was the cop that stepped back while at the call box. Pulling the gun out, the three other cops who were watching me saw it. Saying, "Why, it's a gun," they came close and took several swings at me, and knocked my hat from my head. On finding the gun, they rushed me into the captain's office for grilling. When asked about the gun I gave them a tall story and stuck to it.

I have never been a stool pigeon and I have never tried to get anyone in trouble when arrested. I had no intention of telling them who the owner of the gun was. I knew I would be sent back to the reformatory anyway. I tried my best to clear the fellow with me, but being in the company of a criminal like me went against him. Brought to the police court, I was given a year in the House of Correction, or, in other words, the Bridewell, as it is called. The parole officer had stated at my trial they didn't want me as a violator, and gave me the impression, and also the judge, that whatever the sentence he gave me, I wouldn't be returned to the reformatory. This was the second time I had trouble with the parole office. On the last parole violation I heard a bad report read to me at the parole board meeting. Why the parole officer lied about me I don't know. In his report he stated I never worked or never tried. On hearing that statement I proved it erroneous. At the police court they lied again as I soon found out on entering the Bridewell.

The Bridewell! What a dump this is! I never knew a place as filthy as this existed. I had been in jails and reform schools half of my life. Cleanliness had been the password. Here, it was the other way around. The first sight of this place speaks of filth. This place is a sore spot to the eye. A dismal place, inside and out. A place where cheery souls are made melancholy. The buildings were very old and falling apart. The cell house had no toilets, just pails and some of the odors you inhaled were enough to put you to sleep. Being what they called a wanted man (wanted as a parole violator at the reformatory), I was put to work in the tailor ship where they placed the wanted men and long timers. I got along with the guards here. I never had any trouble with them. If you are not looking for trouble, any inmate can get along any place he may be sent to, be it the Bridewell, Pontiac, or Joliet. The getting along part was a minor thing. Trying to get along with the filthy conditions here was another matter. The food here was the worst that I had ever tried to eat. I would be afraid to feed it to the pigs, let alone humans. If they had tried to feed us food like this at the reformatory there would have been plenty of trouble. Here, many of the fellows have but a few days or a few months to stay, and didn't mind the scummy food. Then again, most of those sent here were derelicts of mankind:

drunks, hopheads, and morons. Many of these living in gutters on the outside, didn't mind the change of gutters! There was no manhood left in them to revolt against conditions here. The few who have a year or more to stay are too few in number to demand better food. Therefore, the conditions will always remain as they are until this place rots to the ground. Washing in what reminded me of a horse trough, trying to down the lousy grub, carrying the toilet pail, through all of this, I managed to pull through the year. On leaving I looked like a bag of bones. After serving the year at the Bridewell, I was sure glad to get out of here. Happy to get away from the filth, the monstrous cockroaches, and the shadows of men. Getting among ablebodied and clean-living men was a pleasure. Just going back to the reformatory again was like going home.

I was given another paddy wagon ride, and transferred to the county jail where I waited two weeks for a transfer back to the reformatory. Having a little over eight months left to serve of my maximum sentence, I didn't mind. During the eight months at the reformatory I began thinking over my past life, wondering if I would end up like the derelicts at the Bridewell. The human wrecks I saw and spoke to had a great deal in making me change my ways, when I received my final discharge from the reformatory some eight months later.

On receiving a discharge I felt a free man. While on parole I was free also, but always under a strain. The parole is a bigger handicap than one can imagine. Although I hadn't stolen or burglarized since my first conviction to the reformatory, I seemed to fall into the hands of the police and having a record and being a parolee, I was given the extreme penalties. Should I have been lucky to have received a discharge instead of a parole, I firmly believe I would never have gone to jail again as a criminal offender. Parole was a handicap to me as they are to most fellows. I don't say this about everybody. Some, a parole helps to keep them out of trouble; some need parole supervision. The parole officers are always under the impression that you are still stealing, and never try to understand their wards, by either a cheery word or a pat on the back. To me, they seemed to carry a chip on their shoulders. Some may say I don't know what I am talking about. I'm only telling what it meant to me. If the parole system is here to stay, the officers appointed will find they will have less trouble with their boys by co-operating in a friendly manner instead of the methods they used with me.

Since leaving the reformatory with a discharge, I have never been in trouble. I have had many chances of making easy money. I still know a lot of fellows I did time with, and with whom I still speak. But, I've come to my senses. I knew crime never paid, but it took a long time before waking up to the fact. Being unable to find a job on my release, I managed to get a few odd jobs in the first two months. Looking about for opportunities, I found I could go to work for myself if I could borrow enough money. I was able to do this and have been working since that time.

CHAPTER X

THE LIFE-HISTORY OF JAMES MARTIN[1]

PREFACE

This story of my life is written so that folks may see the inside of my past, and not only the crust as I think they see it now. Although it may not help me in any way by writing this story, I hope that by knowing the facts and experiences of my life some interested persons may be able to help other children from erring as I have done.

I am now twenty-one years old. I have spent around ten or twelve of these years in various institutions in this state. I am not boasting when I make this statement. In fact, I feel ashamed to be able to say that I have spent half of my life in prison. I merely want to state that I think I have the qualifications to write a story of a boy's experiences in these institutions. This is the first time I ever wrote or tried to write any kind of a story, but I will try to express my thoughts as clearly as I can.

I

My father came to this country from somewhere in Central Europe, the exact location I do not know, sometime in the early nineteen hundreds. He was accompanied by my mother, whom he married there. The three children born in Europe have since died. I don't know of any difficulties he may have had as a kid as I never heard him talk about his life in the Old Country. My father never committed any crimes. His only contact with the

[1] James wrote the life-story presented in this chapter while he was incarcerated in the state reformatory. At the time of writing he had served about four years of a six-and-a-half-year term. The elaborate discussion of institutional life, much of which has been omitted, reflects both the situation in which the document was written and the fact that up to the time of writing James had spent very few years outside of training schools or penal institutions. The idea of a preface as an introduction to his life-story was his own. In addition to the document presented here James wrote some essays and descriptions of the life in his community, some of which are presented in other chapters.

police was as a disorderly conduct and a drunk. I don't know whether or not his brothers or sisters were ever in any difficulty of any kind. I have never seen any of them. Neither have I heard them mentioned. There was no insanity in my father's family that I know of. What the work his brothers and sisters were in was I do not know. I don't believe that my grandparents were in any trouble whatsoever but, of course, not knowing them, or ever having seen them, I cannot say for sure.

My father was a man about five feet, eleven inches tall. Outside of an insatiable appetite for liquor, he was an excellent man in every respect. Only on the demand of my mother did he ever beat us and then the beatings were deserved and only normally severe. He was never brutal with us kids. He was, now that I think of it, a little too lenient with us.

When sober he would talk and joke with us kids, give us pennies for candy and sometimes nickels for picture shows. My mother was the same, only more liberal. He always treated us fairly and did everything he could to prevent us kids from going wrong, but he was bucking the surrounding neighborhood and it was too strong for him. Our contacts and companions were stronger than his pleas. He often told us that the things we were doing would lead us into a lot of trouble from which we would not be able to extricate ourselves, but we were young and thought we were pretty smart and ignored his pleadings.

He was a quiet man and never spoke of himself or his people. My father had no steady trade or profession, but worked on and off at odd jobs. Sometimes he would have no work for a month straight. At the time of his death, he worked as a baker. He died at the age of forty-eight of organic heart disease. Now and then my father would work steadily for awhile and would give mother the whole pay envelope. I think it was at these times that my mother saved every penny she could for the hard days she knew would come. It was this money that pulled us over the hard bumps when my father got drunk and lost his job.

Although my father treated us kids pretty good, I think it was partly on account of him that all the boys in our family have been in prison and reform schools at times. Instead of being a good provider, he would squander almost all his money in saloons, giving only a small amount to my mother.

Mother married my father in Europe and came to this country with him. Since the death of my father she has longed for the country of her birth and the people she knew as a young girl. His death has caused her an awful lot of sorrow. My mother is about fifty-six years old now and is a small woman burdened by the cares that us boys have hanged upon her. She was continually under an apprehension as to where we were, what we were doing, and whether or not we would return home alive. With the exception of a half brother who lives in Chicago and is wealthy, owning three apartment houses, she has no relatives in this country. Around the neighborhood where we live are some people that she knows from the old country and her greatest pleasure in life is derived from her conversation with these people. It usually is about the old country and their younger days.

My mother is very religious and did everything in her power to make us attend church. My mother attends church every day. She sent us to the parochial school and would have liked to see us as altar boys. She tried this but, like the rest of the kids in the neighborhood, we thought more of good times than we did of church. Although not a very religious man himself, father compelled us kids to go to church as my mother wanted us to.

With only the little money my mother received from father, she tried hard to keep us well fed and presentable in appearance. As I think back of all the hardships and troubles my mother went through when I was a small child, I feel ashamed of myself for causing her more trouble by being the kind of a boy I was. I only hope that I may still be able to repay her for the sorrow and trouble I caused her. She was kind to me when I was small. Way back, since I can remember, she was always working, washing clothes, cleaning house, cooking, administering to our needs and so on. About the only diversion she took from work was to go to church. Later when we all grew older, she went out visiting to neighbors a little more.

She has given birth to five children since arriving in this country and has always had a good deal of trouble with us. The death of my father has placed a lot of sorrow in her heart and I don't believe she is as happy now as she should be. My mother never mentioned her family and we kids never asked questions about our parents' lives in the old country. We know that our grandparents on my mother's side are living as she used to send them money but other than that we knew nothing. I don't even know where they are living. She has spoken of bringing them to this country and would be very happy if this could be done but she has never been able to save the money necessary to have this done. My mother and her sisters and brothers never have been in any trouble. I remember her telling of this during the times when she was reprimanding us for our actions. She used to tell me about her sister but never mentioned her name. There was no insanity in the family that I know of.

Her one half brother is a fairly wealthy man, living in Chicago. He owns three apartment houses but refuses to quit his job. He is a large man possessing great strength and vitality. He drives a coal truck and is in a position to quit his job and live comfortably any day that he chooses. He is a strict man and very particular about the children's behavior. None of his family have ever been in any trouble whatsoever. He has never been in a jail of any kind. The only trouble that I know of is that he disowned his boy and has never relented that I know of. His mother forgave him but his father refuses to admit him to the home. Since the trouble with his father, the boy has traveled over the country, as a Marine, and has never spoken to his father since. The father gave him two thousand dollars when he disowned him. I don't know the occupation of any of the other members of my mother's family. There were no criminal actions on the part of my grandparents. I know this from things that I have heard my mother say. I don't know the exact part of the old country from which my mother came.

II

I was born on A—— and F—— streets near the railroad viaduct. The house was squalid looking and near a factory district. The older people of the neighborhood were foreign born and spoke the language of their mother country and taught it to their children. The people were mostly of the laboring class. Most of the men worked in the railroad yards and surrounding factories. Most of the men folk also were habitual drunkards. On pay days they would congregate on the corner saloon and squander most of their hard-earned money.

My earliest recollection is when I was four years old. We then lived on M—— Street right next to a lumber company. A boy by the name of Bob and his brother were my playmates. One day we were playing in the street. We started to race back to our yard, and I fell down the steps leading down to the yard and got a bloody nose. Another event I remember clearly was when my brother Carl was born. He is now seventeen years old, the youngest member in the family.

Another early incident I remember was when my mother was washing the family laundry. She had two big wash tubs filled with the clothes in the kitchen. As the wash tubs were on a stand I could not see what was in them. Curiosity overcoming me I started to climb the stand and just grasped the top of the wash tub when I overturned it, spilling all the clothes and water on top of me. Lucky for me that the water was not scalding hot. I was so frightened when this happened that I did not even complain when my mother undressed me and put me in bed. As I had no other clothes I had to stay in bed till my clothes dried.

Another event I remember clearly is the first time I went "fishing." I was about five years old. A bunch of boys went to the river near N—— Avenue and were fishing. A few younger boys and myself went to the river to watch the older boys fish. One of the older fellows caught a fish and gave it to me, while it was still alive. As I took the fish in my hands the scales bit into my flesh and I let go of the fish which fell into the water. As I dropped it, I made a grab to retrieve it again and I fell into the river myself. After I came up one of the older fellows caught me and dragged me onto the banks again.

The first present I had ever got was a pair of very small turtles given to me by a girl that lived above us. I kept these in an old bucket filled with water and some green weeds. I was then only four years old. I did not know how to care for these turtles properly and they died. I felt pretty bad about it and cried a long time over the loss of these pets of mine. (I call them pets for lack of a better name. They really were pets to me then.)

When I was about five or six years old, we moved on D—— Street. We were living there only a short time when my brother Michael was run over across the legs by an automobile. One of his legs was crooked a long time after that. When I was about seven years old my mother sent me to a parochial school. During the time I was attending this school, I started to be delinquent. I got acquainted with a number of boys my age and a few years older, who skipped school and stole around the neighborhood. My term in this school was very short, as I was sent away just a few months after starting to go to the school.

While going to school one day, I was accosted by William Stock and my brother, Edward. I was about nine years old. They told me if I would do them a favor, they would give me some money. I agreed to do this favor for them. That night, the three of us burglarized a barber shop. The window was boarded up. William Stock and my brother tore one of the boards away. They then pushed me through the small opening they made, and I opened the back door for them. I knew I was doing wrong, but to my youthful fancy, I thought it was brave to do such things then.

A few days later these two fellows were apprehended by the police. They told of my part in the affair, and I was also arrested. This was the first time I ever was in a jail, and the experience was kind of thrilling. The policeman did not put me behind the bars, but kept me in their screened office until my mother came and took me home. They did not "book" me on this charge. While waiting for my mother to come down to take me home, I investigated almost all the drawers, in the desks in this office. As the policemen were playing cards or eating in the next room, there was no one to impede my investigations. I found guns, knives, blackjacks, and other miscellaneous articles. As most of the articles were large, and could not be hidden very well on my small person, I only took a small dagger with its sheath. I carried this out when my mother took me home.

When I was about six years old, my brother Edward and a neighbor's kid, Joseph Wyman, taught me how to beg. I was so small and innocent looking that it was easy for me to deceive people. I would go to the door of a cottage or apartment and knock on the door or ring the bell. If someone would answer, I would tell the person how poor my parents were. In this I was telling the truth. Seldom did I turn away without some money, food, or clothing. If no one answered my call, I took it for granted that the people were not at home. I again made sure by knocking, ringing the bell and making a lot of noise. If no one answered then, I told my older accomplice, and we would break in.

When I said "conditions at home," I meant not enough to eat, no clothes to wear and no money hardly to meet the monthly rent. One landlord put us on the street once, on account of not being able to meet the monthly rent bill.

I started stealing when I was about six or seven years old. I ran around with my brother and his pals, William Stock and Joseph Wyman, who were older than me. With them I used to steal fruit from the peddlers' wagons that used to parade along the streets. As I grew older, I started to shoplift with my buddies and many times with my brothers. We used to go into large department stores, look around and snatch anything that caught our fancy. We used to do this many times because we did not like to go to school, and whenever we got tired of staying in the class, we would sneak out and run away at recess time and hide our books and then go riding on the "L" to some well-to-do district or to the Loop. I was kind of experienced when I quit associating with these older fellows.

When I went out to burglarize and steal with these older boys, I naturally neglected to go to school. Reports from the school to my parents were getting frequent when I missed school day after day. It was then that I first started to lie to my parents. I was threatened with a spanking many times from my mother. This scared me a little and I wanted to go back to school and behave but the older fellows always taunted me saying I was a sissy, etc. Then I would go with them to do "jobs." As I was small and young, I got away with a lot of thefts before I was finally appre-

hended by the police and learned it was wrong. I went out with
William Stock and some of his other friends to burglarize stores
and apartments quite a few times. My older brother Ed used
to go begging and burglarizing also. Now and then he would take
me with him.

I soon found out that the loot these fellows were taking from
their victims was not shared with me. After repeated attempts
to get some money or something for my work, I quit associating
with them and went out stealing for myself. I was pretty successful in burglarizing by myself. Now and then I would go
out again with some of the older fellows, but this time instead of
giving them everything I stole, I kept what I wanted. In my
whole career as a burglar I never burglarized a home at night. I
only worked in the day and evening. It was much easier to steal by
myself. I committed burglary after burglary before I was finally
apprehended by the police. This time I was sent to the Juvenile
Detention Home. I was given trial at the Juvenile Court and
sentenced to an orphanage.

I do not remember how long I stayed in this institution. One
night after every one was asleep I escaped. The night I escaped
was cold, and I sort of regretted that I left my warm bed. I
started to turn back, but as I entered the building from which I
just escaped, I again changed my mind and ran across the fields
towards the cemetery which is near the institution. As I was bare
foot, and running across the field, which I think was some grain
field which was already harvested, my feet were bruised and bleeding by the time I neared the cemetery. Being very young, I was
somewhat awed and a little scared as I entered the gloom of some
trees nearby.

I debated with myself, whether I should cut across through the
cemetery and save a lot of walking, or take a round trip. I do
not know to what conclusion I would have come to, because some
passing motorist decided for me. As I was standing there in the
gloom of these trees, the headlight of a passing automobile shone
on me. I did not stop to reason, but started to run. I was so
frightened that I did not stop running until I was well in the
cemetery. I shall never forget that night. My imagination played

such tricks on me, that by the time I reached the end of the cemetery I was a nervous wreck. In my mind I saw creatures that are
indescribable. Every statue and tombstone seemed to take the
form of a horrible creature.

After I was well away from the cemetery, and walking on the
highway towards the town of J——, I did a funny thing. I
laughed. I laughed so hard and so long that tears started from
my eyes. I do not know what caused me to laugh so. I am sure
I did not enjoy that laugh. It just came on, and I couldn't stop
it. Later on when I grew older, I thought of this experience many
times. I tried to understand why I laughed so. As that was the
only experience I ever had of that kind, I came to the conclusion
that the laughing was the reaction from the fright I just had. As
I had some money, which I received from my mother when she
visited me on the Sunday before, I boarded an X—— street car
in the town of J—— and went home. The conductor of the street
car knew I was a runaway from the orphanage and sympathized
with me. He told me to stay in the platform of the car, as I had
no shoes and was so young to be around myself at that time of
night. When I reached home and snuck into our home, everyone
was asleep.

While undressing to go to bed, my mother came in the small
bedroom where my brothers and I slept. I must of woke her up
as I turned on the water in the kitchen sink to get a drink of
water. I told her I ran away! After looking at me steadily for
about a minute, she went back to bed.

The next morning I was afraid to come into the kitchen and
meet my father. I should have spared myself because my father
went to work before I got up that morning. That night I was
playing with our dog in the kitchen when he came in. I then
thought I was going to get a beatin' from him for running away,
but he didn't.

The following day, my mother told me to go to school. As all
the teachers in the school knew of me being in the orphanage I
hated the thought of going to that certain school, and I told my
mother so. As I would not go voluntarily she took me herself.
After my mother left me in charge of my teacher, she left. At ten

o'clock in the morning, that is "recess" time, I ran away from the school yard. I stole three cents from a newspaper stand and boarded a street car going to a wealthy section of the city.

I generally went there to burglarize people's property. On this occasion, I was pretty successful. After burglarizing about five or six places, and begging from other people I had about forty dollars in cash and many dollars worth of jewelry. I squandered all the money with my young friends on ice cream, candy, and picture shows. As to the jewelry, it was taken away from me by my mother and sent to the police anonymously.

From begging alone, I would procure sometimes three, four, or five dollars in a day and always a lot of food. The food I would almost always take home. Sometimes I would leave it on somebody's doorway. I did this mostly when I was "out of the house." My brother, Edward, was not a novice at the burglary racket. I'm sorry to say that he influenced me not a little, in regard to stealing. William Stock and Edward were buddies and Michael and I were taken out to steal many times by them. I thought what they did was alright. I'm sorry to say that my younger brother Michael was influenced by me later on. I think that if my folks lived anywhere but in a big city like Chicago, I or any of my brothers would never have seen the inside of any institution or prison.

Most of the time when I went out stealing, Michael would accompany me, but sometimes Edward would come along, also sometimes William Stock. On one occasion all three of us boys, Edward, Michael, and myself went to one of the suburbs west of Chicago. I "begged" for about fifteen minutes before I came to a house. I thought no one was home. I rang the bell, knocked and kicked at the door, but no one would answer. I had every reason to think that no one was home. I told my brothers Edward and Michael so. The access to the house was easy enough, and no one tried to impede our way in. While canvassing one of the bedrooms, I heard a commotion in the hall outside of the room. Frightened a little, I ran out to the hallway just in time to see Edward running swiftly in my direction. He told me that a woman was sleeping in the room he went into and accidently woke her up. She screamed, ran to the telephone, and called up the police. Edward told Michael and me to run upstairs. I ran, but not upstairs. I ran into the kitchen and out of the back door. The police responded so quickly that I was just out of the house when they ran in. Some went through the front door and some came into the rear yard. One of them asked me where my mother was. I pointed to the house and told them she was in there. I then casually walked out of the yard.

I knew I could not help my brothers in any way so I ran to the "L" station and boarded a train home. Being so young, the police could not see me connected in the burglary. I guess that's why I was able to fool them.

I do not remember whether my brothers were punished for this this offense or not. Anyway, about this time my brother Ed was sent to St. Charles. I was sent to the orphanage a few weeks later I think for playing "hooky" from school but am not sure. I was there awhile when Michael was sent to this school. In the play yard of the orphanage, Michael and I met.

I have no kind feelings for this institution. Although I know they always meant for the best in anything that was done there, they used the wrong system, at least they did with me. The beatings I received in this institution did a lot to make my heart bitter towards the officials in this and other institutions.

While I was out there, I had the itch. The nurses treated me and other boys. One old corpulent nurse was the one who usually treated the boys for the disease. When treating the boys for the disease in the mornings, she was generally surly and mean tempered. For every little misdemeanor she would whip, slap the boy's face, make the boy take castor oil, or bend the boy's fingers back. My fingers are crooked to this day from this treatment.

As neither of us, Michael and I, enjoyed being in the institution, we decided to escape. One night when the teachers retired at 10:00 P.M. from night prayers, I awoke Michael and we escaped. I was then about ten and a half to eleven years old and Michael two years younger. For the remainder of the night, we slept on the institution grounds, under some cement stairs. At dawn the next morning we walked to the street car lines in the town of J——. I stole some money from the same news stand and boarded a street car home.

When I was a very young boy I was taken out to rich neighborhoods by my brother Edward and William Stock to beg and steal. After they were put into institutions, my brother Michael and I teamed up together. I was about eight years old at that time. Michael and I were very successful together. We stole and begged as often and as much as we could. In order to find out if any body was in a home, we would beg. If some one would answer the door bell or my knock, I would beg for food, clothes or money. Sometimes we would have so much food that we would throw away some of it. If no one would answer my call, we would break into the home. We were very successful in prowling people's property. We each took turns in "begging." I must admit that Michael was a better housebreaker than I. He could crawl through small openings much easier than I could, as he was small and skinny while I was a little taller and much huskier. He found no trouble at all in climbing telephone poles, crawling through the transoms above the doors, etc. I did the heavy work, such as lifting him up to the transoms, jimmying the windows or doors, handling the dogs, etc.

The only trouble we seemed to have was the people's curiosity in wanting to know why we were not in school instead of "begging."

As to burglarizing, Michael and I were very erratic. One day we would burglarize five, ten or sometimes fifteen cottages or apartments a day. On other days, we would play with these people's children. We would go in some back yard and play with them in their sand piles, go in their tents and use their toys with them. Sometimes, we were "snubbed" by these children, but that did not worry us because we played with their toys anyway. Usually when we were not wanted, the boys or girls would yell for their mother. When this happened, we would go away before she came out, but this did not happen very often. I can remember only two occasions when this happened. Other times we would spend lots of time on the beaches. Sometimes we would do nothing but play a week straight at the beach.

I do not know for sure, but I think we were arrested then by the police and sent to the Juvenile Detention Home. The place was then situated on H—— Street and G—— Place. Both of us were sent back to the orphanage. We were there only a short time when my brother Edward came to see us. He asked us if we wanted to go home. As we both agreed, we walked out of the building and home. We did exactly that. We walked out and no one tried to stop us or ply us with questions.

As I was out there three or four times, I do not remember what I did to get sent out there every time, but I do remember distinctly every time I tried or did escape from this orphanage. Once I escaped and my parents took me back. I escaped the very next day and went home. My father was angry and used the strap on me, but did not take me back again. I tried to escape and failed only once. It was on some kind of a holiday that I tried. Everybody was playing in the yard and visitors were coming through the institution. I ran around to the front of the main building and out through the gate. Some one saw me go out, and yelled that I was running away. This started about a dozen boys after me. Needless to say, I was caught.

To my humiliation and sorrow, I was compelled to don a girl's dress and parade among all the boys in this manner. For supper that evening, the boys and girls received ice cream, but I was denied mine. To top my punishment, I was given a thorough strapping. To add to my humiliation and shame, they saw that the back part of my anatomy was bereft of all clothing before the switch was used. That night while laying in bed, I thought of the day's experiences. I decided it did not pay to try to run away and get caught, so I made up my mind to run away again but this time to think out a plan, instead of running off like I did that day. I ran away about a week later after this attempt and was successful this time. I never was sent out there again after that.

[James and his brothers continue to beg and burglarize in the better residential communities. His description of these offenses is presented in chapter iii, page 72.]

One day Michael and I broke into a house in a suburb of Chicago. While canvassing one of the rooms, a woman came into the house without either of us knowing it. As she was in the front room, she did not know we were in the place. Hearing her rummaging around in the other room, Michael and I ducked under the bed. Presently, the woman came into the room. She must of seen us because she started to yell out of the window. Not waiting for the outcome of the yell, Michael and I jumped from under the bed and made our way as quickly as we could out of the house.

You know, the more two fellows go through together, the more they are bound toward each other. It was the same way with Michael and me. As we went through our youthful experiences together, we got to know each other's faults and good points. For one thing, neither of us could pass up a blind or crippled person without giving them some money. One time after a prosperous day, as we were walking along the avenue, we passed up an old blind woman. As I walked on, my conscience started to bother me. I was just going to suggest to Michael to go back and give her some money, but Michael beat me to it. He went back and gave her a ten dollar bill. It made me, and I guess Michael too, feel good. Her "Thank You" and "God Bless You Boys," was certainly a blessing to us, because we went through some experiences without getting apprehended by the police. I believe to this day that if we had not helped this poor old woman, we would have been caught sooner than we were.

Another thing, Michael and I would never burglarize poor people's property. That is why we would go to suburbs and the more well-to-do neighborhoods of the city. Before I induced Michael to accompany me, when I went out to burglarize, I used to take our dog, "Topsy," with me. My brother, Ed, brought her home one day and she stayed with us till her death. This dog was a great help to me in my begging before and after I started to burglarize. I would take her with me almost wherever I went. My brother, Ed, and I taught her a few tricks. One trick, especially, always made a hit with the people in the street cars, was when I had Topsy "pray." She would sit on her hind legs, put her front paws on my knee and put her head between her front paws. I would generally reward her with a piece of candy. I would have her perform this trick in front of the people I begged of, also. Another trick I had her do was to wash herself.

She did this much in the manner a cat washes itself. The street car conductors got to know me and the dog, and we never would have much trouble in getting on the cars after our first few attempts. When I first started to take her with me, I had a basket which I put her in and boarded the car without the conductor knowing what was in it. Once I boarded the car with her in this manner, and had her do her tricks near the front of the car. The laughing of the people attracted the conductor's attention. He came over and ordered me out of the car. I begged him to let me stay on, but he said he'd throw the dog out if I wouldn't get off. Then one big man told him to let me alone or he'd be the one who would be thrown out. This shut him up and he went back to his platform and let me alone.

"Topsy" was the best and smartest dog we ever had. I got arrested with her twice. I guess it was why she always hated a cop. She growled and was sullen when a policeman came to our house to tell my mother that Michael was arrested for some offense and that she was wanted at the station. On one occasion she bit a cop in the leg. He wanted to shoot her, but my mother chased him out with a broom. Topsy not only went with me, she was taken out by Ed and Michael also. Sometimes Michael and I took her along, but as we burglarized more and more we left her at home. Topsy knew whenever we started to go out to steal and we had a heck of a time trying to keep her away. The people we begged of used to coddle her, feed her scraps of meat almost at every house I begged.

I know I and Michael never hung around gangs when we were small. We knew a lot of boys, but we never went out to steal in gangs. Only one or two boys ever went out with me and Michael to burglarize. One was Frank Pepper and another fellow whom I only know by the name of John Olson. It was through Frank Pepper that I and Michael became acquainted with a man whom I only know by the name of Hector. He drove a delivery truck for a Chicago newspaper. Frank would help him to deliver papers in the mornings, so Michael and I decided to help him also. As Hector would start his delivery around three o'clock in the morning, Michael and I stayed away from home and slept in Hector's truck in the night.

Michael and I would burglarize and Hector would get rid of the jewelry and other stuff we stole. He would give us a pretty good price on the stuff and Michael and I kept doing business with him. Sometimes we would sell jewelry to the other drivers in the garage but not often.

It was in the garage that I first learned how to "shoot dice." Needless to say, I was taken in for almost anything I had. Watches, necklaces, rings and other jewelry that I managed to get by burglarizing homes found its way into these men's pockets via the dice. These men knowing I was ignorant of the crooked side of this kind of gambling used "tops" on me.

After my first few losses at gambling with these men, I quit and kept Michael from gambling. He never shot dice with any of them, and never knew I shot dice until a few years later.

One early morning we had a real thrilling adventure. As we started on our route, Hector was a little drunk. He really wasn't drunk, but he had just enough gin in him to feel cocky and adventuresome. Well, as we rode along west on S—— Boulevard, we came to a railroad crossing that I think I almost lost my life at. Hector was speeding along at about forty five or fifty miles an hour when I heard the train whistle and also the warning twang of the bells at the crossing. Instead of stopping, Hector went right across the crossing at about fifty miles an hour and just beat the train by an eyelash. Just as we crossed I could hear the "Whish!" of the train as it passed by. Boy, my heart was in my throat for an hour after that.

As Michael and I did not live at home, we had no place to stay during the day. In spending our time, when not on the beaches or burglarizing, we would go to the theatres during the day. As to eating, we would hardly eat anything but candy, ice-cream, and sweet pastries. This way of living soon made us sick. For weeks Michael and I were troubled with indigestion and sour stomach. This with sleeping in a truck did not improve our health.

I recall an incident in a restaurant when we were troubled with this sickness. Early every morning after we helped Hector deliver the papers, Michael, Frank, and I would go to a restaurant and eat. It was usually five o'clock when the load of papers was delivered. On this particular morning, Michael and I went to a restaurant situated on D—— and P—— streets near the "L" station. We had been patronizing this restaurant quite a while, and the waiter knew us.

Michael and I ordered bacon and eggs. The waiter said nothing but went to get the order, at least I thought so then. When he returned to serve us, he put two bowls of corn flakes with milk and sugar on the table. I told him we ordered bacon and eggs and not corn flakes. He told us if we did not eat what he set before us, he would take us in the back and stuff it down our throats. He said it in such a hard and convincing manner that we believed him. Anyway, we ate the corn flakes. I know that we must have looked pretty run down in health then, otherwise we would have got our order of eggs and bacon as we did every other morning. When we were finally apprehended by the police, it was the best thing in the world that could have happened to us.

In the fall, Michael and I were arrested, after living "out of the house." After being in Juvenile Detention Home about a month or so, we got trial. Michael was sent to the orphanage and I to the St. Charles school.[2]

[2] Although James and his brothers appeared in the juvenile court more than the average number of times, recidivism is not unusual in juvenile court cases. A study of the records of the Cook County Juvenile Court covering the period when the Martin brothers were known to that institution reveals that for the city as a whole on the average each one hundred first offenders reappeared in court an additional 48 times on delinquency petitions. The average number of time boys reappeared in court varied widely between communities within the city, however. It was found that in the areas with the lowest rates of delinquents, on the average, first offenders reappeared 31 times, whereas in the areas with the highest rates of delinquents each one hundred offenders reappeared, on the average, 75 times. Thus the amount of recidivism in the areas of highest rates of delinquents was two and one-half times as great as the amount in the areas of lowest rates. In the area in which the Martin family lived each one hundred first offenders reappeared in court approximately 52 times. This was 1.7 times the rate of reappearance in the areas with the lowest rates of delinquents and more than two-thirds as great as the rate of reappearance in the areas with the highest rates. (See C. R. Shaw et al., Delinquency Areas [University of Chicago Press, 1929], chap. xiv.) These data indicate that the rate of

III

When I appeared before the judge, I asked to be sent to the St. Charles school because my brother was out there at the time. I had not seen him for some time and wanted to see him. The judge granted my request. In this, I feel he made a mistake because I was too young to know what I was asking for. As to the time I spent in the orphanage, I know that it was this institution that started me out to try to avenge myself for the punishment I received here on the well-to-do people, also to make trouble for the police. This, of course, only proved my own undoing.

In October, I was taken to St. Charles. The trip to the school was enjoyable to me. As it was one of my first train rides, I enjoyed myself very much, looking out at the passing scenery as we rode on. The men who took the other boys and me down, bought us candy and fruit and told us tales about the school. The stories were true all right but after we arrived at the school, things were not as glowing as we were led to think.

When we arrived at the town of St. Charles, the day had already started to wane and was dusky. After a hasty meal given to us in the depot restaurant, we were put in a coach-like wagon and driven to the school. The drive was slow and we arrived at the school about seven thirty or eight o'clock P.M.

We were taken to the receiving cottage and went through the regular formality as all new boys; taking a bath, getting all the hair cut off, institution clothes, etc. I was in the receiving cottage, Cottage R, about two weeks when I was transferred to Cottage K. When I was in Cottage R around four or five days, I got my first beating. Here's how it happened. It was about seven o'clock in the evening, and all the work being done, the boys were in the reading room. While sitting in a chair, I sneezed. The sneeze came on so unexpectedly that I couldn't of used my handkerchief and some of the nasal catarrh went on the polished

---

reappearance in the juvenile court on delinquency petition is a variable that is correlated with rates of delinquents. In short, the situations in Chicago that produce the highest proportion of delinquent boys likewise produce the highest proportion of recidivists.

floor. It was an accident I couldn't prevent, but I received a blow in the face from an inmate officer and a strap beating from an officer. That was the forerunner of the many beatings and blows in the face and body I received from officials and inmate officers. Many were probably deserved and many undeserved.

I was in Cottage R about two weeks and then transferred to Cottage K. It was in this cottage where I began and ended "doing time" in this institution. The following three years in Cottage K were simply hell. I went through plenty in my young life, but they were a bed of roses compared to my eleventh, twelfth, and thirteenth birthdays that I spent in Cottage K.

I learned and did my tasks in this cottage with the expectation of receiving a punch in the face or being put through some kind of punishment if I did any of my work or drilling wrong. I cannot fully describe the ill treatments I went through during these years, but they left their mark on me. Work, military drilling and little play was the regular routine in that cottage. Physical torture, whippings, and manhandling were the punishments for the boys who broke some rule in the cottage.

As St. Charles is a military school, every year a competitive drill is held in the autumn. In the three years I spent in Cottage K, our company won third prize twice. The smallest and youngest boys in the institution were in Cottage K, but they managed to beat out Company S that had boys in them fifteen, sixteen, and seventeen years old. How did they do it? Every time anyone made a mistake, he was hit in the face or body by the inmate officers in charge. After repeated treatments like this, the boys were simply afraid to bat an eyelid without getting a command. And weeks before the final competitive drill, we were drilled morning, noon, and night.

A man from outside reading this will think I was lazy and that I am exaggerating all this about work. Remember I was only ten years old when I went out there and I knew nothing at all about work. My teachers (inmate officers) were not patient or kind. They treated me with kicks and blows if I did anything wrong. So it really was not the work that bothered me so much, as the way a boy was treated while doing it.

All of the cottages were not this way. Only the ones who had mean and bullying captains (inmates) and house officers who were hard and strict. The work in the garden was not hard. Strawberries, blackberries, grapes, and cherries were grown in this garden. There also was an asparagus patch, besides the musk and watermelon patches.

A nice place for young boys of ten to thirteen, or fourteen years to work, isn't it? Here's the funny part of it. If a boy was caught eating a berry or cherry or any other of the fruits, he was punished by five or ten lashes with a whip. The man in charge of my cottage and the garden did the whipping. It may seem funny but I can honestly say, that in the three years I worked in this garden, I never ate any fruit while working. I was accused many times of eating some fruit, and always I was whipped by the house father on the inmate officer's say-so. In the winter, we used to work in the garden, turning the manure piles. Sometimes we used to clear the roads of snow.

When I first went out to St. Charles I was put in the third grade. I worked hard at my studies, so that three years later, I was in the eighth grade. I was paroled in September, so I did not graduate that year.

During three years in St. Charles my heart grew bitter and hard at all the officers and inmate officers who were responsible for the manhandling I received. It was due to the treatment in this cottage that afterward caused me to be so bad in the later years I spent in this institution. As I grew older and stronger, I began to assert myself to the inmate officers and officials both. I wasn't born tough. The treatment in this institution made me that way. I realized that if I became hard and tough that the officials and inmate officers would be careful what they were going to do to me.

Although the house officers in various instances did not know it, the fights in the basement were many between the privates and inmate officers. All I can say, I had my share of these fights. I hope that the people who read this will not think that I am a braggard. I am only trying to point out the effect of this manhandling treatment on me when I grew older.

After being paroled from St. Charles, Michael and I again joined forces and did a prosperous business at burglary. This stage of our lives I think was the most adventuresome together. We were "out of the house" most of the time. Being young we did not know how to take care of ourselves and we were sick most of the time. We had new clothes and plenty of money but lack of sleep and improper food were the causes of our ill health.

Sometimes when we ran out of money, we would procure our breakfast by robbing the bread boxes that stood in front of grocery and bakery stores. I had a bread box key and it was a simple matter for us to find a box that our key would open. Occasionally we would break one open. This would usually happen about three or four o'clock in the morning.

It was after I was paroled from the St. Charles School for Boys at the age of fifteen that I started to steal cars. Although I never had driven a car before, I knew how one was operated. A fellow by the name of Anton Macy[3] stole a Buick sedan one day. I accompanied him and when he went home to eat I took the car and started on one of the wildest experiences I had. I knew what I should do to make a car run and I knew the standard gear shift, but the Buick's gear had a universal shift. To begin with, after starting the motor I had all I could do to put the gear in first, or what I thought was first, but was high instead. The car started to shake and quiver at first, but it finally picked up and gathered speed. It was around February and the streets were wet and slippery. I started a few times to put the car in what I thought was second, but every time I bent over to try and shift the gear, the car would seem to swerve a little and it scared me, so I contented myself by leaving it in that gear. At crossings I would push on the clutch and brake and the car would stop.

On one of the street crossings I guess I wanted to show off a

[3] Anton Macy was never taken to court with James, and his name, therefore, does not appear among the names in the official records. His record shows that he was both a juvenile delinquent and an adult criminal. Anton Macy was under the supervision of the Juvenile Court almost continuously for eleven years. He was committed to a home for dependent children, to the Chicago Parental School, and to the St. Charles School for Boys. He served one term at the Illinois State Reformatory for larceny of automobiles.

little and I would push down the hand throttle to make the motor roar. While doing this I unconsciously took my feet off the clutch and brake. The fun then began. The car, after a few hesitating movements, went forward like it was shot out of a cannon. Why I did not kill any people or kill myself, God only knows. The car ran down the avenue at forty or fifty miles an hour. Swerving in and out among the other autos and street cars gave me time to think of nothing but the driving ahead of me. I was too excited to think anyway. Three or four times I sent pedestrians running to safety on the sidewalk. I finally ended the mad drive by shutting the switch and braking the car to a stop. That was my first lesson in driving and I rather liked it after I recalled the events in my mind later on.

· ·

Before being apprehended Michael and I burglarized nearly every day. We averaged around ten flats a day. Now and then we would go to the department stores and shoplift. On one occasion, we went to the dress and coat department for ladies and walked out with about six or seven dresses in a heavy paper shopping bag. We made the trip twice that day.

I was out only a short time when I was brought back to St. Charles. I think it was for burglary. This time I was lucky in getting transferred on a farm. The following two years I spent on the farm were paradise compared to the three years I spent in Cottage K. The work was pleasant. Besides we could eat cherries, apples, and other fruits we picked. Although we hardly ever did any field work, I learned a lot about agriculture. Farm A's work was composed of gardening and orchards. Apples, plums, cherries, and pears were grown on this farm. Navy beans and corn was grown in the fields during the two summers I spent there.

While on this farm my father died. The last time I saw my father alive was in the fall of the year before, when I was out on parole. On this day my father was taking me to school. I had been playing "hooky" for about a week straight and my folks got a call down from the truant officer.

This day my father was taking me to school himself to make

sure I would be there. The children were in school about five minutes when father and I walked into the school building. We walked up the boys' side stairway to the third floor. Just before we reached the third floor, I ran up ahead and down the long hallway to the girls' side of the building and then outside. I never saw him alive again.

I was pretty blue when I found out my father was dead instead of "sick" as the parole officer who drove me home for the funeral, told me. My father's body was put in a vault to await burial. As my older brother John was in the marines, we had to wait for him before my father was to be buried.

The following Monday, Michael and I went riding on the "L." After riding around aimlessly all morning, we finally went to a suburb west of Chicago. We were in this suburb about an hour when we were picked up by a policeman. The police at the station knew us, as we were arrested in this town twice before. As we did not steal anything this time they let us go, but not until holding us for two days. In the meantime my father was buried. A week or so later, I was taken back to St. Charles and Michael was sent back to Parental School.

When I graduated from grammar school, I was sixth from the top in a class of about fifty boys. After my graduation I was again paroled, this time to an outside farm.

I didn't want to go on the farm. I wanted to go home and go to high school the coming term, but I had to go on the outside farm or stay. I was pretty peeved about this but was unable to do anything about it. I believe that if I was given the opportunity to go home and to high school as I wanted, I would never be down here "doing time."

I went on the outside farm all right, but I ran away two days later. The farmer I was to work for came and got me. I was only fifteen years old then. My wages were to be twenty five dollars a month and board. I stayed with the man only two days, and then I ran away. The farmer and his wife were kind to me, and gave me plenty to eat, but he was responsible for me running away.

There was another fellow from St. Charles working for them.

I do not remember his name, but he talked me into going to town [St. Charles] with him, when I was supposed to stay on the farm. The farmer and his wife went to some place themselves in their car so I took the chance of them not knowing I was gone. As there was some kind of show or fair in Potowatomie Park in St. Charles, it wasn't until about midnight that we returned to the farm. Unluckily for me the farmer was back. After seeing me come in, he threatened to send me back to school. The result was that I ran away that night. After walking around two hours on the highway, I was given a "lift" to Chicago by some young fellows not much older than myself. They were driving around and were lost. As I knew the way to Chicago, we got there about four thirty in the morning.

When I got home I knew the authorities would be after me so I started to stay away from home. Again the result was that I went back to my old associates, and back on the racket. Anyway I was apprehended shortly afterward and sent back to St. Charles.

It was after this experience in my life that I began to be kind of hard to handle in the school. The two years spent on the farm put me in good physical condition, and the schooling sharpened my mind. I ran away whenever the opportunity presented itself. I caused the inmate officers a lot of grief when they "picked on" my younger friends.

I ran away quite a few times in the following year. I succeeded every time I tried. Only once I got myself in bad about escaping, that was when I tried to take some boys with me. That experience was enough for me. Every time after that, when I ran away, I went by myself.

Early in the summer of that year I ran away from the "Punishment Line." This "Punishment Line" was where they kept the runaways, and boys who were very bad. These boys were guarded very closely and compelled to work on the pond and zoo. For a month or so I was handcuffed and compelled to stand all day, instead of working. The handcuffs were of inferior quality and easily opened. I and one or two other boys in this "Punishment Line" could open these handcuffs with a pin very easily. One day

I took them off so I could rub my neck and the man in charge must of saw me, because he came over and put another pair of handcuffs on me. I opened these also. The man finally put me to work. I waited for an opportunity to escape. My chance came two or three days later. I was picked up by the police after a few days and returned to St. Charles.

After a few months of this kind of behavior I was made an officer in one of the cottages. I guess the house officer figured if I had a little responsibility on my shoulders I would settle down and behave. For awhile I did behave, but I ran away again and was demoted back to the ranks upon my return back to the school.

In a short time I was again made officer. This time I settled down and behaved myself. In due time I was promoted to the rank of major. While an officer I did not strike a smaller or younger white boy than myself. I did have many scraps with fellows my own age and size and the bigger ones. In fact I used to take the bigger fellows down in the basement and make them fight me. It was funny, I know, but I got a big kick out of fighting. I still do.

When I was returned to St. Charles, I was transferred to Cottage M. I only spent three days here as I was again transferred to Farm B. I stayed on this farm about three weeks and was again transferred to Cottage C. I spent three months in this cottage and was paroled. In December I was sent home. . . . .

Around this time I experienced relations with the opposite sex. A lad by the name of Larry (his last name I do not know) took me and another lad of my age (by the name of Red) to a brothel. I was rather embarrassed during this first experience. I have only patronized a brothel once after that time. Like all the other boys of about this age, I began to play up to the girls. "Gang shags," that is when a group of boys would satisfy their lust on some girl in a school yard or alley at parties, I never participated in. A thing of that sort is not uncommon in the neighborhood.

The older boys would generally get a girl drunk and she would pass out and some boys would take advantage of her. That's one of the results of the 18th amendment. If a man took the statistics on social diseases, he would find them large in neighborhoods of the kind that I spent my early childhood in, mostly because of affairs of this kind.

I worked at various jobs outside and was getting along nicely, when one of my "friends" suggested that we make some easy money. I stole and burglarized awhile before I was again arrested for stealing a car and sent back to Chicago and Cook County School. I escaped twice from here within a month. In the following summer I was arrested for attempting to steal an automobile and sent to St. Charles.

I ran away three months later, but was arrested in a northern suburb with my brother Edward and sent to St. Charles. While the authorities in the suburb were trying to find out who my brother Ed and I was, I attempted to escape from this jail. I succeeded in snapping two iron bars with another long bar, but it was found out before I had a chance to get out. I was taken to the Juvenile Detention Home from this jail. The people in the home knew me. They would not take me in, but sent me to the Maxwell Street Police Station. From there I was taken to St. Charles. Ed was returned to the Illinois State Reformatory. Six months later I was paroled.

During my stay in St. Charles, I had many hours of joy and play as well as my sorrows and work. To this school I have some kind feelings as well as hard and bitter. As I said before, the first three years I spent in this school were the hardest I spent in this life and they had a lot to do with making me as I am today.

IV

After my parole from St. Charles, I worked at various places. As a sticker to a job, I'm sorry to say I was a flop.[4] No work that I tried, held my interest for long. The longest time I held a job

[4] The absence of work habits exhibited here in the failure of James to adapt himself to our industrial system is not surprising in view of his life-experiences. His family did not possess enough unity to furnish effective training or to transmit effectively the Old World traditions of industry and workmanship. Similarly his contacts with the school were too casual to furnish a basis for the development of work habits. The only situations in which he lived where stable work habits might have been developed were the correctional institutions. Obviously the semi-military system of training in these institutions did not prepare him for work situations outside of the institutions.

was when I worked for the Smith Binder Company. I worked for this company about two months. I liked the work for awhile, but it became tiresome after a few weeks of steady grind. In all the positions I held, I was "fired" only once. This happened not because I loafed on the job or because I broke any rule of the company, but because the boss over me found out I was a former inmate of St. Charles. In my other jobs I always quit voluntarily. While I worked for these different employers, I did all the work assigned to me. I did not stall on the job, though occasionally I did come to work a few minutes late.

Now I want to give my opinion on this work problem. From my own experience and from what I learned of other fellows in this institution, I find that a lot of boys are down here because they could not get a job that could hold their interest enough to make them stick to it. It is not because they are lazy and have no ambition. They just haven't got the will to force themselves to work steady. While idle, the nervous energy of the young fellow is misdirected. Instead of buckling down harder, chances are, he is going to gain some money dishonestly, and there is always some adventure in committing a crime. Now if a boy got a job that held his interest until he grew old enough to realize the necessity of picking a vocation and settling down, seven-tenths of the boys would never have been in this reformatory.

It was partly the reason of my not being able to stick to a job that I'm down here. I worked for awhile. When I did not work, I loafed around the parks. This became tiresome after a little while, and I and some other guys from the neighborhood stole automobiles to go out driving.

The experiences I had in shooting dice when a young boy came in handy when I started out with older guys. Anton Macy and some of us fellows would go to a pool room and play. Nearly all of them were pretty good pool players and they would gamble among each other on the outcome of their games. They would always watch for some "sucker" and play him for all he was worth. I never was a good pool player but the money I lost in pool I always won back in the various crap games. I only used the "tops" a few times as it was dangerous to get caught using them.

When I needed money, I stole automobiles and sold the tires. (Since I have been down here a garage that I and my partner in crime used to sell the tires to, has been raided and confiscated by the police. It is located on the near South Side.) My partner, Anton Macy, was known as the "Chrysler Kid" because he specialized in stealing that make of car. The "Kid" and I have known each other since we were kids about ten years old. We stole bicycles when we were small. As we grew older, we started stealing automobiles just for the fun and the rides. Later on it became a business proposition.

My parole officer had me arrested for not working and instead of coming back to St. Charles I was given twenty-five dollars and costs at the boys' court. As I was unable to pay the fine, I spent nearly two months in the House of Correction. Whoever named that place, the "House of Correction" certainly had a funny sense of humor. Instead of correcting, it corrupts the unfortunates who pass through that hell-hole.

About the first of August I was discharged from there. I was out about an hour when I drove off with another person's car for which I was arrested and returned to the Bridewell.

[James steals automobiles, serves two short sentences in the House of Correction for auto theft and is committed to the Illinois State Reformatory on the same charge. James describes these experiences in chapter iv, page 87.]

When I was arrested and sent down here it was the best thing that happened for me I guess, because I was about to graduate from the car bandit to the role of gunman. I had already seen what a gun pointed at some one could do.

I described the neighborhood in which I lived rather roughly before and I mentioned the different classes of petty larceny crooks and boys who were graduating from one class to another while some because of lack of nerve or "guts," as we of the underworld would term it, stuck to the small role of crookedness.

I have been a petty thief, a burglar, and a car bandit and I had my mind set on to hold up stores and prosperous looking men who attended the opera and other high class places of amusement, when I was arrested.

I knew how to drive a car at a high rate of speed. I knew how to use a gun and I guess I had enough "guts," so I thought I would give the stick-up racket a try.

I'm glad to say that my ambitions as a gunman were curtailed. However, in May, a lad we called Whitey accused me of stealing the car he had stolen. I stole his car, a Chrysler roadster, all right but he was drunk and swung at me with a small hatchet. I pulled a gun on him to protect myself. I didn't have to use it, because he got sober mighty quick. The reason I took the car was because my old pal Anton Macy (he's doing one to life in Joliet now) and I had a date with two girls and I had no car at that time and Whitey had stolen a car from me sometime previously.

I used to think then that good times went above everything else. I thought that I did have a good time, but as I look back I find that I did not enjoy living as I did. The fellows I went out with I could not trust, nor did any of them trust me. We did not know the meaning of fellowship. Arguments were frequent, but very few physical combats.

The saying "Honor among Thieves" is the bunk. I've been out with fellows who would knife me in the back if they could squeeze an extra dollar to add to their loot. There are cases, though, where two men team up together that would give their lives for each other. When two fellows go through hell and water together they are drawn closer together then brothers. It is only persons like these that usually keep this so-called "code of the criminal world."

Every crook, and I guess most of the cops, too, hate a "rat." A man after he has been through the mill once and squeals has no business in risking his freedom by being a crook. With the few crooks of my acquaintance the code I understood was: if I was or any of my acquaintances was to get caught with "hot" stuff, we were to take the rap whether we did the "job" or not. We were to keep mum about everyone but ourself.[5]

As I said there is no "honor among thieves," but there is a code among the underworld when it's crooks vs police.

Example No. 1: John Doe and I burglarize a store. John Doe finds a couple of hundred dollars hid away in some drawer. He puts a hundred in one pocket and says a hundred is all he got. We divide. He gets fifty and I get fifty, but I am fifty to the good and he is one hundred and fifty to the good. That is crook vs crook.

Example No. 2: I steal a Chrysler roadster. John Doe borrows the car to keep a date with some girls. Early in the morning he gets pinched by a squad. The car is hot, but he didn't steal it, but he is caught with it. He takes the rap and gets sent to jail. He lived up to the code, "Crook vs Police." If he had squealed he would have been termed a "rat" and never let in on anything by the shrewd crooks. Only fools would have taken him with them on a "job" or fellows who did not know of him squealing to the cops.

As I said before, when I got arrested and sent down here, it was the best thing that happened to me then, but keeping me here may undo what it has done. I have all the intentions of going straight if not for my own then for my mother's sake. We boys have caused our mother a lot of grief and trouble and I am all ready to try and make her happy for the rest of her days on earth, but if she passes away before I'm liberated, God alone knows what path I may lead when I finally am set free.

To end up with, I want to say that my parents always tried hard to keep us kids from stealing and doing other things that are wrong, but they were unable to hold us in check. If my father would have worked and saved his money and moved to a different neighborhood, I'm sure we would have turned out to be different,

---

[5] For a discussion of the codes among thieves see E. H. Sutherland, *The Professional Thief* (University of Chicago Press, 1936); and for a discussion of attitudes toward the police, the rat, and the squealer see C. R. Shaw and H. D. McKay, National Commission of Law Observance and Enforcement: *Report on Causes of Crime*, Vol. II (U.S. Government Printing Office, 1931).

but "Booze" had a strong hold on him and he did not have enough will power to quit drinking. Of the whole family, my mother has suffered the most because of the erring ways of her children but we kids did not know that until we grew older and thought things out.

She was always saving every penny and denying herself many things so that we kids would have some clothes and enough to eat. That is the reason why my brother Michael and I am anxiously awaiting the day we are set free so that we may help her now in her old age, and she needs help I know.

V

As I sit here trying to recall incidents of my past life, the radio music interrupts upon my thoughts and sets me to thinking of the future. I imagine myself at times as aviator, farmer, business man etc. I often think of the wasted years I have spent in prison.

Those who are familiar with my prison record will probably smile to themselves thinking that I am trying to be smart when they read the above statement, but my intimate friends know that I was never cut out to be a crook. The neighborhood in which I spent my early childhood influenced me to steal. That with the maltreatments in city and state institutions, where I spent most of my childhood, induced me to avenge myself against the city and state officials.

As I grew older, I began to suspect that as a crook, I was a failure. Many times I went to work and really tried to stick to the job, but my "friends" lured me back to the racket. I think that if my folks lived anywhere but a big city like Chicago, I or any of my brothers would never even have seen the inside of any state institution or prison.

To put it all in one statement, I didn't want to steal or take any chances in stealing, but I did it anyway. Down in my heart I hated to go out and steal with other fellows, but I went with them to avoid "ridicule." I can't express my feelings like I'd like to, but I hope the people who read this will understand.

I came to this place just seven months after I left St. Charles.

While in this place I have changed in many ways, and I have had, and still have, a lot of time to think, and believe me a fellow doesn't start to think until he is behind the bars with a lot of time to do.

A boy, when he first comes down here, naturally thinks about his home and parents or perhaps his wife and children. Later on he may think of his future. He wonders just how things will be for him when he is given his freedom, but his main thought for the first year will be about his outcome with the parole board. "Will I get out in a year?" he asks himself and his other fellow prisoners. His hopes for the first year were high. He usually thought things out with everything in his favor. I guess I was no exception from the majority of boys, though I did not set my mind on getting out in a year. But after I already had three years in and really expected to go out, I nearly broke down and cried like a baby when I received my slip with the maximum sentence on it. Boy, I felt blue. I couldn't get over it for a couple of weeks. I thought the clerk for the Parole Board had made a mistake.

When I first got the notice from the Board, I felt bitter toward them and everybody in general. I planned to escape, but a friend of mine showed me I would be a fool if I tried to get away. After thinking it over, I decided to stick and do my time. Maybe I would have succeeded in getting away but I do not think it would have been worth the hardships that would follow me. After the thought of escaping had entered my mind and been rejected, I reconciled myself to do my time the best I could, but I have hopes of being able to go out in the world again very soon.

The more human treatment that is being put into play in this institution is having its effect on most of the fellows who are here. When I first came down, I used to be bitter against plenty of the "screws" in here for their free use of the pencil to write reports against me and the other different boys. I used to long for revenge, especially against the big shots of the institution.

In the years I spent in prison and other institutions, penal or charitable, I mingled with all types of men and boys. I made the acquaintance of many men and boys during my incarceration. There are criminals and delinquent boys of all degrees and they were paying penalties of many kinds. Some are gentle, patient, and without the slightest evidence of baseness; others are hardened, bitter, and dangerous. Like myself, some had served many terms in various institutions, and some serving their first term with the prospect, judging from their talk, of serving additional terms.

Some people, if they ever thought about prisoners and prisons, wonder just how hard it is on a boy or man to spend three, four, five or more years behind the bars, especially if he is young. What effect do all these years have on a boy and young man who sees some of the best years of his life glide by while he is incarcerated. Long prison terms only serve to arouse bitterness.

I have seen many boys and men come down here, since I have been here. On almost every face there is a questioning look. Some, especially the younger fellows, act as if being sent down here is a great adventure. It is an adventure, but of a very different kind from what they may expect. The older fellows are more serious. They probably know that everything is not as good as it looks.

Most of the fellows here spend their time as best they can. Some improve themselves both mentally and physically. The majority of the fellows, especially the younger ones, are blue and homesick when they first start doing "time."

They want to know how much time they will do. After awhile, they become reconciled to their surroundings, they turn their minds to other subjects. Some great sage once said, "No matter how hard or difficult tasks may be, people will adjust themselves to them." Well, that's the way it is with the men and boys in prison.

Long and repeated prison terms have no effect in turning the evil doer from his path. His confinement only gives him opportunity to nurse his bitterness and to plan new exploits when he is out of prison. His association with other criminals implants new ideas within him and he is always on the alert to obtain information from those of his kind, which he believes will prove helpful to him in his activities as a law-breaker.

For men who have chanced into prison through a temporary lapse, because of a mistake, or due to unfortunate circumstances and in whom there are no germs of criminality, a long prison term only serves to arouse bitterness. They are unwittingly influenced by the hardened criminals and when they are liberated, they have been saturated with ideas that will ultimately prove their undoing.

For a person who has committed an offense, the penalty for which is prison, if it is his first and committed without intent of criminal practice, a very short prison term will prove efficacious and will do more to protect society and himself than a long and arduous sentence. I believe there should be a schedule of prison terms devised which will enable courts to impose sentences according to the individual temperaments, and not wholly on the person's past record.

The "screens" or "hole" as the boys call it, is the worst punishment that can be given to any boy if given in big doses. The starvation and sleeping on the cement floor poisons a boy's heart and mind towards officials in the institution. Given to a boy moderately, as it is now, it does a lot of good.

How does a man in the "hole" spend his time? He lives in a small space enclosed in steel and an iron barred door. He is conscious of his imprisonment every second. Unseen vermin crawl within his clothes. His mind never ceases to race. It is fed by fantastic maddening sensations of the injustice done to him.

At night, as he lies on the hard cement floor, trying to get some sleep, he curses and damns the official who is responsible for his being down there. Now since the new superintendent and the other new officials came here, we have been treated a little more human, though there still are a few minor officers here that always like to ride a fellow. This though, can always be expected anywhere a man will go.

In the forty months I have been here, this place underwent many changes. Mr. A—— who I knew from St. Charles, was the worst official I ever saw. He was narrow-minded in regard to the prisoners' welfare. He was not fair, and when a prisoner official is not fair he is lower than a snake in the eyes of a prisoner. No matter how hard and strict a prison official may be, if he is fair he will be respected by the prisoners.

Mr. B—— who I now think is in Joliet prison as an official was the same way. Those two men ought to be behind prison bars for awhile and see how it feels to be treated as they treated inmates here.

The men who read this may think I'm prejudiced against these two men. These were the two main cogs in the machine running this institution, that's why I speak of them.

The men in charge now are a million per cent better than the ones who left. Mr. C—— is a good fellow who will treat us like humans, but tighten the reins if the boys get too gay. The first assistant is a tough one, but fair. A fellow wouldn't want a better man to run things. Mr. F——, second assistant superintendent, seems to be all right. He is new yet, but I think he'll make the grade.

As for the minor officers of this place, I can't speak so highly of them. Some take intense delight in reporting a boy. They do not care whether they are reporting the right boy or not.

Luckily for me I finally got a job here that I like. I work in the athletic department under Mr. G——. He is a square shooter and we get along nicely. I take charge of a company of boys and drill them awhile in the yard. This way the boys get a few minutes a day in the fresh air. This is better than having them lay in their cells all day as they used to before the athletic department was formed.

Because of my prison record, I was given the maximum on my sentence. As my mother is poor and my other relatives not willing to help me out of this predicament, I will be twenty four years old when I leave this place. Out of the twenty four years, fifteen or sixteen will have been spent in prison.

I feel an injustice was done to me when the Parole Board gave me the maximum sentence. Didn't I in my early life serve more time than required for the charges held against me? Altogether up to date I have spent over half of my life in state and city institutions. The state institution made me what I am today. Since I have been down here, I thought of many things, but mostly, especially lately, I have thought of my future. I know that I can and will go straight if given any kind of a chance. My main ambition now, is to do a little traveling, then to marry and settle down. I have always been interested in sports and machinery. If possible, I would pick one of the two as my vocation or perhaps take both if possible.

CHAPTER XI
THE LIFE-HISTORY OF MICHAEL MARTIN[1]
I

I, Michael Martin, was born in the city of Chicago twenty-seven years ago, in a very poor neighborhood. My father and mother who were very poor could not afford to live in any other kind of neighborhood. My father and mother were honest and hard working and had to work very hard to support us.

There were three boys in the family when I was born and I made the fourth. The oldest boy was my brother John who was about nine, next came my brother Edward, then James, and then I. After I was about one and one-half years old my youngest brother was born, which made five besides my father and mother. So you can imagine how hard my father and mother had to work to support us children and all of us under twelve years of age when the youngest was born.

My father and mother, who were born on a farm in Europe, were still the old fashioned kind. My mother was very religious; she used to go to church almost every morning. Outside of that she always usually stayed at home, but in the summer time she would work on the farm as an extra. My father who was a laborer 'till a few years before his death was an erratic man. He would work very hard and with some of his money he would usually go to saloons and get drunk and make things a little harder for those at home. The first four or five years of my childhood I cannot remember much about, but by the time I was five

[1] Michael wrote the document which is presented in this chapter while he was incarcerated in a state penal institution. At the time of writing he had served approximately three years of a five-year term. Like James he wrote extensively about institutional life both because he was incarcerated at the time of writing and because he had spent most of his life within institutions for dependents, delinquents, or criminals. In addition to the life-history presented here Michael wrote some essays on the characteristics of his community and on the nature of his home life. This document has been paragraphed and in some instances extremely long sentences have been broken up into shorter ones.

or six years of age I was sent with my brothers, Carl, the youngest
child, and James, who was two years older than I, to a home for
dependent children outside of Chicago.[2] I don't know exactly
what the reason was that we were sent there but I think it was
because my father and mother could not support all of us. Anyway, we all went there and I did not like it there so my brother
James, and I planned to escape. We tried it several times by
running across the fields in the daytime but we were always seen
and caught and punished by the superintendent, who gave us a
good spanking and made us wear girls dresses to make us behave
ourselves.

After being in this institution a few months we finally succeeded in escaping one night from the dormitory. My brother,
James, came from the dormitory one night and woke me up and
told me to get dressed because we were going to beat it. I dressed
myself quickly and quietly and took my shoes outside, so I
wouldn't make any noise. I threw them away because it was summer time and besides I did not care to wear them. After we got
outside we hid under a stairway till about five o'clock in the
morning. Then we started on our way home. We had to pass
through a cemetery and every white piece of paper or any moving
object almost scared me to death. After we passed through the
cemetery we walked to the car lines and my brother stole about a
dime off a news stand so we could ride home in a street car. After
we got home my mother was glad to see us but told us it was
wrong to run away from the orphanage. My father didn't seem
to care whether we stayed there or not.

When I was about seven years old my brother James, who
was about nine, took me out several times to steal pennies from
news-stands and fruit from the grocery stores, which advertised
the fruit in front of their stores. After doing this for a while, we
changed to the worse by starting to be truant from school and
going down-town and visiting all the big department stores and
every time we got a chance we would take something that struck

[2] Michael has confused two separate commitments to homes for dependent
children. According to the official records he was first committed alone and subsequently with his brothers.

our fancy such as candy, toys, and many other little novelties. We kept this up till we got caught and chased out of the stores.[3]

My brother then took me out to the rich districts in Chicago and taught me how to beg. I started doing this and liked it very well because it gave me a chance to see how rich people lived and sometimes I would make about $3.00 or $4.00 a day. To do it I would usually go to the rich neighborhoods with my brother at about eight or nine o'clock in the morning by either sneaking on the "L" lines or hopping trucks and wagons. When we decided the neighborhood was good looking enough we would get off. Then my brother would tell me at which houses he wanted me to beg. I would go to these houses and ring the door bell, while he waited for me in the alley till I came out. If the people were at home I was to tell them my story and then if they were kind people they usually gave me food, clothing or money and sometimes I got both.

Sometimes when I went out begging with my brother, James, we would keep going from house to house till we would finally come to one that did not have anybody at home. Well, I usually made sure that nobody was home by ringing and knocking at both the front and back doors. If nobody was there we'd look around and see if the doors or windows were open and I'd call my older brother who told me how to get in. Sometimes we got in houses by the doors, windows, transoms, ice boxes and even basement doors that led into the kitchen. Then I'd open the kitchen door for my brother who would help me search the house. We took anything that we thought was valuable, such as jewelry, ties, and money and many other things. The police caught both of us in one of the houses and took us to the station, where they searched us and recorded our names and addresses. Finally we were taken to the Juvenile Detention Home, where I had been several times before.

[3] Shoplifting in the Loop was a common practice among boys, especially older boys, in the area in which the Martin brothers lived. Elaborate techniques for securing merchandise without being detected had been evolved and were routinely transmitted through the delinquent group. There is nothing in the official record to indicate that James and Michael were ever apprehended on these shoplifting expeditions.

I remember the first time I went there I was so small and young that they put me on the girls side with the girls till my mother came and took me home. The superintendent of the place always treated me nice and she knew me and my brothers like she would a son of hers. I stayed in the Juvenile Home with James until my mother came and took us home again. She always cried because we got into trouble.

My father then gave us a good spanking and told us if he ever caught or heard of us getting into trouble again he would beat us twice as hard. He usually used a strap on us but I hid it every time I thought I was going to get a beating, so he made one with about 5 or 7 strips of heavy horse harness leather and, boy, I mean it really hurt when he laid it on me. He never did that job half way. I got many beatings from him but I can say now that I didn't get any unless he was sure I needed one.

For about a month or two after that episode my brother James and I went to school and behaved ourselves. Then we again started stealing and bumming from school. We would go to school in the morning and at recess we would quit and go to the rich places and would start to beg again. We did this for about two weeks till we got caught again in a house. We were again taken to the police station and searched and shipped to the juvenile where we enjoyed ourselves till we went to trial. I was only about eight years old then and my mother pleaded for me and my brother, but the judge was stern and told her he was sorry but he thought he had better separate us and make us behave ourselves. So he sentenced me to a private training school and James to St. Charles. After the trial I was taken by a woman who dressed me up in a new suit of clothes, because the ones I had on were too ragged and dirty for me to wear. Then she took me to the training school next day, where I was received by the superintendent and given in care of another person, who took me to the receiving room and gave me a bath and a clean suit of clothes to wear.

After the first few days of getting examined and acquainted with my rules, I was let out with the other boys. I slept with them in the dormitory and was put in the kindergarten class. I had never gone to school very long before that. After being there about two or three weeks I was homesick. I wanted to go home, but I couldn't, so I started to make the best of it.

After a while I started to get acquainted with some small boys who were my age and things were not so bad then. In the summer time we would play marbles, hide and seek, and many other games. During vacation time out there they would take the boys out in the woods which belong to the school, and all the boys would pick walnuts, crab apples, blueberries, and many other fruits which grew on trees. They also would go swimming in a little pond, which wasn't over four or five feet deep. After staying in the woods about four hours, the bugler would blow his bugle and all of us would go back to our line.

Every month I was there my mother came to see me because that's all the visits they allow the people to have. Whenever she came she brought candy, toys, and whatever I wanted and stayed there all day and talked to me and asked me how I was getting along. Then when it was about four o'clock in the afternoon she would leave me, crying, and hating to go without me.

After I was in this institution about one year, I made my First Holy Communion. Every Sunday out there everybody went to Church in the morning. Every morning and night we would say our prayers and they also taught us to say them before and after every meal. So I was raised up right in that school, but I was spoiled after I left it and went to another school.

After being there two years of my life, which I can say were the only happy ones, I was taken home by my father, who treated me very nicely and tried to tell me it was wrong to do any stealing and bumming from school. He said if I did I would only get caught again and go to prison. But I did not take his advice seriously, for I was only a kid about 10 years old then.

II

After I came out of the training school my mother sent me back to the parochial school which was only a couple of blocks away from home, where I was put in the second grade. But I did not like it there because I wanted to go to public school. My

mother said she did not want me to go there. She wanted me to
go to the school I was in and be an altar boy and maybe become
a priest. I went to that school with my younger brother Carl
until I got tired of the grind. I then took my younger brother
Carl with me to the very rich neighborhoods in Chicago and
showed him how to beg and steal like I was shown by my older
brothers.

We got along very nicely until my mother and father started
to get notes from our school, telling them how I would go to
school half a day and run away the other half. My father found
out what I was doing when I wasn't in school, and one evening
when my brother, Carl, and I came home, he searched us and
found some jewelry and money and also a pistol and bullets which
we stole out of some house. Well, he took all of the stuff away
from us and asked us where we got it. We told him because it
was no use denying it, and then he gave us an awful beating and
took all the stolen property to a police station. The police wanted
to know where we stole the stuff from. They asked us if we could
show them the houses. We gave them an idea of the place we
stole the stuff from. The police found the people and told them
how they got it from my father. They agreed to let us go on account of my father returning the stuff, so we went back to school.

The teacher in charge of our room kept an eye on us and did
not let us have recess with the rest of the classroom until she
thought we were behaving ourselves. After that, winter was coming around and we were behaving pretty good and going to school
regular. After school hours and supper I used to go to shows regular and if I was broke and couldn't get the money from my mother
or father I would stand in front of a theater and I would ask
passers-by if they had an odd penny they weren't using. Sometimes I got a penny, nickle, or dime and if I got what I wanted I
would go and see the show.

Well, Christmas was coming around and my mother asked me
what I wanted for Christmas. She said she would write to Santa
Claus and if I was a good boy he might give me what I wanted.
If I was bad I wouldn't get anything, so I was always good when
Christmas came around. The night before Christmas, my father,

who was dressed in Santa Claus' clothes, knocked at the door and made us think that he was Santa Claus. After he gave us our toys and things he would go back out the door, and a few minutes later he would come in so I figured it was he who dressed in Santa's clothes. Then I would have a good time during the following days playing with my toys till the holidays were over.

After my eleventh birthday I started to go with older boys to the beaches, where we would steal pocketbooks till finally I tried it alone and was caught. The way I stole pocketbooks was when I saw some people leave their clothes on the beach. After they would go in swimming, I would keep my eyes on them, search their clothes till I found the pocketbooks, then I put them in my pockets when nobody was looking and went some place to see how much money I stole. If it was enough to last me for a few days I would quit and spend it, but if I didn't get enough I would go back to the beach and steal more till I got enough. Well, I kept this up for about two weeks, until I was caught by the people from whom I was stealing and they turned me over to the police. I was again taken to the juvenile detention home and caused my mother and father a lot more humiliation and shame.

I was then taken before the judge and he told me he would send me to the parental school despite my mother's pleading. Well, I got sore and called him a lot of names and they had to pull me away from the courtroom. The same day I got the sentence I was taken to the parental school and I did not like the place right from the start because the superintendent of the school was pretty mean and did not care how much the kids were beaten or punished.

The first day I got there I was given to a house officer who was to be my "boss" while I was there. After I got in the cottage with the other boys I was given a bald head by one of the boys who was a pet of the officer. I was given a different suit of clothes till mine was washed and fumigated. My boss lived there with his wife all the while I was there. A few years after I left he was fired, so you can see that I didn't have a good time there.

The first few days I was there I got to learn what some of his rules were. They made me eat everything they set before me. If

I didn't eat every bit of it, I would be punished. Sometimes we were served with some food that I didn't like and I had to eat it anyway, whether I liked it or not. I used to give my food, that didn't agree with me, to some other fellow who liked it. I was finally caught and punished for this.

If a fellow ever broke any of the rules of the cottage he was given a mark. At night, when all the work was done, the house officers made all the fellows who had marks get in the middle of the room, and for each mark they had to do seven minutes of squats and eight minutes of muscle grinders. If they didn't do them right, they either got a kick in the face or hit with a club over your head and shoulders. Some of the fellows were punished so bad that they fainted and others begged for mercy. All the mercy they got was a kick or blow.

When it was bed time each of these fellows would receive about twenty to twenty-five blows on their bare bottom with a paddle about an inch thick, while some fellows held them down. I know how it feels because I happened to get a little more than my share. I remember after I was there about two months I was caught soaking my hair in the water when I was washing myself one morning. One of the officer's pets squealed on me and I had all my hair cut off, besides doing about two hours of some punishment. Then I was given a beating that night.

I wanted to run away but I was too scared to do so. After I spent four months of that kind of punishment my mother came and took me home.

III

I stayed home till my brother James came home from St. Charles. After a while he and I ran away from home and met up with a former pal of mine, whose name was Frank Pepper.[4] He

[4] Frank Pepper did not appear in court with Michael or with any of the other brothers, so that his name does not appear in the official records. Since he was one of Michael's early companions his long record is of value in the study of this case. Frank Pepper was arrested and taken to the juvenile court on seven separate petitions alleging truancy, incorrigibility, larceny, burglary, and larceny of automobiles. He was committed to the Chicago Parental School, the Chicago and Cook County School, and the St. Charles School for Boys. He was subsequently killed by members of a rival gang.

came along with us and took us to a newspaper garage where he knew a fellow whose first name was Hector. He delivered the papers on his truck from 3 to 6 o'clock each morning. We slept in this fellow's truck all the while we were bumming from home. At three o'clock we would help him pile the papers on his truck and then sleep on them until he delivered them. While he delivered them from block to block, I used to steal cases of milk from the milk man and break into bread boxes in front of grocery stores. I did this many times and only once I almost got caught doing it. If we had too much to eat we usually put the rest of the cakes and biscuits and milk in front of some house where we knew some poor people lived and knocked at the door and awakened them and then beat it before they could see who we were.

A number of times I went with Frank to some big downtown department store and he taught me the tricks of shoplifting. I believe I just learned the trick from him. He took me to many places I had never been before, such as the Haymarket Theater, and the newsboys lunchroom, in some alley downtown where you could buy a big meal for 15 cents and get also three packages of gum for a nickel. He took me to several of these places when we didn't have much money. He also showed me around Maxwell Street where the streets were crowded with Jews and Dagos who were trying to sell their wares. While I was bumming from home and school, I was going with this fellow and my brother and many times we got away with stealing anything that we could lay our hands on.

I was doing this for about four or five months when I was again caught and arrested and went through the same details as before. I was sentenced to parental school again, this time for seven months and my brother went to St. Charles while the other fellow went to Cook County School. I went back to the same cottage and house officer that I had been with before, and this time I was treated twice as bad for being a second offender.

After I was there about two months I was taken very sick and rushed to the County Hospital by an ambulance which came there and got me. On the way over to the hospital I felt a lot better, the fresh air did me a lot of good. When I got to the hospital I was examined and given some medicine and put to bed for a few days. Then I was sent back to parental school with orders to return two weeks later so I could get operated on for my tonsils and adenoids.

After two weeks I was taken to the hospital by my house officer who left as soon as I was in charge of the hospital authorities. I was then put in a ward with the rest of the children who were to be operated on and that night I was given a bath and put to bed because I was to be operated on in the morning. So I slept all night and in the morning we did not receive any breakfast. At nine o'clock we were given our cards and put in a line by the nurses who were taking care of us. I was the ninth one to be operated on and every time they took a child in to the operating room I felt like jumping out of the window I was so scared.

Well, I finally managed to live through the agony of waiting and I was taken to the operating room by a nice looking nurse who was cheering me up and gently leading me to the operating table. Then I was told to get on the table and lie down with my hands on my side. I did this all without a murmur because I knew if the rest of the children went through this and lived, why I could do the same. I laid my hands on my side and the doctor cheered me up as he put the ether cup over my nose. I remember telling him I couldn't breathe and for him to take the cup away but the next moment I was seeing blue and pink colors, then everything grew dark and I fell in a deep sleep.

The next thing I remember is when I awoke I was in the ward and crying for my mother. A girl who was about 18 years old and was supposed to go home that day was helping the nurse take care of us children. She was calling me dear names and told me not to cry, and at the same time wiping the blood away from my mouth which was still bleeding from my tonsils. I stayed in bed for a couple of days, then I was sent home for a few days before I was to return back to parental school.

After I returned to parental school I went back in the same routine of work and waiting for my time to end. My mother often came to see me and brought along fruits and sandwiches but no candy for it was prohibited there. She would stay all day and tell me what a bad boy I was and ask me to behave myself. I always told her I would but I seemed to forget it when I got out because I'd be in trouble again. After staying there about four months after my sickness a great blow was struck to our family. My father, who was only 48 years old, died one night without previously ailing or feeling sick. He died suddenly after coming home and waiting for supper.

My mother had gone to the grocery store. I was in parental school and my other three brothers were absent also, one in St. Charles, one in the reformatory, and one in the army. I was sent home for the funeral. My father died exactly three days after my 12th birthday.

After the funeral I got a notice to go back to parental school and my brother had to go back to St. Charles. When I went back to parental the officer felt like putting me in the guard house because I didn't return in time, instead he had my hair cut off again and gave me a beating in the night. The three weeks I was there seemed like three years because I was worried about how we would get along now that my father was dead. The company he worked for was good enough to send my mother an extra pay envelope. She got a little help from the city. Every month she would go and get rice, coffee, flour, and many other things to eat.

Well, after my three weeks were up at parental school I stayed with my mother and cheered her up. I know it must have been pretty lonely for her. After about six months of going to school and behaving myself I went back to my old ways. This time I had to go with my brother Carl, and we went to various places and started to bum school together. I took Carl with me around H—— P—— and many other rich neighborhoods and I started at the old game of begging and stealing again.

We kept this up for about two months till finally we were caught by a neighbor who saw me crawl in the house next to his. It happened in R—— P—— and I was taken to the police station there and they searched me and took all the money and jewelry and other valuables off of me and my partner. I was sent to the juvenile again and this time when I came before the judge he sentenced me to St. Charles School for Boys.

IV

A few days after my sentence I was taken there with a few more boys and we arrived there about 11 o'clock in the morning. I was put in a receiving cottage where I was given a hair cut, took my bath, and put on the institution clothes that were given to me. When I got through it was about dinner time and we all got our dinner and then washed the dishes and cleaned the place up.

After staying a few days in the receiving cottage I was assigned to G—— Cottage which was Company "O." The first few days I was taught what some of the rules were by the boy officers and then was placed in a steady position as dining room boy.

It was my business to clear off the tables and reset them. Things were getting along pretty good for the first few months I was in the Company. When we had a competitive drill we won 2nd Prize which was $30.00. The first Prize was $50.00, the second was $30.00, and the third was $20.00.

The first year I was there I got along pretty good, although once or twice I was punished by my house officer, who was a pretty good old man. I was punished because one of the boy officers hit me in the face for disobeying his orders and I hit him back. Then we made a good fight of it and I'm proud to say I got the best of him.

I went out there when I was about 12 years of age and after staying there a little over a year, I suddenly decided to run away from the place because they were a little too strict for me and besides I was getting a little homesick. I hadn't seen or heard from my mother or any of my other brothers. Another reason which made me decide to run away was my brother, James, who had run away the day before I did. I decided I'd like to join him at home, so the next day after he ran off, I decided to do the same. When breakfast and dinner were served the following day, I got ready to take a few boys to church.

After reporting to the house officer, who was in charge, that I was going to church with the boys, I took them there and instead of returning I circled around the little pond and zoo which was built by the boys and jumped over a wire fence into the woods. After running about three miles away from the school, I went to the Northwestern Railroad tracks and walked along the track for about four hours. Finally I saw a freight train coming in my direction. As it got along side of me I started running with it and then jumped for a ladder on the side of the box car. I got on the top of the car and sat there for a while till I started to get chilly, then I moved over nearer to the engine where it was a little warmer.

After I spent half the night riding toward Chicago and passing all the small towns on the way, the train finally stopped at Bellwood, Illinois, where the engines were being changed. I got off the box car and as it was about two o'clock in the morning, I decided to sleep in some box car till morning. I woke up several times during the night on account of it being so cold and besides I didn't even have a coat or cap. After several vain attempts to fall asleep, it started to get daylight and then I got out of the car all dirty, hungry, and cold and started to walk out of the railroad yard. I walked what seemed to me a mile and finally came into the town of Bellwood and roamed the streets for a while. About 7 or 8 o'clock I was so hungry and tired that I decided to beg for some food, whether I got caught or not. At the first house I came to, I asked the girl who came to the door for a bite to eat, but she told me she would have to see her father first. Her father came and he asked me what I wanted and after telling him a hard luck story he finally came across and gave me a few sandwiches which his girl fixed up.

I knew I'd have to get me some different clothes on because the ones I had were the same ones that I ran away with and they belonged to the institution. So after going about four blocks farther down the street, I went to another house and asked for food and clothes. They invited me in the house and questioned me till I finally told them that I ran away from St. Charles. The father of the house wanted to have me sent back but his wife and his two daughters, who were married and living with him, caused him to change his mind. Well, anyway, after spending all morning in their home and eating breakfast and dinner there, they fixed me up with a lot of clothes. After dinner one of the girl's husband who was there took me to a street car and gave me directions to Chicago. He asked me to write them and let them know how I was getting along. After getting in the street car and paying my fare I sat down and wondered how long it would take me to get in Chicago and how I would surprise everybody at home, especially my brother, James. After about two hours riding in the car I finally reached home.

After getting in the neighborhood of my home, I walked around a bit then went home and met my mother and two brothers. My mother was kind of sorry to see me run away because she knew I would get in trouble over it.

That night my brother, James, and I slept together because our home wasn't very big and besides there were only two bedrooms. One of them was for my mother and the other one for my brothers and me. Besides that we had an extra folding bed at home, but the way things were at home there were hardly over two or three of us boys together at one time, because one or two of my brothers were usually in jail or in prison.

Ever since I was a young child I don't believe the whole family were together in one bunch. The way things happened at home when one of my brothers was about to come out of jail or some school, another one would go to jail. The last time I saw my oldest brother was seven years ago. And since then I have been going along from bad to worse by associating with older and more experienced companions.

After sleeping that night my brother and I decided not to go to school because we were both fugitives from St. Charles. We did not wish to get caught right away, so we both walked around the neighborhood and looked the city over the rest of the day. The next few days we spent in the same way until finally we decided on making some extra money some way. I tried looking for a job selling newspapers but I was too young and nobody seemed to want me, so I went to work on a farm with my mother for a dollar a day. My younger brother, Carl, was going to school then and I don't know what my other brother, James, was doing. My two brothers were in jail, one of them was in the state reformatory for receiving stolen property and was doing from one to ten years. My oldest brother was in some other jail or prison.

After working with my mother on the farm for about two weeks, my brother and I got caught by a probation officer who was looking for us and he took us back to St. Charles the next day. After he left us there we both went to our cottages and I was punished by having all my hair cut off and all my play and privileges were taken from me for thirty days. I also was put on the punishment line, where I had to sit all day on a bench about two feet by one foot with arms folded across my chest and back up. I had to do this for ten days, if my marks were good, otherwise I had to do a day more for each mark. Besides all that I lost 30 days for running away. After a fellow who runs away and gets caught goes through all that punishment he is put on the coal detail for 30 more days and then he can earn the privileges the rest of the boys earned. After I went through all this punishment I was sent back to the mending room where I worked before I ran away.

After doing 19 months out in St. Charles I got my parole papers but I couldn't get a job, so they kept me there five more months after my papers were signed. But as I couldn't get a job they finally let me out. Altogether I did two years out there my first time. After I went home I tried to get another job then but still I was too young. For the month that I was out I went swimming and enjoyed myself all kinds of ways.

After I was out of St. Charles three weeks I met my former pal, Frank Pepper, who had taught me all I knew about stealing. When I first met this fellow I was about eight or nine years old and he was about three or four years older than I. When I was a kid, he and I used to go to big department stores and steal everything we could. Later on I started to burglarize stores at night with him and I also ran away from home with him too. He used to come to my house about every morning when I was going with him and holler my name out loud so I could hear him and then we would go anywhere and try our luck in stealing things. My mother and father used to hear him call for me many times and instead of letting me out they would go and scold him for trying to take me out with him. I remember my father used to chase him away a lot of times and tell me if I ever got caught with him he would give me a whipping. Instead of listening to him, I used to sneak out and meet my pal on the corner of the street and we would go all over and steal things.

I remember once when we went to R—— Department Store and he told me to steal a box of red dice, while he kept jiggers. The result was I got caught and he got away. The head of the department store took my name and address and let me go with final orders that if I got caught in the store again he would not let me off so easy. I gave him a different name and address so that did not worry me any because about four days later I was back in there but I did not try to get anything because the floor walker had his eyes on me and my buddy. I never blamed my buddy for any of the times I got arrested, because I was only a kid and never realized that if I kept going with him I was bound to get in trouble.

For a few days after meeting him everything was going along fine until one day he came around my house with his father's car and took me for a drive. After we rode a little while he told me to get out of the car for a few minutes till he saw his father and then he would be back. Before he went he saw a nice looking radiator cap on a Hupmobile that was standing in an alley and he told me to try and get it for him. I told him all right I would try and then he drove off, saying he would be back in 15 or 20 minutes and pick me up. As soon as he left, I went into the alley and I saw a Ford truck with a young boy in it and I started to talk to him and tried to get him to get out of the car and go and see if he could find something for me. I wanted him to go around the corner so he wouldn't see me steal the radiator cap. Despite my arguments he stayed in the car till his father came from a bank and got in the car. He saw me talking to the boy and I guess he asked him what I was talking about because as soon as he got in his car and turned it around towards me he jumped out and grabbed a hold of me and started accusing me of trying to steal his car. He figured I tried to talk the boy into getting out of the car so I could steal it because he had his keys in the lock. I told him he was mistaken and to let me go. He was a copper off duty and he took me right over to the traffic officer and told him I was trying to steal his car and then he called up the patrol wagon right in front of a busy corner.

When the wagon came he turned me over to them and then told them he'd be down with a charge against me. After the wagon took me to the police station I was taken in front of a probation officer and he told me they were going to send me back to St. Charles. I tried to tell him I couldn't even drive a car but he wouldn't listen to me. He told the policemen to take me to the juvenile home and for me to wait there till they got a chance to take me back. Well a couple of days after staying in the juvenile home I was taken back to St. Charles by my parole officer.

After I got there I was put in the receiving cottage where I had to change clothes and take a bath. Following a week in the receiving cottage I was put in the H—— Cottage or otherwise Company N. It was right next to the receiving cottage and had nice house officers. They had a son about 12 years old and a daughter about 16 or 17 years old. After I got in the cottage I was treated like the rest of the boys for about a week and then the house officer called me to his office and told me that he and his wife liked me and would appreciate it very much if I would take charge of the kitchen and see that the boys did their work good. They said I could do this because of my past record in the school as a clean boy besides my experience in that kind of work. So I did everything in my power to help these kind people who thought so much about me and liked me too.

After I was in St. Charles a few months with my brother, my older brother got out of Pontiac Reformatory and came to visit us. The authorities of the school would not let James see him because he was on punishment line for something, so they just called me out for the visit and I had a good visit with my brother and the fellow he brought with him. While he was visiting me he told me to try and run away because he would wait for me that night about 7 o'clock on the side road, so I told him I would try my best and do it that night. So after the visit was about over he told me to tell my brother James the same thing and not to fail to do so.

Well that evening I sent my brother James a note telling him about the visit from Edward and what he told me to do. So that night after about 7 o'clock I was in the basement looking for a chance to get out but I couldn't get away so the next day I tried and got away but I was caught in the town of Geneva three miles away. After I was caught I was transferred to Company A or otherwise called C—— Cottage. The cottage was run by an ex-prize fighter and his wife and he was a good guy if you did not cause him any trouble. After I ran away and got caught I was sorry I did it because it only caused my house officers a lot of trouble and besides it was very rotten of me to take such advantage of them after they been treating me like one of their sons while I was in their care.

After I got in C—— Cottage I was appointed to do all the hard work with the rest of the fellows who were being punished. About two months it continued that way. If I got through with the work, I was put on a line and was told to face the wall with the other boys for about 2 or 3 hours at a time. If the rest of the boys in the cottage went out in the yard and played, all the punishment boys would have to face a tree. If we moved our head around and started to talk to the next fellow, they would make you do squats for about a hour or so till they thought you had enough.

At home my brother Edward was working for awhile, till he quit his job for some reason or other. My youngest brother Carl was still going to school and was getting along pretty good till one of my former pals started to take him out and showed him how to steal bicycles and cars. He got caught after a bit and was sent to parental school where he did four months and then got out and went back to school.

After I was in C—— Cottage about six months and was getting along fine my brother James ran away from the coal detail one cold day in November and got away. There's one thing I got to say about my brother James, after he was out in St. Charles about 2 years he used to run off whenever he cared to and nobody could do anything about it either, because punishment would only make him all the madder and the only thing they could do would be to treat him as nice as possible. He made his reputation out there by running away and being popular too. If I went back to St. Charles today and asked several of the officers if they knew my brothers I'd be willing to bet they did. After he ran away, the house officer kept an eye on me because he thought maybe I would try to run away too, but he was mistaken, for I never ran away anymore that time.

. . . .

After doing my eleven months I was again paroled. My brother was paroled a few months ahead of me and when I got home in eleven months he just went to the Bridewell with another fellow for stealing a car. Well, when I got home I met my younger brother, Carl, and my mother and I asked her where James was and she told me he was not at home for the last 3 days and nights. I asked several of the fellows who went around with him where he was, and they did not know. I called up the county jail and asked if he was there and they told me he was not. I looked around the neighborhood and other places and wondered where he was. Finally a fellow who came out of the House of Correction told me James went in there the day he came out.

In the meantime, while I was looking for my brother, I was looking for a job too. I could not get one myself, so I tried an employment agency. They got me a job in the A—— Engineering Works on R—— and N—— Street. I worked there for about a week and was fired for some reason or other. I guess it was because I was not experienced enough. Well after I got fired my mother told me to try to get another job or go to school. She wanted me to stay out of trouble. Anyway I had no business going to work, because I was only 15 years old then, and I had not finished school.

. . . .

Well after I heard my brother was in the Bridewell, I decided to go and see him. I told my mother and she told me when I got ready to go to take along some food so he could have a good dinner. I did not know the direction to the Bridewell, so I met a fellow who knew my brother and used to go out with him on the corner around the street and he told me he would take me over to the Bridewell to see my brother. He said he would like to talk to my brother because he and my brother were good pals. Well I told him all right lets go and we went there. I asked to see my brother but they said they did not have a fellow by my name there, so I went back home with this fellow, whose name was Clyde Jones. We told my mother that the authorities in the Bridewell said my brother was not there. My mother was pretty worried about him but then she got over it, because many times my brothers or I would be away from home for about a week at a time and nobody would know where we would be till finally we landed up in jail some place.

V

When I was between 9 and 13 years old and used to go with my two brothers and burglarize homes, I used to get caught in nearly every suburb around Chicago. I used to be caught stealing bicycles or coaster wagons and my mother would not know where I was till about three or four days later. It was no use of her worrying because we would only worry her to death if she worried over us every time we were sent away.

After I came from the Bridewell with this fellow, I started to hang around the corner, because I couldn't find work to suit me. I did not want to go back to school, so after a few days of staying on the street corner and picking up the acquaintance of a few more fellows I was treated as one of them and stayed around the corner as late as one o'clock at night. Many times I was offered a drink but I turned it down because I never drank a drop of any kind of whiskey or booze. I had made up my mind I never would when I found out that whiskey was partly the cause of my father's death.

[Michael became associated with two adult offenders and with them engaged in armed robbery. Two weeks later the St. Charles parole officer and two detectives arrested him in his home. His description of these robberies is presented in chapter iv, p. 90.]

Well, then my parole officer did all the talking and he told me to put my shoes on and wanted to drag me to his car like that without my coat or cap. I resisted and told him I would like to get my cap and coat. Then he finally let me get them and one of the detectives gave me a crack in the face and told me to speed it up. My mother came in and told them to keep their hands off of me if they did not want to get into trouble so after getting dressed they took me to the police station where I was put in a cell till the following afternoon. They asked me where I got the gun and what I was doing with it. I told them where I got the gun but I lied to them about what I was doing with it, because I knew I was in for it bad enough. They did not get any satisfaction out of me, so they threw me back in a cell till I was ready to tell the truth. In the meantime my brother came out of the Bridewell and heard all about me getting arrested. He came down the same day and told me not to tell them anything and he told me what my two partners were doing to try and help me out. The cops were busy, too, because they knew from my home that I had been associating with a couple of crooks and stickup men. The police rounded up all the people who were robbed in the last two weeks and they asked them if any of them could identify me. Well, there was only one who I held up and she identified me as one of the two who held her up. She was the first one I held up with my partner and she remembered me well. After that I was put back in a cell and stayed there till the next day. Then they took me out again. They asked me my age, and I told them I was seventeen, but my parole officer who was there told them I was lying. They took me to the church where I was baptized and found that I was only fifteen years old. After staying in a cell at the station for about three or four days they finally caught one of my buddies and then they got the other one a few days later. He was caught with my brother, James, and charged with stealing a car with my brother, besides the holdups he had done with me.

After the three of us were together we were again identified by some woman we had robbed. After seeing we were trapped, we confessed to all the holdups we committed. We were then taken to the detective bureau for some more show ups, but nobody

had anything against us here, so we went to the bureau of identification. From there I was taken over to the Cook County Jail.
All this was new to me and I wasn't caring much because I was
only a kid yet and I did not take things seriously. My brother,
myself, and my two partners were taken to the county jail and
when we got there it was about nine in the morning and we were
thrown in the bull-pen with the rest of the inmates who had just
come there. We were searched, one at a time, and had to take a
bath, while a couple of experts went through our clothes while
we were bathing. After we went through having ourselves
searched we spent all day in the bullpen with nothing to do.
After supper we were examined by a few doctors and had to
answer a few questions concerning our health.

When bedtime came we were put in a cell just for the night
and the beds were so dirty and full of bedbugs that I had to stay
awake half the night trying to keep them off of me. Next day
we were awakened by a guard who came around and tapped on
our cell door. We got dressed and again went into the bullpen
where I was served with black coffee and a heavy bun for my
breakfast. I stayed in the bullpen with the rest of the bunch
till about eight o'clock. Then we were assigned to the new part
of the jail where we were going to stay till we left the place.
I was put on the same tier that my brother and my younger
partner were put on. My other partner went on the third floor
where they had fellows about his age. After I was appointed to
a cell everything was new to me and I got acquainted pretty
quick for the jail was pretty crowded and I had three other cell
partners besides myself and they put me wise to things in there.

Time went by pretty fast on the second floor because they
had a school up there during week days and on Sundays we all
went to church in the morning and in the afternoons we played
several different games, which helped to make the time fly. After
I was in the county jail two weeks, my mother came to see my
brother and me and left us each a big bundle of eats so it would
last us about two days or so. My mother came regular after that
and each time she seemed more worried and older because the
only one left at home with her was my kid brother. After a few

months went by even my younger brother got arrested and was sent to St. Charles for stealing a machine. Out of five of us boys all of them were gone. Three of them already sent away and my brother James and I about to get sent away too.

After about two months in the jail, I was taken with my brother and partners for a hearing, but the case was continued for a month. The court appointed a state lawyer for my defense, because I could not afford a lawyer of my own. I did not care anyway because I was ready to take the rap with one of my partners because I knew I did not have a chance. If possible, we were going to try to throw the other partner of ours out of the trouble, and take the whole rap ourselves. That didn't work, because when I went for trial with my brother and buddies I pleaded guilty to three robberies, a burglary, and larceny, and was sentenced for one to ten years in the Pontiac Reformatory. My brother also pleaded guilty to the stolen machine, with my partner, and he also was sentenced for one to ten years in the Pontiac Reformatory. The younger one of my partners also pleaded guilty to the robberies committed with me, and the stolen machine with my brother, and he was given the same sentence. My other partner took a jury trial, because he thought with the help of my partner and me he could beat the charge. After wasting another month getting a jury he was tried and despite the fact that my partner and me tried to deny that he ever had anything to do with any of the robberies with us, he was found guilty and sentenced to ten years to life in Joliet Penitentiary.

After we were all sentenced we went back to the county jail and my mother came to see us during the last two weeks that we stayed there. She cried over me and my brother because she knew we were not going to St. Charles or any of the other kids schools, but to a prison where they treat a fellow worse than they do in bigger prisons. I told her not to worry because I would only be there one year instead of five or six because I wanted her to stop crying and worrying over me and my brother. A few days after her last visit, we were notified early in the morning to pack our belongings because we were going to Pontiac. After an hour of waiting in the lower office of the jail we were handcuffed, four in a row, and taken to the depot where we took the Chicago and Alton train. A few minutes later we were Pontiac bound.

It was the first time I ever was going so far away from Chicago, so I looked at everything that we went by. After riding about an hour we came to Joliet, and I caught a glimpse of both Joliet prisons, the old one and the new one, as we went by. I felt sorry for the poor devils who were perhaps locked up in that tomb of living death for life. My brother sat across from me on the train and we discussed the family affairs and what my other brother Edward would say when he saw us come in Pontiac, to do time. My brother Edward was there for his second term and he had been in about four years altogether both times.

After we reached Pontiac depot we were dumped into an institution truck and were taken to the prison right past the iron gate and into the captain's office. After we were there about five minutes the Recorder of the Institution came in and called out the fellows' names till he came to mine and then he asked me how old I was. I told him, 15 years old. He asked me if I had told my age to the judge who sentenced me and I said, yes. He told me to say goodbye to my brother as I was going back to the county jail because I was too young to come out there.

Well I told my brother James goodbye and then I was taken to the institution front office where I had to wait for a couple of hours till the guards who brought us down were ready to take me back. About four o'clock in the afternoon on the same day I was taken back to the county jail in Chicago and put back on the second floor in my old cell. Soon as I got there I wrote home to my mother and told her all about them not accepting me at Pontiac reformatory on account of me being only 15 years old.

My mother came to see me the following visiting day and I told her I probably would go back to St. Charles for the third time. She was pretty glad that I wasn't going to the Illinois State Reformatory and she told me if I did go to St. Charles I better behave myself out there and then be a good boy when I got out. I promised her I would because I found out it didn't pay to be a crook. So the next week that I was in the county jail

I was again tried by the same judge who sentenced me before. He was pretty mad at me because I didn't go to Pontiac but he couldn't do anything about it so he sentenced me to St. Charles. After he gave me my sentence, I was taken back to the jail and I told the fellows I knew where I was going, so the next week I was notified again to pack my things to be taken to St. Charles.

· ·

I was put in the charge of two big bailiffs who took me to the juvenile court right across from the detention home. I waited in the hall till dinner time with the bailiffs and then they asked me if I was hungry. I told them I was and told them I didn't have a square or decent meal in the jail outside of the food my mother brought me. Well, they took me into a restaurant around the corner and then took my handcuffs off with a warning that if I tried to run away on them they would kill me. Well, I told them to cease to worry because if I wanted to run away I could wait until I got to St. Charles. After eating till I was filled up we went back to the juvenile court and waited till some fellows were sentenced to St. Charles so they could take them along. About an hour later I was put in the county bus with one colored fellow who was going with me to St. Charles and a small colored girl who was going to Geneva Girls School.

On arriving at the institution the superintendent told me to behave myself because if I didn't I would be taken back to Pontiac. So I promised him to behave and be a good boy while I was out there. After that I was taken into the receiving cottage and took a bath and changed into institution clothes. I recognized many of the boys there and things were not so bad out there for me because I was an old timer and I knew all the ropes of the place. I asked to stay in the receiving cottage because I knew it was a lot better in many ways and also it had many more privileges than most cottages out there had. My request was granted as long as I showed them I was trying to behave myself.

A few days after my return there, I was appointed to take charge of a group of boys who worked in different parts of the cottage and I was to see that they did their work and did it right. The family officers told me that they appointed me to this position because of my experience and good former record as an officer out there before. So for the first month in that cottage everything was going along fine.

I saw and spoke to my younger brother Carl and he was in the B—— Cottage. He and I were in the same class room and saw much of each other while I was there. I did not hear from home very often because my mother cannot write English, aside from a few words.

I went to St. Charles this time a week before my sixteenth birthday. I stayed there only about two and one-half months before I ran away again. I was transferred to C—— Cottage one day and I asked the supervising officer who transferred all the boys why he transferred me when I was behaving so good. He told me that was the trouble because I was behaving too damn good to please him. He told me he was wise to me and let it go at that. I was working in the electric shop at that time and when I got transferred out of the receiving cottage into a former cottage of mine I planned to escape because I did not care to stay there. So I got a friend of mine who was out there several times and he and I planned to get a pipe cutter and cut the bars that were on the basement windows when our regular family officer had a day off.

So a week later I stole the pipe cutter out of the plumbing shop and carried it in my belt to my cottage and hid it until after supper. Then we would get it out as soon as it was dark and cut the bars which were only a half an inch thick. That night my partner was going to stay in the basement and keep a look-out for me, while I cut the bars. When I got them cut we let two other fellows go with us. As soon as the bars were cut I got my cap and went through the window first and then my partner and the other two boys followed him. We all dashed across the yard and then into the fields heading toward the town of St. Charles. We got into the town about an hour later because we had to hide in the fields while searchlights from cars were flashing all around us.

After we got in town we started looking for a machine of some kind. We looked for about a half hour and finally we found a car that was unlocked. It was an old time make and I did not know how to drive it. One of the other fellows, who knew how to drive, got in and then we started to go towards Chicago.

My partner Joe, who knew the directions towards Chicago, got in the front seat and directed the way till we came into Roosevelt Road. It was about eleven o'clock at night then and the driver opened the car up to see how fast it would go. It couldn't go over 65 miles an hour because it was an old type of car. We traveled at the rate of 40 miles an hour and there was nobody on the road all night but us.

Just before we reached Cook County we were pretty low on gas so the next gas and oil station we came to we saw it was closed and besides it was a refreshment stand. In the dead of the night one of the fellows and I broke the glass on the window and crawled in and helped ourselves to everything that we came across. After we got all the candy, peanuts, and gum and other things we took a five gallon can that was full of gas and setting in the corner of the gas room. We put the can and all in the car and started for Chicago again. We got there about an half hour later.

We rode for about an hour till I decided to see what clothes I could find at home. I told the other three fellows that I was going home and had the car stopped in front of the house and went in through a window, because I figured the door was locked and everybody was asleep. But as soon as I started to get in the window our dog started barking and woke my mother up. I got in the house and as soon as the dog saw who it was he started jumping all over me. He was so glad to see me again. My mother got out of bed and when she saw me she just stared at me a few minutes and asked me what I had done. I told her I had run away and had come home to get some clothes and was going out and sleep some place for the night. She wanted me to stay at home and sleep but I told her the police would probably be here in the morning and I did not wish to get caught.

As I was getting the clothes I looked the house over and saw a few changes. On of them was that the house was installed with electric lights and my mother bought a new white range stove.

After getting the clothes and giving them to the three fellows in the car, I came back to the house and got me some food because I was pretty hungry after riding in the car and open country for two or three hours. My mother wanted me to stay at home and I told her I could not do it. After eating a hurried meal, I told my mother I was going to ride around with the fellows for awhile and I would notify her in the morning where I was staying. She told me I would get killed riding in the car with the other boys but I just smiled at her and told her I would have to take my chances on that. I went out and left our home for the last time.

I got in the car with the other three fellows and we went to one of the other fellow's home. He couldn't get in the house because it was one or two o'clock in the morning, so he got back in the car and then we didn't have any place in particular to go so one of the fellows suggested breaking into some stores around his neighborhood. So off we went and we broke into about three places that night. We rode around all night and any grocery or butcher shop that looked like an easy job to break into, we did. After riding around till about four o'clock we got a flat tire and Joe and I sent the driver and other fellow out to hunt for some heavy thing so we could knock the heavy padlock off the spare tire that was on the car. After the two fellows were gone about ten minutes a Flint car approached our car and stopped about 12 feet in front of our car and I saw two detectives come out of the door. Well, when I saw who it was I crawled out of the car and sneaked in behind it, and then ran around the corner into an alley and into the top floor of a four story apartment building. I stayed there till about what seemed to me as fifteen minutes and then I got down and looked around the corner of the alley and I saw that both cars were gone.

Well I thought that Joe, my partner, had been arrested with the car and all, so I decided that I better go home. I started to walk across the street into the other alley and I saw one of the two fellows who were out of the car when the police came. I asked him where the other fellow was and he told me he went back to the car just as I got out. So we both thought the other two fellows were arrested and in jail so we walked around a bit till the fellow decided that he would go home to G——— City where he lived. I told him I wouldn't mind going with him as I did not have any place to go. We looked around the streets for about half an hour trying to find a car with the ignition opened. Finally we came across a brand new Velie Sedan that was standing in front of a lighted apartment building. The clutch was open and the key was in the ignition so everything was just fine for us. We got into the car and started away with it. We headed toward the outskirts of the city but as the neighborhood was strange to me we were lost so we turned back towards the city and it was about 5:30 A.M. when we got to 63rd and Stony Island Avenue.

We were just about to turn a corner on 63rd Street when I looked around and saw a Cadillac Squad right in back of us. Well, I told my partner, who was driving, that they were there. He turned around and saw them and then started to step on the gas. The police squad saw the sudden move of our car and they followed us for about a block. Then they clanged their gong for us to stop but my partner only stepped on the gas a little more. The police squad rang their gong for us to stop but as my partner wouldn't stop, they opened fire at us for the next four miles. Our car was swaying from one side of the road to the other and we almost killed about three pedestrians. The Cadillac Squad was only about 40 or 50 feet behind us and they were continually firing a stream of bullets towards our direction, but as luck was with me I never got hit, for I was next to the driver and had my head between my knees and every now and then I peaked out of the back window and told my partner what side of the car they were trying to get on, and before they could get on our side we would steer the car in front of them.

The chase continued for about 5 miles and all the while they were shooting I was mumbling a prayer and calling myself a fool for not taking my mother's advice and staying home. After they chased us on a straight road for about 5 miles I told my partner to try and turn some corners because the squad car was more powerful than ours and we could not beat it on a straight course. The next block came and he tried to turn a corner 55 miles an hour and instead of turning the corner the car hit the street lamp on two wheels and we crashed into the sidewalk with two of the right wheels broken under us. When the car stopped I was cut up a bit by the broken glass. I opened the door and was going to get ready to run but the four detectives were out of the car and had their guns pointed at me and my buddy. I just stood there beside the wrecked car and waited for them to come and get me.

They thought we were desperate crooks and they asked us for our guns but as we did not have any to give them, we told them we did not have any. They started to beat up on me till they knocked me senseless. Everyone of them took a turn beating up on me and when they got through my body was all black and blue and my temple was swollen about an inch from the blow of one of the detectives' guns.

After they found out that we were only a couple of runaway kids from St. Charles, they treated us a little better, and then took us to the police station and threw us in a cell for awhile and then took us out for a talk. A reporter from an evening newspaper was there and made a story about us which he put on the front page of the paper that night.

In the afternoon a few officers from St. Charles came and handcuffed us and took me and my partner back to St. Charles and put us in separate cottages. The first thing they did to me when I got in my new cottage was to cut off all my hair as part of my punishment. The week that I stayed in that cottage everything was made miserable for me. After doing a week of standing in the corner and doing all the dirty jobs in the cottage, I was again taken out of the institution because the general superintendent swore out a warrant and did not want me out in St. Charles. On Saturday, a week after I ran away and got caught, everybody was in the gymnasium and watching a basketball game, while I was in the punishment line and facing the wall. After facing the wall for about twenty minutes, I was called out to the front of the gymnasium and a Chicago parole officer was there to receive me. They took me to the tailor shop and outfitted me with a cheap suit and then I was taken back to Chicago and then to the County Jail.

My mother came to see me the first week I was in the jail and worried over me as usual. I felt ashamed of myself and I thought what a big fool I was for running away from St. Charles and making trouble for everyone including myself.

VI

Well, for the following three weeks I was in the County Jail and things did not look bright for me. I was so sick for about two weeks of the time that I seemed to be in a trance. After I had been in the jail three weeks I was given a hearing and my case was continued for one week. A week later I went into court and was sentenced to the reformatory for one to ten years. I asked the judge to change it to some other place because I did not care to let everybody know that three of us boys were in the same reformatory. The judge just called me a Hoodlum and did not change it, so a few days later I was bound for Pontiac and to join my other two brothers. I went down to Pontiac with eleven other boys. All the boys in my family were arrested at that time. My brother Carl was in St. Charles, two other brothers, Edward and James, were in Pontiac reformatory with me, and John was in a prison in another state.

After I worked in the extra detail for a few months I was picked out and assigned to the furniture factory, where I worked for the first eight months I was in this institution. My brother Edward went up to the Parole Board then and was paroled and then he started to write to me and told me how things were at home and what he was doing.

After my brother Edward got paroled, I was transferred to live with my brother James because I thought things would be a lot better. My brother was working in the tailor shop then and he seemed to get along fairly well there, with the exception of going to the hole every now and then for minor offenses.

The screens, or what the inmates called the hole, is a solitary vacant school room at the north end of the north cellhouse. This room is filled with 24 tiny cells about 4 feet wide by 6 feet, and there is not a thing in a cell except a small bucket and cup. The cup is for water which is passed to the poor devils in there two times a day, morning and night. And the bucket is for toilet purposes. Each morning at about 7:30 o'clock it can be emptied. The fellows that go there are supposed to have violated some rule of the institution, probably talking in line, passing a book or articles to the next cell or fighting and many of the other rules. A great many of them are foolish ones and I think they should not have them but I can't say or do anything about it except obey them or get thrown in the hole for maybe one, two, and up to ten days, without anything to eat except one slice of bread each morning and no more.

The first time I went to the hole was when I was still a fish (newcomer) and was boxing with my cell partner. The night guard wrote us both a ticket and turned it in to the assistant superintendent and we both were called over to the court in the morning and he bawled us out and threw us in the hole for one day. The hole was so hot and stuffy that I could hardly breathe. I could not sleep at all that night because if I tried to lay on my side the cement floor would hurt my hips so I sat up all night and thought of all the wrong I did in my past life and just what did I gain besides a lot of time in jail. That night seemed like an eternity to me because I was so anxious for the morning to come and for the guard to let me out of that damned hole. After I got out I made up my mind not to break any rules if I could help it, because that hole did not agree with me. It was the cause of more than one inmate getting tuberculosis and dying, so I made up my mind to stay out of it if possible.

I did not hear much from home. Once in a while I'd get a letter a month and maybe sometimes I went three or four months at a time without a letter, so I did not know very much of how things were progressing at home. After twelve months in the reformatory I went before the Board of Pardons and Paroles and they asked me how the robberies were committed and what I done. Well, I told them all about the robberies and asked them for a break because I was only 15 years old when all these robberies were committed and I did not realize what I was doing till I got caught. But the answer I got of the Parole Board was parole denied, and a few months later my case went up again and I was continued for three more long years.

After my first year here I got out of school entirely because I did not get any farther along in my education than I was when I went there. I got out of the furniture factory also because I wasn't interested in that line of work. I was then assigned to the print shop and put in the bindery department and now I'm the head bindery man and pretty well advanced in the art of book binding and making other leather goods.

In the summer time I was allowed with the rest of the boys to spend 45 minutes each day in recreation. Outside of that there is no other playtime or recreation for me or the boys. In the winter the fellows saw a picture show each Saturday and maybe on special holidays. During the second winter I was there, I was on no play privilege for almost 9 months and I missed all shows, chapel services, and many other privileges the rest of the fellows had.

I was in the hole several times then and did not seem to care whether I went or not because it was no use of me trying to be an angel because you're bound to get a bum rap off some of the guards and besides I was used to the hole. I only went there for one serious charge and that was for fighting with another inmate who thought the world was wrong and he was all right. I done five days in the hole for that offense and when I came out I looked like I was dying on my feet. After I celled with my brother for about a year and a half we had a few arguments and he seemed kind of disgusted with everything. One thing which led to arguments was because we did not hear from home and because he was two years older than I he seemed to think he could run me but as I'm no kid any longer I let him know that and so he got mad and started a fight. I won the first one and he did not like it, so about a month later he started another one and that fight came out about a draw.

In the meantime my brother, Edward, went to work for the first few months and was doing fine, but soon after my brothers, Carl and John, got their releases and came home, Edward was caught with a gun and was charged with carrying concealed weapons and was sentenced to the House of Correction for one year. My brother, Carl, who was still under age, got his working license and got a job and helped my mother by working in the Western Union. My mother, I heard was getting along alright, only at times money was pretty scarce at home.

After I had the second fight with my brother I decided it was best for me or him to get out of the cell before we grew to hate each other as some of the brothers do, so I tried to get a transfer with no results 'till finally again my brother did not seem to like some of my habits. I was a pretty heavy sleeper and used to snore once in awhile and he did not like it. One night he kicked my bunk and swore at me and I told him to lay down because I couldn't help it. Well I went back to sleep again and in the morning he got up and started to argue with me and get smart so I didn't want to fight any more but he hit me first and then the fight began and it was one of the toughest and dirtiest fights I have ever been in. He wasn't satisfied with only using his fists so he used his teeth and feet. I tried every way to calm him down but he wasn't satisfied till he saw I was bleeding from a cut in my head and blood was all over the cell. Well the result was I had to go to the hospital and get two stitches sewed in the cut and I was transferred to a different cell. For a while I did not talk to him because I wanted to give him a chance to feel sorry for his mistake in fighting me. A few months later after the fight he started talking to me and asking me to do little favors for him such as loaning him some tobacco or getting him some paper or any other thing he wanted out of the Print Shop.

I got twelve times in the screens to my credit from the time I came here till now. Some of these twelve tickets I got were unavoidable because when a fellow hits you in the mouth and tells you to come on and fight, I could not stand there and let him get away with it because if I did the rest of the fellows would know that I was a yellow coward and that's one word I don't take from anybody.

The twelve tickets I got since I been here I will write down what they were for. The first time I went was for wrestling a friendly match with my cell partner; the second one was for neglecting my work; the third one for throwing water off my finger tips on the fellow who sat across the aisle in school; the fourth ticket was for talking in line, I did four days for that charge. The fifth was for talking in line again; I did four more days for that too. The sixth ticket I got was for passing a book to the next cell; the seventh was for using a bum Y.M.C.A. card to go to the meetings. I did five days for that; the eighth was for having unauthorized articles in cell; the ninth offense was for fighting with another boy; the tenth time was for talking to the next cell; the eleventh time for talking in line again—this charge was a bum rap, the officer who wrote the ticket had it in for me. He also wrote the twelfth ticket too which was for unauthorized articles in my cell.

. . . .

Since I been here I started reading books and magazines and I've read about 500 books in this institution besides all kinds of magazines. After about two years in this institution I never thought of what I was going to do with my life when I got out. I didn't care because I thought I never got a break in my life and no one to help me when I got in a jam, so I used to talk with my cell partner who was working with me and celling with me. I used to tell him of my experiences in all the places I had been in and also how I came to get caught and come down here. I thought of going out again and instead of going to work all the time, I was only going to work for the first few months, then go in a higher priced racket and make up for lost time, but when my cell partner went home and a few months later got caught for robbery with a gun, I decided to cast all of them foolish ideas and thoughts out of my head because now I know that sooner or later a fellow will get caught and pay the price. My former cell partner paid dearly because he got life in Indiana prison for his crimes and also I know of many others who went out of here with the idea of paying society back for their incarceration in this place and they always usually came back here or went to Joliet State Penitentiary. I banished all thoughts and ideas of that kind out of my head because I know now that it never pays to be crooked. It took me a great many years to find out, but now that I'm old enough to reason for myself I know that the old policy of crime never pays, is right.

. . . .

Our new superintendent is also trying to see that we get loud speakers in the cell houses and it makes an inmate a lot better instead of worse. Since they got the radio I never thought of all the good times I was missing, and when the radio is turned on and all the music and outside news is broadcasted, it makes me wish I was out and enjoying those things instead of being out in this reformatory. I can't remember of one Christmas or any other holiday in the last seven or eight years that I enjoyed at home. In the three years that I done time here a few things changed at home.

My brother, Edward, who came back here for the third time got the maximum before the parole board and went out six months later on a discharge. He had all his time in six years and three months and got out on a discharge. Since he got out he has been behaving himself pretty good and I guess he finally realized that it never paid to steal and never will, so now he's working and making things lighter for everybody at home. My brother, James, still has three years to do before his maximum is up and then he also will go out on a discharge. I think he got a pretty rotten deal from the parole board, because he only has a larceny charge against him and I don't see why the parole board gave him this maximum and give other boys who have worse charges and records than he has about two years. The only reason I think they gave him all that time to do is because when he went to the parole board there were two of us brothers out here and they thought when a whole bunch of brothers come down here its a hopeless case to reform him and gave him the maximum and forgot all about him.

. . . .

[Michael describes how he and his brothers used a dog "Topsy" in their begging and burglary. See chapter iii, p. 74.]

VII

What I think is partly the cause of a young kid getting into trouble is associating with older and bad companions. Take for instance many of the cases now where the kids usually start by being truant from school and a few weeks later they are either sent to Cook County School, Parental School, or St. Charles. And when they get into one of those places they might happen to meet some fellow they take a liking to and this fellow who happens to be an older boy and more experienced in many ways, tells of his experiences of making easy money in an easy way and tells of a great many other things he has done. This youngster who never had had a chance, gets mighty chummy with this fellow and is taught many tricks. He tells the big fellow that he's going to go out and try and get some of that easy money. And all the time he's in these institutions he learns more and more on how to get this and get that without getting caught. I know this to be a fact in many cases because I was in a great many institutions and in each one of them I was taught more and more about the different kinds of rackets.

When I was in Parental School I used to listen to three or four boys talking about how they got arrested and what they did and what they were going to do when they got out. In St. Charles it was a little worse, because there I was made a little more experienced because there were older fellows. In my opinion I think the worst place for a small boy is one of these institutions. He ought to have at least a good chance to make good and if he still thinks of bumming school or stealing bicycles, he ought to be given a bicycle and that will satisfy him. If he bums school give him a good beating if he don't pay any attention to your kindness and speeches. Make the kid respect you and you'll get along a lot better with him than you will if you continually beat him or send him to an institution.

When I got arrested this last time I was sent to the county jail. During the time I was there and in this institution I learned more in these places than I did in all other places combined. I did not know much about the city or world and when I came into the County Jail and the Illinois State Reformatory, I learned more, because as I said before a bunch of the inmates would get together and start telling about their experiences all over the world. They would tell one another just how to get rid of a stolen machine, how to pull off robberies without getting caught and many other things in that line. I've heard about a thousand fellows' tales and adventures and have learned quite a bit, but even at that I never gave a thought that these fellows were all the same as I was and they probably would find out some day that the only and safe way to make money was to work for it. When I get out of this reformatory, which I hope will be soon, I'm going to go to work and take care of my mother who is pretty old and probably won't be with me very long. Then as soon as I get some money saved I'll probably get married and settle down. Well, since I've been in this institution I've made up my mind to behave myself because I cannot afford to spend all my life in jails. I've been in this reformatory three years and I've only seen my mother once. My mother and younger brother came with other boys' folks who happen to live in the same building we do. Everyone is now at home with the exception of my brother and I. It's been quite a good many years ago since the whole family had a reunion, and I hope it won't be long before my brother and I get out of this institution and get a chance to make good. You ought to have a little consideration in my case—I've never tried robbery with a gun before and I never would of now if I had a little help in getting a job. I was only fifteen years old and just beginning to realize what I was doing to myself after about a year or so of working now and then. I believe nobody need to be afraid of me getting into trouble again.

Before I came down to this place I was too young to listen to the advice of my mother. I'm very sorry I didn't because maybe I'd never have come down here. I hope I never see any of my old associates again because they were partly the cause of me being down here. If I stayed away from them like I should of, I probably would be behaving myself and working now because I never had the least idea of ever committing a crime till I was talked into it by my partners. I don't want to throw the blame on them because I'm here, because if I hadn't been so young and foolish and had stayed away from fellows older than me and had told them to go to hell like I should have done, things would be different.

In my earlier life I never had a chance to have things I liked such as bicycles, roller skates, and many other things because as I mentioned before we were too poor. My mother and father could hardly make ends meet when we were youngsters and too young to help. It was still worse when my father died, because after the funeral and other bills, my mother could hardly make a living. My father had no money to leave for my mother and the county took care of her and us kids for one year after my father's death. She also used to go to the settlement house where she was given a little help now and then. She took me there many times and she told me about them places.

My mother, I believe, likes me a little better than the rest of the boys because many times she told me when I was a kid to grow up and try to be a good boy and get married and live with her. She used to tell other folks how good and gentle I was and she told people who had children or babies not to be afraid of me minding them because I liked babies and children.

I've been in some institution or other for the last twelve years and you ought to know that I really haven't had a chance to really enjoy life. From the time I was about six or seven years old till now, I haven't been out of jail for four or five years altogether, and I've spent most of my holidays as well as my life in jail. I'm only nineteen years old now and pretty young to face life alone because I haven't had much education. I quit going to school when I was in the 8th grade. I would like to go away from home for about a year after my parole and go to some strange part of the country where I'm not known or anything is known about me. I could stay and work there till I met new and better people instead of going home back to the old familiar neighborhood where I would see familiar faces and get back into the habits of my former days with my old street pals who might be out again.

I think a stay of a year or so will do me good out in some nice warm climate and build up my health as well as my character again. Out of the whole family I'm the second to the tallest boy, yet I'm the lightest one in the bunch. I only weigh one hundred and thirty-five (135) pounds and according to the health book I'm about fifty pounds under weight for my height which is five feet, eleven inches. At home my mother used to think I was the sickest boy in the family because I usually got sick pretty often. In the last four years I was only sick twice which I call pretty good for an institution of this kind where they treat and feed the inmates a lot worse than they do in Joliet or in the Atlanta Government Prison. Some of the food which is dished out to us isn't fit for a dog to eat and yet they expect the boys to eat it and then turn out a days work on an empty stomach. If you don't turn out the required amount of work the officer in charge will send you to the hole. I could write a book about this place if I wanted to, but it wouldn't do any good so why should I bother about it. I could tell about some of the guards who don't seem to be human. They make a young kid slave and if the fellow was sick or something he wouldn't get any rest. The institution hospital is run by a strict and mean doctor and many young fellows who are newcomers get beat over their head and face because they won't give the doctor a satisfactory answer as to their offense in coming down here. This is something the doctor has no business asking a fellow to tell him.

There are a few officers in this institution who have lived here quite a number of years and they seemed to have formed a habit of sending an inmate to solitary or to the hole for almost any kind of petty offense. Some of these officers do not think of the welfare of the inmates and when something new is given to the inmates they try to prevent its use by sending many boys to the hole for almost nothing.

When our new superintendent of this institution first came here he treated the boys fine and told us to keep away from the court line here and he would see that we would get many other privileges. Well when the radio was being tried out in the north cellhouse many of the officers thought we were being treated too good and they wrote many boys a ticket for bum raps. By doing that they thought the superintendent would abolish the idea of a radio being installed in this place. Its such officers as these who make many of the old timers bitter against them and they usually start trouble.

Several men who I think should be fired are the dietitian, cook, and baker because the food we have been getting since I came is terrible. The dietitian is to blame for not getting us the right kind of food and seeing that we get plenty of it and the cook is to blame for not serving the food clean and not cooking it right. The pies and bread the baker puts out aren't worth two cents especially what they call pumpkin pies. We got these every Sunday for dinner for about fourteen months straight and only about one or two fellows out of a dozen ate the pies. The food we got between the first of January and the first of March of this year was pretty good because the superintendent used to inspect the pans but since he quit inspecting them all the fellows complain about it. Besides we did not get any butter for the last three weeks. This ought to give you an idea of the food we get. A few of the fellows here who have been in government prisons tell me they feed the fellows here worse than they do in any other kind of institution or prison. I know for a fact that the food I got in the other institutions was better by a whole lot than it is here. For a month before each holiday they almost starve us in order to make up for what they give us to eat on a holiday. Well, since I been in this institution I've grown to be a whole lot wiser to everything.

I spend my time in here like many of the other boys do. In the daytime I work in the print shop here and have learned a fair trade and in the evening when supper is over I read a book, magazine or any other thing which interests me. I've read quite a number of books since I've been in this place and I am familiar with many authors and their books. I like to read as long as books interest me. If I have no books or anything to do I wash my socks and handkerchiefs and either play cards or start a conversation with my cellpartners, till bed time. We go to bed at nine o'clock and wake up at 5:30 o'clock in the morning. I seldom have dreams but when I do dream I dream of things that seem to have interested me or have effected on me during the day. Many times since I been here I dreamt I was home and going to work or doing other things and when I awoke I had a great disappointment when I found out I was in this place.

A Sunday or any other day is just another day in this jail to me and its the same old daily routine day in and day out. Many times I grow tired of being in here and think of home and other pleasures I'm missing for four years or maybe six, just because of the few paltry dollars I stole.

A Sunday in this place is very boresome because time drags and if you haven't anything to do it's still harder because a fellow is locked in his cell for the whole day except for breakfast and dinner. After dinner you're locked in till next morning because they do not serve any supper to the inmates here and that's what makes time drag along.

Well, I've been here in this institution for a little over three years and have told all I think is necessary. During the three years I've been here I've decided to lay off anything outside the law and go to work when I get out. Since I've been here in this institution I've only seen my mother and kid brother once and about nine months later my two oldest brothers came out to see me and I've decided to go straight just like my two brothers have. I'd like to go to the parole board soon and get a parole so I can go to work and help my mother take care of things. I've decided to move out of the old neighborhood as soon as we can afford it and then get a good job and enjoy the luxuries of life.[5]

At the present time everyone but me and my brother, James, is at home and if we could get out soon and go to work I'm sure the city or state will not have any trouble with me any more.

[5] When Michael was released from the reformatory he was ambitious for himself and his family. He wanted to secure work and earn money to make it possible for his mother to move into a better community and to buy new furniture for the home. He did not realize the extreme difficulty which he would encounter in securing the employment necessary for the realization of these ideals. Actually Michael had spent so many years in institutions that he knew very little about securing employment or making a living. In addition he was released during a period of widespread unemployment when he could not secure work either through his own efforts or the efforts of others who were interested in him. His inability to find employment and thus achieve by legitimate means the ends to which he aspired was probably important in his failure to make an adjustment in conventional society. (For a discussion of the factors involved in post-institutional success and failure see Glueck and Glueck, *500 Criminal Careers* [New York: Harvard University Press, 1930]; A. A. Bruce, E. W. Burgess, and A. J. Harno, *The Workings of the Indeterminate Sentence Law and the Parole System in Illinois* [Springfield, 1928]; George B. Vold, *Prediction Methods and Parole* [Hanover, N.H., 1931]; Helen L. Witmer, "Some Factors in Success and Failure on Parole," *Journal of Criminal Law and Criminology*, November, 1927, pp. 18-384-403.)

I'm old enough to realize that all my life I've been foolish, and I've paid for every single offense I've committed, so all I want now is a chance to go straight. I'd like to get out soon because a few more years in this place would only harm me instead of doing any good to me, because I'm reformed and I'll tell the world that if it was necessary. I know I'm reformed because I've had many temptations to steal things which would do me some good in here and some inner feeling in me would tell me not to do it. I know how a fellow with a family feels when he works all week for about 25 or 30 dollars a week and then someone steals it from him. I feel sorry for the person and I've decided to quit the crime racket and instead grab a lunch box and go to work. I've made the popular policy of "Honesty is the Best Policy" my policy, and all I need is a good job with a good salary and then the State of Illinois can check another boy off their hands as reformed.

CHAPTER XII

THE LIFE-HISTORY OF CARL MARTIN[1]

I

The earliest recollections that I have of my home life are when we moved into a house with a rather large yard. From that time on we always have lived in this building. The reason for remembering that incident was that on the first day after we moved there I had a fist fight with one of the neighbors. We had no electricity there and the building was rather run-down. There was no bath and the toilets were outside in a hall way.

My father was working regularly at that time and as far back as I can remember he worked fairly regular. But my father's regularity in work did not mean anything because when he got paid he went on a spree and spent half of his check, drinking and playing cards with his friends. So, in general, his working did not do us any good. I was about eleven years old when my father died. My mother worked on and off during the summer months on a farm in order to support the family. My mother never worked in the winter except for about three years when she got a job in a factory. She worked in a pickle factory for two of these years.

The neighborhood I lived in was rather deteriorated in appearance as the buildings are rather old. They are not modern in construction and have no bathrooms which causes the people to rely on the public bathhouse. The alleys are very dirty and they are not of concrete and are full of tin cans and garbage most of the

[1] Carl wrote this life-history within the last year. Approximately ten years had elapsed between the time he was released from St. Charles School for Boys and the time he wrote this document. He wrote primarily for a small monetary consideration. Carl is the least articulate and has the least literary ability of the five brothers. He wrote with difficulty and he required continuous encouragement and some assistance. About five years ago he wrote two short life-histories, parts of which have been presented in other chapters. All of these materials have been repunctuated and re-paragraphed.

time. The neighborhood is adjacent to the Chicago River and near a railroad where some of the residents go and pick up coal. It also has quite a few factories adjacent to it. The streets around there have very high walks and the yards have drops of six or seven feet below the street level. The people in the neighborhood are very old fashioned as most of them have come over from the old country and still believe in their old fashioned ways and dress in their old fashioned way. Most of them are very poor and many now are dependent on the city for support. Many of them work on WPA projects. Most of the old people there believe in going to church two times a day if possible as they are very religious.

The attitude of these older folks toward stealing is very strong and they have a very bad opinion of anyone who steals. Most of the older men are of the drinking type and quite a few of them are drunk most every day. But seldom do the older people get in trouble with the police.[2] No more are arrested in this neighborhood than in any other as they are very old fashioned and they probably feel that if they did try to steal something they would not get away with it. The parents in the neighborhood do not know much about what their children are doing. The kids don't tell their fathers and mothers what they do and the parents are ignorant of how the kids play. Lots of other kids indulged in stealing. Of course I know the gang I and my brothers went around with stole. Outside of them I don't know much about what other kids did.

The situation at home was something like this: When my mother and father were at work us children were left pretty much to ourselves and we did what we thought was best. We had to get our own food because there was not much food at home. We were not locked in so we had the run of the house and if we

[2] This statement is supported by studies of the rates of crime among the foreign-born as compared to native-born population. In the conclusion of an exhaustive study made for the National Commission on Law Observance and Enforcement Miss Edith Abbott quotes Aleda C. Bowler as follows: "in proportion to their respective numbers, the foreign born commit considerably fewer crimes than the native born" (National Commission on Law Observance and Enforcement, *Crime and the Foreign Born*, Report No. 10 [United States Government Printing Office, 1931], p. 400). This same conclusion has been reached in the other studies of this problem.

wanted to go anywhere we just went. This kept up for a while until I was, with my brothers, sent to an orphanage. I do not remember very much, only that I was homesick and lonesome. I was there about two or three months until one day my father came to see me and took me home.

II

It was soon after this that I started going to school, but schooling somehow just did not seem to agree with me.[3] I believe the first time I played hookey from school was with my brother Mike. I was about seven years old when I started to bum school. When we were truant from school we would go for long walks, down to Lincoln Park, along the beach, to the zoo and all the other interesting sights, and when we were hungry we would go around and knock at back doors and ask the people for something to eat. I had gone out begging before I went to school when I was about five years old with Mike. On these trips from school which my brothers and I took we would sneak up on the "L" and ride downtown, transfer and ride to where we felt the neighborhood looked nice enough. We would walk up and down the alleys and choose a prosperous looking house. I would go to the back door of the house and knock at the door. I would go because I was smallest at the time and as such we figured the people would feel a little more sympathetic towards me. I would ask them if they couldn't please help me as my father was ill and my mother was not working, and we did not have enough to get along on. Well, if the people had a sympathetic nature they would feel sorry for me and would give me a basket of food and whatever change they could afford. I did this quite often, almost every time I was away from school.

[3] Although Carl's life-history furnishes fewer details about his earlier experiences than are found in the documents written by his brothers, it can safely be assumed that he was a product of the same general influences that were so evident in their lives. He started in delinquency at an early age in the company of his brothers and other older companions, and he continued to engage in delinquent behavior until he was committed to the St. Charles School for Boys. Unlike his brothers, however, he did not serve time in adult penal institutions. The records show that he was arrested for disorderly conduct on several occasions after his release from St. Charles but that he was discharged in each instance.

On some of these trips, after I got to be a little older, my brothers would wait in the alley and when the people were not at home I would go out and let them know. Then we would break into the house. In order to find out if anyone was home I would ring the back door bell and knock on the door and in general create a big disturbance. If I got no answer I would go to the front door and ring the bell for quite a while and if no one answered I knew that everyone was away. After I let my brothers know I would go back with them.[4]

On the North Side the back entrances used to contain ice boxes which would open up from the back window and I would go through the ice box into the pantry and open the doors or windows and my brothers would come in. Sometimes we got in through the transoms. When we were in the house we would take whatever attracted our attention at the time. Being small I didn't know if a thing was valuable or not so I just took anything that happened to please me. If I took a liking to a toy I would take that, since a child's toys attracted me. As to what my brothers took I could not say. This went on until either my brothers were sent to St. Charles or I was sent to the parental school for truancy. I don't remember which. I don't think we thought that there was anything wrong in what we were doing. It was just a means of gaining food and having a little money.

I was caught a couple of times on some of these trips, but was let go on probation. When I was about eleven years old I was brought to court for bumming school. I was then sent to the Chicago Parental School. When I was sent there I couldn't eat or sleep for about a week. After I got used to the place I did not mind it so much. As far as I can remember the parental school is

[4] It should be noted that the early delinquent experiences of Michael and Carl are telescoped into a brief span of years with the result that they engaged in serious delinquencies at a much younger age than their brothers. Their initial delinquencies as recorded in their life-histories correspond to the more serious types of crime in which their older brothers were engaged at the time. For example, Carl was implicated in prowling expeditions before he was of school age whereas John and Edward were still engaged in junking at that age and did not become involved in burglary until they were some years older. Carl's earlier initiation into the practice of burglary was due to the influence which was exerted upon him by his more experienced older brothers.

a pretty nice place for boys. It is a very fatherly place. They give you books to read and you can play all you want to and they have a Scout group out there. I joined the Boy Scouts while there and learned all the signals, knots, and all that sort of stuff. You got to go to a show once a week outside of the building and we had singing there. We had to go to school every day too. They were not very strict with us. It was almost like home. You had your regular duties there, washing dishes or something like that. The food was pretty good and the place was clean. In general, I don't remember very much about it.

My father did not know what was going on because my mother was afraid that if he did he would beat us severely, and as we never did anything seriously wrong she never told him. I believe that if my father had known what was going on he would have taken a different attitude towards his own life. My mother used to scold us and tell us that we would get into trouble and go to jail if we did not cut it out. She finally got tired of the constant going to court and sort of gave up her efforts to keep us straight. My mother had entirely different attitudes on stealing and begging. She did not know we were stealing things but when we came home with any food she was glad to get it. She would ask us where we got it and we would tell her we got it from somebody and that was all there was to it. The food came in very handy. As we had to pay the rent, which was not very much, but still as my mother did not make very much it was quite difficult and we had to go without a lot of food to pay the rent.

We never had the things that a lot of kids have such as roller skates, baseballs, etc. What we had, we had to go out and get for ourselves as my mother could not afford to get it for us. My mother does not understand sports but understands that it is good for one and I believe it was her not being able to afford it that she did not give any of these things to us. I believe that if she could have she would have given us these things.

I never stayed away from home much like my other brothers. There were a few times when I would go out and stay all night, sleep in a Park or in somebody's attic. It was then when we would steal from milk wagons or bread wagons or go out and pick up a bottle of milk from somebody's back porch and have something to eat and drink. I did this too with my brothers and we would bring home the stuff. We used to tell my mother that we begged the stuff from the bakery and houses.

When my brothers were put away somewhere I acquired a buddy, Joseph Herman, who lived next door to me and we used to arrange upon a given signal before we went to school. Any time we felt like going out we had a signal agreed upon. This was throwing a stone at the door from the alley and no one knew about it but me and if anyone in our home looked out when this noise was created they wouldn't see anything and just thought it was some kind of a noise. But as this was a signal I knew what it meant. It meant another truancy from school and going downtown around the department stores, ten cent stores, and stealing candy out of the counters somewhere or little articles easily hidden in the palm of the hand. I never went junking very much. It was too much like work. I relied on begging and burglary for my show money. We also shoplifted in the neighborhood. I first went out on these excursions with my brothers, mostly Mike. I quite frequently would steal bicycles on these trips with Joseph Herman.

When we got tired of begging or had too much in our baskets we would throw some away in the garbage cans and then take some of the food home with us. If we got tired of walking we would go through the alleys and if we saw any bicycles one of us would go in and the other would watch in front and when no one was around one of us would go in and steal the bicycle. Each of us would get one apiece and we would ride them home, leave the bicycles in some secluded spot and keep them for our own use. I believe the way we would lose these bicycles was that I would tell someone about them and they would steal them from me. The usual take when we went begging was about fifty cents or a dollar and this would be enough to get along on. We would go to a show, buy candy and we were well satisfied.

When we went shoplifting we just took candy, small toys, nothing very valuable. We got caught shoplifting downtown on one of our trips in a department store. We had taken some small things off the counter and I don't remember what it was and one of the floor-walkers asked us what we were doing. We just said we were looking around and didn't know if we wanted to buy anything or not. He asked us to come with him. He took us down to the basement, I think it was the warehouse, and searched us and found we had taken some things off the counters. So he threatened to call the police and have us arrested. We said that we were sorry and wouldn't he give us another chance. He held us there for what seemed a long time to us, but really was only an hour and let us go home for which we were grateful.

On one of my trips up to the North Side while burglarizing a home the lady of the house started to come home. We saw her on the walk and coming up the stairs. We decided it was time for us to leave. She came in the front way as we ran out the back way and I guess she heard us for she ran through the house and saw us going out the back gate and started to scream and hollering for help. We got out of that scrape but it gave us the wim-wams for awhile. Michael was with me at this time.

I went out one day with a friend of mine, John Olson, who was seven or eight years older than me and we went out to the north-west side and broke into a house. I crawled in through the icebox which had an opening from the back window and got into the home. I opened the door and let my friend in and both of us were in the house when the people who owned the place started to come in the front way. As we did not have any time to go out the back door I jumped under the table in the kitchen and stayed there about an hour until they moved into the front room. My partner had gotten out of the kitchen before I did and went out through the icebox, and got away. Well, the people went into the front room and I got out onto the porch which was enclosed. It had a door which was locked and I couldn't open that door as I did not know just how the lock worked. There was a day-bed on the back porch and as the lady started to come into the kitchen from the front room, I jumped under the day-bed and stayed there about two and a half hours while she was preparing supper. When she moved out from the kitchen I got out from underneath the day-bed and tried to open the lock again but I just could not open it. The lady started coming into the kitchen again so I jumped under the day-bed again. But this time she had heard me and just let me stay there while she called the police. Well, after the police got there she asked me to come out from under the day-bed and took me into the kitchen.

She was very nice and asked me how long I had been there and if I had taken anything or not and whether anyone was with me at the time. I told her that a friend of mine had been with me and she asked if he had gotten anything and when I told her that he had not she asked me if I was hungry. I told her that I was, so she gave me something to eat and then the police took me to the station and questioned me about this other fellow that was with me. Well, I went with them to this fellow's house and as none of us had taken anything we were both put on probation. In the meantime I was kept in the juvenile detention home.

My first impression of the juvenile detention home I don't seem to recall much about it. I do not know how old I was but I was very homesick and lonesome and it really looked like a prison to me as it was the first time I had been incarcerated for a period of time and the idea did not appeal to me. The food seemed very good to me because I was not used to getting good food. The bedding was clean and in general the recreational program was very good. I would go out and play ball and games with the other kids. This was at the old detention home.

The new juvenile detention home I remember a little better as I was a little older then. We had very good food there and we would read a lot and we would also go to school, and there was a lot of boxing. We were just kids there and talked just like kids would. We would ask each other what we were there for and it never led to anything serious. We never talked of stick-ups because we were still children. I do not remember any conversations about crime. There was one time while at the juvenile detention home that I, my brother and another fellow tried to escape. There was a chapel adjoining the dormitory and somehow or other we picked the lock on the chapel door and got into it and hid ourselves for awhile. When we saw we were not missed we got out from behind where we were hiding and opened the windows and took the screens off. We had a couple of sheets with us which we had taken off the beds which we tied up to make a sort of rope. Well, my brother went out the window and the other lad had started to get on the window sill, and I was still in the place when one of the guards finally missed us and located our hiding place and came barging in and caught me and the other fellow that was just going down the rope. He threatened this kid and said he would shoot so the fellow came back up and my brother was captured around the corner. The guard did not have a gun, just a handkerchief in his pocket, and bluffed this one lad.

III

My brothers, James and Michael, used to go out at night and what they did I don't know, but anyway one or the other of them used to come about two or three o'clock in the morning and ask me if I wanted to take a ride in an automobile and I was always glad to go. I was about eight or nine years old at this time. I would get dressed and we would go out for a ride. This happened a number of times and finally several years later I decided to get a car for myself, and my brother, Ed. I went out to a suburb with the intention of securing an automobile and at a country club we found a Studebaker touring car. We stole it and drove around all evening and after riding around we went home to bed. I arose early the next morning and took the car out and rode around until I ran out of gas. Then I parked the car and having no money for gas I walked home. In the late afternoon, after getting some money for gas, I went back to the car and while putting in some gas an officer came up to me and asked me whose car it was. I told him it was my uncle's and that I was just riding around in it. As I was under age, and I don't think he believed me in the first place, he took me to the station and questioned me. They looked up the history of the automobile and found it was stolen. For this I was sent to the Cook County School for Boys.

When I found out I was going to go to the Cook County School for Boys for three or four months I did not feel so good. Because it was three or four months off my life I felt blue about it. But the officer who was taking us out there was very nice and spoke kindly to us and asked us if we could not see that we were doing wrong and that we ought to stop. He told us to do our time and make the best of it. He offered us cigarettes but I felt bad and refused everything that was offered me. When I entered the Cook County School for Boys I found it pretty nice place to be in and I tried to make the best of things. I went to work in the woodwork shop there and made a few things such as benches, candle sticks, and book racks. We had a large gym to play around in when we were not working and we were let out of doors to play. The food there was very good and they gave us the general run of the cottage we were staying in. It is a very good place for a boy as they are not very strict and they treat you with a little decency.

After about a month of this I got rather lonesome and with three other boys we decided to try to escape. One morning while the man in charge of the ward detail was calling out each crew assigned to special details the four of us who had been sent out together previously went out on a four person detail. We just walked out of the grounds and succeeded in escaping. One of the fellows had fifty cents on him and we walked to the "L" station and got home safely. I went home, had something to eat, and deciding it was not a safe place to stay as I knew the officer would come and try to catch me. I would sleep in attics at night and in the mornings I would go home to eat and change clothes and then go off again for the day. Sometimes I would go to a show.

This kept up for about a week or a week and a half until I was finally caught at home by the probation officer and returned to the Cook County School for Boys. As a punishment for this I was compelled to stand in line and mark time for three days, with the exception of meal times. After that I decided I would make the best of it and serve out my time and get it over with, which I did. In this school they try to get you a job, that is, if you have any training in any line the head of the school will try to place you in outside work and you can go to work every day and come back at night and sleep there. Since you are sentenced to the school you have to spend the night there. This was very good for some of the fellows who got to do outside work as it was like being home except for sleeping there. The workshop was not really a workshop as you were there just to while away the time and it was very interesting to make something all by yourself. They also had a very good library out there and if any of the inmates had any musical instrument which they could play they were allowed to do so. Finally, they released me.

When we would steal a car it would be late at night. We would ride around with the car for an hour or two and then we would get tired of driving and take it to a garage, jack it up and take the spare tires, spotlights, and any tools in the car which we thought we could sell. We would sell them to friends. For a tire we would get about a couple of dollars. We never took them to fences, just sold them among our friends. However, we did not do this very often and after I was sent to St. Charles and released from there I decided it was best to stop everything when I saw how my brothers were progressing, which was not very good. They were in jail more than anywhere else and I decided I would stay out of jail after that.

If we took anything valuable, and we never did take anything really valuable, we would sell it for a dollar or two or whatever we could get.[5] Being just kids we did not know the value of things and took anything offered to us. It was, I might say, just a business to us, just a way of getting money. If we could have gotten a job we would have taken it.

One night we were walking around in the evening about eight or nine o'clock and while walking through Humboldt Park we decided we would go out and get a car for ourselves. I had acquired a Chevrolet key, how I do not know. At that time the key for a certain make of car would open all other cars of that make. We walked around till we saw a Chevrolet which we stole. We rode around all night and in the morning we got kind of hungry so we decided we would have something to eat. As we had no money we thought the best bet would be to wait for the bakery trucks

5 Carl minimizes the seriousness of the offenses in which he was involved both as regards their moral implications and as regards the value of the property that was taken or destroyed. He also makes more justificatory statements than any of the other brothers.

to start their deliveries. About three or four o'clock in the morning we saw one of these trucks and followed it. We got ourselves about half a dozen rolls, half a dozen loaves of bread and we thought that would be enough so we decided we should have some milk to go along with it. When the milk wagons started to make their deliveries we followed one and took a whole case. Then we went out in the country to have a party. We took a muddy road and the car got bogged under. Well, we saw a farmer coming down the road with two horses and a wagon and we asked him if he would help us get our car out. He did and we had just got the car going when somebody started to chase us and we took to our feet and left the car there. One of us was caught. The two of us who were not caught ran up the road and would take to the bushes when a car approached. But when we got close to the street car line a squad caught up with us. For this I was sent to the police station, then to the juvenile detention home, and finally to court where I was sent to the St. Charles School for Boys.

When I was committed to St. Charles School for Boys I really felt very bad. After I walked away from the court room I cried for about a whole day and I also cried on the way out there. After I got there I was given a bath and had my clothes changed. In the receiving cottage where all of the new inmates are brought I was asked what kind of work I would like to do. As I was there for about eighteen months they wanted to make the best possible arrangement they could for me. I told them I liked music a lot and would like to get into the band. In about a month I was transferred to the band and I liked it from the beginning. I was given a picolo and one of the inmate officers was assigned to show me how to play the instrument. I liked this very much.

The rules of the institution were very strict. You could not talk out loud at the table in the dining room, and if you did you were struck by a captain of the table with an open palm and it was no love tap either. You could not strike back because if you did you would be sent to solitary confinement. You were not given much freedom and your recreation time amounted to only about two hours a week. Out on the field you would play either baseball or football.

The first month there I was working on the coal pile and you had to put out quite a bit of work. The shovels used were big ones. I also worked in the dining room detail in the cottage where I set the table and saw that the plates, dishes, cups and saucers were in order. I would not say that I liked St. Charles as they were very strict. In fact, they were a little too strict. You were not allowed to talk in the library either. The means of punishment for talking out loud were that you had to stand up in line every evening for a period of two hours while the rest of the boys would read in the library.

I went to school there and graduated from the eighth grade and I also got in a year of commercial work. I do not think St. Charles is a good place to send kids for the simple reason that boys there come from all over the state and they talk about what they have done and why they are there and what they would do and just how they would do it if they were out. They always referred to the crimes for which they were committed and you got to know a lot more about crime than you did when you got there. The fact that I had a brother in St. Charles and one in Pontiac gave me a little prestige among the other inmates. As some of the inmate officers there had been there two or three times and had known my brothers they were not so severe with me as with the rest of the boys. One of the house officers did not trust me at all as one of my brothers had stolen his automobile in escaping and it was not until I had my blue slip (release) that he trusted me with a message from the cottage to the hospital. That's the kind of a drag I had at St. Charles.

The day previous to my release the house officer took me into his confidence and talked to me in a very fatherly way. He told me to go straight as it would not pay to do otherwise. He pointed to my brothers as examples of how useless it was to keep on as they had done. After I got home one of the boys who was paroled with me was caught in a burglary of some kind and was shot and killed and that made kind of an impression upon me. I read about it in the newspapers. He was quite a nice young fellow too.

IV

I think my stay in St. Charles helped me to go straight because I had a lot of time to think to myself there. The conversations I had there did not mean anything to me because I was convinced that crime did not pay. I saw that all criminals got was years and years in prison and saw that my brothers too had only got into jail again and again. I decided to put a stop to it as far as I was concerned. I felt sorry that we had caused my mother so much trouble and grief. I don't know what you could call it but I just made up my mind that it does not pay and that I would rather starve than steal. I never went on a single job after I was released from St. Charles.

The next day after I was released from St. Charles I went over to a telegraph company and secured a job as an errand boy. I worked there for about a year or two. I quit this because I was working nights. Then too I didn't agree with the clerk in charge of the office and didn't make enough money, only about twelve dollars a week. I had to work a full day to make this. After that I went to work for another company and did not make much money there either. I worked there about six months. Then I worked for a radio company and was very well satisfied with the job I had there. It was factory work. I worked there about four months and received about eighteen dollars a week. However, conditions got bad and I was laid off.

After that I grabbed any jobs that offered themselves. I worked on punch presses, kick presses, drills, etc., and I can still operate these machines. Then I worked for a department store for about a year and nine months. After I quit this job the foreman of the garage came around to the house and tried to get me to go back to work as they were well pleased with my services, but I was very much disappointed in the company and decided I would try elsewhere. During one year there they did not give us the bonus which we were promised, and the next year I heard that we would not receive the bonus even after they had given us a cut in wages. They also worked us a little too much, sometimes about eighteen hours a day, and never paid us any overtime, so I decided I would try to find other work.

After this I was out of work for a few months. I worked as a drug apprentice for about three years. It is hard to know what my future is going to be just as it is hard to know what the future is for anybody. I am hopeful for the best, and I will try to make the best of myself. I do not think there is any future for me in the tree trimming job on which I am now employed. A fellow doesn't know whether he will have work the next week or not.

The way I would try to explain why we got in trouble is that there was not enough to eat at home and we had no money. When we went out to steal and beg we did not look upon it as stealing, just a way of getting money or something to eat. In other words, it was just like a job to us. I believe it was the poor conditions at home that started us off wrong. Then too, we probably got in with a wrong bunch of fellows, that is fellows who did stuff like begging and stealing. I believe I was started out by my brother Mike. I think that each of us was started out by another brother in the same way. It is the only explanation I think there can be for it. After a certain length of time it gets to be a habit like working in a factory or office and receiving pay for it.[6]

[6] It is interesting to observe that the brothers who had the longest careers in delinquency were the ones who possessed personality traits which are usually regarded as being most desirable. John, Edward, James, and Michael are sociable, friendly, and loyal persons who adapt themselves readily to other individuals. Carl, on the other hand, possesses fewer of these traits, yet he continued in delinquency for a shorter period of time than did his brothers. It is suggested that perhaps socially desirable personality traits may be related to satisfactory adjustments in the delinquent group in the same manner in which they are related to adjustments in conventional groups. In short, they may be social assets in both situations. Conversely less desirable traits may complicate the process of adjustment in delinquent and in nondelinquent groups. (For another example see *Judge Baker Foundation Case Studies No. 1* [Boston, 1922].)

PART IV

PHYSICAL, MENTAL, AND PERSONALITY
CHARACTERISTICS OF THE
MARTIN BROTHERS

INTRODUCTION

The two chapters included in Part IV are concerned with the study of the constitutional, mental, and personality characteristics of the brothers. In chapter xiii, Dr. Harold B. Hanson of the psychiatric staff of the Institute for Juvenile Research gives a brief summary of the various clinical examinations which were made during the years in which the brothers were active in delinquency. In addition to the findings of these early studies, he includes the results of examinations which he has made during the last few months. He has had repeated contacts with John, Edward, James, and Carl at the Institute for Juvenile Research. His final examination of Michael was made in the penal institution in which he is incarcerated.

Chapter xiv has been prepared by Professor Ernest W. Burgess of the Department of Sociology of the University of Chicago. In this chapter Dr. Burgess gives an analysis of the personality of each of the five brothers.

CHAPTER XIII

CLINICAL SUMMARIES

HAROLD B. HANSON

The careers in delinquency of the Martin brothers present an unusually favorable opportunity for study, inasmuch as all of them engaged in essentially the same kinds of delinquent activities during the early years of their lives. What is more important, they present a longitudinal picture of sufficiently long life-periods to bring into relief some of the principal contributing factors in their individual and collective behavior.

This discussion of certain psychiatric features of the case is based upon materials secured from a variety of sources. These materials include autobiographies, the reports of probation and parole officers, the records of a family-case-work agency which maintained contact with the family for a period of many years, and the findings of physical, psychological, and psychiatric examinations which were made at the Institute for Juvenile Research and in the juvenile and penal institutions in which the brothers were confined. These records, along with the findings of the examinations which the writer has made during recent months, provide the basis for this brief discussion.

The oldest boy, John, was examined at the Institute for Juvenile Research when he was twelve years of age. Some deformity of the left ear which involved the helix was found, but in other respects he was reported to be in good physical condition and without other physical stigmata. His nutrition at that time was rated as good. On a recent physical examination the most striking characteristic noted was the discrepancy between his physical appearance and his chronological age. He has the appearance of a man of middle age. It is possible that his chronic moderate alcoholism is responsible for his physical appearance. He has several devitalized teeth and a marked nasal septum deviation associated with a chronic nasal congestion. Liver and kidney function tests might possibly demonstrate some evidences of degenerate changes due to alcoholism, but he presented no symptoms suggesting organic dysfunction. His blood pressure was normal and the findings of a neurological examination were negative. He has a prominent habit-tic consisting of frequent sudden sniffing.

The second brother, Edward, in a physical examination which was made by the Institute for Juvenile Research when he was fourteen years of age, was found to be in good physical condition. It was noted at that time that the lobules of the ears were not clearly defined. There was some slight roughness of the heart sound but this was regarded as probably not significant. In a recent complete examination he was found to be in good physical condition, with the exception of several devitalized teeth. His blood pressure was normal. It was noted also that he was ambidextrous. A neurological examination was entirely negative.

The third brother, James, was examined at the Institute for Juvenile Research at the age of ten, but so far as can be determined a physical examination was not given at that time. However, the reports of subsequent physical examinations which were made at the time of his confinement in juvenile and penal institutions showed that he was in good physical condition. A complete physical examination which was made recently by the writer showed that he was in excellent physical condition. The distal phalanges of the right third and fourth fingers were partially amputated, but no other physical defects were found. His blood pressure was normal. The findings of the neurological examination were negative.

The fourth boy, Michael, was examined at the Institute for Juvenile Research when he was eleven years of age and was found at that time to be in good condition and without any obvious physical defects. Since that time he has had repeated examinations at various state institutions and in all of these the report showed him to be in good physical condition. In our recent interviews with him, he has complained of some recurrent lumbago which he attributed to the dampness of his cell in the state prison where he is still confined. A recent examination showed that his blood pressure is normal. The neurological findings were negative. There was no indication of any serious physical diseases.

The youngest brother, Carl, is the only one of the brothers who was not examined at the Institute for Juvenile Research during the course of his delinquency. He was given a complete examination recently and was then found to be in good physical condition, with the exception of several carious teeth. He has a slight visual defect, not sufficiently severe, however, to require glasses. His blood pressure was normal and a neurological examination was negative. It was noticed that he has a habit-tic of the jaw consisting of a cracking sound upon retraction of the jaw.

The four oldest boys were given psychological tests during the original examination at the Institute for Juvenile Research. Three of the boys were classed as having average intelligence, while Michael was classified as dull. Subsequent examinations at the Illinois State Reformatory classified Edward and James as having high average intelligence, while Michael was classified as having superior intelligence. Carl was placed in the group having average intelligence at the time he was examined in one of the juvenile institutions.

It is interesting to note the psychiatric diagnoses which have been made from time to time on the four older brothers. In the case of the oldest one, John, there was only one psychiatric comment made when he was examined at the age of twelve by Dr. Healy, who remarked that John seemed to be under considerable emotional tension during the examination. This was evidenced by apprehension and a blueness of the lips. Dr. Healy suggested that this reaction might have been due to the interview situation rather than to any underlying emotional conflict. He predicted that if the boy continued to live in the same neighborhood, his behavior would continue unchanged. The validity of this prediction was amply corroborated by John's subsequent delinquent and criminal career.

Since his last period of confinement approximately ten years ago, John has remained out of further difficulty. He has maintained a fairly consistent work record and has supported himself and contributed to the support of his mother with whom he and the youngest brother live. He was found to be an outwardly friendly, sociable, carefree, easy-going person with a good sense of humor. He appears to have developed a cheerful, fatalistic type of philosophy which appears in his autobiography and in his social and economic attitudes. On the other hand, he is largely indifferent about his personal appearance and to the opinions of others.

As noted above, he is a moderate chronic alcoholic and becomes irritable and outspoken when intoxicated. In addition to his underlying attachment to the mother, there is some evidence of identification with the father which is suggested in the following excerpt from his autobiography.

> At times we were without food because occasionally he [the father] would go to the corner and partake of the cup that cheers and . . . . drink had too strong a grip upon him. My father was an easy-going man, just a little bit inclined to follow the path of least resistance. If he had been a bit more determined, he could possibly have advanced more in life. But when he became riled, it was a horse of another color. I shall have to admit that I've inherited some of his characteristics in that direction.

It is quite evident from this brief description that John presents many of the traits of the typical "alcoholic character." His service with the Army and relatively smooth adjustment to institutional life would appear to further substantiate this. It is in keeping with these characteristics that this boy's early delinquencies occurred in the form of begging. It is not implied that this underlying dependency was necessarily the chief motivating factor in his delinquencies, but rather that this form of delinquency, ready at hand with family and local social approval, provided a vehicle for the expression of his particular strivings and needs, just as his indulgence in alcohol later in life serves as an expression and an attempt to satisfy these same needs. It is quite probable that this boy's needs would have found expression in some manner other than delinquency if the physical, economic, and social factors described in other chapters had not been present or had been of less intensity.

In respect to Edward, the statement was made when he was examined at the Institute for Juvenile Research that there was no evidence of psychopathology or of emotional disturbance. The factors which were thought to be contributing to his behavior were: "bad neighborhood, bad companions, poor home interest, and poverty."

The psychiatric reports which were made in the reformatory as well as the findings of more recent examinations indicate that Edward is quite realistically oriented to his entire situation. There is no evidence of emotional disturbance or of psychopathology.

In his autobiography and in his remarks in personal interviews he is clear and blunt in descriptions of his family, neighborhood, and his delinquent and institutional experiences. He presents no definite evidence of identification with either parent, although he expresses the same loyalty to the family as all his brothers do. He does not attempt to minimize the parental defects as much as the others, yet, despite this greater frankness, there is no hint of resentment toward the parents. He is a cheerful, frank, outgoing person, with rather definite economic ambitions, and deep concern for the welfare of his family. Although he expresses regret for the many years of his life that he considers to have been wasted in institutions, he apparently entertains no definitely antisocial or paranoid attitudes at this time.

In the case of the third brother, James, when seen at the Institute for Juvenile Research at the age of eleven years, the clinical report described him as "a very alert child who does not let much pass his notice." He was thought to have a great deal of initiative. The same contributing factors of bad neighborhood and bad companions together with poor home supervision and poverty were regarded as the principal causes of his delinquency.

James is obviously the most aggressive, dynamic, and ambitious of the brothers. He is friendly and outgoing and more talkative than the others. He gives the distinct impression that he has been less unfavorably affected by his experiences than the others. He recalls many of them, for instance, with a good deal of zest and humor and still obtains satisfaction in telling of the techniques he and his brothers developed in their particular "racket." In his contacts with James, the writer has found no evidence of any crystallized antisocial or paranoid attitudes, mental pathology, or emotional disturbance.

In later years when James was incarcerated in the Illinois State Reformatory, the psychiatrist classified him as a psychopathic personality. It is usually understood that such diagnosis carries with it the implication that the behavior and personality characteristics of such an individual are unalterable. In view of the adjustment which James has made since his last incarceration, it would seem that this original diagnosis was not valid. This case raises serious questions with regard to the validity of the psychiatric classification of prison inmates and of the still somewhat prevalent belief that only an intrinsically abnormal individual can exhibit criminal behavior. The writer's recent examination of James did not reveal any evidence suggestive of psychopathic personality or mental abnormality.

The fourth boy, Michael, when examined at the Institute for Juvenile Research at the age of nine years, was described in the clinical reports as a "bright, alert, promising child, wide awake, with a great deal of energy which unfortunately has been misdirected for a long period of time." The absence of any notation suggesting psychopathology or serious emotional conflict in the report would indicate that no evidence of this was found at that time.

When examined at the time of his incarceration in the reformatory, Michael was classified by the prison psychiatrists as an egocentric personality. In a later examination he was described by a psychiatrist in the following manner: "According to formal tests, we are dealing with a boy of superior intelligence. At Pontiac he has been classified as an egocentric personality and we find no occasion for changing this classification at the present time. We feel, however, that the biggest factors in this inmate's criminal career are environmental and that there is nothing intrinsically characteristic of this boy to prevent an adequate social adjustment if environmental stress is not too great. We are bound to consider him recidivous; yet in the light of a fairly adequate personality and a good mental endowment, plus his present attitude, we are inclined to think that under adequate supervision and with the assurance of a job he might make good."

Michael impresses one as being more introspective than his brothers. He is quiet and unassuming and has little to say in direct conversation. This latter characteristic was no doubt influenced by the fact that the interview was carried on in the prison where he is still confined. Inasmuch as his case was then being considered by the parole board, he was naturally somewhat reticent and cautious. His general manner and attitude, however, impress one favorably. His autobiography, in contrast with the others, is more detailed and careful as to time relationships and as to relationships within the family. He gives evidence of being more deeply impressed with the parental defects and deprivation of parental care and affection. His attachment to James, the next older brother, and his dependence upon him in earlier years is apparent in his written material. He dwells more definitely on the severe treatment and punishment he has received in his institutional life. Although he does show evidences of embitterment and disappointment, neither the material in his autobiography nor his institutional record in the last few years gives any indication that he has developed any crystallized antisocial or paranoid attitudes. He is apparently encouraged by the success of his brothers in making good and seems sincerely interested in establishing himself socially and economically.

We do not have the advantage in this case of a long, post-institutional observation. If our estimation of points of conflict in this case are accurate, one is inclined to question the extent to which this boy will make a satisfactory adjustment even though he remain out of further criminal activity. He seems to have attained a degree of insight into his difficulties in the last few years which may assist in obviating further criminal activity.

The youngest brother is a rather stolid person who is inclined to be defensive in his attitude. He is less at ease during an interview than his brothers and is considerably less responsive. However, the examinations did not reveal any definite existence of psychopathology. While he gives the impression of being more socially maladjusted than his brothers, his career in delinquency was shorter than that of any of the brothers. He accounts for this fact by the single statement: "I saw what happened to the others and I got smart."

In conclusion it should be stated that in this discussion very little effort has been made to trace the early development of the personality organization of the brothers. As previously indicated, they differed in regard to personality traits. The influences which determined these divergent developments are not known. It must be recognized, however, that despite differences in personality, physical stature, and intelligence, all of the brothers engaged in the same forms of delinquent conduct throughout the early periods of their careers. It is probable that their delinquencies were due in large part to the lack of unity and security in the family situation and the influences which were exerted upon them in the delinquent play groups and gangs with which they very early became associated. Bromberg and Thompson[1] recently reported that in a study of 9,958 men who had pleaded guilty or had been convicted in the Court of General Sessions in New York City, only 18 per cent were of such mental, physical, and emotional condition as to warrant a diagnosis of mental defect, psychosis, psychopathic personality, or psychoneurosis. The mental defectives comprised 2.4 per cent, psychotics 1.5 per cent, psychopathic personalities 6.9 per cent, and psychoneurotics 6.9 per cent of the total group of offenders. Of the total, 82 per cent were classified in the group designated as "normal" or average individuals. Upon the basis of the available evidence, it is assumed that the Martin brothers would properly be classified in this latter group of offenders.

[1] Walter Bromberg and Charles B. Thompson, "Relation of Psychoses, Mental Defect and Personality," *Journal of Criminal Law and Criminology*, Vol. XXVIII, No. 1 (May–June, 1937).

CHAPTER XIV

PERSONALITY TRAITS OF THE BROTHERS

ERNEST W. BURGESS

The life-histories of the five brothers make it possible to give a preliminary answer to the crucial question: To what extent is a criminal career a result of personality traits and to what extent is it a product of the situation in which the person is born and reared?

With each of the five brothers social factors are much more important than personality traits in influencing their behavior. The entrance and progress of each brother in a delinquent career appears to be almost a direct outcome of the residence of a poverty-stricken immigrant family in a neighborhood of boys' gangs and criminal traditions. Counteracting factors, it is true, were present, such as parental concern over the behavior of the boys and opportunity for them to follow law-abiding careers in school and at work. But the appeal to the boys of conventional patterns of behavior was weak in comparison with the thrill of adventure and the easy rewards of stealing.

It must, therefore, be conceded that in the criminal career of each of the brothers social factors are much more important than personality factors. This does not mean that in all cases of crime social influences predominate. The spectacular crimes that make headlines in the newspapers are generally those in which some particular constitutional or psychological characteristic is present and appears to be an essential factor in the crime.[1] There is good reason to believe, however, that the vast majority of cases of delinquency and crime in American cities is due to social influences. It is this fact that gives this volume its significance for

[1] In the two case studies presented previously by Mr. Shaw the egocentricity of Stanley in *The Jack Roller* and the precocity and inferiority complex of Sidney in *The Natural History of a Delinquent Career* were important factors in connection with social factors in determining their behavior.

the understanding of delinquency. The cases of the brothers may be taken as typical of the formation of criminal careers. They are usual and not exceptional cases.

Full recognition of the play of social factors in delinquency does not and should not mean the neglect of the study of individual differences in personality. Occasionally criminal behavior can be significantly related to particular personality characteristics. In many cases personality traits undoubtedly enter to a greater or less degree as secondary influences. In nearly every case an understanding of individual differences may be of great importance in working out a plan of reformation.

Personality and social factors are of course intertwined in every human act. The person—or social self—is a result of interaction with the social environment. The five brothers in their personalities embodied characteristics of the culture of their family, of their companions, and of their neighborhood.

However, for purposes both of research and of treatment, a distinction needs to be made between personality traits that are psychogenetic and those that are cultural. Edward Sapir defines the psychiatric personality as an "invariant reactive system" made up of inherited tendencies as conditioned and fixed by the experiences of infancy and early childhood.[2] This reactive system of psychogenetic traits is believed to persist relatively unchanged throughout the life of the person. Examples of psychogenetic traits are aggressiveness, lack of inhibition of temper, dominance, egocentricity, and emotional instability. In contrast with psychogenetic traits are the cultural traits of the person, such as his ideas, ideals, interests, and values which are acquired from the social environment.

The psychogenetic traits of the person and his cultural characteristics are to be considered as separate and independent. The five brothers might have widely divergent psychogenetic traits and yet each be inducted into the same criminal culture and

[2] "The psychiatrist's concept of personality is to all intents and purposes the reactive system exhibited by the precultural child, a total configuration of reactive tendencies determined by heredity, and by prenatal and postnatal conditioning up to the point where cultural patterns are constantly modifying the child's behavior" (Edward Sapir, "Personality," *Encyclopaedia of the Social Sciences*, XII, 86).

exhibit apparently uniform criminal behavior. Such, in fact, was the case. The cultural traits of the five brothers are, as demonstrated by their life-histories, practically identical. Our problem then is to determine (1) how similar or how different their psychogenetic traits are and (2) how these differences, if any, affected their criminal career and reformation.

The materials available for an analysis of their psychogenetic traits were (1) their life-histories, (2) the findings of examinations upon two standardized tests (the Bernreuter Personality Inventory and the Humm-Wadsworth Temperament Scale), (3) the comparative ratings by two of the brothers of certain personality traits of all five brothers.

The life-histories of the brothers are quite different. Each document reveals the personality of its author.

1. John's life-history is an apology. As he reflects over his life he attempts to justify his career, not so much to his audience as to himself. In fact, he, of all the five brothers, seems the most oblivious of his readers. For his criminal career he puts the blame, first upon his eldest brother who died, then upon his father, next upon the neighborhood, later upon his partner in his last offense, and finally upon women, but never on himself. His moralizing, his philosophizing, and his formal language also substantiate the point that he is the most egocentric of the brothers.

His trait of egocentricity, however, appears to have no causal relation to his entrance into crime, his continuance in it, and his exit from it. He adapted himself rather readily to army life and later, without much resistance, relapsed into the offense for which he paid heavily. Criminal attitudes seem to have been none too deeply ingrained in him and yet they appear to persist relatively unchanged although he has no record of criminal behavior for the last ten years.

Feelings of depression and defeatism find expression in the closing paragraphs of his life-history. This is in marked contrast with the optimism and plans for the future which animate the writings of the other brothers. At present he appears to be the least well adjusted to life.

2. The life-history of Edward is that of a normal, well-balanced

person. His account of his experiences in delinquency, in crime, and in prison are objective and impartial. His story shows that as a child and adolescent he was as responsive to conventional as to delinquent patterns of behavior. On two occasions, one at eight or nine years[3] and the other at fourteen years,[4] he seemed particularly susceptible to sympathetic approaches for his reformation. He appears more conscious than the other brothers of the alternative between conventional and criminal behavior.

At the time of the writing of his document he is definitely oriented to success in a legitimate career. "I am a determined sort of fellow and I am going to succeed somehow." He appears to be well adjusted at present to conventional society.

3. James shows a greater degree of self-consciousness and therefore of a sense of his audience than any of the brothers. The first sentence of the preface to his life-history evinces this attitude. "This story of my life is written so that folks may see the inside of my past and not only the crust as I think they see it now."

More than in the case of the other brothers, his document indicates his interest in the changes taking place in himself as a result of his institutional experience. "I wasn't born tough. The treatment in the institutions made me that way." "My heart grew bitter and hard at all the officers and inmate officers who were responsible for the manhandling I received."

He appears more concerned than his brothers with an analysis of the conflict of his impulses to follow a legitimate career or to continue in crime. "Many times I went to work and really tried to stick to the job, but my 'friends' lured me back to the racket." "Down in my heart I hated to go out and steal with other fellows, but I went with them to avoid 'ridicule.'" His document, as his preface promised, discloses to the reader his inner feelings and attitudes toward his past, present, and future. With apparent candor, but with implicit reservations, he states, "I have all the intention of going straight if not for my own then for my mother's sake. . . . . I know that I can and will go straight if given any kind of a chance." At present he appears well adjusted to society.

3 P. 176.   4 P. 123.

4. The life-history of Michael is a matter-of-fact, generally objective, but somewhat defensive, account of his life. It lacks the vivid, vigorous, and original style of the writings of his three older brothers. It does not admit the reader, as did James's story, into the inner world of his feelings and attitudes. Unwittingly, however, his document reveals personality traits of self-pity, hypercritical attitude toward the institutions and officers, and a tendency to put the blame for his career and present predicament upon society and upon others. At the time of writing his document he has not definitely and unreservedly given up a criminal career. He tells of planning with his cell partner that after his release he would "go in a higher priced racket and make up for lost time" but later, because of the sorry ending of his cell-mates' attempt to follow this plan, he decided that "it never pays to be crooked." He concludes his story with his bargaining proposition to society: "All I need is a good job with a good salary and then the state of Illinois can check another boy off their hands as reformed."

5. Carl's life-history is the least revealing of the five documents but tells us much about its author. It exhibits him as the most divergent of the five brothers in psychogenetic traits. He is the most objective, the least outgoing, the least communicative, and, with the possible exception of Edward, the least susceptible to the impress of the criminal culture of the neighborhood. He prefers apparently to write about his environment rather than about himself. His document, shorter than the others, gives evidence of brief and defensive responses to the direct questions of the interviewer.

Much of his difference from the other brothers may be due to the fact that he is the youngest child with characteristic ambivalent attitudes of dependence and independence. He stayed home at nights more than the other brothers. He seems more aware of the condemnation of delinquency by the adults of the neighborhood. His entrance into crime is by tagging his brothers and older companions, but when, like Edward and James, he decides in his adolescent years to go straight, he persists and does not, as they did, succumb to the influence of companions.

At the time of writing the document he appears to be well adjusted.

The derivation of psychogenetic traits from life-histories is largely a matter of sympathetic introspection and is essentially subjective. Therefore the interpretations of the marked divergence in traits of the brothers as shown by the personality documents need to be checked by the findings upon objective tests such as the Humm-Wadsworth Temperament Scale, the Bernreuter Personality Inventory, and a list of specific psychogenetic traits.

The Temperament Scale, which was filled out by the five brothers, was developed by D. C. Humm and G. W. Wadsworth, Jr., "through a statistical comparison of normal and abnormal or atypical subjects."[5] It is based on Rosanoff's theory of personality and seeks to give an objective comparative measurement of the temperamental components which actuate the conduct of the individual.

For purposes of the present analysis[6] the temperamental components are named and defined as follows: (1) The normal component, or control mechanism, which provides rational balance and temperamental equilibrium, making for the "well-balanced" individual. (2) The self-preservation component,[7] an excess of which denotes ethically inferior motivation as judged by the standards of conventional society. In persons with delinquent experience this component perhaps measures the impress of criminalistic attitudes. (3) The manic component, or manifestations of some degree of elation, pressure of activity, and distractibility, together with manifestations of excitement, such as enthusiasm and impatience. (4) The depressed component, or manifestations of some degree of sadness, lessened activity, dearth of ideas, and associated characteristics such as worry, timidity, feeling of

5 See *The Humm-Wadsworth Temperament Scale* (Los Angeles, 1934); see also *Personnel Journal*, April, 1934.

6 Two components are omitted here, since on both of these the brothers show little or no divergence from the average: (1) the autistic phase of the schizoid component characterized by seclusiveness, shyness, and suggestibility and (2) the epileptoid component characterized by inspirations to achievement.

7 Called by Humm and Wadsworth the "hysteroid component."

malaise, etc. (5) The paranoid component, or manifestation of fixed ideas, conceit, suspicion and contempt for the opinions of others.

On this temperament scale the ratings of the brothers are as follows: John, depressed paranoid, with self-preservation component above average; Edward, well balanced; James, well balanced, with self-preservation component above average; Michael, quite well balanced, manic-paranoid with self-preservation component above average; Carl, well balanced. These ratings correspond closely to the findings upon personality differences as revealed in the life-histories.

The object of the Personality Inventory devised by Robert G. Bernreuter, was to measure at one time several different aspects of personality.[8] When first constructed, it was designed to measure (1) neurotic tendency, (2) self-sufficiency, (3) introversion–extroversion, and (4) dominance–submission. It was later found that neurotic tendency and introversion–extroversion had very high intercorrelations and that both were moderately correlated with dominance–submission.

Intercorrelating the scores on the foregoing four scales, J. C. Flanagan,[9] by means of factor analysis, arrived at two new measures of personality, practically independent of each other, which accounted for nearly all the variability.

These he named Factor One and Factor Two. For convenience Factor One will be designated as "social adjustment" distinguishing between individuals who are self-confident, socially aggressive, and "thick-skinned" and those who are self-conscious, shy, and emotionally unstable. Factor Two will be called "independence," differentiating individuals who are dependent upon social contacts and those who are not.

The ratings of the five brothers upon these six scales show marked differences between them:

John is markedly below the average in social adjustment;

[8] Robert G. Bernreuter, *Manual for the Personality Inventory* (Stanford University, 1935).

[9] J. C. Flanagan, *Factor Analysis in the Study of Personality* (Stanford University, 1935).

average in independence; somewhat below average in emotional stability and extroversion; below average in self-sufficiency and dominance.

Edward is average in social adjustment; markedly above the average in independence, self-sufficiency, and dominance; and unusually high in emotional stability and extroversion.

James is average in social adjustment and independence; above average in emotional stability and extroversion; somewhat above the average in self-sufficiency; and average in dominance.

Michael is below average in social adjustment; somewhat below average in independence; average in extroversion; below average in emotional stability and dominance; and markedly below average in self-sufficiency.

Carl is markedly above average in social adjustment; somewhat below average in independence; markedly above average in emotional stability, extroversion, and dominance; and somewhat below the average in self-sufficiency.

The third comparison of the brothers was upon a list of psychogenetic traits, with comparative ratings of the five brothers by two of them. These two reports were in substantial agreement and indicated that Edward, James, and Michael were much alike in psychogenetic traits but that John diverged somewhat and Carl markedly from the others. (1) None of the brothers but Carl gets angry easily and all except him get over it quickly. (2) John is the least aggressive of the brothers, and Carl and he do not assume responsibility as willingly as their other brothers. (3) Michael and Carl are less likely to attempt to dominate than the other brothers. (4) John has the greatest and Carl the least sense of humor. John makes friends more easily and Carl less easily than the others. Both care less than their brothers about belonging to organizations or about what people say and think about what they do. John is considered the most easygoing. (5) Carl is reported as being more stubborn, more easily hurt, more irritable, and more likely to be moody than the others. He also is considered to be the most selfish.

These findings are sufficient to indicate that John and Carl are quite different in a number of traits from Edward, James, and Michael, who appear to resemble each other quite closely.

The personality differences between the five brothers revealed in the content and style of the life-histories are corroborated in the findings upon the three tests. Both kinds of data are important for an understanding of the brothers. From the story of their lives the reader gets a feeling of acquaintance with them and insight into their sentiments, attitudes, and conceptions of themselves. From the finding of the personality tests the student obtains, not this personal touch, but rather a quite exact comparative rating of the brothers upon clearly defined and measurable psychogenetic characteristics.

The cultural traits of the brothers were very similar and for all practical purposes, identical. Their participation with companions and with each other in the delinquency patterns of the neighborhood initiated and sustained their criminal careers. The relation of their specific psychogenetic traits which differ markedly from each other to definite aspects of their criminal careers is not apparent either from official records or from the life-histories of the brothers. It seems, therefore, that in the main their criminal careers were not a resultant of psychogenetic factors but a function of the neighborhood situation.

Experience in institutions for juvenile delinquents had little or no deterrent effect upon the brothers. Carl is the exception in that confinement in St. Charles led to a decision to abandon a criminal career, a resolve probably implemented by the fact that he had observed that the crimes of his brothers had led only to repeated incarceration. Confinement in reformatories and prisons, however, had a marked effect on the other four brothers in bringing about a realization that crime does not pay. This attitude is undoubtedly quite general and genuine among inmates of reformatory and penal institutions. But in the case of the three brothers who served time in Illinois institutions the probabilities of reformation under ordinary circumstances upon release from prison were poor. Based upon their previous behavior the prediction of the probability of parole violation within the first year after release made by the sociologist-actuary was for Edward 59 per cent, for James 50 per cent, and for Michael 43 per cent.

The fact that John, Edward, James, and Carl made good upon their last release from institutions is, in the judgment of the writer, due not only to an attitude upon their part favorable to reformation, but also to the type of intelligent assistance that was made available to them. The success of this kind of sympathetic and discerning treatment adapted to the attitudes, temperament, interests, and aptitudes of each brother is of great significance for the development of policies and programs of crime prevention. Case work with individuals divorced from an understanding of their social relationships has, in the majority of cases, been proved a failure. The treatment of delinquency and crime to be successful must be oriented to a community approach, with emphasis placed upon work with the gang and with neighborhood conditions.

PART V

METHODS OF TREATMENT AND ANALYSIS
OF THE CASE

INTRODUCTION

Two chapters are included in Part V. Chapter xv is a short description of the methods which have been used in the treatment of the brothers, while chapter xvi gives a brief analysis of the influences which seem to have been instrumental in determining the development of the five careers in delinquency and crime.

This discussion of the treatment and the etiology of the careers of the brothers is entirely tentative. To provide an opportunity for various interpretations, all available materials pertaining to the successive experiences, the social background, and the mental, physical, and personality characteristics of the brothers have been presented. While the following analysis of the five careers has been made in terms of the conditioning effect of the social milieu of the brothers, it is recognized that the materials presented may afford a basis for other analyses by persons with different points of view.

CHAPTER XV

METHODS EMPLOYED IN THE TREATMENT
OF THE MARTIN BROTHERS

As revealed in the official records in chapter i, most of the traditional methods usually employed in the treatment of delinquents were tried in the cases of the brothers throughout the period of their childhood and early adolescence. These methods included numerous arrests, repeated appearances in the court, probation, confinement in detention homes and correctional schools, foster-home placements, parole supervision, clinical studies, and the efforts of family-case-work agencies during a period of more than fifteen years.

That these methods were ineffective throughout the period in which the brothers were wards of the Juvenile Court is amply demonstrated by the official records. The failure of these efforts does not in any sense impugn the intentions of the large group of workers who had the responsibility for the supervision and custody of the five brothers. It may indicate, however, that their methods were not formulated in terms of the nature of the problem at hand. If, as it is here assumed, the delinquencies and crimes of these boys were functions of the complicated system of interpersonal relationships and cultural patterns which comprised their social environment in the community, it is not surprising that the attempts to treat them in individualistic terms proved to be ineffective.

PROBATION AND PAROLE SUPERVISION

The records of the activities of the probation and parole officers reveal that their efforts in behalf of the brothers included frequent visits to the Martin home, interviews with teachers in the schools, filing petitions in the Juvenile Court, securing financial aid for the family from relief agencies, providing for clinical examinations and medical service, investigating complaints, and making arrangements for foster-home placements. For the most part, the treatment consisted of attempts to deal with the problem of delinquency by direct manipulations of each individual boy. The officers seemed to have depended chiefly upon the use of admonition, threats of punishment, the authority of the court, and incarceration to effect the desired changes in conduct.

With few exceptions, each time the brothers were placed on probation or released under parole supervision, they were returned to the same community situation in which their initial delinquencies had occurred. Here they renewed their contacts with former associates or established relationships with new companions and with them continued their careers in delinquency. There is no evidence in the available records nor in the autobiographical documents to show that any effort was made to deal with the neighborhood groups to which the brothers belonged, or to introduce them into the recreational programs carried on in the local public and private institutions. Although the brothers lived within the vicinity of such institutions they were never identified with them.

TREATMENT IN JUVENILE INSTITUTIONS

More than fifty-five of the one hundred and fifty years of life of the five brothers have been spent in dependent, correctional, and penal institutions. During the first seventeen years of their lives the brothers spent a total of more than twenty-eight years in institutions for the treatment of problem and delinquent children. Despite these many years of confinement in the Detention Home, the Chicago and Cook County School, and the State Industrial School for Boys at St. Charles, four of the brothers subsequently served sentences in institutions for adult criminals. It appears from the materials secured in personal interviews and in the autobiographical documents that these early institutional experiences were contributing influences in the continuance of the brothers' criminal careers. In various concrete ways they furthered the process of education in delinquency which had originated in the gangs and play groups in the local community.

The brothers state that while they were in these institutions, particularly the Detention Home, delinquency was one of the most common topics of conversation among the boys. As Edward and James indicate in the following statements, these conversations proved to be a fruitful source of information with regard to the various aspects of the practice of stealing.

Although I had been doing things that are considered to be criminal before I was put in one of these institutions, on entering one I learned more than I knew before. The Juvenile Home is where I really learned a lot of things. While in here I spent most of my time in conversation.

Kids as a rule, are very frank with the friends they make in a place like this and they discuss their problems together. Having to stay in the Detention Home and other juvenile institutions many months at a time I met lots of other kids in crime. We would tell each other stories about all the crimes we had committed and how we tricked the police and a lot of other things. I heard of stealing and stripping cars, strong-arming people, picking pockets, hold-up with a gun, stealing from telephone boxes, and breaking into stores. Some of the things I heard of for the first time in the Detention Home. Here I heard about sexual intercourse with girls. I learned many new ways of committing crimes.

Here is the way they talk. Every kid tells what he is in the Juvenile for and how he got caught. His friends ask him if he ever tried such and such a way to keep from getting caught. Each kid tells him how he does it and that way they all learn to use more strategy. By discussing their crimes from all angles, the kids learn more about crime and how to evade capture.

In this same connection, James makes the following comment.

The next time I was sent to the Juvenile Home was after I had spent three years in the St. Charles School. This time I was not a dingbat any more (boy under twelve years of age). I was put on the second floor with the older boys. While in groups, sitting or walking around, the boys naturally spoke of their homes, and the reason for being in the "Home." During these conversations we spoke of our experiences and picked up different methods and ideas. Outside of the Barber Shop affair, with two older accomplices, it never occurred to me to try my luck at burglarizing small stores, until the thoughts were put in my mind through the talks I had with some of the fellows while at the "Home." The result of my contacts there was a misfortune not only to myself but to several store owners, whose stores I had burglarized with the aid of Michael and other partners. Another thing I picked up there was to put my shop-lifting on a more profitable basis. Instead of taking small trinkets I began to take clothing, such as dresses, shirts, shoes, etc.

After my stay in the "Home" on this occasion was when I burglarized my first store. I can picture it as vividly as if it was yesterday. Michael, myself and a fellow partner of ours by the name of Olson decided to "take" an ice cream parlor. I had found out that cigarettes and cigars are easily disposed of.

Due to the fact that it was a night job, and that people could probably see you and you couldn't see them, I didn't relish it very well. But I was "in" and I couldn't very well take the chance of being called "yellow"—I went along with Michael and Olson. Arriving at the scene of our little adventure, Olson and I boosted Michael in through the transom window above the door. Michael then opened the door for Olson and myself. Everything was going along all right until a few minutes after we had broken our way in. I received a pretty good scare that night and Michael and Olson did also. After we all began to raid the candies and tobacco, I heard a funny noise. I couldn't imagine what it was and I stood perfectly still trying to locate it. In a little while I heard it again and I really was scared. I thought the owners were sneaking in on us. Again I heard the noise and something pressing against my legs. I jumped away and almost knocked the counter over. I looked where I had stood and there in the ray of the street light was a young cat! Boy, was I angry. The noise we heard was the meowing of the cat. Anyway the cat was put in the ice cream can while we went along pilfering the store. After leaving the store I thought of the poor cat in the ice cream can. I felt so bad about leaving it there that we all went to the back of the store and left our loot in the alley while we went in again and released the cat. After that I felt better.

Usually the boys who are most habituated and sophisticated in stealing are the ones who are most advantageously situated for transmitting information about delinquency to other boys. By virtue of their greater experience in delinquency, they often occupy positions of superior status and prestige. Thus they are emulated, idolized, and respected. The beginners are especially receptive to their influence and instruction. This point is emphasized in the following comments which were made by Edward and James. Particular attention is directed to the sentence in James's statement in which he describes how superior and proud he felt when he was in the Detention Home because " . . . . none of the other boys had a brother in St. Charles like I had."

During the first time I was placed in the Juvenile Home, I met many thieves. Some fellows had been in there many times for stealing things. I admired these fellows. There was a clique of fellows in there from the neighborhood of Grand Avenue and Western. They were a well-known bunch of car thieves. I met these fellows and admired them. When I won a fist-fight one day in the Home, the auto mob became friendly with me. I got a great kick out of this. I wanted them to like me, because I looked up to them for the deeds they had already done.

In the Home the kid who has been sent in for a little theft is afraid to tell the other guys what his charge was. He tries to save face by telling a big story about all the things he has done. He does not want to lose the respect of the other guys. The other fellows would rib him if they knew what a little thing he had done.

Later, after I had been in the Detention Home many times, the kids would flock around me and wanted to be my friends. I had a reputation because I had been in there so many times, had escaped from the place, and my escapades had been written up in the newspapers. Naturally, my reputation was made as a big guy as far as the kids were concerned. I had a bad influence upon the younger kids, just the way the older kids had been when I was in the Home the first time. I talked to them, gave them advice on delinquency, and of course they listened to me because of my reputation.

In this connection, James makes the following comments.

My first journey to the Juvenile Detention Home was when I was approximately seven years old. I felt out of place and a little scared of everything and everybody for a while, but in a few days I became accustomed to the new surrounding. I did not make many friends, nor was I really able to acquaint myself with any, as I was isolated most of the time with tonsilitis. If I wasn't sick, I was always falling down the stairs or hurting myself one way or another. If I remember correctly I was taken to the Eye, Ear and Nose Infirmary to have my tonsils removed while there at that time. In between the bruises and illness, I liked going to the class rooms in the basement. I took delight in making figures out of clay, and I also enjoyed the singing classes.

The second trip was a little better because I not only was a little older and able to comprehend things a little better, but I wasn't as sickly as I was during my first sojourn to the "Home." It was while here that I began to take pride that I was pretty slick, because I felt that I was a little better than any one there at my age, as far as stealing was concerned. After hearing a few of their stories I kind of bragged of what I had done, and besides none of them had a brother in St. Charles like I did. I told them I was going to ask the judge to send me there also as I felt as every kid did that if you're sent to St. Charles you really are a tough guy. A perverted outlook on life, that I know now, but I sometimes wonder if I really knew the difference between right and wrong as I know it now. I knew I had to go to church on Sundays and that I should be good to dumb animals, but stealing from rich people didn't strike me as being very bad.

The experiences of the brothers in juvenile institutions seem to have had the effect of intensifying, rather than resolving, their conflict with society. It appears that the rigorous discipline and formal routine widened the cleavage between the brothers and the society which was ostensibly seeking to adjust and assimilate them. Three of the brothers comment on the resentment which grew out of their experiences in these institutions.

During three years in St. Charles my heart grew bitter and hard at all the officers and inmate officers who were responsible for the manhandling I received. It was due to the treatment in this cottage that afterward caused me to be so bad in the later years I spent in this institution. As I grew older and stronger, I began to assert myself to the inmate officers and officials both. I wasn't born tough. The treatment in this institution made me that way. I realized that if I became hard and tough that the officials and inmate officers would be careful what they were going to do to me.

On leaving St. Charles I lost the rosy outlook about life. I had a subconscious feeling that I was going to make somebody pay for the treatment I had received here. I had no intentions of behaving myself, and I didn't have any intention of quitting my burglaries. Having exchanged stories with boys about their causes of being here, I learned to be more careful in the future. Being seventeen years of age I knew I would be taken to the County Jail if I were caught again, as I had passed the age of sixteen, which was the limit of the Juvenile Home.

I learned and did my tasks in this cottage, with the expectation of receiving a punch in the face or being put through some kind of a punishment if I did any of my work or drilling wrong. I cannot fully describe the ill treatments I went through during these years, but they left their mark on me. Work, military drilling and little play was the regular routine in that cottage. Physical torture, whippings, and manhandling were the punishments for the boys who broke some rule in the cottage.

When I was in the different juvenile institutions I didn't consider the officers my friends. I had learned in my neighborhood as a kid that officers are not to be trusted. In the institutions they considered that the inmates were just crooks; they let the inmates know how they felt in a hundred different ways. Sometimes they would call us thieves, lousy jail birds, and any despicable name. Because the inmates and officers were on different sides of the fence, each one was suspicious of the other fellow.

It is a well-known fact that the delinquent group in its initial stage of development is usually organized upon the basis of propinquity. Very often its members reside in a very limited area of one or two blocks. As the members increase in age, they establish contacts with delinquents living in other sections of the local community and in other parts of the city. Not infrequently these new relationships are established in juvenile institutions. Sometimes the boys who thus become friends in institutions continue to engage jointly in delinquency after their release, as Edward points out in the following statement.

After being placed on adult probation at the age of 17, I went home. Having nothing to fear, I tried to find a job. I had no luck, but kept looking for a month. One day when I was answering an ad in the paper, I ran into William Sloan and Earl Wooms at the place where I went for the interview. Since we didn't get a job, we walked out together. Since we had met in St. Charles, being in the same cottage, we exchanged tales as to what happened since we last saw each other. Telling each other where we lived, we made dates to meet the following day to look for work.

Having no success in getting jobs, we began discussing ways and means of getting some money as we were all broke. All of us having burglary experience, we decided to break into a place the next day. Over-sleeping that night I missed my appointment with them. Hoping they had waited I dressed hurriedly, and went to where I was to have met them. I found they had gone. Walking about the neighborhood, I met Joseph Wyman, who I also knew from St. Charles. Telling him I had missed my date with Sloan and Wooms, he said he wanted to come in with us. Meeting them that evening, I told them about Wyman and what he had said. We all agreed to let Wyman in with us, and went to his house to tell him.

Even if the juvenile institution is successful in inculcating conventional ideals in the child, these are often destroyed on his return to his delinquent groups in the community. This is particularly the case when the values of the boy's groups are in opposition to the values which the institution has sought to inculcate. This point is illustrated by the following experience as related by Edward.

Although I was punished a few times at the beginning of my first period in the Parental School, the officers polished me down, and at the end of my seven months' stay here, I had learned many things. I became a model boy. The folks in charge of my cottage treated me like a son, and I got along fine with the rest of the kids. In a way, I was sorry I had to leave, but the homing call is always stronger, no matter how bad home may be, especially to a little tot like me, who hadn't had any experience of being away from home.

A few days after I came out of the Parental School I was walking down the street with my brother, John. We met a friend of his who had just been in a fight with a kid. Hearing this kid swear, I told him it's wrong to swear, and that he would get punished for it. He, in turn, wanted to know since when did I become a sissy and a teacher's pet.

I soon found out that I was getting into fights for sticking to the new ideals I had been taught. When some of us kids would get in groups and talk about something, the kids would use a cuss word here and there. When it was said in my presence I would resent it by telling the kids that it was a sin and not to swear. As a rule, the kids were a little bigger than myself and would resent my butting in. After a verbal fight, it usually would end up with, "You want a punch in the nose?" After declaring himself, the kids would take sides, for or against him, which usually ended in a fight between the two of us. I found out I would have to fight every kid I knew, because every one that I knew swore like a trooper.

Eventually this ideal wore away, as I began to mix with the kids. Before long the Parental School was a thing in the past, and I was doing the same things I had done before. While fighting for my new ideals I received a name for being tough. And, because the kids found out I had been in the "band-house" as they called it, the tough character stuck.

Presumably, the methods of treatment administered in juvenile institutions not only failed to deter the brothers from further delinquency but contributed rather to their continuance in careers of crime. In this respect the careers of the Martin brothers are not exceptional. They are representative of hundreds of young delinquents in Chicago who pass through these juvenile institutions each year and subsequently are committed to reformatories and prisons. The magnitude of the number of such cases is convincing evidence of the need for a continuous experimentation to discover more effective procedures for the treatment and prevention of delinquency and crime.

EXPERIENCES OF THE BROTHERS DURING RECENT YEARS

As stated in chapter i, John, Edward, James, and Carl have been engaged in legitimate employment for a number of years, while Michael is still serving a sentence in a penal institution. John has not engaged in crime for ten years, Edward for eight years, James for six years, and Carl for ten years. The influences that contributed to the termination of the careers in crime of these four brothers are difficult to ascertain. The following considerations are entirely tentative.

From the point of view of the follow-up study of the Gluecks in Massachusetts, and the parole prediction studies of Burgess in Illinois and of Vold in Minnesota, the probability was very great that the brothers would continue in crime after their final release from institutions. Particularly in view of their long careers, their environmental situation at home, and the usual difficulty encountered by parolees with long records in securing legitimate employment even in times of prosperity, the prospects for adjustment were not favorable. Even if they did not continue in crime, there was a great probability that they would become involved in one or more of the marginal rackets.

The essential feature in the treatment efforts of the writers has been to provide various employment opportunities for the brothers. In so far as possible, types of work were secured which appealed to their interests. During the early years of the depression, when work in private industry was not available, it was necessary to raise money from private citizens to create the necessary employment opportunities. At that time financial assistance was given to John and Edward for the purpose of establishing a small business enterprise for them. This small business provided them with employment for more than seven years. The total expenditure was much less than the cost of incarceration for one person for one year.

Employment was originally provided for Carl in a large department store in the Loop. He worked at this job for almost eighteen months. When James was discharged from the Illinois State Reformatory, funds were secured to provide the same type of employment for James and Carl as had previously been secured for John and Edward. James and Carl were thus provided with employment for four years, after which other work opportunities were arranged for them. Later, financial assistance was given to James to provide him with educational opportunities as a preparation for professional work.

Michael was discharged from the Illinois State Reformatory six years ago. At that time he had a genuine ambition to secure employment and thus make it possible for him to provide more favorable home conditions for his mother. In fact, his ambition to succeed was much more intense than that of his brothers. Despite repeated efforts, it was not possible to secure work in private industry for Michael at that time. Before funds could be secured to create employment, he became involved in armed robbery with a former companion. Within three months from the date of his release he was again in custody.

Along with the provisions for employment, personal relationships of a friendly, informal, and confidential character have been maintained with the brothers. When they had work difficulties, desired small sums of money, needed medical assistance for themselves or for members of their families, they came on their own initiative for aid or advice. They were always regarded as persons who could make an adjustment if given the necessary facilities.

In conclusion it should be observed that the early attitudes of the brothers toward delinquency and crime seem to have changed during their periods of confinement in penal institutions. During the early years of their careers they regarded their delinquencies as stimulating, interesting, and enticing experiences. During their later incarcerations, however, delinquency lost much of the glamor and color which it had held for them in former years. As a matter of expediency they realized the importance of legitimate employment as over against further participation in criminal activities. Employment was not necessarily more desirable from an ethical standpoint, it simply did not entail the hazards of further incarceration and deprivation of their liberty. Perhaps this change in attitude helped to prepare the way for their favorable consideration of the employment opportunities which were later made available to them.

CHAPTER XVI

ANALYSIS AND IMPLICATIONS OF THE STUDY

This analysis is based upon three assumptions, namely,. (1) that the brothers were not different from large numbers of persons in conventional society in respect to intelligence, physical condition, and personality traits; (2) that their careers in delinquency, from the first simple acts of stealing to the more serious crimes which occurred in later years, represent a gradual, progressive process of informal training, education, habituation, and sophistication in the practice of stealing; and (3) that their induction into the practice of stealing, the formation of their habits of theft, their progressive sophistication in the knowledge and utilization of criminal techniques, and their sustained interest in stealing during a period of from twelve to twenty years were products of the varied influences exerted by the many delinquents, groups, and institutions with which the brothers had personal contact. Presumably, these five brothers, had they lived in a homogeneous, conventional milieu, might have acquired occupational skills and developed socially approved attitudes and ideals with the same facility that they became accomplished in the practice of stealing.

Franz Alexander and Hugo Staub, in *The Criminal, the Judge, and the Public*, have differentiated three general classes of offenders, namely, (1) the neurotic criminal, (2) the criminal who is organically conditioned, and (3) the normal criminal. The neurotic criminal is the individual whose criminality is assumed to be the "result of an intrapsychic conflict between the social and antisocial components of his personality." In the second class are included "those criminals who were either retarded in their development because of defective biological growth or those whose psychological personality was destroyed by some organic processes (idiots, paretics, schizophrenics and epileptics)." The class of "normal criminals," numerically the largest of the three groups according to Alexander and Staub, comprised those offenders who "are well adjusted to a totally different community, and that within the limits of that community they are normal social beings. The internal conflict between Ego and Super-Ego is not present, or, at any rate, not greater than in the case of a normal person. Only the exaggerated conceit of a scientist, who is bound and determined to defend the standards of a definite social organization, will make one seek biological points of differentiation between these individuals and ourselves.

"We think, therefore, that these criminals are to be looked upon as normal persons who had the misfortune of adjusting themselves to a weaker part of the community. Many of these, if they were brought up outside the criminal environment, would have grown up to be highly adjusted social individuals in our sense of the word."[1]

In view of the materials compiled in this study, it is assumed that the brothers fall definitely into the group designated by Alexander and Staub as normal criminals. The fact that they deviated from conventional persons in conduct, attitudes, and interests may be explained in terms of their life-history, rather than upon the basis of organic defect or mental pathology. Under different conditions they probably would have become law-abiding citizens rather than offenders against society.

If the brothers possessed constitutional defects, mental abnormalities, or traits of personality which are not present among law-abiding persons in conventional society, they were not revealed in the numerous clinical examinations which were made at various times during the years in which they were engaged in the practice of stealing, or in the examinations which have been made by psychiatrists in recent months.

The physical examinations revealed such defects as devitalized teeth, peculiarly shaped lobules of the ears, slightly impaired vision, a "slight roughness of the heart sound," in one or more of the brothers. The observed physical abnormalities consisted of defects which are common to large groups of children in the gen-

[1] Franz Alexander and Hugo Staub, *The Criminal, the Judge, and the Public* (New York: Macmillan Co., 1931), pp. 52–53.

eral population.[2] Aside from such defects as these, the reports of medical examinations were negative. With few exceptions, the various examiners characterized the general physical condition of the brothers as good.

The psychological examinations which have been made in recent years indicate that the brothers have average or superior intelligence. For the most part, the psychiatric reports did not present any factual evidence suggestive of mental pathology. It is true that, while Michael and James were confined in the reformatory, the former was referred to as an egocentric and the latter was classified as a psychopathic personality. However, in his recent examination of James, Dr. Hanson reported that there was no evidence to support the diagnosis of psychopathic per-

[2] In connection with this statement the following quotation is presented from William I. Thomas and Dorothy S. Thomas, *The Child in America* (New York, 1928), p. 449. The estimates given in this quotation are especially pertinent because they were made during the period in which the brothers were engaged in delinquency.

"In 1918, Thomas D. Wood, chairman of the Joint Committee on Health Problems in Education of the National Education Association and the American Medical Association, submitted the following estimates on the physical condition of the school children of the United States:

'At least 5 per cent—1,000,000 children—have now or have had tuberculosis, a danger often to others as well as to themselves.

'Five per cent—1,000,000 of them—have defective hearing, which, unrecognized, gives many the undeserved reputation of being mentally defective.

'Twenty-five per cent—5,000,000 children—have defective eyes. All but a small percentage of these can be corrected, and yet a majority of them have received no attention.

'Fifteen to 25 per cent—3,000,000 to 5,000,000 children—are suffering from malnutrition (not always due to poverty). . . . .

'From 15 to 25 per cent—3,000,000 to 5,000,000—have adenoids, diseased tonsils, or other glandular defects.

'From 10 to 20 per cent—2,000,000 to 4,000,000—have weak foot arches, weak spines, or other joint defects.

'From 50 to 75 per cent—11,000,000 to 16,000,000—have defective teeth. . . . .

'Seventy-five per cent—16,000,000 of the school children of the United States —have physical defects which are potentially or actually detrimental to health. . . . .'

"In 1923, Dr. Wood wrote that he believed these figures were still essentially accurate for the country at large, although he supposed that the percentages would be considerably lower in a few of the cities where rather intensive programs of health care have been undertaken during recent years."—Moore, H. H.: *Public Health in the United States* (New York: Harper & Bros., 1923), pp. 56–57.

sonality which had been made in the reformatory. Furthermore, if the crime for which James was committed to the reformatory could be explained in terms of psychopathic personality, upon what basis would his present long record of regular and successful employment be explained?

There is much evidence to indicate that the label of "psychopathic personality," which was ascribed to most of the inmates of the Illinois State Reformatory at the times James and Michael Martin were incarcerated there, did not have a high degree of reliability. The concept was not clearly defined, the methods employed in the diagnosis were not standardized, and the examiners apparently operated upon the preconceived assumption that criminality was a psychopathological trait. Sutherland has made the following observation with regard to the methods used in making such diagnoses. "The methods of diagnosis of the psychoses and of psychopathic personality are not standardized and the diagnoses are not reliable. The large proportion of criminals found to be psychopathic is explained by this lack of standardization and by the preconception that criminality must be due to psychopathy. This preconception is shown in extreme form in the editorial in the *Journal of the American Medical Association*, which was approved by the sub-committee on the medical aspects of crime, to the effect that a diagnosis of mental disease is 'permissible even when the criminal has shown no evidence of mental disease other than his criminal behavior.' A diagnosis of mental pathology assumes a criterion of the normal, and the normal in regard to thoughts, feelings, and sentiments is not stated in objective terms but is determined by the psychiatrist's preconceptions."[3]

During the period in which James and Michael were incarcerated in the Illinois State Reformatory, the reports of the psychiatric diagnoses showed that of 5,976 inmates examined, 5,950, or 99.6 per cent were classified as pathological. In the total group, 5,278, or 88.3 per cent, were diagnosed as psychopathic

[3] E. H. Sutherland, *Principles of Criminology* (Chicago: J. B. Lippincott Co., 1934), pp. 105–6. Used by permission of the publisher.

personalities,[4] as contrasted with the 6.9 per cent so diagnosed in the New York study reported by Bromberg and Thompson.[5] It seems probable that this wide discrepancy in the findings in these two reports reflects differences in the methods and points of view of the examiners, rather than actual differences in the offenders examined.

It has been traditional to impute to the criminal certain distinctive and peculiar motivations and physical, mental, and moral traits and characteristics. Historically crime has been ascribed to innate depravity, instigation of the devil, constitutional abnormalities, mental deficiency, psychopathology, and many other conditions inherent in the individual. Criminals have been thus set off as a distinct class, qualitatively different from the rest of the population. The current wide-spread practice of diagnosing all or a large proportion of the inmates as pathological personalities probably has no more validity than the former extravagant claims that feeble-mindedness or constitutional abnormality was the chief cause of delinquency and crime. The validity of this thesis depends, first, on whether the extent and character of pathology existing among offenders has been accurately determined and, second, on whether such pathology, when it does exist among criminals, has causal significance. If objective methods of diagnosis were used, comparative studies might reveal almost as large an incidence of egocentric and psychopathic personality traits among the noncriminal as among the criminal population. In the light of all available evidence, it may be assumed that the diagnosis of James and Michael as egocentric or psychopathic personalities amounted to little more than the assigning of labels according to a traditional practice in which criminality was assumed to be a psychopathological trait.

The delinquent careers of the brothers had their origin in the delinquent practices of the play groups and gangs with which

[4] State of Illinois, Department of Public Welfare, *Twelfth Annual Report of the Criminologist* (July 1, 1928—June 30, 1929), p. 11.

[5] Walter Bromberg and Charles B. Thompson, "Relation of Psychoses, Mental Defect and Personality," *Journal of Criminal Law and Criminology*, Vol. XXVIII, No. 1 (May–June, 1937).

they became associated at the time they began to participate in the play activities of the children in the community. The first act of stealing of each of the brothers was a group experience in which other boys, who were already delinquent, were implicated. John and Edward initially engaged in theft while associating with the group which was described in chapter vii. They, in turn, along with certain of their companions, were instrumental in inducting James, Michael, and Carl into the practice of stealing.

The origin of delinquent careers in the activities of play groups and gangs, as illustrated in the lives of the brothers, is typical of a very large proportion of the boys who are taken into the Cook County Juvenile Court each year. Among those boys who appeared in this court in 1928, 74.4 per cent were known to have committed the offenses for which they were first taken into the court while in the company of one or more boys. Among those charged with acts of theft, only 6.9 per cent were lone offenders, as contrasted with 93.1 per cent who were implicated with other boys.

In the cases of the brothers, as in numerous other cases, the initial acts of theft were part of the undifferentiated play life of the street. Gradually, however, stealing became a more distinct and specialized practice which required appropriate skills, insights, and knowledge. At the outset these were provided by the gang and by the more experienced delinquents with whom the brothers had personal contact in the community and in juvenile institutions. The delinquent groups not only furnished the fund of appropriate knowledge but they provided the stimuli, the encouragement, the incentives, the approvals, and the necessary sanctions. From the simple forms of stealing the brothers progressed to more complicated, more serious, and more specialized forms of theft.

As indicated earlier, the aspect of the life of the community in which the brothers engaged was such as to give encouragement to and justification of their participation in delinquent practices. The community as a whole offered little organized resistance to delinquency and crime, although a very large proportion of the immigrant parents were individually moral and law-abiding in their conduct and attitudes. Economic insecurity, confusion of cultural standards, traditions of delinquency, crime, racketeering, and graft in its varied forms, and the basic changes that have taken place incident to the threat of invasion by industry and commerce, all combined to render the community relatively ineffective as an agency for transmitting to the children a consistent tradition of conventional practice and for maintaining effective discipline, training, and control consistent with the requirements of the larger society. In addition to this general situation, there were many specific influences which contributed directly and indirectly to the delinquency of the brothers and their companions. These included the junk dealers, professional fences, and residents who purchased their stolen goods, contact with older offenders in the community who set the pattern for adult forms of crime and symbolized success in the criminal world, the presence of dilapidated buildings which served as an incentive for junking, the acceptance by the parents and neighbors of such forms of stealing as junking and stealing from the railroads, the lack of preparation, training, opportunity, and proper encouragement for successful employment in private industry, and, as previously mentioned, the presence of play groups and gangs with long-established traditions of delinquency. In short, the careers of the brothers developed in a social world in which stealing was an accepted and appropriate form of conduct.

As a protection against the delinquency-producing effects of the gang, play group, and community, the family influence was negligible. Extreme poverty, the lack of group unity which resulted from the widely divergent social backgrounds of the parents and of the brothers, and the discontinuity of family traditions precluded the development of those intimate, stable relationships, loyalties and mutual interests essential to normal family life. Parental control was almost entirely absent. Consequently, in the absence of restraints in the family, the early controlling influences in the lives of the brothers were limited largely to whatever group or groups they might perchance become associated with in the community.

As the brothers began to be taken into the court for playing truant from school and for burglary and other forms of theft, the parents were faced with a variety of problems with which they were largely unfamiliar. They knew relatively little about police regulations, the laws of compulsory school attendance, the procedures of the courts and juvenile institutions. Furthermore, in their attempts to train, discipline, and control their children, they did not have the support of an effective community organization, as would have been the case in the Old-World community in which they grew up. In the new community the forces outside of the home operated to counteract the efforts which they made to impose conformity to conventional standards. In this situation the parents, like the school authorities, the police, the officers of the court, and officials of institutions, resorted to coercive and punitive methods of control. The brothers reacted by resorting to protective lying and increased cunning, caution, and adroitness in their truancy and delinquency. The coercive methods of discipline had the additional effect of solidifying the allegiance of the brothers to their delinquent groups and further alienating them from conventional society. Perhaps these methods failed because conventional norms, which these agencies were seeking to impose, were inconsistent with the traditions, sentiments, and practices of the groups which provided for the brothers the only security and satisfactions which they knew.

It should be noted that the community situation in which the brothers lived is neither unique nor unusual. It is part of the large area of deterioration that surrounds the Loop and extends out along the north and south branches of the Chicago River. Physical deterioration, low rentals, confusion of cultural standards, and a disproportionately large number of school truants, juvenile delinquents, and adult offenders are characteristic of this whole area. These conditions are not of recent origin; they have persisted in the area for a long period of years. The cultural characteristics, social types, institutions, opinions, and practices which prevail here are forms of accommodation which the occupants of the area have made in their struggle for a living in the economic and social life of the city.

As the city has grown, the central business district and industrial centers have expanded and incorporated additional land for industrial and commercial purposes. In view of the low financial return in the form of rental and the threat of invasion by industry and commerce, property-owners have not invested capital in the construction of new residential buildings nor in the repair of old properties. Hence, this section of the city has become increasingly deteriorated. Along with the physical deterioration, important changes have taken place in the character of the institutions and social practices. The lowest income groups in the population of the city have been forced into this area, while the more successful groups have been distributed in communities that represent higher gradations of economic attainment. In this process of segregation, the newly arrived immigrant groups have settled in this area. As each of these groups has prospered it has moved into other residential communities. The succession of national and racial groups with varying cultural backgrounds, the extreme difficulty involved in securing remunerative employment in private industry, the diversity of standards of conduct, and the fact that many of the families regard their residence in the area as temporary are among the influences which have contributed increasingly to the breakdown of conventional forms of neighborhood control.

In this process, conventional practices have given way progressively to forms of conduct which are inconsistent with the norms of conventional society. The presence of vice resorts which operate under protection, the prevalence of varied forms of delinquency and crime, organized criminal gangs, the availability of professional fences for the disposal of stolen goods, the universally low resistance to delinquency, the willingness of many residents to purchase stolen merchandise from children, vote frauds, the practice of bribery in connection with criminal cases are a few of the concrete social forms and adaptations which have developed in these areas and which comprise a community environment particularly conducive to delinquency. It is assumed that these attitudes, social groups and practices are functions not of individual perversity, incompetence, or pathology, but, rather, human reactions to the cultural disintegration which has resulted from the natural processes involved in the growth and expansion of the city. From this point of view, delinquency in this area and the various forms of conduct associated with it are the ways in which the individual assimilates the ideas, beliefs, and practices of his group and under their control carries out his life-processes.

In many respects, the careers of the Martin brothers are illustrative of the lives of hundreds of boys who become delinquent in this physically deteriorated and socially disintegrated area of the city. As indicated by the findings of other studies, the social experiences of many of these delinquents are essentially not unlike those of the Martin brothers.

The breakdown of traditional forms of control in these deteriorated areas represents a more advanced stage of the process of disorganization which is taking place in society at large. The moral code and social practice are undergoing marked modifications in all classes of society as a result of such changes as the movement of populations, new developments in the industrial system, and the introduction of new modes of communication and transportation. With these changes the controls traditionally exercised by such social groups as the family, the neighborhood, and the church have been weakened. The effects of these changes in relation to delinquency are most marked in the physically deteriorated and socially disorganized areas adjacent to the centers of commerce and industry in the city. The careers of the brothers are presented as a concrete illustration of the manner in which the conditions in these areas of the city give rise to delinquency and crime.

As illustrated in the present study, the experiences of the habitual delinquent in these areas may involve various aspects of the life of the local community. The wide ramifications of these experiences suggest the need for developing treatment and preventive programs of a community-wide character. Programs which seek to deal with single individuals or small segments of the community life are not likely to be any more effective in the future than they have been in the past. If the delinquencies of the brothers were representative of the social character of the careers of a very large proportion of the habitual delinquents in the deteriorated areas—and there is much evidence to support this assumption—it appears that to bring about a substantial reduction in the volume of delinquency in these areas it will be necessary to develop an effective organization of conventional sentiments, attitudes, and interests as a substitute for the present situation in which socially divergent norms and practices prevail.

Effective procedures for bringing about such changes in the organization of the social life in these areas are not known at the present time. Efforts to impose from the outside programs of ready-made activities have not yielded satisfactory results in the treatment and prevention of delinquency. There is reason to believe that more satisfactory results might be achieved by programs in which primary emphasis would be placed upon the responsible participation of the local residents, as contrasted with the traditional practice in which the responsibility for determining policies and planning programs is vested in groups residing outside of the community. In such an enterprise the objective would be to effect a greater unanimity of attitudes, sentiments, and social practices in the community by giving to the local residents every possible assistance in developing their own programs to promote the physical, moral, and social well-being of their own children.

INDEX

INDEX

DATE DUE